DEAR EDITOR

DEAR EDITOR

A HISTORY OF *POETRY* IN LETTERS

The First Fifty Years, 1912–1962

EDITED AND COMPILED BY
JOSEPH PARISI AND STEPHEN YOUNG

Introductions and Commentary by Joseph Parisi

Foreword by Billy Collins

W. W. NORTON & COMPANY

New York • London

The text and display of this book are composed in Bembo
Composition by Carole Desnoes
Manufacturing by the Haddon Craftsmen, Inc.
Book design by JAM Design
Production manager: Julia Druskin

Library of Congress Cataloging-in-Publication Data

Dear editor : a history of Poetry in letters : the first fifty years,
1912-1962 / edited and compiled by Joseph Parisi and
Stephen Young ; introductions and commentary by Joseph
Parisi ; foreword by Billy Collins. —1st ed.
p. cm.
Includes index.
ISBN 0-393-05092-0 (hardcover)
1. Poetry (Chicago, Ill.) 2. Monroe, Harriet, 1860–1936—Correspondence. 3. Monroe, Harriet,
1860–1936—Contributions in editing. 4. Periodicals—Publishing—Illinois—Chicago—History—
20th century. 5. Literature publishing—Illinois—Chicago—History—20th century. 6. American
poetry—20th century—History and criticism. 7. Shapiro, Karl Jay, 1913– —Correspondence.
8. Rago, Henry, 1915–1969—Correspondence. 9. Editors—United States—Correspondence.
I. Parisi, Joseph, 1944– . II. Young, Stephen.

PS301.P623D43 2002
811'.509—dc21   2002010991

W. W. Norton & Company, Inc., 500 Fifth Avenue, New York, N.Y. 10110
www.wwnorton.com

W. W. Norton & Company Ltd., Castle House, 75/76 Wells Street, London W1T 3QT

1 2 3 4 5 6 7 8 9 0

To the Memory of Harriet Monroe,
Her Successors, and the *Poetry* Staff
1912–1962

Contents

List of Illustrations

Acknowledgments

Without the great generosity of the poets, heirs, and literary executors listed at the back, most of whom waived fees, this book would not have been possible. Stephen Young and I are especially grateful to the widows, children, and other relatives of the past Editors, who in several instances verified facts and gave us vital information unrecorded except in their memories. To Ann Monroe, Evalyn Katz Shapiro, Juliet Rago, Derek and Jon De Vries, Bonnie Larkin Nims, and Sophie Wilkins Shapiro, our heartfelt thanks. Bonnie Nims provided us with several letters from her personal collection, as did Nan Bright Sussmann, who also gave us the photograph of George Dillon as a young man.

Most of the *Poetry* archives are preserved and divided into two collections, at the Regenstein Library at the University of Chicago (1912–1960) and The Lilly Library at Indiana University (1961–present), and include original manuscripts, letters, financial records, proofs, and other documents—some 300,000 items in all. Beginning in 1998, we examined the entire correspondence and many of the other files; almost all the letters we selected from *Poetry*'s first fifty years were transcribed from the originals at Chicago.

Alice Schreyer, Curator of Special Collections, was unfailingly helpful, as were all the staff: Jay Satterfield, Daniel Meyer, Barbara Gilbert, Debra Levine, Benjamin Stone, and Jessica Westphal. They responded to our queries and several special requests with remarkable speed and good cheer, and we deeply appreciate their personal kindness on our many visits. The Lilly Library at Indiana University granted both of us Everett Helm Visiting Fellowships, which enabled us to make several trips to Bloomington to research the post-1960 files. To then Director Lisa Browar and to Curator Saundra Taylor, Rebecca Cape, Joel Silver, and the rest of the very gracious staff at the Lilly Library, our warm thanks. We should confess that on too many occasions in the course of searching the files we burst into laughter, groaned aloud, and shouted variations on *Ah-ha!* and *Eureka!* We appreciated the forbearance of the librarians, and apologize again to them and to the scholars who were offended by such unseemly violations of reading-room decorum.

In the Newberry Library, we also found several items, including unindexed correspondence and memoranda deposited by *Poetry* trustees of the forties and fifties, which shed new light on the financial and editorial crises at the magazine after World War II. We are indebted to our colleague Aaron Fagan, a former aide in Special Collections, who alerted us to this trove, and to Curator Diana Haskell, who allowed us to reproduce photographs and other rare documents from *Poetry*'s early years conserved in the Newberry.

Additional letters, information, and leads on literary executors were provided by several other libraries and their staffs, including: Patricia Willis, Curator of American Literature, and archivist Timothy Young at the Beinecke Library, Yale University; David Koch, Curator of Special Collections at Southern Illinois University Library; Houghton Library, Harvard University; The Huntington Library, San Marino, California; University of Arkansas Library; Smith College Library; and Harry Ransom Humanities Research Center at the University of Texas. Present and former *Poetry* staff members Helen Lothrop Klaviter, Judy Olson, and Damian Rogers also helped uncover several records, clippings, and photographs in the archives housed in the magazine's offices. Jayne Marek's *Index to Poetry* 1912–1997 (Poetry Press, 1998) was indispensable in tracking publishing histories.

To Stephen Young fell the formidable task of identifying and locating the many (and often very elusive) heirs and executors of poets represented in this history. Several scholars, critics, editors, independent researchers, and publishers gave clues for searches, shared their knowledge of various poets and periods, and offered valuable suggestions. Particular thanks are due to Murph Henderson of the Library of America, Dennis Palmore of New Directions, Professor Sandra Spanier, Lisa Szefel, Jean Burden, Dan Campion, David Hilliard, and J. D. McClatchy.

Ellen Williams's *Harriet Monroe and the Poetry Renaissance: The First Ten Years of Poetry, 1912–22* (University of Illinois Press, 1977) remains the most thorough study of the magazine's first decade, and was an invaluable resource in compiling the history for that period. *The Little Magazine: A History and a Bibliography*, by Frederick J. Hoffman, Charles Allen, and Carolyn F. Ulrich (Princeton University Press, 1946), provided abundant data on *Poetry* in its early years and on its many fellow laborers in literary journalism over the next three decades. Karleen Georgiana Redle's meticulous annotations in her Ph.D. dissertation, "Amy Lowell and Harriet Monroe: Their Correspondence" (Northwestern University, 1967), clarified both general background and many specific references. Likewise,

John Tytell's incisive, even-tempered biography of *Ezra Pound: The Solitary Volcano* (Doubleday, 1987) was a major source for the broad cultural context as well as particular details of the poet's early life and years in London. Diederik Oostdijk confirmed numerous facts and shared several discoveries that are now related in his Ph.D. dissertation, a comprehensive examination of "Karl Shapiro and *Poetry: A Magazine of Verse* (1950–1955)" (Katholieke Universiteit Nijmegen, 2000).

Since the start of research, we have enjoyed the support of the Board of the Modern Poetry Association and the warm encouragement of many poets and friends. Stephen and I are much beholden to Susan Estes and Andrew Rojecki for their great kindness in offering us lodging during our visits to Indiana; to Barbara Stufflebeem for lightening the burdens during our many travels; and to Edward Gubar and Stephanie Zaiser for their hospitality in Bloomington.

I am particularly grateful to Alice Fulton, Sandra M. Gilbert, John Hollander, and Helen Vendler for their support and wise counsel; to Billy Collins and Chris Calhoun for their faith in this project, friendly advice, and continuing generosity; and to the John Simon Guggenheim Foundation, whose award of a Fellowship was of immense assistance as I was completing the research for and writing this book.

—J.P.

Foreword

As I was reading all this lively correspondence between *Poetry*'s editors and its contributors, two questions began buzzing around my head. First, what is the true nature of the editor-poet relationship? And, second, what ever happened to that rejection letter Henry Rago wrote in response to the poems I sent him in 1957?

The second one is easier to answer: it got lost. But not as lost as some of the theorems of Pythagoras, because I remember what it said. And I remember its length as well—a full page, typed, single-spaced, more than it would take most editors to reject the work of a high school junior—with the accent on the junior. In 1957, I was probably moving out of my Ersatz Beatnik Period into my languorous *Brideshead Revisited* Phase, so I can only wince when I try to imagine how bad the poems—which thankfully are as lost as those theorems—must have been. Yet Rago, who edited the magazine for fourteen years (in third place behind Harriet Monroe's twenty-four and Joseph Parisi's nineteen, so far), took the time to write a patient, detailed letter of encouragement—not encouraging me to submit more poems, I hasten to add, but to continue to write and, with greater emphasis, to read more poetry.

I was not surprised, then, to learn from these letters that Rago had his first poem accepted by *Poetry* when he was only fifteen and that, as editor, he often wrote such warm letters of rejection that some of the rejected wrote back to thank him. I didn't—in fact, I let thirty years go by before I tried the magazine again—a respectful silence that was rewarded when Joseph Parisi conferred legitimacy on me in 1987 by applying Harriet Monroe's famous "Open Door" policy to all three of the poems I'd sent in.

The graciousness of its editors is only one of many themes that run through *Dear Editor*, a collection that takes us backstage into the lives of many editors and poets, notably the figures who have come to define Modernist poetry in English. Eliot proclaimed famously that the poet was beyond personality, but there is plenty of it on display in these letters. Pound remonstrates, Amy Lowell wheedles, Williams quibbles, Wallace

Stevens rolls over, Hart Crane explicates, Yvor Winters gets nasty, and Sara Teasdale and Vachel Lindsay launch an uneasy liaison through the intercession of Harriet Monroe. The dominant markers of High Modernist poetry may be irony, image, and ambiguity; but the recurrent themes of these letters are vanity, anxiety, reputation—and money. The number of requests for advances, loans, and emergency cash was probably due to the magazine's unusual generosity in paying contributors well and offering an array of annual cash prizes.

Having to deal with not only poets' work but also their opinions and their personal lives, the editors, particularly Harriet Monroe, show an admirable evenhandedness and patience. While Monroe is blue-penciling with one hand, she is cutting a needy poet's rent check with the other. While she is leading American poetry out of the nineteenth century by providing a showcase for experimental poems, she is obliging many conservative voices as well. And while struggling to keep the magazine afloat financially, she is weathering the criticism of her contributors, most of whom are convinced that they know better than she how to run the magazine and what poems it should promote, besides their own. One can only wonder how Miss Monroe absorbed such announcements as "After May 1st all poems by William Carlos Williams will be $50.—a piece minimum."

So back to the first question. No one set of terms can stabilize the complex interplay of personalities that form the editor-writer relationship. If the family is taken as a model, such relationships can range from the maternal to the avuncular, from the intimacy of sisters to the remoteness of distant cousins. The connection is a written one, the editor being first a reader and, sometimes, the poet's first reader. The writer's attitude toward authority colors the association, for an editor can be seen as standing between the poet and the public rather than simply providing the poem with an audience. Each wants something of the other. The poet wants approval and access to a readership; the editor wants to advance the cause of the magazine and to be made proud, or at least not embarrassed. When an editor insists on a textual change, he or she is posing that imperative question: "Surely, you're not leaving the house looking like that?!" I was surprised to discover how often *Poetry*'s editorial suggestions, some regarding poems now considered canonical, were obediently followed. Wallace Stevens even allowed Harriet Monroe to change the order of the stanzas in "Sunday Morning." (Like some other cooperative contributors, he returned the poem to its original form when it appeared in a book.) There are also writers present here who would resist altogether the intrusions of an editorial hand. Nabokov seemed to speak for them all when he wrote in a letter to his publisher: "By editor, I assume you mean proofreader."

The status of contributor is very different from the status of poet. The absolute control that the poet enjoys on the page in the privacy of composition gives way to a reliance on an often faceless stranger to give the poem a public existence. The editor is the agency that leads the poem out of the monk's cell of ink-work into the light of day. Short of the last resort called self-publishing, the poet cannot do it alone. Perhaps this dependency is what brings out the worst in some writers. If the editor serves as a kind of absentee parent, the contributor may respond as a child. Thus, the tantrums of Pound, the show-off behavior of Williams, and the regular appeals for aid to Mother Monroe from Vachel Lindsay.

As in the model of the family, there can be many contributors but only one editor, a situation that puts the writer in the position of vying for a parent's attention with a host of invisible siblings. Rejection is bad enough in itself, but coming from an editor, it implies the acceptance of other, more favored competitors.

To see these letters as negotiations with mother and father figures is just one way to enjoy them. Besides offering a spirited drama of personalities, the letters keep pace with twentieth-century history, touching on the two World Wars, the Leopold and Loeb trial, the Great Depression, and the jittery years of the Cold War. Winifred Bryher's warnings in regard to rising anti-Semitism in 1933 Germany are particularly chilling.

Plus, there is a fund of trivia here. It is not essential to know that Yvor Winters bred Airedales or that Crane's father invented the Life Saver. But that the first half-year royalties for Wallace Stevens's *Harmonium* totaled $6.70 will offer consolation to some. And what young poet will not be encouraged to learn that the first submissions of both Frost and Williams were—to use the dreaded word—rejected.

—BILLY COLLINS

*The histories of modern poetry in America and of
Poetry in America are almost interchangeable,
certainly inseparable.*

—A. R. AMMONS

Introduction

Dear Harriet Monroe—

   Spring is here, —and I could be very happy, except that I am broke. Would you mind paying me *now* instead of upon publication for those so stunning verses of mine which you have? I am become very, very thin, and have taken to smoking Virginia tobacco.

                              Wistfully yours,

                                        Edna St. Vincent Millay

P. S. I am *awfully* broke. Would you mind paying me a lot?

When she appealed to the Editor of *Poetry* in March 1918, Millay was already well known, though still living a Bohemian life in Greenwich Village. She got the advance, and became even better known when "First Fig," one of the stunning items in question, was published in August. "My candle burns at both ends, / It will not last the night," it begins, prophetically, and closes with an insouciant snap: "But ah, my foes, and oh, my friends— / It gives a lovely light!" While Millay's once-high luster has dimmed, her lovely light verse has joined the long list of works first presented in *Poetry* that are now the staples of anthologies and have settled into cultural consciousness.

   Millay was only one in a multitude of writers who turned to Harriet Monroe during her long editorship. Unlike Millay, most of them were obscure when the magazine first printed them, and wrote in styles less conventional than her clever quatrain. In fact, soon after it began, in October 1912, *Poetry* became notorious for presenting the earliest important work of Ezra Pound, Carl Sandburg, William Carlos Williams, T. S. Eliot, Marianne Moore, and Wallace Stevens, among several then-unknown, now-classic authors. Promoting such radical innovators and their experimental techniques, *Poetry* became *the* forum for the New Poetry, and a center of controversy.

   By the time Millay wrote in 1918, the "Poetry Renaissance," usually dated from the magazine's founding, was in full swing. The practice and

very perception of poetry would never be the same. In the years follow-
ing that first revolution, the magazine has continued to help launch sev-
eral waves of New Poets and an ever-evolving series of poetic styles. Even
when its shoestring budget has been stretched to the snapping point,
Poetry has managed to come out every month, without interruption—an
achievement unsurpassed in the field. Now in its tenth decade, it has pre-
sented, often for the very first time, virtually every poet of note in the
twentieth century.

Poetry's improbable success has become a "Cinderella" story in Ameri-
can letters, and the stuff of legend. Far less known—and much more fas-
cinating than the myths that have arisen—are the behind-the-scenes
relations between the poets and editors through the years. That inside
view is the principal subject of this book. In the chronicle that follows,
Poetry's history and its part in the development of modern poetry over its
first fifty years will unfold primarily through the words, the voices, of the
distinctive artists who helped shape them both.

Since the beginning, poets have written to the Editors of *Poetry* to
introduce themselves and their work, to share news of their professional
and private lives, to ask for advice or favors, to say thank you, and to
complain—especially about the magazine's contents—often in detail and
with surprising candor. Poets in its first decades could write with a
directness and acerbity unthinkable now. Before creative writing began to
be institutionalized in the fifties, authors were perhaps less fearful of
offending: promotions and tenure, prizes and fellowships, and other
aspects of "po-biz" (as insiders call it) didn't hang in the balance. It is
doubtful that many prospective contributors today would tell an editor,
"You are an intangible coward" (as Maxwell Bodenheim did in 1916),
or term "damnable . . . ninety five percent of the stuff you print" (Yvor
Winters, 1920).

Decade by decade, the letters in the *Poetry* archives indicate the
give-and-take between authors and editors and the practical aspects of
publishing; the suggestions offered, debated, adopted, or rejected; the
"career counseling" and frequent financial aid; the running arguments—
and the sometimes acrimonious partings. Many contentious authors
wrote to takes sides in literary battles or to weigh in with strong opinions
on controversial poets or historical events, giving the editors a multifac-
eted perspective on current affairs. This diverse, contemporaneous testi-
mony depicts the real-life conflicts, uncertainties, not to mention
politicking, that underlay the making of modern literature.

For most poets, too, letter writing is itself an art. Authors in the early
part of the century, without "benefit" of cheap and fast phone calls or e-
mail, took time and special care to *compose* missives, often very long ones.

Some conveyed their "thoughts and impressions" with such eloquence that their letters—like Cecily Cardew's diary entries in *The Importance of Being Earnest*—were obviously "meant for publication." As the narrators of their own stories, the poets display an immediacy, an intimacy of tone, and a degree of frankness—about their aspirations, setbacks, and rivalries—otherwise impossible to convey. Who better, then, to recount the rise and twists and turns of modern poetry than those who created and molded it?

Beyond their inherent literary value, these Letters to the Editor hold a broader interest. Among the most articulate and perceptive observers of their times, the poets convey a dramatic sense of what it was like to live through the major social and political events of the last century. In memorable words and images, they evoke the experiences of successive generations engaged in or reacting to the Great War, the twenties, the Great Depression, World War II, and the several cultural upheavals and artistic transformations that came in their wake.

In the fragile world of literary journals, life is fleeting. Most are lucky to last two or three years, before fatigue and financial problems overtake them. Very few persist beyond the term of their original editors. During Harriet Monroe's twenty-four-year tenure, hundreds of competing poetry and general arts reviews started up and stopped, and the founder believed her own periodical would die when she did. But after she collapsed on her way to Machu Picchu in 1936, at age seventy-five, grateful poets and loyal readers rallied to keep *Poetry* going, and Monroe's successors carried on the traditions she established. Gambling on untried talents, providing moral and more tangible support, the magazine has attracted ever-growing ranks of aspiring poets. Now the largest of the "little magazines," *Poetry* receives upwards of 90,000 unsolicited poems a year. For young authors especially, it remains, as Gwendolyn Brooks once called it, "The Goal."

"There is nothing quite like it anywhere else," wrote T. S. Eliot, during the magazine's financial crisis in 1954. "*Poetry* has had its imitators, but has so far survived them all. It is an American Institution." If that is true, it is a very unusual one. Few writers in regular contact have remained neutral about the magazine. As their letters indicate, the emotions *Poetry* can arouse in writers and readers, whether great affection or deep animosity, go beyond the ordinary responses to a mere "Institution." They take it *personally*.

From the beginning, Harriet Monroe made it difficult to view the magazine's work dispassionately, because she got so intimately involved herself. While she helped advance the art of *Poetry*'s "discoveries," the Founder-Editor took an active interest in their lives, as well, and with a degree of individual attention that went well beyond usual author-editor transactions. She not only gave authors feedback on manuscripts but actually fed them. Besides a discerning place of publication and a pay-check—both rarities for emerging poets at the time—Miss Monroe provided hospitality in the office and at home, a sympathetic ear, and, quite often, loans and gifts of cash in emergencies.

She also helped arrange first-book contracts, wrote letters of recommendation, made introductions, and on at least one occasion tried to play matchmaker. Through her innumerable, unpublicized acts of generosity, as much as her receptiveness to artistic quality of many kinds, Monroe set the standards of the magazine, securing *Poetry*'s singular status. In return, the majority of authors she championed maintained lifelong allegiance. Less happily, some authors to whom the Editor was extremely gracious repaid her with slurs and rank ingratitude.

"Her job brought Miss Monroe into contact with the most ferocious egoists. I mean poets in general," Wallace Stevens wrote in his homage shortly after her death. Reading some of the letters she and her successors received, one is dismayed, even at this remove, to discover just how self-centered and arrogant they could be. Stevens himself was exceedingly modest, and in writing to H.M. he took an aloof but amused stance toward his more pretentious contemporaries. William Rose Benét, another of her witty correspondents (and a fellow editor), mocked the pomposity of submitters when sending in some of his own poems in 1915:

> Here are some gems—or germs, according as you look at 'em!—Every one of 'em is to me tremendous, epic, glorious, superb! To you they may not be even poetry. But how can that affect me? I say they're *great, magnificent, wonderful, supernal!* Read them & be stunned with their impact! My God, must I *beg* you to read them? All right, I beg you to read them. . . .

Many who wrote to grouse doubtless tried the Editor's patience. During the magazine's formative first decade, as Ezra Pound, Amy Lowell, and other strong-willed, enterprising types vied for attention and tried to sway her toward their particular styles or aesthetic theories, Monroe often found herself caught between warring factions. Those who didn't get their way considered her woefully inadequate, and many told her so in the bluntest terms. Yet when they berated and insulted her, she let them rant without fear of retribution. So a sizable number of disgruntled correspondents continued to argue with her—and to seek admission to her "rotten" magazine—many submitting their work year after year, even

Cover letter from William Rose Benét to Harriet Monroe, 17 April 1915.

when acceptance seemed unlikely. Sending for the first time in August 1930, J. V. Cunningham told Monroe that, although he disagreed with its policies,

> particularly in late years, *Poetry* still remains the one standard dependable magazine of verse . . . . They (the poems) are not what I could wish

them to be, neither, however, could you discourage a budful talent by rejection. I could not stop writing, even should you wish it.

Some poets corresponded for two, three, or more decades, developing close or cross relationships. In scores of letters to successive Editors, they present vivid and sometimes less-than-flattering self-portraits, while exchanging literary ideas and gossip, tart opinions about their competitors, and details of their lives. Many correspondents are fine raconteurs and stud their letters with amusing anecdotes; and unlike certain academic critics, they speak for themselves in clear, concrete English. A fair number of future contributors began dropping by the *Poetry* offices or sending in poems while they were still in high school. Several of the most humorous letters came from very young writers. After a visit with H.M. in 1927, seventeen-year-old Elder Olson wrote in mock despair:

> I've waited awfully long, trying to get something really lovely to send you; but alas, everything I did sounded like a collaboration of Longfellow and Eddie Guest. . . .
>
> Do you suppose poetry can go quite so utterly from one? Can one lose everything in that line? I worry myself sick about that . . . not that I've a great deal to lose, but it's all I have. A penny is so much to a man nearly penniless. As it is, I'm continuously haunted by the notion that I'll never be able to do anything any more—not write poetry nor prose nor plays nor even play the piano. Isn't that dreadful? A sort of death-in-life affair.

Harry Brown, another Monroe protégé, also started submitting when he was seventeen. She published some of his first poems in 1935, and helped him get into Harvard, despite his poor grades. In June 1936, on the eve of his entrance exams, he wrote "Dear Miss M":

> I honestly don't think that I'm prepared, especially in the Histories, but there's nothing to do but take them, do my best, and pray that the powers that be will be lenient to me, a poor sinner. . . . I am writing a very nice poem called COMPLETE DISINTEGRATION to send to you.

Most striving artists never "arrive," of course, and those who do gain fame, or at least publicity, often go into eclipse shortly after, sometimes before, their demises, as did Millay. Several of the poets represented here never made big names for themselves. But all wrote letters that still retain a freshness that their poems today may lack. In their back-and-forth with *Poetry*'s editors, they reveal conflicting attitudes toward poetry, as well as the individuality (not to say idiosyncrasy) of artistic temperaments. Dealing with so wide a cast of characters, many of them "difficult," Monroe and her successors displayed remarkable fairness, civility, and good humor, even when provoked. A sense of the ridiculous was often necessary to maintain sanity in the face of certain authors' more absurd notions, gripes, and demands.

All editors must say no far more often than they can say yes. *Poetry's* have been notable for trying to soften the blow, and often received appreciative notes from people whose offerings were returned. Of course, the great bulk of creative work is mediocre or worse, whatever the medium, and doesn't survive its era of production. Like every other literary journal, *Poetry* devoted much space over the years to works that proved ephemeral. Ironically, the correspondence about these poems sometimes holds more lasting interest.

Many of Monroe's choices seem dull, if not downright embarrassing, now. Her contemporaries, too, thought a lot of pieces she presented were dreadful—such as the ones beginning: "Hog Butcher for the World, / Tool Maker, Stacker of Wheat . . ." and "Let us go then, you and I, / When the evening is spread out against the sky / Like a patient etherized upon a table. . . ." When *Poetry* introduced them in 1914 and 1915, Monroe's subscribers were baffled and sent irate letters to her and other editors. Hostile critics and satirical columnists found "The Love Song of J. Alfred Prufrock" pathological and "Chicago Poems" simply incompetent—that is, if such formless, "fantastic imaginings" could be called "poetry" at all. (Sappy couplets such as "I think that I shall never see / A poem lovely as a tree"—also first published in *Poetry*, in 1913—now, *that* was poetry.) When it appeared in 1915, "Sunday Morning" was ignored, except by Wallace Stevens's friends, who said it was impressive, but cryptic.

Within its first four months, *Poetry* attracted attention with the thumping rhythms of "General William Booth Enters into Heaven," by an obscure but upbeat vagabond minstrel named Vachel Lindsay. In the same issue (January 1913), the magazine printed something completely different: the finely sculpted "Hermes of the Ways," by the young Hilda Doolittle, who was identified only (and forever after this, her first publication) as "H.D." Her poems were pared then proffered from London by her old college sweetheart, Ezra Pound, who labeled her an "*Imagiste*" and informed her she was thus a follower of Imagism, a "movement" he had just made up.

Pound appeared in Vol. I, No. 1 with "To Whistler, American," wherein the expatriate ingratiated himself by declaring his Stateside countrymen "a mass of dolts." Replying to the Editor's solicitation letter in August

```
            Trees

I think that I shall never see
A poem lovely as a tree.

A tree whose hungry mouth is prest
Against the earth's sweet flowing breast;

A tree that looks at God all day,
And lifts her leafy arms to pray;

A tree that may in Summer wear
A nest of robins in her hair;

Upon whose bosom snow has lain;
Who intimately lives with rain.

Poems are made by fools like me
But only God can make a tree.

                    Joyce Kilmer
```

Original typescript of Joyce Kilmer's "Trees,"
the most popular poem Harriet Monroe printed.

1912, he also volunteered to scout out "whatever [was] most dynamic in artistic thought" in London and Paris, and predicted a Renaissance in American poetry was "inevitable." She immediately appointed him *Poetry*'s first Foreign Correspondent. So began one of the most productive and tempestuous alliances in literary history.

Over the next five years, in Chicago and London, the odd couple of intrepid editor and bull-headed impresario found and promoted a series of upstarts, introducing fresh approaches to poetry. Besides giving Eliot, Stevens, Williams, Moore, and H.D. their first professional publications, *Poetry* presented early work by Robert Frost, D. H. Lawrence, James Joyce, Edgar Lee Masters, and many other future Standard Authors. From the start, the magazine also featured poems by already recognized masters like William Butler Yeats and Edwin Arlington Robinson, as well as by younger writers who wrote in conventional modes, such as Sara Teasdale and Rupert Brooke. But in the public mind *Poetry* would forever be identified with free verse. Both the high-strung imports by Pound's *"Imagistes"* and the folksy, homegrown products of Midwestern populists drove conservatives to distraction, and drew flocks of novice experimenters to *Poetry*'s door. Thanks to abundant publicity, by its second year the magazine was getting about fifty poems a day.

Poetry appeared at a propitious moment, just as the disparate elements that would transform American poetry were about to coalesce, and it was Monroe's extraordinary good fortune to present a string of masterpieces in a very short space of time. Indeed, no poetry or general literary journal since has matched *Poetry*'s record in just 1914–1915. Many critics continued to scoff, while lovers of traditional verse remained outraged. But with the aid of her irascible Foreign Correspondent—and her shrewd Associate Editor, Alice Corbin Henderson—the Editor had put *Poetry* on the map and inaugurated the Modernist movement in poetry.

They didn't quite realize it at the time, of course. Monroe certainly didn't foresee the course American poetry would take. Her motive in founding a journal was simply to provide an outlet for serious work others were unwilling to print. But *Poetry* also became an apologist for the new and a meeting place that ended the isolation of independent poets, making them aware of one another's ideas, thus hastening developments. Monroe began work in a gloomy period of neglect for poets, and was as surprised as anyone by what followed from her initiative. In *Harriet Monroe and the Poetry Renaissance* (1977), the most thorough study of *Poetry*'s first decade, Ellen Williams observes: "It was not conceived in response to other glimmerings. Surely never has a candle lit against darkness been so suddenly rewarded with an explosion of light."

Ezra Pound's part in that spectacular production was central. It has also been greatly exaggerated, foremost by Ezra Pound. With the exception of Eliot and Frost (who was already in print), most of Pound's "finds" proved to be minor poets; he himself became disillusioned with them within a few years. More important in the long run, to the art in general, were his dictates for radical reform. Pound's checklist, "A Few Don'ts by an Imagiste," and his practical criticism helped strip away ornate diction, artificial devices, and obsolete notions, while fostering concrete language and direct presentation: foundations of literary Modernism.

When the Editor refused to let Pound run *Poetry* his way, he became increasingly frustrated and belligerent, as the correspondence below shows. Even eighty years on, his unveiled contempt and diatribes about H.M.'s picks and policies make Pound's letters to Monroe amazing reading. (In even harsher letters to others, he disparaged her taste and ability, calling "'Arriet" a "bloody fool," "old maid," "silly old she-ass," and other charming epithets.) But Miss Monroe's and Mrs. Henderson's discoveries were also important, and in many cases had greater staying power—above all, Wallace Stevens. During Pound's very heavy early correspondence with H.M., it is curious to note, he does not mention Stevens's name, even though he salutes, slams, or jots a capsule commentary on almost every other contemporary poet worth attention.

Pound's contributions to *Poetry* were perhaps fifty poems. Yet, with the passing years, he claimed more and more credit for Monroe's enterprise, while deprecating her substantial labors. Always gracious, Monroe in her autobiography, *A Poet's Life*, not only gave Pound his due but downplayed his negative impact on the magazine (and his hostility to her personally) with dry humor. She printed only a handful of his letters, and those tactfully edited. Pound was an effective propagandist, and his acolytes and later historians have tended to accept his version of events. The records, particularly his complete correspondence with *Poetry*, paint a more complicated and less edifying picture.

Though many, the Pound letters printed below are only a fraction of what he sent: his files, spanning fifty years, are among the largest in the *Poetry* archives. The originals of H.M.'s letters to E.P. before 1919 apparently are lost; perhaps he didn't think them worth saving. Fortunately, she kept carbons of her more official missives to him, as well as drafts, which indicate how carefully she chose her words to her hot-tempered collaborator. The strife in their partnership, as well as the satisfactions and positive excitement, may be gathered from the correspondence quoted here.

Pound's generosity to struggling authors is legendary. His efforts on behalf of Eliot and many others less renowned are well documented in the chapters to follow. Pound was always eager to "modernize" writers with potential. In one of his earliest letters to Monroe, in October 1912, he offered private tutorials: "If any of the younger writers . . . think my criticism would be any use to them, I shall be glad to give it. I remember how I used to be starved for some one with whom one could talk about poetry." Ironically, Pound never managed to modernize Monroe. In 1915, when she availed herself of his services and asked his opinion of "The Turbine," a poem on a "modern" subject (and one she was especially proud of), he savaged it for its "absolutely literary, bookish syntax" and "vague blobby gernerlizing [sic] words," and asked: "Have you ever let a noun out unchaperoned???"

His critiques of the magazine were not so amusing. Sooner or later, all of Pound's friends came to feel his sting. Many broke with him, while others (including H.M.) learned to take his scathing remarks in stride. For years after he left his official position, Pound continued to heckle the Editor—and to contribute to *Poetry*. Although she published two of his later Cantos in 1933 and 1934 (she printed the first ones in 1917), Monroe told him they would be "the last of your political manifestos which *Poetry* will care to have the honor of printing." When she told T. S. Eliot of E.P.'s "unspeakable" response, he replied: "I hope that you don't take the violence of his style too seriously; I am completely habituated to it myself."

"The wrecks of his wild runs strew the path of progress," Monroe pointed out in 1931, in a rare act of self-defense from Pound's unfair remarks. If she had let E.P. run *Poetry*, especially the business side, she noted, it would have gone the way of the many other journals with which he was also fitfully associated. Assessing his tortuous first five years with *Poetry*, Ellen Williams totaled up Pound's many quarrels over payment and concluded that he viewed the magazine primarily as a "cash box" that he used, by right of his genius, until it ran out: "When it did he left it, glad to be rid of a connection that he found embarrassing from every point of view but the financial one." Still, the gadfly couldn't completely let go. Although he continued to needle the Editor and her "family magazine," when *Poetry* was in deep fiscal trouble in the early thirties, Pound again volunteered his services.

Enormous human energy is devoted to "getting and spending." And although it is a major concern to most people, money is the rarest of topics in American poetry. Dark family secrets, psychological dysfunctions, sexual transgressions—all are now discussed in poems, endlessly and shamelessly. But seldom money, the last taboo. In their letters, however, poets do not hesitate to talk about it with the editors. Along with inquiries about publication dates, problems over finances are among their most frequent topics, occasioning the most poignant letters in the files.

Although in its most precarious days rates had to be cut, *Poetry* has always sent checks to its contributors. How the magazine managed to keep going with slim resources, a challenge that has undone so many other little magazines, is a story that has never been fully told. The exceptional loyalty and effort of editors, poets, and friends are indicated in several letters and introductions to chapters that follow.

If *Poetry* had closed up shop in 1917, its place in American letters would have been assured. In some ways, its reform campaign had already become *too* successful. Although traditional rhymed and metered verse (and sentiments) did not perish, they seemed hopelessly passé as more and more poets, young and old, adopted free verse à la mode. By 1918, Mrs. Henderson could write that it had become "a staple of the market":

That is the way with all rebels—they will go and get accepted and become fashionable. Nowadays everyone is writing imagist vers libre, or what the writers conceive as such, particularly those who at the beginning made the most outcry against it. Free verse is now accepted in good society, where rhymed verse is even considered a little shabby and old-fashioned.

Amid the triumph, the Editor was disappointed when the "great audience" she envisioned didn't materialize and *Poetry*'s artistic accomplishments weren't reflected on its balance sheet. Monroe's dream of financial security turned out to be wildly optimistic, and was never fulfilled. For her successors, that blessed state would prove equally elusive.

As with everything else, the Great War had a severe impact on the magazine. Most of *Poetry*'s best English writers went to the trenches, and many Americans later joined them. Monroe tried to support the effort by printing several "war" poems, most notably by Rupert Brooke and Isaac Rosenberg, as well as letters from the Front sent by soldiers and women volunteers. Poets who survived the carnage were profoundly altered and slow to recover. Letters from H.D.'s husband, Richard Aldington, convey the sense of disillusionment his generation suffered through their horrific experiences.

In the late teens and twenties, as many of the most talented in the new generation of writers went abroad, *Poetry* received submissions and letters from expatriates, including Ernest Hemingway. In a gossipy letter from Paris in 1922, he gave Monroe updates on Gertrude Stein, James Joyce, and a mutual friend from St. Louis who planned to stay, "[he said] indefinitely, but that usually means two years." The Editor herself visited Paris in 1923, and met several of the avant-garde writers, artists, and musicians, including Tristan Tzara ("the original dada-ist"), Constantin Brancusi, and Erik Satie.

But Monroe's editorial position after the war looked homeward. Monroe always felt that European influences had stymied American originality. In several editorials she stated her belief that English tradition, reinforced by the arbiters in Eastern universities and magazines, had imposed a cultural "colonialism" on U.S. artists that instilled a sense of inferiority and inhibited their growth. To her irritation, E.P. repeatedly warned her about being "provincial." In October 1913, she shot back: "If we are provincial, we shall always be so until we cease to take our art and art opinions ready-made from abroad, and begin to respect ourselves." After dealing with feuding theorists and in-group antagonisms for years, Monroe became disenchanted with "coteries" and turned away from experiments.

Much of what *Poetry* printed in the twenties was undistinguished. Far more stimulating were the letters received, especially from feisty, uninhibited younger writers. Some met the Editor in the *Poetry* offices. Others wrote out of the blue after reading the magazine or Monroe and Henderson's popular anthology, *The New Poetry*. The brightest of the new generation professed allegiance to no "schools" but followed Emerson's counsel to do their own thing. Monroe got several earfuls from these avowed amateurs and free spirits.

By far, the most self-assured, perceptive, and sardonic of her independent correspondents was Yvor Winters. He exhibited no fear in telling Miss Monroe exactly what he thought of his elders and contemporaries, and of the things in her magazine. His letters began in 1919, and so impressed her that she wanted to hire him. Winters's early missives are wickedly entertaining. Critiquing the January 1920 issue, he told H.M.: "I still think H.D.'s poem ["Hymen"] an abomination. Worse than Aldington's love poems, if that is possible. Why Williams should like it is beyond me. And how H.D. could write it is beyond me."

Eventually his relations with *Poetry* soured when, like Pound, he became frustrated in his attempts to "enlighten" the Editor. He told Monroe in October 1930: "Believe me, then, for I speak it as a great critic, Edna sounds like a sack full of old kitchen utensils, and Lindsay sounds worse." In a parting shot, after she suggested a change in a review, he sneered: "There are not more than two or three writers living from whom I would even consider taking such dictation, and you are not one of them." As usual, H.M. took the reproaches calmly. She was also humble enough to admit it, publicly, when she did not understand some new work, as in her correspondence with Hart Crane in 1927.

By the end of 1929, *Poetry* was the lone survivor among the many little magazines that started up in the teens. It too came close to extinction, on the eve of the 20th Anniversary. *Poetry* was saved after newspapers nationwide decried the threatened loss of such an "asset" and many small donations came in. During the Depression, the younger poets were among the most hard pressed. Despite their own difficulties, the editors went to great lengths to answer calls for help. The letters gathered here are but a small portion sent by struggling, often nomadic, authors. Norman Macleod, for example, was stranded in Holland in 1932 after he was kicked out of France for singing the Communist anthem. An advance from Monroe tided him over. (The next year he joined the *New Masses*.)

At the same time, H.D.'s friend Bryher (Winifred Ellerman) sent early and very disturbing reports from Europe revealing the growing violence against liberals, intellectuals, and the Jews by the Nazis. She also warned of another war. Monroe did not live to see it. After her death in Peru, papers across the country ran eulogies, and there was an outpouring of condolences such as is hard to imagine today for a literary editor.

Poetry's staff, faithful subscribers, and devoted authors refused to let the magazine end, and Morton Dauwen Zabel held things together for a year. He was succeeded in November 1937 by George Dillon. He had been Monroe's Associate Editor in the late twenties, while still in college. He then gained a reputation as a lyric poet (and a Pulitzer Prize in 1932), and published a noted translation of Baudelaire with his erstwhile lover, Edna St. Vincent Millay. Dillon had the unenviable task of preserving *Poetry* as war was breaking out.

At this unpropitious juncture, a young humorist, Peter De Vries, sent in some poems, and Dillon asked him to join the staff in 1939. Together, they found both funds and several promising poets. When Dillon was drafted, De Vries became Editor, and needed all his wits to keep the issues coming off the press. Supporters put on several programs (readings, lecture series, musicales, anything short of bake sales) to raise money. Even under wartime pressures, *Poetry* was also very active on the editorial side, and regained much of the strength it had lost. The correspondence reflects a new energy, too. Despite the grim times, the letters to and from the office are among the most amusing in the archives, particularly those by De Vries and John Frederick Nims, who would himself serve as a *Poetry* editor, three times.

Through the forties the magazine presented, usually for the first time, a string of young talents who went on to produce substantial, sometimes groundbreaking, work. John Ashbery, Frank O'Hara, Kenneth Koch, James Merrill, Randall Jarrell, John Ciardi, Gwendolyn Brooks, Robert Lowell, John Berryman, and Karl Shapiro were among the rising stars on the roster. Shapiro and several other servicemen-poets sent in work from war zones and military barracks. As in the Great War, *Poetry* printed letters from soldiers and news from the Front. In January 1944, the staff was surprised to read in the papers that a Liberty ship had just been christened the *Harriet Monroe*—probably the first (and only) time a piece of military equipment has been named after a poet or editor.

Editorially and financially, the postwar period was extremely difficult, and by 1949 Dillon had had enough. Hayden Carruth, then a graduate student, became Acting Editor in the midst of the controversy over the award of the first Bollingen Prize to Ezra Pound. Things went from bleak to near bankruptcy at *Poetry*, but, at the last possible moment, the magazine was saved again.

In 1950, Karl Shapiro began what became the stormiest editorship in the magazine's history. Shapiro debuted in *Poetry* in 1940, and won the 1945 Pulitzer Prize for *V-Letter*, his book of war poems. He also acquired a reputation as a provocative critic, and controversy followed him when he joined the magazine. Shapiro printed strong work, especially by poets of his generation, and the letters from Jarrell, Ciardi, and Berryman are among the most engaging in the files. But many of the harsh reviews

Shapiro ran generated bad feelings, as well as angry letters from (among others) Conrad Aiken and Tennessee Williams. Endless money troubles plagued Shapiro's tenure, and when finances hit rock bottom in December 1954, he left for Berkeley and Henry Rago took charge.

Rago had his first contact with *Poetry* while still in high school, and Harriet Monroe first printed him in 1931, when he was sixteen. Rago was indefatigable and quickly restored *Poetry* to fiscal health and wide regard. He was also a prodigious correspondent and, like the first Editor, receptive to a wide diversity of talents, marginal and major, well known and aspiring. Among the scores of younger poets he encouraged were Robert Creeley, James Dickey, Thom Gunn, Donald Hall, Robert Duncan, Carolyn Kizer, John Hollander, Richard Howard, Denise Levertov, Philip Levine, Mona Van Duyn, and James Wright. He also had good relations with authors *Poetry* had presented in its earliest days, including William Carlos Williams, Robert Frost, and Marianne Moore.

Thus, as the second major revolution in America poetry was beginning to stir, Rago made the ideal intermediary to bridge the great divides between the many new stylists and their conflicting ideas about the art. The trust he earned from poets across the spectrum enabled him to bring them together, at least on paper, in *Poetry*.

In the letters that follow, the very large, very mixed group of creative personalities who wrote the Editors give their firsthand accounts as explorers on the major routes, roads less traveled, detours, and dead ends that the art took in the half-century after *Poetry*'s founding. Many of the poets (and editors) could sympathize with the sentiments D. H. Lawrence expressed to Harriet Monroe on the eve of World War I:

> But, my dear God, when I see all the understanding and suffering and
> the pure intelligence necessary for the simple perceiving of poetry, then
> I know it is an almost hopeless business to publish the stuff at all, & par-
> ticularly in a magazine.

To the many hundreds of writers *Poetry* has published over the decades, the elation Williams Carlos Williams conveyed to the Founding Editor in 1916 would also be familiar: "You make me feel it worthwhile to be alive."

A Note on the Text

In transcribing the letters from the originals in the archives, we have retained the spelling and punctuation of the individual authors. In the early years, for example, "dont" is often used for "don't"; and the placement of commas and periods outside quotation marks is common. Collectively and individually, many of the poets are inconsistent, however, in these and other practices. Most of the obvious misspellings have been silently corrected, but certain idiosyncratic usages, including English spellings by American authors, have been retained. For various reasons, a few curious spellings, (deliberate?) misspellings, and oddities have been retained; they are indicated with [sic].

Ezra Pound's letters have the greatest number of "irregularities" in that regard, particularly when he employs archaic slang or his pseudo-rustic American ("Amur'k'n") dialect. Pound's punctuation is often erratic, especially in the use of commas for periods (and vice versa), slash marks [/] for commas or periods, and so on. Occasionally, standard marks have been inserted or substituted silently to clarify syntax.

All ellipses in the letters are editorial ones, unless indicated by [sic]; thus, . . . [sic] indicates the author's own ellipsis. In a few instances, the writers use ellipses that are expressed as ..... (i.e., without spaces between the periods); these have been retained, without use of [sic].

As a general rule, terms or phrases underlined in the original letters are printed in italics here.

CHAPTER I

Beginning Again

I. Poetry before *Poetry*

The verses we print are rather of the progressive, uplift type, the kind that Kipling might do if he were writing in this country. Anything more graceful and delicate is unbecoming to the contents of our magazine.

—rejection letter from *Hampton's Magazine*
to Harriet Monroe

In 1911, when she had the improbable idea of founding, in industrial Chicago, a magazine devoted exclusively to verse, Harriet Monroe was a failed playwright, obscure poet, struggling freelance writer, and almost fifty-one years old. Most founders of literary journals have been young people, like the editors of the *Little Review*, the *Seven Arts*, *Contemporary Verse*, and other periodicals that followed *Poetry* in the teens—not to mention the countless "little" magazines that have come and gone since. The young possess the energy, innocence, and impatience with benighted authority that seem prerequisites for such ventures. Monroe had these qualities, and considerable frustration, too, but she was not naïve. She had had her share of negative experiences in the publishing world.

Monroe's unhappy encounters were in fact typical for poets who wrote serious, longer works or dared to deviate from the standards of the marketplace. Newspapers and magazines of her time preferred short, generally light verses—as the editor of *Hampton's* reminded her—mainly to fill out columns at the end of articles. Since poetry books weren't profitable, trade houses demanded subsidies; friends underwrote Monroe's own first collection, *Valeria and Other Poems*, in 1892. Her first poem appeared in the *Century* in 1888, and others followed at irregular intervals. In 1906, of twenty-five poems she sent out, three were accepted. In that "typical year," she said her verse netted a total of $5.

Recalling "The Middle Years" in *A Poet's Life*, Monroe wondered "how

Harriet Monroe, c. 1892, when her
"Columbian Ode" was performed at the
dedication of the Chicago World's Fair,
The Columbian Exposition.

I managed to live on such small returns; indeed, even my frugal habits did not yet make me wholly self-supporting." As her "unbecoming" poems continued to be met with indifference, she became increasingly discouraged. By 1910, she had received so many rejections that she "well-nigh ceased sending poems to periodicals." So, at an age when prudent people begin to give serious thought to retirement plans, she decided to start her own magazine dedicated to that least attended of the arts. She should have known better.

Monroe's one moment of national attention had occurred twenty years earlier. In 1891, she maneuvered to get a commission to write an inaugural poem for the World's Columbian Exposition in Chicago. She then upset the fair's organizers by presenting a bill for $1,000. She justified the unheard-of sum by noting that architects and painters routinely commanded even higher fees. Why, she asked, shouldn't poets be paid equally for their skill and labor? It was a question she would repeat often in future fund-raising campaigns.

After much controversy, Monroe prevailed. But about a month before her "Columbian Ode" was to be performed by a chorus of five thousand at the dedication on 21 October 1892, the New York *World* pirated the text. Monroe sued for copyright violation, and won a judgment of $5,000. The episode instilled a lifelong commitment to protecting poets' rights. When she finally collected the settlement in 1897, she was able to sail to England, where she met Thomas Hardy, Robert Louis Stevenson, Alice Meynell, and Francis Thompson. The money also helped sustain her in the lean times that followed.

Monroe managed to make a meager living by lecturing and selling freelance articles and the travel pieces that helped finance her many trips. In 1890, she briefly enjoyed a position as art critic for the Chicago *Tribune*, writing incisively on Saint-Gaudens, Gauguin, Van Gogh, Cézanne, James McNeill Whistler (whom she had visited in his London studio),

Matisse, and other innovators. She was delighted when the *Tribune* invited her back in 1909. The position offered no job security, she wrote, but brought her interesting friends, and left her enough time for travel "and even for the founding of a magazine." The timing was auspicious. During her five years on the paper, she was an enthusiastic analyst of what she realized was "a period of revolutionary change in the arts of painting and sculpture." And, she might have added, poetry.

For younger and more astute poets, the avant-garde artists offered exciting new models for expressing the modern world that were unavailable in current literature. (Realistic novels gave hints, but the "decadent" French Symbolistes were suspect, and that true American original, Walt Whitman, was still kept in the closet.) In the meantime, mainstream "magazine" poets remained content to moralize and provide "uplift," while genteel ladies and gentlemen with three names aped the pallid manners of their supposed betters in England, as they churned the last dregs of Romanticism.

Surveying the "name" poets of turn of the century today is a depressing task; many are virtually unreadable now. In stilted diction and contorted syntax, versifiers solemn and silly recycled the same stale subjects and pious platitudes in the prescribed manner. From their gentle musings, one could conclude these soporific songsters were unaware that the electric lightbulb or the telephone, automobiles or elevators had been invented.

To the generation coming of age in the new century, the archaic language, lofty abstractions, and overworked conventions seemed increasingly empty, irrelevant, and incapable of dealing with the present realities of a rapidly changing, urbanized society. In the advanced theories of the visual artists and particularly in their use of collage and other disjunctive techniques, aspiring poets saw fresh ways to approach the complexity of modern consciousness and to express the sense of uncertainty, fragmentation, and alienation in modern life.

As an art critic during this pivotal era, Monroe was ideally placed to track the latest movements—"wild" Fauvism, "crazy" Cubism, and Futurism. In *A Poet's Life*, she said "the grand climax" of her time at the art desk was the famous New York Armory Show, which she persuaded the *Tribune* was so important that she had to have "an expense-account trip to give Chicago news of it." At the 1913 exhibition of dissident artists, she had "a grand time" and enjoyed the viewers' puzzled and indignant reactions. Monroe herself didn't always appreciate some works. ("Duchamp's *Nude Descending a Staircase*," she wrote, "looks like a pack of brown cards in a nightmare or a dynamited suit of Japanese armor.") But she approved: "They throw a bomb into the entrenched camps, give to American art a much needed shaking-up." When the show came to the Art Institute of Chicago, drawing unprecedented crowds and protests, she wrote:

> Either these pictures are good or they are not. If they are good, they will make their way in spite of objections; if not, they will perish without the aid of objections. . . . Better the wildest extravagance of the cubists than the lifeless works of certain artists who ridicule them. . . . They represent a search for new beauty, impatience with formulae, a reaching out toward the inexpressible, a longing for new versions of truth.

More than she knew, she was describing the attitudes that would surface among the younger poets. The work they submitted, and from which she had to reject or select for her own "exhibition," would put her broadmindedness to the test.

Modern architecture was Monroe's allied and even greater interest, dating at least to the early 1880s, after her older sister, Dora, married the brilliant John Wellborn Root. With his partner, Daniel H. Burnham, Root devised new engineering methods for tall structures and designed Chicago's Monadnock and Rookery Buildings. She knew both men well, and became a champion of Louis Sullivan, creator of the Auditorium Theater and Chicago Stock Exchange. She admired Sullivan's originality as a designer, and his progressive spirit and democratic idealism, which mirrored her own. (She was less fond of his student, Frank Lloyd Wright, who "was by no means Sullivan's equal," but had "a genius for publicity.") With these leaders of the Chicago School of architecture, she often discussed the latest developments and shared their optimistic visions of the future.

By 1910, urban landscapes were crowded with skyscrapers their early Chicago experiments had inspired and defined. Architects, painters, fiction writers, dramatists, all had entered the new age and were trying to come to terms with the modern world created by science and technology. Taking their lead from the scientists, artists were appropriating their methods, propounding theories, performing "experiments," or at least adopting scientific-sounding vocabularies. Challenging conventions, advanced thinkers in almost all artistic media were reconsidering basic principles and attempting to find fresh modes of expression. Looking over the scene in the first decade of the twentieth century, Monroe had to admit that only poetry seemed stuck in the nineteenth, or earlier.

Given its dated perspective and dullness, it seems little wonder that poetry had diminished in importance and lost its once-wide audience. But Monroe didn't see it quite that way. She fixed responsibility for the decline in production—not on the mediocrity of the rhymesters or their disregard for the altered perceptions and actual experiences of modern life—but on crass publishers and a callous public.

2. The Birth of an Idea

Returning from an around-the-world trip in the spring of 1911, Monroe found Chicago "surging with art activities and aspirations beneath its commercial surface." Chicagoans could well boast of their city's cultural progress, and no one was prouder—or a greater booster—than Harriet Monroe. She inventoried the artistic assets of the metropolis: the Chicago Symphony Orchestra, the Little Theatre, the new dance troupes, the renowned high-rises. And, of course, the Art Institute, symbol of Chicago's new status and of special interest to her, personally and professionally. Generously endowed privately and publicly supported by tax dollars, it could afford to give large prizes to painters and sculptors, as well as scholarships to its school. Monroe couldn't help making comparisons with her own métier and feeling resentment. She put the question in the chapter "The Birth of an Idea" in *A Poet's Life*:

> Why this difference between the respectful attitude of donors and press and public toward painting and sculpture ... and the general contemptuous indifference of all these powers toward the poet and the beautiful art he practices or aims at, the art which, more than any other, has passed on the "tale of the tribe" to succeeding generations?

The phrasing captures Monroe at her most self-consciously grandiloquent. But couched in the rhetoric is a concept well understood in Chicago. Indeed, it is the unofficial motto at City Hall: *Ubi meum?*— Where's mine?

Monroe never tired of offering her Defense of Poetry. She truly believed that community support was warranted; while conferring private benefit upon striving poets, it contributed to the public good. Thus, from the start, she viewed her project in the old-fashioned way, as a civic enterprise. "Gradually, during the half-year after my return," she recalled, "I became convinced that something must be done; and since nobody else was doing anything, it might be 'up to me' to try to stir up the sluggish situation. But what could I do?" Instead of envying the Art Institute and the other successful Chicago cultural organizations, she decided to copy their methods and create one herself.

Afraid that "such a harebrained project" as a poetry monthly would be ridiculed, she sought reassurance from several artistic confidantes. Then, on 23 June 1911, she consulted her friend Hobart C. Chatfield-Taylor, a novelist, biographer, and trustee of several high-profile Chicago institutions. He agreed that poets needed help; then he offered a financial plan. Get one hundred people to underwrite the magazine at $50 a year for five years. With a $5,000 annual budget, the editor should have enough to cover expenses. Counting subscription income, she could even pay the poets. The magazine should also offer annual prizes. To start the Guarantors Fund, he wrote a check for $50.

Monroe set to work. Though far from rich herself, she had many friends among the social elite, and her sterling reputation gained her entrée to the best addresses in Chicago and the suburbs. Between calls to matrons on Astor Street, she knocked on the doors of businessmen on LaSalle. In visiting offices, she remembered, "I would not be stopped by secretaries, those polite evaders whom big men placed at their doors to turn away importunate solicitors like me." Face to face, Miss Monroe was not easily denied. Whether they were persuaded to her cause or just wanted to be rid of her, she had little trouble acquiring her first thirty sponsors.

By the spring of 1912 she had seventy subscribers, which "gave the project plausibility." She then printed up a brochure stating her case: Poetry alone had no endowment, prizes, scholarships. Publishers "almost never" printed books of verse without subsidies. Editors of "most literary magazines" refused to accept long poems, "no matter how meritorious." Poets were paid "less than one-tenth" what artists received. And, the syllabus of errors concluded, if a book of verse got printed, the critics ignored it and few bought it: "In short, the vast English-speaking world says to its poets: Silence!"

More persuasive perhaps than her plea in the brochure was her list of first Guarantors to the Fund, which read like a Who's Who of Chicago commerce and society: Charles Deering and Chauncey and Cyrus H. McCormick (McCormick Harvester Company), Mrs. Potter Palmer (The Palmer House hotel), Edith Rockefeller McCormick, Mrs. George M. Pullman (railroad cars), Mrs. Julius Rosenwald and Albert H. Loeb (Sears, Roebuck), Edward L. and Martin A. Ryerson (steel), Samuel Insull (utilities), Charles H. Swift (meat packing). Other patrons included newspaper editors, professors, bankers, architects, and several attorneys, including Clarence Darrow.

By June 1912 Monroe had surpassed her goal. With 108 people signed up, she stopped soliciting—a decision she would later regret. Most of the Guarantors weren't deeply interested in poetry, which left her free in the editorial department. They didn't supervise her on the business side, either. Monroe's probity was assurance enough that her "experiment" would reflect well on them and the city. She did appoint an advisory board—Chatfield-Taylor, the poet and critic Edith Wyatt, and the novelist Henry Blake Fuller—who helped select prize winners, but did little else after the first six months.

Monroe then chose her Associate Editor. Alice Corbin Henderson had attended the University of Chicago, and in 1905 she married the painter and designer William Penhallow Henderson. (In 1913, he did murals for Frank Lloyd Wright's Midway Gardens project and was instrumental in bringing the Armory Show to Chicago.) Alice Corbin's first poetry book, *The Spinning Woman of the Sky*, appeared in 1912, and she was well liked in Chicago artistic circles. In August, Monroe discussed her project with the couple, and Mrs. Henderson agreed to come on as first reader of manuscripts, at $40 a month. Her eye for new talent and strong critical sense would prove crucial to the magazine's early success.

3. "The Open Door"

With venture capital secured and staff assembled, Monroe now set about finding authors. She had no fixed idea of who they might be, and no sharply defined editorial policy. Not unlike some Internet entrepreneurs today, she seemed more concerned about founding a company, and had devoted more time and thought to getting the financing than considering the actual product the enterprise might offer. Her working assumption about both contents and customers appeared to be: If we build it, they will come.

Monroe drew up two new flyers, one for use in soliciting subscribers, the other to attract potential contributing poets. The "poets' circular" featured the Pegasus logo and the complete title: *Poetry: A Magazine of Verse*, as well as the first appearance of the motto from Whitman which would appear on each issue: "To have great poets, there must be great audiences too." Informing the poets of the backing for "this experiment" and of the $250 prize for the best work published in the first year, the circular promised:

> First, a chance to be heard in their own place, without the limitations imposed by the popular magazine....
> Second . . . we hope to print poems of greater length and of more intimate and serious character than the other magazines can afford to use. All kinds of verse will be considered—narrative, dramatic, lyric,— quality alone being the test of acceptance.

Third, besides the prize or prizes above mentioned, we shall pay
contributors.... [T]his magazine is not intended as a money-maker but
as a public-spirited effort to gather together and enlarge the poet's pub-
lic and to increase his earnings.

The Editor concluded:

We promise to refuse nothing because it is too good, whatever be
the nature of its excellence. We shall read with special interest poems of
modern significance, but the most classic subject will not be declined if
it reaches a high standard of quality.

Aside from the earnest tone, the appeal is notable for its generality. The
chief motives of the magazine are support of poets and development of
an audience; the character of the "best verse" is left undefined.

Monroe did not see herself as the leader of a new movement. She
issued no manifesto listing revolutionary objectives. There was no "move-
ment" as such when she was setting up the magazine. "Modernism" is a
term applied by critics, after the fact, to the radical transformations in
literature dating roughly from the founding of *Poetry* to 1922. And it is a
misleading term, suggesting more unity of ideas and methods than
existed. The emerging poets who would later be identified with literary
modernism were, in 1912, isolated individuals, obscurely published if at
all, groping their way to their own distinctive styles, not an organized
group with a clearly outlined agenda.

Harriet Monroe was far from a revolutionary, and certainly no theo-
rist. She didn't issue a "policy" statement until the second issue, and then
only to declare her lack of allegiance to any one aesthetic viewpoint. She
intended to be inclusive not restrictive, as she announced in a brief edito-
rial in November 1912:

The Open Door will be the policy of the magazine—may the great
poet we are looking for never find it shut, or half-shut, against his
ample genius! To this end the editors hope to keep free of entangling
alliances with any single class or school. They desire to print the best
English verse which is being written today, regardless of where, by
whom, or under what theory of art it is written. Nor will the magazine
promise to limit its editorial comments to one set of opinions.

4. First Responses

Monroe was nothing if not systematic in soliciting authors. During the summer of 1912, she spent several weeks in the Chicago Public Library reading the recent poetry books. She also perused American and English magazines from the previous five years for verse. In early August she sent out letters to fifty poets, asking them to submit. Among the Americans who received personalized requests and returned cordial responses were: Madison Cawein ("The Keats of Kentucky"), Floyd Dell (editor of the *Friday Literary Review* of the *Chicago Evening Post*), Arthur Davison Ficke (a lawyer in Davenport), Agnes Lee, Edwin Markham, John G. Neihardt (a bard from Nebraska), Grace Fallow Norton, Edwin Arlington Robinson, Louis Untermeyer, Edith Wharton, Helen Hay Whitney, John Hall Wheelock, Willa Cather, and George Edward Woodberry.

Robinson didn't reply until 14 January 1913, explaining he was not writing poems now, only plays, "the first and last infirmity of noble and ignoble minds." But he added:

When I have satisfied myself and all my friends that I cannot write one, I hope to be able to write some more poetry—or verse, if you insist. Will you pardon me if I presume to ask why you have concentrated so much deadly emphasis into the sub-title of your magazine?

Robinson would not be the only poet to question the redundant or (depending on point of view) contradictory subtitle. It stayed on the cover for thirty-eight years, until Karl Shapiro—who insisted distinctions be drawn between "verse" and "poetry"—made its removal one of his first acts upon assuming the editorship.

Deliberately *not* invited were successful "magazine" poets such as Olive Tilford Dargan, Clinton Scollard, Edith Thomas, Lizette Woodward Reese, and Ella Wheeler Wilcox, a popular author for whom Monroe seems to have had a particular dislike. Grace Hazard Conkling was not sent a circular, but got word of it very early. She wrote on 9 August, asking if she might send a suite of poems called "Symphony of a Mexican Garden." Monroe printed the "Symphony" in the very first issue. Conkling would be published dozens of times into the twenties. (Her daughters, Hilda and Elsa, also appeared several times, first in July 1916, when they were four and five years old.)

Newcomers like Joyce Kilmer, Conrad Aiken, and Sara Teasdale also escaped Monroe's notice. Others who would figure prominently in the history of American poetry and *Poetry* did not make the list, either, including Robert Frost, who had moved to England; Edgar Lee Masters, then using the pen name Webster Ford; Carl Sandburg, whose one book had appeared in 1904; and William Carlos Williams, whose privately printed first *Poems* of 1909 probably wasn't in the Chicago Public Library. All would make appearances over the next several months, gaining wide attention that would start, or restart, their careers.

Most of the poets solicited responded within a week or two. One of the very first was Floyd Dell, a fellow critic. Before he moved to New York in 1913 to join the staff of the *Masses*, Dell was a leader of Chicago's younger, "Bohemian" artistic set. Although Harriet Monroe's closest friends were older, more established figures, it is clear from the cordial tone of the Dell correspondence that she attempted to have good relations with the new and more radical generation in town, as well. Dell wrote her in August: "If I come across any young poets—but having said that I think of several—I'll send you their names and addresses. But I refuse to be considered responsible for any of 'em." When Dell himself did not submit any work, Monroe repeated her request. He wrote to apologize on 1 April 1913:

> I have been discouraged from writing by the rumor that you pay for such matter. I have not the heart to take any of "Poetry's" money. I have a feeling that money devoted to the cause of revolution should be spent only for bombs. . . .
>
> The only thing I should suggest about "Poetry" is that it needs a little more the controversial note . . . . I would like to come around to your office on Monday . . . first to show you that my advice is probably not so valuable as you think, and second to offer it to you in any amount. . . . But I shouldn't wonder if you are not much more revolutionary than I . . . .

Vachel Lindsay and Amy Lowell were particularly eager in answering the Editor's call, each beginning a voluminous (and often problematic) correspondence with Harriet Monroe that would continue the rest of their lives. Although at the moment she had no poems to offer, Lowell wrote on 7 September that she found *Poetry* "a most excellent undertaking," and enclosed a check for $25. Monroe had extraordinary faith in Lindsay, for she wrote him, care of the *American Magazine*, 6 September: "Dear Sir: I have not seen your verse but your prose articles make me hope that you will give me the chance to look them over. Can you not submit a few poems for early publication in our magazine?"

Lindsay replied from Los Angeles on 18 September, informing her he was from Springfield, Illinois: "If I may be confidential I have been horri-

Vachel Lindsay's grateful bow to Harriet Monroe, 22 November 1912.

bly homesick for a month—and fear that (spiritually speaking) I shall hobble through the rest of my expedition." From Springfield, he wrote again on 22 November, enclosing "General William Booth Enters into

Heaven," which was to be the most widely noted poem *Poetry* published in its first year.

> My Dear Miss Monroe:
>
> I hereby make my best bow and extend to you my grateful thanks for taking some of the moon-poems. Here is one more that you need not print.
>
> Any corrections you desire to have made in General Booth I will gladly undertake. I have set my heart on having you spread that work throughout the Anglo Saxon world.

About a third of Monroe's circulars and letters went to British poets, several of whom she had met on her trips to England. Among them were the "Georgians" John Drinkwater, Alfred Noyes, Wilfred Wilson Gibson, Lascelles Abercrombie, and the recently prominent John Masefield. Others from the English group included Frederic Manning, Alice Meynell, Harold Monro (proprietor of the Poetry Bookshop and editor of the *Poetry Review*), Ernest Rhys (editor of Everyman's Library), Lady Margaret Sackville, James Stephens, Allen Upward, Joseph Campbell, and William Butler Yeats—in short, virtually all the notable poets then writing in the British Isles.

On 15 August, Monroe solicited work from Yeats, whom she had met when he was on tour in Chicago and whose international reputation would lend invaluable prestige and credibility to the new magazine: "I trust that you may be interested in this project for the relief of the muse. It will be a great pleasure and honor if you are willing to testify to that interest by sending us a poem or a group of poems for early publication. Indeed, I can think of no contribution which would delight me more." She was unaware he was not in London at the time. In November Ezra Pound forwarded five of Yeats's poems, which he had taken the liberty of "correcting."

5. The First Pound Letters

Of all the overseas poets who replied, no one was more enthusiastic than Pound, then a twenty-seven-year-old expatriate living in England and little known in America. With her circular, Monroe sent a personal invitation on 7 August, in care of his father, Homer L. Pound, assistant assayer at the U.S. Mint in Philadelphia. Pound responded immediately, not only promising to give her exclusive American rights to his poems, but offering to gather material from "other sources." He also enclosed "Middle-Aged" and "To Whistler, American." By return post, Monroe accepted both offerings for the inaugural issue and asked him to be *Poetry*'s foreign agent.

From his top-floor bed-sitting room at 10, Church Walk, Kensington, Pound began sending a steady stream of long letters, as many as three a week in the first months, filled with encouragement, advice, and exhortations. Besides the celebrated Yeats, he eventually forwarded poems from the Bengali poet Rabindranath Tagore, soon to be awarded the Nobel Prize, as well as submissions from his unknown protégés, Richard Aldington and Hilda Doolittle.

In the October 1935 issue, Monroe published an article, "*Poetry*'s Old Letters," in which she glanced back gratefully on Pound's help: "He looked on *Poetry* almost as his organ during its first year or two; indeed, it *was* partly his organ because, through his contacts in London, he sent to Chicago not only his own poems and articles, but poems by people otherwise most inaccessible . . . . He didn't mind being 'didactic' in his letters even to the point of violence; and since he was born to be a great teacher, the editor felt herself being rapidly educated."

In *A Poet's Life*, she repeated the sentiments and published extracts from Pound's first letters. But she did not go into much detail about their later exchanges, drawing a discreet veil over Pound's many disagreements. While his lengthy missives reveal a great deal about Pound's personality, they are also curiously impersonal. He mentions almost nothing about his extraliterary life, but issues a steady stream of bold opinions about the current state of the art, with suggestions for editing the magazine.

Pound's letters bristle with energy. In the first, scrawled in longhand, his pen often stabs the paper: a portrait of agitation. The poet was a very speedy but not a very well-organized letter writer. (In a letter to Alice Henderson, he mentioned writing from dawn to late into the night.) He was no better as an essayist, as he was the first to admit. Though Pound is full of arguments, his points are seldom neatly arranged. Usually he keeps two or three main subjects in play, jumping from one idea to the next, then returning to themes as further thoughts occur. Nearly all the letters have postscripts or comments inserted between the lines.

To preserve their flavor in the presentation here, Pound's idiosyncrasies in spelling and punctuation have been retained, except in cases of obvious errors, which have been silently corrected. In December 1912, Pound began typing his letters. This was not a great improvement; he was a poor typist, working perhaps on a bad machine. His punctuation is erratic, and to avoid confusion or to make syntax clearer, commas or semicolons have sometimes been inserted. Pound neglected to supply dates on many of his early letters; these have been supplied from H.M.'s pencilled notations and internal evidence. For her most important communications, Monroe made carbon copies or kept drafts; they are the sources for the texts of her correspondence here.

Harriet Monroe to Ezra Pound

7 *August 1912*

Dear Sir:

Your poetry has given me very special pleasure ever since Mr. [Elkin] Mathews introduced me to it in his London office, a fact which I am acknowledging in an article on American Poets, in the Poetry Review.

I strongly hope that you may be interested in this project for a magazine of verse and that you may be willing to send us a group of poems, for very early publication.

Very truly yours, / Harriet Monroe

Ezra Pound to Harriet Monroe

[18 August 1912]

Dear Madam:

I *am* interested, and your scheme as far as I understand it seems not only sound, but the only possible method. There is no other magazine in America which is not an insult to the serious artist and to the dignity of his art.

But? Can you teach the American poet that poetry *is* an *art*, an art with a technique, with media, an art that must be in constant flux, a constant change of manner, if it is to live[?] Can you teach him that it is not a pentametric echo of the sociological dogma printed in last year's magazines? Maybe. Anyhow you have work before you.

I may be myopic, but during my last tortured visit to America I found no writer and but one reviewer who had any worthy conception of poetry, the Art. However I need not bore you with jeremiads.

At least you are not the usual "esthetic magazine", which is if anything worse than the popular, for the esthetic magazine expects the artist to do all the work, pays nothing, and then undermines his credit by making his convictions appear ridiculous.

Quant à moi: If you conceive verse as a living medium, on a par with paint, marble, and music, you may announce, if it's any good to you, that for the present such of my work as appears in America (barring my own books) will appear exclusively in your magazine. I think you might easily get all the serious artists to boycott the rest of the press entirely. . . .

? Are you for American Poetry or for Poetry[?] The latter is more important, but it is important that America should boost the former,

Ezra Pound responding to Harriet Monroe's invitation, August 1912.

provided it don't mean a blindness to the art. The glory of any nation is to produce art that can be exported without disgrace to its origin.

I ask because if you do want poetry from other sources I may be able to be of use. I dont think it's any of the artist's business to see whether or no he circulates, but I was nevertheless tempted, & on the verge of starting a quarterly, and it's a great relief to know that your paper may manage what I had, without financial strength, been about to attempt rather forlornly.

I don't think we need go to the French extreme of having four prefaces to each poem and eight schools for every dozen of poets, but you must keep an eye on Paris. Anyhow I hope your ensign is not "More poetry!" But, more interesting poetry, & *maestria* [mastery]!

If I can be of any use in keeping you or the magazine in touch with whatever is most dynamic in artistic thought, either here or in Paris—as much of it comes to me, and I *do* see nearly everyone that matters—I shall be glad to do so.

I send you all that I have in my desk—an over-elaborate post-Browning "Imagiste" affair ["Middle-Aged"] and a note on the Whistler exhibit ["To Whistler, American"]. I count him our only great artist, and even this informal salute, drastic as it is, may not be out of place at the threshold of what I hope is an endeavor to carry into our American poetry the same sort of life and intensity which he infused into modern painting.

Sincerely yours, / Ezra Pound

Any agonizing that tends to hurry—what I believe in the end to be inevitable—our American Risorgimento, is dear to me. That awakening will make the Italian renaissance look like a tempest in a teapot. The force we have, & the impulse, but the guiding sense, the discrimination in applying the force, we must wait and strive for.

Ezra Pound to Harriet Monroe   *21 September 1912*

My Dear Harriet Monroe:

All right you can put me down as "foreign correspondent or foreign edtr." if you like, and pay me whatever or whenever is convenient. If I were in this trade for the cash there is to be gotten from it, I should have quit some time ago. There is a rather fine saying of Browning's which is not so well known as it might be: "Money! If I'd made matches with my hands I'd have made more out of it. . . ."

I'm sorry I had nothing more important to send you for the first number—but I've already explained that at length in my other letter. You'll get whatever I do that is fit to print as soon as I can manage it: you could just as well have had some of "Ripostes" only it's too late now, and was when you wrote. I shan't want to send you very much prose, for I am the surviving saducee [sic] and my hatred of bad verse is only measurable by my care [for] poetry. . . .

I have also some of young Aldington's stuff here, but I can hardly send it to you without asking him.

As touching exchanges with the foreign journals. Perhaps you had better send me some stationery and I'll have my self and address added to the heading as "foreign editor" or what ever I'm to be called, and try to arrange the exchanges with Paris, Vienna etc.—if you will have copies sent to the offices of such papers as I name and I will then have them send their issues to me direct., s.v.p. Let me know how many copies you care to distribute in this way. I could manage with 25 but might want a few more. . . .

As touching Boston & New York—if their press is too much amused by Chicago's having a Poetry magazine you might send me some of the clippings and perhaps I can riposte on them from a less expected quarter. . . .

Ezra Pound to Harriet Monroe   *[late September 1912]*

Dear Miss Monroe:

I've just written to Yeats. It's rather hard to get anything out of him by mail and he won't be back in London until Nov. Still I've done what I can, and as it's the first favor or about the first that I've asked for three years, I may get something—"to set the tone."

Also I'll try to get some of the poems of the very great Bengal poet, Ramanath [Rabindranath] Tagore. They are going to be THE sensation of the winter. . . . [sic] but I don't know how much of my knowledge has been imparted to me in confidence so I couldn't mention them in my note on "Status Rerum."

W.B.Y. is doing the introduction to them. They are translated by the author into very beautiful Eng. prose, with mastery of cadence.

I shall leave the "literati" to themselves. They already support themselves very comfortably—unless there is someone whose work you particularly want. . . . [sic]

As soon as I know what rates (exactly) we can offer I shall start on Paris. It might pay to spend a little freely at the beginning. We must be taken seriously *at once*. We must be *the voice* not only for the *U.S.* but internationally. [*H.M.'s note between the lines:* "I think we might print one French poem a month."] . . .

My idea of our policy is this: we support American poets—preferably the young ones who have a serious determination to produce master-work. We *import* only such work as is better than that produced at home. The *best* foreign stuff, the stuff well above mediocrity, or the experiments that seem serious and seriously & sanely directed toward the broadening and development of The Art of Poetry.

And "TO HELL WITH HARPER'S AND THE MAGAZINE TOUCH."

Have you a list of the "Patrons". I don't see why we should stop at $5000 per yr. subsidy if we can get more. At least I shall tackle a few people here—if there's no objection. These —d expatriates might as

well come in on the deal. I see no reason why Chicago should be
bounded on the east by Manhattan Island. In fact, if our 'colony' on this
side of the water doesn't make some sort of showing in the subsidy list I
shall do my little to make them "ashamed of theirself."

I have gone through certain knot-holes in the cause of American Art
and I have earned the right to speak my mind.

(I might say, I have ruined my digestion, & achieved a liver prematurely
and my "mind" on the subject of "slackers" is somewhat acidulated.)

I think a few words of approval (of us) from Henry James might do
more to quell the facetious east than anything I could say. He is sup-
posed to hate poetry, so it may be difficult to elicit them. I must bide
my time, but I'll do what I can with him. Do send me some circulars,
the first sort: I've sent my only copy to Yeats.

Yours, / Ezra Pound

6. The Rush to Publication

By late summer, with positive responses coming from around the country
and promises of more manuscripts from London, Monroe went canoeing
in northern Wisconsin. Her idyll was rudely interrupted when a friend
sent her a circular for a projected Boston magazine of poetry that threat-
ened to use "her" title and begin publication in October. (She had
applied to the Library of Congress to protect the name *Poetry*, but was
informed that there was no provision in copyright law for magazine
titles.) In a panic, she returned to Chicago and started stamping "Octo-
ber" as the publication date on her flyers—and hoped her "rival" would
be delayed with his first issue.

Arthur Davison Ficke had also received the brochure, and on 24 Sep-
tember he wrote Monroe that "it seems to me it will do no harm to
insert a knife very gently a little way between the gentlemen's ribs." On
his law office stationery, Ficke suggested to Edward J. O'Brien, Esq., Edi-
tor of "Poetry" (Boston), that confusion would result and advised he take
another name. In the event, the *Poetry Journal*—actually a project of the
Boston Evening Transcript critic William Stanley Braithwaite—did not
appear until November.

Taking no chances, Monroe hastily assembled her first issue with what
she had on hand. When she discovered there was only enough material to
fill fourteen pages, Mrs. William Vaughn Moody came to the rescue with
an unpublished poem by her late husband. Monroe then turned to her
friend, the publisher Ralph Fletcher Seymour, who advised her on type-
faces and paper and rushed to design the magazine's cover and layout.

Henry Fuller sat up nights proofreading, "the editor being then untrained." Through a hectic three weeks, they kept the project secret from Boston and the rest of the world. Dated October, *Poetry: A Magazine of Verse*, Volume I, Number 1, came off the presses 23 September 1912, Monroe recorded, "nearly two months before the laggard Bostonians."

With a bow to the past, the issue opened with Ficke's double sonnet "Poetry," followed by Moody's long poem, "I Am the Woman," and Pound's two first appearances. Short lyrics by Emilia Stuart Lorimer and Helen Dudley (their first publications) and Conkling's "Symphony" completed the poetry section. Short essays by Edith Wyatt and Monroe and the Editor's remarks on "The Motive of the Magazine" made up the

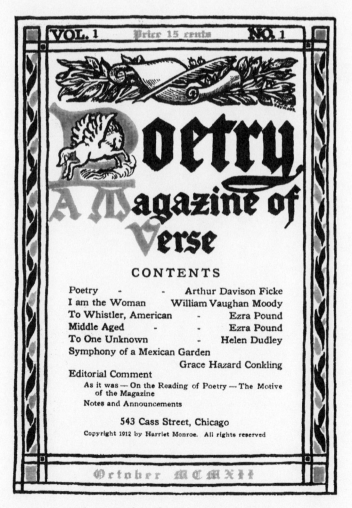

Title page of the first issue, October 1912.

prose section. The first press run of 1,000 copies was gone within two weeks. Monroe had instructed the printers to hold the type, and another 1,000 copies were ordered. She recalled: "It was an exciting day for the editor and all the staff when their impertinent little organ of the muse first lifted its voice for the 'Cinderella of the arts.'"

CHAPTER II

The View from Cass Street

1. "Hopes and Hospitalities"

Adding to the pressure as she rushed to publication, the Editor had to find a permanent office. In September, she moved from the Fine Arts Building to 543 Cass Street (now Wabash Avenue) and set up operations in the former living room of a converted mansion. When the magazine was forced to relocate in 1922, Monroe printed an article, "Moving," in which she looked back on the old office, with "our gallery of poets' photographs and other pictures, our tempers and temperaments, our hearts and hopes and hospitalities." The small space was usually crowded with staff, advisors, and visitors. *Poetry*'s "Open Door" policy was taken literally, and poets and friends felt free to drop by to chat, read and discuss poems, or help with clerical chores. "During those first years," Monroe recorded in her autobiography, "Alice Corbin was not only a well-nigh indispensable member of *Poetry*'s staff, but also one of the gayest and most brilliant slingers of repartee in the groups that soon began to gather in the *Poetry* office."

In the course of these gatherings, the Editor was known to brew coffee over an open fire in the vacant lot next door. At four o'clock, she would produce a box of chocolates, and the staff took a break. Special guests were taken to Victor's, an Italian restaurant around the corner. Visitors discovered that, despite her stern appearance, Miss Monroe was rather a soft touch, and writers down on their luck knew they could depend on her for a handout. She was particularly fond of young people, and many an aspiring college poet and even some high school students were invited to tea. Several, like Janet Lewis, Yvor Winters, and Elder Olson, got their starts in *Poetry* after such meetings and kept in touch for decades. George Dillon and Henry Rago (who met H.M. in 1929, when he was fourteen) joined the staff and eventually became Editors themselves.

As a major railroad hub, Chicago was a frequent transfer point, and many roving poets used their time between trains to visit the office. Shortly before receiving the Nobel Prize in 1913, Rabindranath Tagore

H.M. in the Cass Street office; the windows looked out on the
vacant lot where she brewed coffee for guests.

came to Chicago with his son, a chemistry student at the University of
Illinois. Since *Poetry* had few funds for entertaining, Monroe's old friend
Harriet Moody put them up at her house, as she would many others.
During the visit, Will Henderson painted the poet's portrait. In 1915, soon
after his return from England, John Gould Fletcher spent several months
in Chicago, and H.M. helped him when his funds ran out. In his autobi-
ography, *Life Is My Song* (1937), Fletcher left an account of his visits to the
office, where he found Carl Sandburg correcting proofs with his feet
propped on Monroe's desk, a derby over his eyes, and a cigar in his
mouth. Sandburg didn't bother to say hello. At their first meeting,
Fletcher recalled, Monroe seemed cool and aloof. "I scarcely realized
what a degree of crusading ardor lay beneath her exterior."

Fletcher grew to admire Mrs. Henderson, who he discovered was a
southerner like himself, and sympathetic to his poetry. He concluded,
"Without her influence Miss Monroe's paper might have been, I felt, nar-
rower in its scope and less epoch-making in its effect." Fletcher eventually
met Edgar Lee Masters, who "baffled" him but whose work he respected.

He did not see Vachel Lindsay, which was just as well. He admitted he had "already taken a strong and possibly unreasoning dislike to 'General William Booth Enters into Heaven,' with its tone of a backwoods revival meeting."

Lindsay's unusual piece was published in January 1913, and in large part fixed *Poetry*'s early reputation, at least in the mind of the general public, as a radical journal that printed all manner of strange new things. But from the start, the magazine also published a great deal of traditional verse. Even more widely noted than Lindsay's dramatic tribute to the founder of the Salvation Army—and certainly more crowd pleasing than anything Pound submitted—was a six-couplet lyric

Carl Sandburg, author of "Chicago Poems" and sometime proofreader for *Poetry*.

that became the most often quoted and beloved poem that Monroe ever presented. Replying to H.M.'s acceptance notice (and suggestions), the author wrote from Mahwah, New Jersey, 26 May 1913: "I thank you for your note of May 24th. Six dollars will satisfy me for 'Trees'. I like the line about 'a nest of robins in her hair' but if it offends you seriously you may omit it and its predecessor. . . . Joyce Kilmer."

"Trees" was reprinted innumerable times and, set to music by Oscar Rasbach, brought in large sums of money over many decades to the music publisher G. Schirmer, Inc., as well as to vocalists, arrangers, record companies, broadcasters—everyone, except the author and the magazine that originally printed the poem in August 1913. Had *Poetry* shared in the royalties, its editors might never have had to worry about deficits.

Writing to H.M. 13 September 1913, even the normally dry-eyed Ezra Pound allowed that, "Of your things, Kilmer seems the best: a simple Blake-esque tone, bad reasoning but poetic—can he sustain himself?" Like Fletcher, Pound disliked the productions of Vachel Lindsay, and became ever more convinced that he was a lightweight. Fletcher's instant antipathy toward Lindsay's style indicates how quickly lines of demarcation were being drawn within the magazine's first year. By the time the first four or five issues had come out, many of the poets were already formed in opposing camps.

Writers in conventional modes—together with the more conservative subscribers and literary critics—seldom approved of the works of the experimentalists. Pound's contributions, both his own poetry and that of the younger people he promoted, provoked the greatest derision. In June 1913, for example, John G. Neihardt, a poet of the old school, complained that Monroe was turning her magazine into "a freak." For their part, the innovators—who often disagreed among themselves—found the writers in traditional forms hopelessly passé or merely dull, and tried to ignore them. Each side often felt uncomfortable appearing between the same covers. And each complained to the Editor that she favored or was a partisan of the opposite side.

One thing is clear from the outset: Harriet Monroe did not approve of "magazine poets." A case in point was the highly successful, "inspirational" Ella Wheeler Wilcox. One of the best-known poets of her time, Wilcox (1855–1919) is virtually forgotten today, but not her immortal lines: "Laugh and the world laughs with you, / Weep and you weep alone." In May 1913, Monroe printed an uncharacteristically harsh editorial, "In Danger," in which she asked: "How may a man be a popular poet and yet save his soul and his art?" Rather cruelly, she added, "Some popular poets, of course, have no souls to save—none, at least, which emerge about the milk-and-water current of their verse, the [Martin Farquhar] Tuppers and Ella Wheeler Wilcoxes of this generation." The summary dismissal elicited a spirited response on 8 September from the "soulless" but uplifting author, who felt (not without reason) that Monroe was being vindictive:

Miss Munroe [sic],

I have just chanced upon your sweet womanly reference to me in the May Poetry Magazine. It gave me a sharp hurt; but stronger than any other feeling, was my pity for you.

Criticism is as needed in the world of art, as skilled surgery in the world of medicine. But the doctor who thrusts a rusty nail into the flesh of a patient because he chances not to like him, is not practicing surgery. You thrust a rusty pen into a poet you chance not to like. That is not criticism. It is spitefulness.

There are, undoubtedly, people whose souls are not sufficiently developed to be saved. Foremost among them, is the self styled critic who wantonly wounds an author whose works have not been read with an unprejudiced mind.

Poetry to me is a divine thing. I love it with all my heart; (yes even with my soul, which I dare believe is well evolved). There are as many kinds of poetry as there are intellects in men. I have followed the bent of my own talents, since I first *thought* in verse, and have worked according to my own light. I have never made a bid for popularity. If I chance to be a popular poet, it is just because I have loved God and life and people and expressed sentiments and emotions which found echoes in other hearts. If this is a sin against art, let me be unregenerate to the day of my death. . . .

Hoping you may develop a sense of justice, which will cause you to study your poets before criticising them, and that you may also grow at least a sage bush of heart to embellish your desert of intellect, I am,

Sincerely yours / Ella Wheeler Wilcox

She also attached a letter from a devoted reader, a lonely invalid who found consolation in her work, with a note: "This is a sample of letters which come to me by the thousands. I confess it is a kind of 'popularity' which appeals to me." Monroe replied, rather curtly, on 6 October: "We all have our standards, and if your verse is not according to ours, yet it has such a vogue as not to be quite negligible—hence my remark in our May number, which was intended, of course, not for you personally, but for you as an artist. If your feelings were hurt, I am sorry, but the integrity of the art is more important than anybody's feelings."

It's hard not to sympathize with Mrs. Wilcox, whose perception of Monroe and her magazine was probably shared by many another writer and lover of conventional verse. Fletcher, who was more conventional than he knew, was of the opinion that Monroe seemed "disconcerted and bewildered" by the modernist experiments *Poetry* was "provoking," and he claimed H.M. was "in awe of Pound." (Fletcher himself had several differences with E.P. and the avant-garde in London during his years there.) According to Fletcher, the only "ultramodern 'discovery' about whom Miss Monroe was deeply enthusiastic was Wallace Stevens," perhaps because of their interest in Chinese art. He also thought that her main interest was to discover new Midwestern poets.

That Monroe favored Midwesterners is a claim that has been often repeated. But in issue after issue she presented all sorts of poets from widely scattered places. As numerous letters below make clear, even when she did not particularly care for poems and had good reasons not to like certain poets—even people she helped could be incredibly rude to her—she set aside her personal feelings or aesthetic preferences and printed them if their offerings were good, on their own terms, or at least "interesting." And she didn't hesitate to reject poems in whatever styles when they were not.

But during the first months there was positive feeling on all sides. The first issue met with approval in the papers, and many letters arrived commending the enterprise. Amy Lowell wrote 30 September: "It is exceedingly interesting and to have such a magazine is a most cheering thing to all who care for poetry, and for us who are trying to make it, to know that there is an editor who really knows and feels, does make a very great difference." On 27 October, Louis Untermeyer offered praise, as well as the first of many complaints about E.P.: "There are one or two things in it that I do not care for (the Pound contributions particularly), but the average is high—several miles higher than that of any magazine I know of in America . . . . And the format is more pleasing."

2. Editing Practices and Pitfalls

Within the first months, a great many unsolicited poems began arriving at Cass Street. In *A Poet's Life*, Monroe recalled Mrs. Henderson's perusal of the slush pile: "She was a pitiless reader of manuscripts; nothing stodgy or imitative would get by her finely sifting intelligence, and we had many a secret laugh over the confessional 'hot stuff' or the boggy word weeds which tender-minded authors apparently mistook for poetry." Often H.M. and A.C.H. would pencil suggestions on manuscripts—some of which were actually followed by the authors. Ficke, for one, wrote 26 December 1912, accepting with good grace H.M.'s advice offered during a visit:

> Here are the verses, cleaned, pressed, and with the buttons sewed on. I think the "Swinburne" is the better for your objections. . . .
> You were extraordinarily good to let me descend upon you so disturbingly on Monday: and I enjoyed the party to which I invited myself far more than was decent of me. Mrs. Ficke always says that these poets are terrible people to deal with; you never can tell what they will do.

Just how terrible and unpredictable, Monroe soon discovered. When she sent out her circulars, she hadn't expected such an overwhelming response and had imprudently accepted, sight unseen, a verse drama by John Neihardt. When *The Death of Agrippina* arrived, she was appalled to find it was in pseudo-Elizabethan blank verse and hopelessly bombastic. She had said she was willing to print long poems; now she felt she could not allow such a piece to consume an entire issue. She tried to be released from the poem, to make cuts, or to divide it over two issues, but Neihardt was adamant. As Monroe tried to bargain, the poet proved a very tough negotiator, and summer turned to winter. In the end, much as she disliked doing so, Monroe felt duty bound to print the poem.

After it appeared in May 1913, Neihardt was far from happy. Having harbored bad feelings about free verse and the other experimental work the magazine had also presented, he vented his irritation in a tart letter that offers a good summary of the objections many other traditionalists were leveling against the New Poetry. Monroe answered him point for point in her letter of 24 June 1913, which lists her arguments against prolonging moribund tradition and clearly indicates her modernist sympathies in editing the magazine.

John G. Neihardt to Harriet Monroe   Bancroft, Nebr., 18 June 1913

Dear Miss Monroe:-

I have just now received your note . . . . I'm here on vacation for 2 months.

Thanks for the letter you enclosed. I would be grateful if you would let me see all the other letters you have received. . . .

Why do you take so much trouble to yourself by way of fighting sincere work? [Yone] Noguchi and Tagore are wonderful poets; but what of that wretched drivel in the April number? [The issue included Pound's "Contemporania" and Yeats's "The Grey Rock."] In your heart you must know it is insincere & highly imitative of the worst in Whitman. Yelling isn't poetry. Billingsgate isn't beautiful. Rebellion gets no where. Only slow growth ever counts. There is no *new* beauty. Literature *is* organic. We can not banish our ancestors with a fiat. Important changes are not abrupt. Did the French Revolution bring democracy to France? Violence is the manifestation of hysteria. Real growth is imperceptible. You & Pound can't change natural laws. Why repudiate sincerity & careful workmanship?

Don't you know that all this bother that is being made in various lines of human endeavor is the wave crest whitening to no purpose? The depths change slowly, slowly.

Why make your magazine a freak? You could print formless nonsense as an exhibit of transient tendency. But why defend the indefensible? My God! Have you forgotten that we are endowed with a great heritage? Will you & an impudent young man wipe out a tremendous past that has produced us?

Sincerely, / John G. Neihardt

P.S. Don't imagine that this letter has anything to do with pique. You are running a magazine supposed to represent modern American poetry. You did *not* begin with the idea of fostering blatant crudities. That came later. Are you going to show us up as a nation of ignorant roughnecks? The majority of any nation is vulgar; but art can not stoop to the mob. The mob must rise if it wants art, and the matter of bringing art & the mob together is a problem for sociology, not for art. . . .

Harriet Monroe to John G. Neihardt   *24 June 1913*

My dear Mr. Neihardt:

First, I hope you will enjoy your vacation . . . .

You ask to see all the other letters we have received about *Agrippina*. We have received very few—[Madison] Cawein's is the only one of any importance that I remember and I will enclose that with pleasure. You see he agrees with you about E.P. I must say, however, that a great many people don't—people I mean whose opinion is of value for various reasons. I am not speaking now of Mr. Pound's friends or followers, but of men and women of the World . . . .

You say "In your heart you must know it is insincere & highly imitative of the worst in Whitman". Now, as a matter of fact, in my heart I don't know any such thing. I think that Ezra Pound is passionately sincere and that some of the poems are extremely beautiful and full of rare and exquisite rhythmic effects. Of course, in some sense of the word, there is no such thing as new beauty, but all things are relative in this World and one has to use language as one finds it, to express not always the absolute, but usually the relative, and so the phrase "new beauty" has a certain meaning for me and I should be inclined to justify its use.

Of course there is hardly time to argue out some of your propositions. You say "Rebellion gets nowhere. Only slow growth ever counts" and you don't think the French Revolution brought democracy to France. Well I think rebellion does get somewhere and I think volcanic outbursts like the French Revolution are very effectual, even if you cannot sometimes analyze them, are all making for the final result of long hidden growth. You ask, "Why repudiate sincerity and careful workmanship?" I don't, but I think sincerity and careful workmanship are of very little use by themselves and I am tempted to say you must think so too. I fancy, from everything I hear, that Pound is one of the most sincere and careful workers we have—he writes poetry in no slapdash fashion, but very slowly—at least so I am informed by those who know. You ask "Why make your magazine a freak?" I don't see why a few poems or editorials that we print should place it in that category, even if they seem to you freakish, for surely we have been hospitable to all kinds and have not confined ourselves to any one school. You, at least, ought not to accuse us of limiting ourselves to the radical group.

I suppose it comes down at last to a question of innate preference. I find that my instincts are rather with the radicals than with the academicians. This feeling is so emphatic that I devoutly hope a man of your calibre will not spend any more time over Roman tragedies. I feel that that sort of thing is not for our modern World. It has been done and done better and more instinctively than we can possibly do it now. Probably it is that sort of feeling which has prevented any notice from the critics....

This seems to be quite a volume, but I am tempted by the points you raised. Of course I wish you to talk freely to me and your extremely emphatic language does not hurt my feelings in the least....

Well, I might go on forever, but I guess I had better stop. I wish you were returning to Minneapolis, via Chicago. Why don't you? And then we can talk all day and night on these questions.

It was typical of Monroe to try to end disputes on a conciliatory note. Many who quarreled with her continued to correspond; although she might not persuade her opponents to her side, they still remained on friendly terms. Even those who strongly disagreed were forced to give her at least grudging respect. In any case, in explaining the *Agrippina* fiasco to Pound (who never let her forget it), she vowed not to make the same mistake again. In fact, after her first circulars went out, she almost never solicited poetry: it was just too awkward to have to reject someone who kindly responded to a request for work. But she really didn't need to ask. Marion Strobel calculated that by the time she joined the staff, in 1920, *Poetry* was receiving about 3,000 poems a month.

3. More Manuscripts, and Advice, from London

Transatlantic mail sometimes took as long as two weeks in either direction, and so Pound did not receive his copies of the first issue until mid-October. Monroe would have to wait to see his reactions until November. Meanwhile, the manuscripts he had promised arrived in a steady stream, along with more declamatory letters. Besides Tagore's work, Pound sent groups by Richard Aldington and H.D., whom he identified for the first time as "Imagistes." He then forwarded five poems by Yeats; Monroe published them in the December 1912 issue, after restoring the original texts, as Yeats demanded.

Pound also submitted an article on the state of poetry in England, entitled "Status Rerum." Monroe felt the essay was too strident and asked for revisions. The request called forth an impassioned, twenty-one-page letter on 22 October, in which Pound tried to defend his extreme positions.

Despite her misgivings, the Editor acceded to the author's wishes, and printed the piece, almost exactly as he first sent it, in January 1913—with very negative consequences. Many of her critics now had further evidence to support their feeling that *Poetry* was becoming an organ for Pound and his theories.

Ezra Pound to Harriet Monroe   London, [October 1912]

Dear Harriet Monroe:

I'm sending you Aldington's poems (four). They are I think the best stuff now lying loose about London....

Re/ the Sappho fragment. I think you could well print the greek also, as it is very little known. We had both intended to make translations, but I was too much pleased with R.A.'s version to attempt one after I'd seen it.... This will be the first of his work to appear seriously.

It's rather hard to get all I want to say into such small compass as that which follows ["Status Rerum"].

You may think my criticism rather drastic, but I think you could make no greater mistake than that of trying to interest the public in mediocre work. We must be severe if we are to count, and if our voice is going to be, as it should and must be, *the* authority.

If we print slight verse, or young verse, let us do so, saying "This is slight," or "young," or this is a sketch, an experiment.

And let us for gods sake stick to the sketches and experiments of those who really mean to go on and whose sketches and experiments are made in the serious determination that their own later work and that of their successors is to be better and is to profit by their present labour. I don't think it will do "les jeunes" [the young poets] any harm to know what they look like from this side of the water....

I make such a rotten fist at writing prose!!! However, I think I've jabbed down the facts. I can't get 'em into briefer form....

Ezra Pound to Harriet Monroe   London, [3 October 1912]

Dear Miss Monroe:

This is THE *Scoop*. Reserve space in the next number for *Tagore*. We'll be the only American magazine to print him, or even to know.

I don't remember what I wrote you. But he has sung Bengal into a nation, and his English version of his poems is very wonderful. Yeats is doing the introduction and WE'RE to hold down the American copyright. I've known for weeks that he was *the* event of the winter. Yeats greeted me with "some one greater than any of us"—"I read those things and wonder why one should go on trying to write," *etc.*

It's the only real fever of excitement among the inner circle of litera-ture that I've ever seen here. *And* we—"Poetry"—have got six poems, at the least; and nobody else will have ANY. . . .

This means at least that we have *got* to be taken seriously and *at once*. That we rank as a serious magazine. *Weltlitteratur.* . . .

P.S. You needn't spread this. Let the bomb burst in our next issue.

Yours / E. Pound

Ezra Pound to Harriet Monroe   London, October [1912]

Dear Harriet Monroe:

I've had luck again, and am sending you some *modern* stuff by an American. I say modern, for it is in the laconic speech of the Imagistes, even if the subject is classic. . . . At least "H.D." has lived with these things since childhood, and knew them before she had any book-knowledge of them. . . .

This is the sort of American stuff that I can show here & in Paris with-out its being ridiculed. Objective—no slither—direct—no excessive use of adjectives, etc. No metaphors that won't permit examination.

It's straight talk—straight as the greek! And it was only by persistence that I got to see it at all.

It is requested that no biographical note appear, the signature is by initial H.D. and in small italics "Imagiste" sic. H.D. "Imagiste". . . .

Ezra Pound to Harriet Monroe   London, [11 October 1912]

Dear Miss Monroe:

Recd. £10. Thank you. *Please* don't worry about prose rates, now, at the start. Your initial expenses, printing *adv*, circulars, etc must have cut into the 1st yrs. $5000. . . .

I do want money to get the best stuff from Paris. I'll try by mail, but if necessary I want to be able to go over after it. Also I want to be able to close with Yeats, whenever he does a good thing. He writes so little verse now, and he wont be bothered with magazines. But when he reads me a good thing, I want to be able to say "Here, you don't want it. I'll give you £5— or £10" (as the case may be).

If I can help you make "Poetry" *the* centre of the best activity, that will mean more to me than "rates". And I do want a high standard kept. . . .

And I'm so tired of the Poetry Review and its constant labour to bolster up mediocrities.

Nobody does *much* good work, in the sense in which I use the word. I think your format is big enough as it is. Few people want more or can stand more than 20 pp. of poetry at once. . . .

I haven't sent you any more verse of my own for I think it more important to print Aldington & "H.D." to say nothing of the promised Tagore, than anything I've done. . . .

You probably find my note "status rerum" a bit drastic. I'll do you one on "Survivors" if you like—men like Blunt, Plair, Rhys, etc. who are exactly what I've called 'em "food for Anthologies"—who show to their best advantage by a poem or so, rather than by their whole works—but who have done one or two poems well worth knowing & who help to make the milieu "London" a mecca. . . .

Back to my "bete noir"—the charlatans! They do more harm to the arts than any indifference. And it is to them that we owe so much the general mistrust of "the muse." When poetry is really good the people will take it fast enough. My war is not on the public taste, it is on editors and on pretenders. —

How I do deluge you with epistles. Of course, we ought to be able to talk over campaigns, then I wouldn't need to fuss so much.

This month between speech & answer is a bother. . . .

Ezra Pound to Harriet Monroe   *London, 15 October 1912*

Dear Miss Monroe:

I've got you four (possibly five) lyrics from Mr. Yeats. Two in his best manner. And there seems a good chance of getting a longish-shortish narrative poem that he hasn't yet finished. This ought to be enough to establish the fact (which I have mentioned before, to wit) that we are a serious international publication, to be "taken seriously" by all the elect.

Yours— / E. P. / 1 a.m. Oct. 15. 1912

Ezra Pound to Harriet Monroe   *London, [22 October 1912]*

Dear Harriet Monroe:

Oh Lord! . . . Let us be patient with each other. . . . I'm willing to stand alone for my position. Not because I think I'm omniscient. For example, I make 3 enemies in a line—"[Alfred] Noyes, [Darrell] Figgis, Abercrombie". I do no one any harm. I assure myself six bad reviews, at least, for my next book. . . .

Can't you see that until someone is *honest* we get nothing clear. The good work is obscured, hidden in the bad. I go about this London hunting for the real. I find paper after paper, person after person, mildly affirming the opinion of someone who hasn't cared enough about the art to tell what they actually believe.

It's only when a few men who know get together and *disagree* that any sort of criticism is born. If you want "Harper's" I can't help you. . . .

It isn't as if I were set in a groove. I read any number of masters and I recognize any number of kinds of excellence. But I'm sick to loathing of people who don't care for master work. Who set out as artists with no intention of producing it. Who make no effort toward the best. Who are content with publicity and the praise of reviewers.

I think the worst betrayal you could make of American poetry is to pretend for a moment that you are content with a parochial standard. You're subsidized, you don't have to placate the public at once. . . . Whistler and Walt Whitman, I abide by their judgment. Print me with an asbestos border & deplore my opinions in a foot-note or in an editorial. . . .

I know perfectly well that my criticism seems like the speech of a conceited fool. I accept this burden along with a few other loads. . . .

Good art can't possibly be palatable all at once. You can't possibly pat all the semi-defunct on the head & be sincere. . . .

When I say a thing is *good* I mean I can read it and enjoy it & do so without fear that it will harm my style (god knows I have none in prose), sap my energies or blunt my perception of το καλον [the beautiful]. I can find little contemporary work (*some in france*) which does not seem to me the worst possible stuff for a young poet to fill his or her mind with.

Great god. If a man writes six GOOD lines he is immortal, isn't that worth trying for. Isn't it worth while having *one* critic left who won't say a thing is *good* until he is ready to stake his whole position on the decision.

There's been so much of the caution which you praise that no review has any value—or at least it may have some but when I think of one friend who had 32 splendid reviews and sold 17 copies, I am skeptical as to the value of cautious support; of the continuous placation of publishers, public & poets. . . .

But to return to our first question, the "tone" of my "Status Rerum". I've got a right to be severe. I'm not a masked reviewer—a non-producer—I'm not shielded by anonymity. For one man I strike there are ten who can strike back at me. I stand exposed. It hits me in my dinner invitations, in my week-ends, in the reviews of my own work. Nevertheless it's a good fight, but you are welcome to believe me Thersites if you see it that way. . . .

Oh Lord, what a volume this is getting to be. I should have used this copy & sold the same for £.s.d.

Anyhow, I've got to go out now. Vid. the altered article. / E.P.

Harriet Monroe to Ezra Pound   *9 November 1912*

My dear Mr. Pound:

We feel very grand with "Yeats" and "Tagore" who have arrived safely. I feel a little uncertain about the expediency of printing both in the December number. Have not quite decided, in fact, although since you want me to and since I owe them both to you it seems as if we ought to do it. . . .

I am glad you promised to be frank, though perhaps that is what the journalists would call a work of supererogation. I will try to do likewise. . . .

I enclose a draft for "Yeats" and "Tagore". I should say about $75.00 for Yeats, and the rest for the Hindoo. You will know where to send the money. . . .

Ezra Pound to Harriet Monroe   *London, [early November 1912]*

Dear Miss Monroe:

Please print Yeats' things exactly as they were in the type written copy and reject my emendations and changes, reinsert the phrase *as it were*. In the line

seemed, as it were, a burning cloud. . . .

Oh *la la*, ce que le roi desire! / E.P.

CHAPTER III

The View from Church Walk

When the first issues of *Poetry* finally reached London, Pound was disappointed, though he couched his misgivings in humorous terms. The early numbers were in fact quite uneven, and Pound provided critiques of their strong and weak points. While she welcomed Pound's own first poems and essays and gladly published "his" authors, the Editor of course printed her own discoveries, as well. When H.M. presented particularly substandard items, E.P. was disdainful, as in the case of the uninspired Mrs. Schuyler Van Rensselaer, whose "Aubade" and "Nocturne" appeared in the November 1912 issue.

Several of the American authors chosen in Chicago wrote graceful verses in conventional forms, and clearly bored the foreign editor. But gradually Monroe and Henderson were able to find more original native talents. As first reader, A.C.H. plucked from the slush piles several works that created much attention, above all Carl Sandburg's "Chicago" poems (March 1914). While the Editor was away, Henderson returned Robert Frost's first submissions from England in 1913. Pound, who never fully appreciated Frost, consoled H.M. and A.C.H., saying: "I don't doubt that the things Frost sent you were very bad." After due apologies, new Frost poems arrived, but they also were rejected.

On the third try, Monroe accepted "The Code—Heroics," which appeared in February 1914, marking Frost's first appearance in an American magazine after his success in England. From his doctor's office in Rutherford, New Jersey, William Carlos Williams sent his first submissions to Pound for approval and forwarding, but soon mailed poems directly to Chicago, beginning a voluminous and amusingly cantankerous correspondence with Harriet Monroe. Most of Pound's English discoveries eventually bypassed him, as well.

By late fall, the number of submissions increased, along with Monroe's selectivity. Rejections might be ill received, but returned poems seldom prevented their authors from sending more: hardly surprising, since on many manuscripts H.M. and A.C.H. offered comments. Monroe wrote Pound in March 1913, "frequently our suggestions for emendations result in distinct modernizing of the tone and general improvement." But well before the *Agrippina* affair in May, Pound was having his doubts. Issue to issue, Pound's enthusiasm waxed and waned, and he grew less than confident about Monroe's judgment. He confessed to having "a twinge of curiosity about what is being cast out." Monroe deflected his intrusion into the selection process by assuring him: "nothing that has any life in it gets by us."

For her part, Monroe kept her faith in Pound and defended him even when doing so further alienated readers. The Chicago *Tribune* ran parodies by Bert Leston Taylor in his "Line o' Type" columns, but Monroe told Pound that she didn't mind jokes. This being so, she must have enjoyed a ditty sent in by Louis Untermeyer in March 1913:

CHANT MONROE

Dear Miss Monroe, let added be
This to the Muse's Litany
Deliver us—Oh welcome sound!
Deliver us from Ezra Pound!

Enough! The cry goes up, enough
Of his crack-brained, distorted stuff:
If you would be with blessings crowned,
Deliver us from Ezra Pound!

Virile—you say—a thing apart—
The acme of the new in art;
Profound—well, if he *be* profound,
Deliver us from Ezra Pound!

Genius—do you aver? Oh, tush!—
A maze of egotistic mush!
Sense?—nay, conceit and empty sound!
Deliver us from Ezra Pound!

Are you a patroness of pose?
If not, have pity on our woes,
And evermore, while suns wheel round,
Deliver us from Ezra Pound!

Attacks by the *Dial*, a conservative journal also published in Chicago, were less amusing. Scornful of *Poetry* from the beginning, in May it printed a scathing article by Wallace Rice, who attacked Pound for his egoism and Monroe for fostering bizarre items that betrayed the great traditions of poetry and the trust of her backers. She immediately defended Pound and her own work as Editor, naming several poems she had printed on modern subjects. Rice replied that each of them was a failure, Lindsay's in particular.

Far more damaging to the magazine's reputation than Monroe's poetry selections were Pound's polemical essays. In January 1913, she had printed "Status Rerum," his particularly dogmatic "letter from London," in which he praised his friend Ford Madox Hueffer and the still-obscure "Imagistes," declared "Yeats the only poet worthy of serious study," and dismissed the "Georgians" as mere "food for Anthologies." The article immediately provoked angry reactions at home and abroad. Writing from London, Conrad Aiken sent an open letter in January:

To POETRY: a Protest.

I wonder if Poetry is willing to listen for a moment to a benighted outsider . . . [sic] even if he be rude? And whether it will listen tolerantly or cynically? . . . the Editor, or at least the Editor and Mr. Pound, are using Poetry too egotistically, in order to give expression and scope to their own personalities. Instead of at once putting this new magazine on a basis of broad and sympathetic tolerance towards all poetry . . . the Editor, or the Editor and Mr. Pound, have made it propagandist. And propagandism has no place in a magazine of this sort.

It is all very well for Mr. Pound to hold certain convictions: all young men do. I do myself! But that out of these convictions should be shaped a law, and that by these convictions should be established a magazine whose speech is as oracular as though it were the voice of an Academy—there I protest, and I am sure that poetry protests with me. Why must we accept Mr. Pound's views as final? Because his voice is loud and insistant [sic], louder than ours? Or because Poetry was started to obtain a hearing for Pound . . . [sic] and incidentally for poetry?— Really, Mr. Pound becomes at times autocratic, high-handed. He writes good poetry, when he is not too intent upon writing good poetry, for which I am one among many who are grateful. But must we also have his opinions thrust down our throats? *Must* we agree with him, for instance, that Whitman is the poet most worth imitating, and that *vers libre* or some form evolved from it is the poetic form of the future? Must we share all of Mr. Pound's growing pains with him, pang by pang? And must we believe him when he says with lazy indifference (January number) that there is no new poetry in England at present . . . [sic] and that there are no new poets?

This last has annoyed me not a little, that Mr. Pound, in his self-created position of authority, should so abuse his authority, so deceive his audience.

While Aiken continued to criticize *Poetry*, that did not prevent him from sending large quantities of his verse, most of which was returned. Even when he was accepted, Aiken argued with Monroe (and several of her successors) about changes or manner of presentation. But he didn't stop contributing, or complaining, until 1962.

Even before "Status Rerum" was published, Pound was aware that his contributions were too extreme. Following the negative publicity generated by the piece, he became more amenable to modulating his tone and said that he was willing to have H.M. reject some of his things rather than jeopardize the magazine. Despite his dissatisfaction, Pound's correspondence into the spring of 1913 was fairly positive, even jocular. Monroe was particularly pleased to send him Floyd Dell's glowing editorial, "To a Poet," printed in the Chicago *Evening Post Literary Review*, 4 April 1913:

> Ezra Pound, we salute you!
>
> You are the most enchanting poet alive.
>
> Your poems in the April Poetry are so mockingly, so delicately, so unblushingly beautiful that you seem to have brought back into the world a grace which (probably) never existed, but which we discover in an imaginative process in Horatius and Catullus. . . .
>
> There is no mistake about you, Ezra Pound. You are a creator of beauty in the world where only by a divinely creative process does beauty exist. (Quarrelsome poet, do not stop to discuss the matter now; besides, your prose is not convincing anyway.) The point is that you are a Poet.
>
> Salve!

Ezra Pound to Harriet Monroe   *[London, November 1912]*

Dear Miss Monroe:

My GORD! but this stuff of Mrs. Van *Rensselaer's* is *twaddle*. . . . Surely this good lady should shine as a patron rather than as a contributor. . . .

Of course I know some of her friends and I know she is a charming & gracious lady & I wouldn't want her feelings hurt, & this is in secret council. *But* you aren't fostering Am. letters by printing her . . . she is utterly unprintable.

Dio sanctissimo, what muck. For once I'm not harping on technique. This stuff is rotten at the root—lies & *lies* & *lies*. If the woman could be persuaded to tell the truth for an instant?? No, not on the rack, she wouldn't. It would never occur to her. I don't accuse her of malign intent. They are as they are, god help 'em. But they are the curse of art. . . . YAH! . . . I wonder if she has ever read a poem. . . . (burn this document, s.v.p.)

Yours. E.P.

Ezra Pound to Alice Corbin Henderson   London, [December? 1912]

Dear Mrs. Henderson:

. . . I wonder if "Poetry" really dares to devote a number to my *new* work. There'll be a *howl*. They wont like it. It's absolutely the *last* obsequies of the victorian period. I wont permit any selection or editing.

It stands now a series of 24 poems ["Contemporania"], most of them very short. I'd rather they appeared after H.M. has published "The Garden" (as sort of a preparation for the on coming horror) and whatever else of that little lot she cares to print. There'll probably be 40 by the time I hear from you.

It's not futurism & it's not post-impressionism but it's work contemporary with these schools, and to my mind the most significant that I have yet brought off.

BUTT [sic] they wont like it. They wont object as much as they did to Whitman's outrages, because the stamina of stupidity is weaker. I guarantee but one thing: the reader will not be *bored*. He will say ahg, ahg, ahh, ahhh, bu-bu-bu-but this isn't Poetry. . . .

I expect a number of people will regard the series a pure blague [nonsense]. Still, I give you your chance to be modern, to go blindfoldedly to be modern, to produce as many green billious attacks throughout the length and breadth of the U.S.A. as there are fungoid members of the American academy. I announce the demise of R. U. Johnson [editor of the *Century*] and all his foetid generation

Sta così. / Yours, / E. Pound

Leading off the April 1913 issue, the "Contemporania" group included "Tenzone," "The Condolence," "The Garret," "The Garden," "Ortus," "Dance Figure," "Salutation," "Salutation the Second," "Pax Saturni," "Commission," "A Pact," and "In a Station of the Metro," the most famous Imagist poem. On 3 December 1912, E.P. told H.M., "if you print 'em *all* it will certainly cause a riot and bring our glorious periodical to a sudden & ignominious end."

Ezra Pound to Harriet Monroe   London, [3 December 1912]

Forgive the *messiness!*

Dear Miss Monroe:

Yes, the "Related Things" is more to my fancy. I had no intention of trying to exclude you from your own magazine but you know as well as I do that you could have written the Nogi [H.M.'s own first appearance in *Poetry*, in November 1912] in four lines if you'd had time to do so.

I've sent the 30 dollars to Tagore.

For GORD'S sake don't print anything of mine that you think will kill the Magazine, but so far as I personally am concerned the public can go to the devil. It is the function of the public to prevent the artist's expression by hook or by crook. Ancora e ancora [again and again]. But be sure of this much that I won't quarrel with you over what you see fit to put in the scrap basket. . . .

Given my head I'd stop any periodical in a week, only we are bound to run five years anyhow, we're in such a beautiful position to save the public's soul by punching its face that it seems a crime not to do so. . . .

Ezra Pound to Harriet Monroe   *London, 27 January 1913*

Dear Miss Monroe:

Having spent two days in rage and depression—"more in sorrow than in anger" etc—I shall procede [sic] to show my innate weakness of character, and forgive you your sins.

Re/ my own stuff, do as you like, you've my answer already to that question in my other letters. (Only it IS tactless of you to betray to me, that you confuse me in your mind with Mssrs Ficke and co. Very tactless!!) That is not however the cause of my teeth gnashings.

Nor is Lindsay's blague ["General Booth"], rather a good blague [hoax], and his own, ONLY he mustn't be let to use that manner of speech on other subjects. He ought to do you instead of Masefield. I don't think we need to import Masefield as long as we've got him. It's not our place to follow somebody else's boom but to make our own.

As I've said to Mrs Henderson, If we can bring good stuff to its own so that the other magazines will have to accept it, we will do a lot more for poets and poetry than we could ever do with our own $5000 per yr.

Old Rhys's poem ["A Song of Happiness"] is very good for him also, but why you felt it necessary to apologize for H.D. I am at a loss to imagine. She's the only thing in the number [January 1913] that I can expect any one here to take the slightest interest in. I simply don't understand your note. Whether you misread my note and applied something I said about my own work to hers or what ??? or what ????. Non capisco. ????? No! non capisco [I don't understand]. . . .

How are we to be two decades ahead of the country and cater to news stands at the same time?? We've simply GOT to lead. Otherwise we sink to the level of a dozen other dilettantes. We can't compete on business terms with the Home Journal. We *can't afford* to give the public what it wants. . . .

I wish I could make you see the standards I'm fighting for aren't merely a caprice of my own but they are the standards of the few here who matter. They are NOT the standards of the English press, not by a long ways. . . .

Ezra Pound to Harriet Monroe   *London, 8 February [1913]*

Dear Miss Monroe:

. . . As I've written to A.C.H., [Witter] Bynner is endurable. If he, by any miracle of the just and avenging gods, should have for just once and for 8/9ths. of a second something resembling a poignant emotion he might begin to write poetry. A much too pleasing and pleased personality. I think he works in the right direction. God send him an ounce of guts or some lingering tortuous disease to put some edge on his nerves . . . .

Ezra Pound to Harriet Monroe   *London, 10 March 1913*

[*Sent with corrected proofs for "Contemporania," published April 1913*]

Dear Miss Monroe:

I'm deluded enough to think there is a rhythmic system in the d— stuff, and I believe I was careful to type it as I wanted it written, i.e., as to line ends and breaking *and capitals.* Certainly I want the line you give, written just as it is. . . .

In the METRO hokku, I was careful, I think, to indicate spaces between the rhythmic units, and I want them observed.

Re/ the enclosed sheet from your letter [objecting to several passages in the poems], it never occurred to me that passage (A.) would shock anyone. If you want to take the responsibility for replacing it with asterisks, go ahead. . . .

Passage (B.) honi soit! Surely the second line might refer to the chastest joys of paradise. Has our good nation read the Song of Songs? No, really, I think this ought to stay. The tragedy as I see it is the tragedy of finer desire drawn, merely by being desire at all, into the grasp of the grosser animalities. G-d! you can't emasculate literature utterly. You can't expect modern work to even look in the direction of Greek drama until we can again treat actual things in a simple and direct manner.

Morte di Christo! Read the prefaces to Shelley written just after his death, where the editor is trying to decide whether Shelley's work is of sufficient importance to make up for his terrible atheism!!! . . .

As to getting out a number that will please me; I think it is a possible feat, tho' I'd probably have to choose the contents myself. When you do finally adopt my scale of criticism you will, yes, you actually will find a handful of very select readers who will be quite delighted . . . .

I want the files of this periodical to be prized and vendible in 1999. Quixotic of me! and very impractical? . . .

I DO hope you'll print my instructions to neophites ["A Few Don'ts by an Imagiste"] (sent to A.C.H.) soon, that will enable our contributors to solve some of their troubles at home.

Oh well, enough of this, if I'm to catch the swiftest boat.

Yours etc. ever / Ezra Pound

Pound's corrections for typesetting of "In a Station of the Metro," the most famous Imagist poem.

Ezra Pound to Harriet Monroe   London, [March 1913]

Dear Miss Monroe:

I'm sending back both sets of proofs because I have to work on a clean one, more or less . . . I've made further notes on the sheets attached. . . .

The station of the METRO: give this whatever space there is left on the page, i.e., in centre of whatever white space there is. And group the words as follows:

The apparition   of these faces   in the crowd:
Petals   on a wet, black bough.

. . .

Ezra Pound to Harriet Monroe   London, [late March 1913]

Dear H.M.:

Congratulations on "March". While it contains nothing wildly interesting, it contains nothing or rather no group of poems which is wholly disgusting. I think the average "feel" of the number is as good as you've done. . . .

I'm glad you're going to print "Bill," i.e. Wm. Carlos Williams [three poems recently forwarded by E.P.]. . . .

I think you are probably taking the best of what comes in, but I do now and then have a twinge of curiosity about what is being cast out.

Honestly, besides yourself and Mrs. Henderson, whom do you know who takes the Art of poetry seriously? As seriously, that is, as a painter takes painting? Who Cares? Who cares whether or no a thing is really *well* done? Who in America believes in perfection and that nothing short of it is worth while? . . .

I know there are a lovely lot who want to express their own personalities, I have never doubted it for an instant. Only they mostly won't take the trouble to find out what is their own personality. . . .

I want to know [you], we've got to get acquainted somehow. I don't think I underestimate the difficulty of your position. . . .

Harriet Monroe to Ezra Pound   31 March 1913

My dear Mr. Pound:

Just a word to explain our May number, which I suppose will make you say "damn". I accepted Neihardt's play [*Agrippina*] in the very beginning of the enterprise. . . . I was terribly disappointed to find it a Roman tragedy of Elizabethan origin. Of late I asked him to release me from my promise to print it in a single number, but he declined, so I am fulfilling the promise. It has some strong passages, I think, in Nero's Soliloquy, but much of it is bombast, and it isn't drama. However we will get it off our hands and our files and will never do such a thing again, please God. . . .

I will use the rest of H.D.'s things, if you say so. Of Flint I like three of the four which you sent recently, but I don't like the one you sent some time ago.

You needn't bother about the things we reject. You can be pretty sure that nothing that has any life in it gets by us. As for some of the stuff, you would dance a can-can if you could see it and your hair would stand on end.

I am glad you like the March number fairly well. It is true that a lot of our versifiers think they must talk in Tennysonian or Elizabethan, but if you could see the letters we write them you will realize that we [are] trying to train them out of that. And frequently our suggestions for emendations result in distinct modernizing of the tone and general improvement.

I am gratified by the kind of comment that the magazine is receiving over here, also our subscription list is growing gradually and I begin to think we may have a Future, but I don't permit myself to think very much about that phase of it. Please send me anything you read or hear about the April number.

We are deep in the Insurgent Art Exhibition in these parts. I am going to send you a very clever article on it by Floyd Dell, who is Literary Editor of our Evening Post. His view of Matisse is very interesting, but perhaps you are not interested in ART.

Yours very truly, / HM

Ezra Pound to Harriet Monroe   Sirmione, Italy, [April 1913]

Dear Miss Monroe:

My hair does stand on end. Habitually. I was born with it in that position. . . .

Yes, naturally I'm interested in painting. The only competent criticism of "Ripostes" came from a painter. "Post-Imp" [Post-Impressionist] at that. . . .

Ezra Pound to Alice Corbin Henderson   London, [March 1913]

Dear A.C.H.:

I enclose some more Tagore for the May number. . . .

Have just discovered another Amur'k'n [Robert Frost]. VURRY Amur'k'n, with, I think, the seeds of grace. Have reviewed an advance copy of his book [*A Boy's Will*], but have run it out too long; will send it as soon as I've tried to condense it . . . also some of his stuff if it isn't all in the book.

YRS / E. P.

Robert Frost in a photograph inscribed to
Associate Editor Eunice Tietjens, late teens.

Ezra Pound to Harriet Monroe   London, [March 1913]

Dear H.M.:

. . . Frost seems to have put his best stuff into his book, but we'll have something from him as soon as he has done it, "advanced" or whatever you call it. Lawrence has brought out a vol. He is clever; I don't know whether to send in a review or not. We seem pretty well stuffed up with matter at the moment. (D. H. Lawrence, whom I mentioned in my note on the Georgian Anthology.) Detestable person but needs watching. I think he learned the proper treatment of modern subjects before I did. . . .

E.P.'s review of Lawrence's *Love Poems and Others* was printed July 1913.

Ezra Pound to Harriet Monroe   London, [March 1913]

Dear H.M.:

Sorry I can't work this review [of Frost's *A Boy's Will*, printed May 1913] down to any smaller dimensions! However, it can't be helped. — Yes it can. I've done the job better than I thought I could. —And it's our second scoop, for I only found the man by accident and I think I've about the only copy of the book that has left the shop.

I'll have along some of his work, if the book hasn't used up all the best of it. Anyhow, we'll have some of him in a month or so.

I think we should print this notice at once as we ought to be first and some of the reviewers here are sure to make fuss enough to get quoted in N.Y. . . .

Harriet Monroe to Ezra Pound   5 April 1913

My dear E. P.

Three [letters] from you this morning. Enclosing your own things, the review of Frost and Tagore. I had a fine time with your things which [are] certainly immense. We will see about them later.

Alice says *mea culpa* about Frost. For we did find him among our returns and it was done while I was in New York. She has the grit to stand up however, and say if it was returned it deserved it, or at least those particular poems did. You can apologize for us and say we are very contrite and would like some more some day.

Tagore declines your emendations, and gives us carte blanche to do exactly as we please. To print however and whatever we want to. I must say I agree with him about your improvements with a few exceptions. You are alright for yourself but you had better let him run his own

English. He is leaving for good today. Having made, I think, some rather warm friends here. In fact, he is trying to annex the Hendersons. W.P.H., who is, I will privately inform you, in the way of being a great painter, has made the best portrait of him, Tagore says, which he has ever sat for. And now, he wants the Hendersons to get a contract from some magazine for illustrated articles and go to India for a year. . . .

Well WE are cut, and I enclose the first gun [Dell's review of "Contemporania" in the Chicago *Evening Post*, 4 April 1913], which seems to be loaded with roses. This *Post* Friday supplement is, I think, the cleverest literary review in the country, and its editor Floyd Dell, who is about your age, is an interesting chap. He occasionally plunges into verse himself, but of late not much.

Well I guess that's enough for today. Oh No it isn't. I enclose a check for your contributions in March and April, less about ten dollars you owe us for subscriptions. I wish it were bigger. Next year if we prosper as I hope I shall certainly raise rates for my very specialest contributors. . . .

E.P. wrote his mother in January 1914 that it was Tagore who convinced the "imbeciles" at *Poetry* that the "Contemporania" series was good and should be printed.

Harriet Monroe to Ezra Pound   *12 April 1913*

My dear Mr. Pound:

I enclose the second gun [review]. B.L.T. is Bert Leston Taylor, whose daily column ["Line o' Type"] in the Tribune has more readers than anything else in town. . . . Walter [Wallace] Rice, who is a space writer and ballad monger poet about town, and Will Henderson were discussing your April contributions rather shortly the other day. Walter Rice read the poem and said that he had to work a devil of a time to get it. Taylor smiled yesterday and said he had had it in for you ever since you parodied "The Shropshire Lad". I don't know how you feel about jokes, I don't mind them in the least. . . .

Your last bunch of poems, of course, we need not decide now which of them we had better use since we cannot use any for a few months. Some of those epigrams have a very complete little sting. Others do not seem to me quite so firm. After all, Alexander Pope did that kind of thing pretty well. I like "Lustra" but I rather wish that the next bunch we print of yours might be an oblation to pure beauty, something in the vein quite different from "Contemporania". However, of course, that is for you to decide. . . .

Your April poems have had some high praise in some more or less unexpected quarters. Mrs. [Anita McCormick] Blaine, a prominent millionairess here and one of our double guarantors, and one of the most public spirited and wholly inspiring women I know, thinks they are grand. Likes their social tone. . . .

Ezra Pound to Harriet Monroe   *Sirmione, Italy, 22 April 1913*

Dear H.M.:

Gord knows *I* didn't ask for the job of correcting Tagore. *He* asked me to. Also it will be very difficult for his defenders in London if he takes to printing anything except his best work. As a religious teacher he is superfluous. . . . So long as he sticks to poetry he can be defended on stylistic grounds against those who disagree with his content. And there's no use his repeating the Vedas and other stuff that has been translated. In his original Bengali he has the novelty of rime and rhythm and of expression, but in a prose translation it is just "more theosophy". Of course if he wants to set a lower level than that which I am trying to set in my translations from Kabir, I can't help it. It's his own affair.

Rec'd £28, with thanks, salaams etc.

Dell is very consoling. It's clever of him to detect the Latin tone.

I don't doubt that the things Frost sent you were very bad. But he has done good things and whoever rejected 'em will go to hell along with Harper's & The Atlantic. After my declaration of his glory he'll have to stay out of print for a year in order not to "disappoint" the avid reader—serieusement, I'll pick out whatever of his inedited stuff is fit to print when I get back to London.

About W.P.H. [Will Henderson]—I should *hope* his portrait *was* the best. T[agore]'s beloved friend [William] Rothenstein can't paint for nuts. Even in the drawing, which might be worse, poor Rabindranath is shown with a busted forearm. Of course *if* A.C.H. departs I [underscored six times] shall come back and subedit—and then THEN what will happen?!?✳?!!✿!??! . . .

Yeats is interested, likes some of the things, trembles for my 'unrestrained' language. (That was, I think, in a poem you're not using). . . .

I expect my book to be attacked when it's published over here, but they may have the cunning to ignore it. I am getting even that much disliked.

Yours sincerely, / Ezra Pound

CHAPTER IV

The Editor and the Impresario at Odds

By the summer of 1913, relations between Editor and Foreign Correspondent started to shift. For Monroe, it was a period of trials, personal and financial. In May, her older sister, Dora Root, died suddenly. Then the Editor discovered, despite the Guarantors' fund, the magazine would have a deficit by the end of the year: a sign of things to come. By early 1914, she was forced to cut the rate from $10 to $8 a page for poetry. The hoped-for poetry "boom" in the later teens did not really help her cause. Subscriptions remained at about 1,100, and never rose beyond 2,000 during Monroe's editorship. Every year, she was obliged to find additional, often emergency, funding.

On the surface, Pound seemed pleased, or as contented as he could be under any circumstances. But by late summer 1913, his patience seems to run out, and there occurred the first of a number of serious flare-ups, at least on Pound's side. (As usual, Miss Monroe remained calm.) The proximate cause was a disagreement over the Guarantors' Prize, which Pound insisted go to Yeats. But deeper resentments had been simmering concerning the general direction of the magazine. It was not unusual for Pound to have strife with partners. Indeed, a pattern of initial enthusiasm and high hopes, then gradual disillusionment, quarrels, and caustic breakups characterized many of his relationships.

In his very first letter, Pound overstated the prominence of his position in England, or at least neglected to mention its negative side, when he told Monroe, "I *do* see nearly everyone that matters." Had she known Pound's tangled literary and personal connections in London—and his need for control—the Editor might have been better prepared for what lay ahead when she invited him to join her enterprise.

1. Pound before *Poetry*

Harriet Monroe first encountered Pound's work during her around-the-world trip in 1910. En route to Peking for a visit with her sister Lucy and her husband, William J. Calhoun, the U.S. Minister to China, she stopped for six weeks in London. Monroe met with old friends like Alice Meynell and had dinner with Herbert Hoover, who had been the railroad engineer for the last emperor of China. She also began a friendship with the novelist May Sinclair, who introduced her to Elkin Mathews. Mathews recommended Pound's *Personae and Exultations*, which he had published the previous year. Monroe bought both books, and later "beguiled" the long trip on the Trans-Siberian Railroad "with the strange and beautiful rhythms of this new poet, my self-exiled compatriot."

Pound had left the States in 1908. He had been a graduate student at the University of Pennsylvania, where he met the nineteen-year-old Hilda Doolittle and William Carlos Williams, then a young medical student. Pound was stymied in his academic career when a fellowship was not renewed

H.M. in Chinese dress; she read Pound's first books on the Trans-Siberian Railroad, on her way to visit her sister in Peking in 1910.

and he couldn't complete his Ph.D. Then he was cashiered from his first teaching position, at Wabash College; it was the only regular job he ever held. Pound was making no headway in publishing his poetry, either. Believing that America was incapable of recognizing true genius, particularly his own, he went to Europe. He spent three months barely scraping by in Venice, but printed, at his own expense, his aptly named first book, *A Lume Spento* (With Tapers Extinguished). He moved to London in September.

From Italy and then England, Pound tried to place poems in *Harper's*, the *Century*, and *Scribner's*, but with even less success than Harriet Monroe. All his submissions were rejected. With funds dwindling, he got a job lecturing on Provençal literature in a night school. Meanwhile, he began making his way into English intellectual circles. At Harold Monro's Poetry Bookshop, he became acquainted with other aspiring poets and writers, including F. S. Flint, Maurice Hewlett, Lawrence Binyon, and Frederic Manning, who introduced Pound to Olivia Shakespear and her daughter Dorothy. On first meeting Pound, Dorothy was smitten. Her parents were less thrilled with the idea of her marrying the impecunious poet; but after six years they consented, and Olivia settled £150 a year upon Dorothy, which sustained the couple.

Over tea at the Shakespears', Pound recited the poems of William Butler Yeats and extolled his idol, whom he had yet to meet. Olivia Shakespear had known Yeats for years—he later married her cousin, Georgie Hyde-Lees—and they shared an interest in theosophy and telepathy. Olivia, of course, reported Pound's admiration to the poet. The young man was soon introduced to the great man and invited to his Monday night at-homes at 18, Woburn Buildings. By then, Pound was being invited to many other "evenings" and teas, where he continued to widen his artistic contacts. Most important among them were two established men of letters who would be crucial for his development as a poet and critic: T. E. Hulme and Ford Madox Hueffer, later Ford. (Because of the war, he changed his Germanic last name.)

Elkin Mathews took Pound to the Poet's Club, where he met George Bernard Shaw, among others, and was introduced to Hulme, the leader of the group. Soon Pound was admitted to the inner circle. A philosopher by training, Hulme discoursed at length on the need to reform English poetry. He felt it was still caught in an outmoded romanticism that had degenerated into sentimentality and empty decoration in the hands of the Victorians. This feeble state, he believed, had been protracted by the genteel platitudes of Edwardian verse. Like the rest of the Poet's Club, Hulme thought the young fogies in the Georgian group (so named after the recently installed monarch) were too conservative or insipid to effect a change. Hueffer referred to them as the "Gargoyles," including John Masefield, Lascelles Abercrombie, Rupert Brooke, W. H. Davies, Wilfred Gibson, Walter de la Mare, James Stephens, and John Drinkwater. If English poetry was to be brought in line with the modern age, it would have to be pruned of obsolete notions and the meaningless verbiage of the dominant modes. The new poetry, Hulme proposed, should focus clearly, describe accurately, present directly—through sharp images, not hazy abstractions—precision being the truest sign of sincerity in art. Hulme's theories and others stemming from Poet's Club discussions on free verse and Japanese haiku became central to his own practice and the program for reform he would try to effect through *Poetry*.

In Hueffer, he found a mentor whose ideas would prove even more significant for his evolving style. As the editor of the *English Review*, then the most distinguished literary journal in England, Hueffer was also helpful in advancing Pound's publishing career. Only a few weeks after meeting him, he printed Pound's "Sestina: Altafore" (June 1909); he then asked him to be an advisory editor. Hueffer himself was a clear and fluid prose writer; after reading the convoluted syntax and overblown rhetoric of Pound's *Canzoni*, he encouraged the young poet to listen to how people normally speak and to write more naturally. Hueffer's first principle, with a dash of Hulme's philosophy, became Pound's own creed, summarized in his most famous letter to Monroe, written in May 1915:

> Objectivity and objectivity and again objectivity, and NO expression, NO hind-side-beforeness, No Tennysonianness of speech, nothing, *nothing*, NOTHING that you couldn't in some circumstance, in the stress of some emotion, ACTUALLY say. . . . Every literaryism, every book word, fritters away a scrap of the reader's patience, a scrap of his sense of your sincerity.

During 1909 and 1910, more of Pound's poems were getting into print, and his books were receiving notices in the better journals in both England and America, but the reviews were mixed. Many critics found his style pedantic; others saw originality and genuine talent amid the distracting display. When *Provença* was released in the United States, the Boston *Evening Transcript* suggested he read Longfellow, who was in fact his great-uncle. Floyd Dell wrote a perceptive review for the Chicago *Evening Post*, comparing Pound with the avant-garde painters:

> Mr. Pound is a very new kind of poet. . . . Like the Neo-Impressionist painters, like the Impressionists in their day, Mr. Pound is open to misunderstanding, and even to ridicule. . . . But though these poems have often an unconventional form, bizarre phraseology, catalectic or involved sentence structure and recondite meanings, yet it is always apparent that the poet knows what he is doing. . . .

By 1911, Pound was beginning to acquire a reputation, in more ways than one. At first, the disciple sat at Yeats's feet, but soon he was dominating the room. As their friendship grew, Pound was a frequent guest of Hueffer's, and of his partner, the novelist Violet Hunt. Hunt was the daughter of the noted Pre-Raphaelite painter Holman Hunt, and South Lodge, her villa in Kensington, became a gathering place for the *English Review* set. There Pound met many upcoming artists, and writers from whom he would soon gather material for *Poetry* and other journals. Women at the parties were often charmed by Pound. Proper English gentlemen were not so taken with his flamboyant manner, or taken in by his loudly voiced opinions. First, they were put off by his accent and pseudo-rustic patois. (His letters are well larded with this "Amur'k'n" lingo.) Then there was his appearance: the bushy red hair, the cape, the sombrero-like hat worn even indoors, the walking stick, the pince-nez spectacles in imitation of Yeats. To Establishment authors this figure out of opera (or operetta) seemed a Bohemian; many of them, like the eminent Victorian Sir Edmund Gosse, considered him a charlatan.

Some in the younger generation eyed Pound with suspicion, as well. On first meeting him, D. H. Lawrence was impressed, then came to feel the self-proclaimed expert in all manner of art was a poseur. Ever the diplomat, T. S. Eliot kept his opinion of Pound to himself. Robert Frost, who resented his patronizing air, was less polite; after meeting him in London in 1913, he wrote a friend that Pound was "an incredible ass." Pound didn't let his personal feelings interfere with his artistic judgments, and he promoted several authors he didn't particularly like. But many he helped publish viewed his efforts with ambivalence. Because of his strongly held positions and aggressive manner, Pound could be a formidable advocate, or opponent.

In his autobiography, *Life for Life's Sake* (1941), Richard Aldington remembered him as "a bit of a czar," who controlled traffic to *Poetry*. When she met him in Paris in 1923, Gertrude Stein, rather a benevolent despot herself, found Pound unpleasant. In *The Autobiography of Alice B. Toklas*, she referred to him as "a village explainer—excellent if you were a village, but, if you were not, not." Frequently he overstepped the bounds. When he dared to "correct" Yeats's first poems in *Poetry*, the master was not pleased. With younger authors he could be even more heavy-handed. Though many were initially willing to submit to his "guidance"—he was, after all, getting them into print—eventually they rebelled. After Pound got Aldington published and placed as an editor at the *English Review* and then the *Egoist*, they had a falling out, and Aldington remained bitter. (Which created an awkward situation; they lived cheek by jowl at 5 and 8 Holland Place Chambers in Kensington.) It was a pattern that would repeat itself many times—so often, that by the end of the decade Pound was alienated from almost everyone who had helped him and whom he had befriended in England.

In the summer of 1912, however, Pound had much reason for optimism. His own career was taking off, and the first stirrings of the "new poetry" were beginning to be heard. Harriet Monroe's circular announcing couldn't have arrived at a more opportune moment. But neither he nor Miss Monroe foresaw how quickly the "American Risorgimento" he prophesized in his first letter would come to pass.

2. Pound and the "Imagistes"

In his letter of 18 August 1912, Pound had told Monroe that he himself had been "on the verge of starting a quarterly." Now, with H.M. handling practical details like printing, distribution, and finances, he could concentrate on literary matters. In *Poetry* he would have not only a stable, paying place for publication of the authors he favored but a bully pulpit in America from which to proclaim his aesthetic doctrines and wage his "educational campaign." Or so it seemed.

Monroe agreed with Pound on the need to reform the art, and as part of the process she welcomed his new Imagist principles and poets, starting with Richard Aldington and Hilda Doolittle. When Pound met her in 1905, Doolittle was at Bryn Mawr. She fell in love with Pound (her father did not), and when they met again on his visit to New York in 1910, he advised her to come to London. She arrived in 1911, and in 1912 she married Aldington, who knew he was second choice. Pound eventually forwarded poems by his two young protégés (Aldington was only nineteen), Lawrence, James Joyce, F. S. Flint, Fletcher (just out of Harvard), and other, rather disparate, authors whom Pound herded under the banner of Imagism. The "movement" was created, on the spur of the moment and almost as a stunt, by a stroke of Pound's pen.

According to Aldington, the locale was the tearoom in the British Museum, where Pound read over Doolittle's poems, cut and altered "Hermes of the Ways," then dubbed her "H.D., *Imagiste*." (In 1915, Pound admitted to Monroe that "the whole affair was started not very seriously chiefly to get H.D.'s five poems a hearing without it's [sic] being necessary for her to publish a whole book.") Monroe published the poems in the January 1913 issue, signing them as Pound had instructed, with a contributor's note identifying the enigmatic author only as "an American lady resident abroad."

In the March 1913 issue, Pound defined an "Image" as "that which presents an intellectual and emotional complex in an instant in time." More helpfully, he also provided "A Few Don'ts by an Imagiste": "Use no superfluous word, no adjective, which does not reveal something"; "Go in fear of abstractions. Don't retell in mediocre verse what has already been done in good prose"; "Use either no ornament or good ornament." Pound suggested the article be printed up and used as a rejection slip— along with an essay on "Imagisme" (drafted by E.P. but signed by F. S. Flint) that defined Imagist doctrine:

1. Direct treatment of the "thing," whether subjective or objective.

2. To use absolutely no word that did not contribute to the presentation.
3. As regarding rhythm: to compose in sequence of the musical phrase, not in sequence of a metronome.

Although these dicta and "Don'ts" became foundations for modern poetry (and remain fundamental to all good writing), Imagism didn't arouse great interest at first. By mid-1913, Pound himself seems to have lost interest in the "movement." Aldington dropped out early, having become increasingly irritated with Pound's intrusive "help," as may be gathered from the letter he wrote from Paris, 5 July:

> I am sending you some of my poems, with comments by Mr. Pound. In no. one he says "trunks" sounds like elephants. That is unfortunately true; but I might just as well sound like a deposite des bagages. "Trunks" is—are—what I *meant*; but if it strikes you as elephantine, or anything of that sort, pray substitute "trees". I have corrected the mistakes Mr. Pound made in typing—hope the corrections are legible? I may say that we have fought over these poems during the last six months, & I don't believe either agrees in the least with the other as to the respective merits! ...

H.D. wrote Monroe from Sirmione, Italy, in the spring of 1913, asking that the "Imagiste" tag be removed from her name with her next group of poems: "If they are not already in type, will you please sign with the simple initials *H.D.*—I feel that the 'Imagiste' in the first series has sufficiently identified me." She repeated the request from London, 24 October: "I saw your annoncement [sic] in the end of 'Poetry' anent my poems. When you publish them will you be so good as to sign them 'H.D.' simply, cutting out the affectation of 'Imagiste.'"

In his first letter to Monroe, dated 29 August 1913, John Gould Fletcher wrote from London to separate himself from Imagism, as well. Fletcher had become friends with Pound and was for a time associated with the Imagistes; but they had a falling out when Fletcher accused Pound of stealing his ideas. Fletcher's letter summarized points made by other critics about the limitations of free verse and imagist theory:

> Mr. Pound, as you know, is the greatest apostle of 'vers libre' and 'Imagisme', and the MSS he sent you were 'vers libre', but not 'Imagist'. I do not know in what direction your inclinations may tend, but I may say that I am not exclusively a 'vers librist' ... I have experimented in many forms, and shall continue to seek for a more supple and less monotonous technique than that of the average cutter of verses to

measure. Whether I shall ever find my own technique is questionable. I have too great a regard for independence, in my own case and in others. . . .

I hope that 'vers libre' will develop. But so far as it has gone, I think it useful merely in extremely short poems, especially in descriptions of a single brief emotion or small scene, where the play of rhyme would interfere with the full intensity of the color and the words. For long narrative poems, dramatic poems, or a mixture of narrative, descriptive and dramatic, I am convinced—against my will—that vers libre is at present impotent, and that rhyme and regular metre are essential to give the speed and unity that are required.

With Mr. Pound's 'school' of 'Imagisme', I am in even greater disagreement. 'Imagisme' is an attitude towards technique, pure and simple. I am unable, and I wish that everyone else were unable, to impose upon myself the pedantic yoke of any particular technique. . . . I have informed Mr. Pound that I do not intend to hamper myself with technique and his 'don'ts'.

Fletcher would soon ally himself with Amy Lowell, who had little trouble drawing most of Pound's disaffected "protégés" to her side after she visited England in 1913.

3. Further Disagreements

If the acerbic tone of his correspondence with Monroe is any indication, it is easy to understand why so many of Pound's English colleagues, who had to endure his pontificating face to face, became offended and broke with him. In the beginning, Pound had been very sanguine about *Poetry*'s prospects—but also wary. In his very first letter, he asked: "But? Can you teach the American poet that poetry *is* an *art* . . . Maybe." He had also declared: "My idea of our policy is this: We support American poets— preferably the young ones who have a serious determination to produce master-work. We *import* only such work as is better than that produced at home."

Harriet Monroe took him at his word. By early 1913 she was becoming much more selective about which of the "imports" she accepted. Perhaps Pound had "educated" her too well, for she turned down several poems by Frederic Manning and F. S. Flint, feeling that, by Pound's standards and her own, they were weak. She also became less enthusiastic about H.D.'s pieces. She told Pound she would use them "if you say so," but she decided to space out their presentation, because she didn't want the magazine to become lopsided with English (or Imagist) material. Then she had the temerity to start rejecting or demanding changes in Pound's own work, some of which she found trivial, too bitter, and possibly indecent. Since he had altered texts of Yeats and Tagore, without informing them, he was hardly in a position to object; but of course he did. Pound's little patience was tried, friction increased, and his letters took on a more hectoring tone.

He began sending poems by "his" authors to other magazines, on the pretext that they were pieces *Poetry* wouldn't want, even though Monroe should have been offered the chance of first refusal. And despite the fact he had offered her exclusive U.S. rights to his own poems, within a year he broke his promise. Monroe discovered in August 1913 that he had sent the same poems to both *Poetry* and the *Smart Set*. Pound tried to justify this breach of faith by placing the blame on W. H. Wright, the editor, and excused himself thus: "Incidentally his rate is higher than ours. ALSO he had the good sense to divide all the poets here into two classes: Yeats and I in one class, and everybody else in the other. Such illumination can not pass without reward."

Apart from his disagreements about the poetry selections, Pound was dissatisfied with the prose section, and wanted to enlarge the back of the book, particularly with critical articles by himself. Finally he advised that the entire prose section be edited by him and Hueffer. Monroe pointed out that she couldn't afford to add pages, and noted it would not be "expedient" to have the prose edited in London. She had no intention of turning her magazine into an organ for advancing Pound's, or anyone else's, special agendas. In her "Open Door" editorial, she said *Poetry* would avoid "entangling alliances with any single class or school. . . . Nor will the magazine promise to limit its editorial comments to one set of opinions." A sound policy—and one followed at *Poetry* to this day—but Pound's prominent appearances seemed to belie it.

No editor can hope to please everyone, and even one as fair minded as Monroe couldn't placate such temperamental egoists as Pound and Amy Lowell. The ever-ambitious Miss Lowell, too, was anxious to present her views in the back pages. Miss Monroe kindly but firmly let her know who was in charge. With Pound, the situation was different. Monroe genuinely admired him and was grateful for his assistance, though she became less confident of his judgment and more displeased with his prose style as time passed. But, as he had with so many others, Pound kept pushing until he wore her down.

More than a few of his contemporaries remarked on the appropriateness of Pound's name, and he himself used the term "hammer" often, and less facetiously perhaps than he intended. He saw himself, in general, as engaged in a kind of literary warfare—his letters to Monroe are well seasoned with martial imagery—and in his association with *Poetry*, he saw their effort as a campaign for supremacy in the field. The Editor herself was not afraid of a fight, and seemed to relish the controversy the early issues of *Poetry* provoked among the establishment journals.

In her article, "The Enemies We Have Made" (*Poetry*, May 1914), the Editor declared, with more than a touch of bravado: "Next to making friends, the most thrilling experience of life is to make enemies." But, in truth, Monroe did not wish to become endlessly embroiled in controversy, and preferred to accentuate the positive, by assisting the authors she believed in. Pound's fear, voiced in his very first letter, that *Poetry* would be provincial, a mere booster of American work, seemed confirmed by 1913 with the appearance of Lindsay, whom she promoted at every opportunity. But Monroe devoted ample portions of the magazine to Pound's choices, as well, even after his own faith in them had faded, as in the case of Tagore.

Pound's irritation grew until, in the autumn of 1913, he erupted over the awarding of the $250 (£50) Guarantors' Prize, *Poetry*'s first. Monroe wanted to give it to Lindsay, who was her first big "find" (and always in need of cash). Pound was incensed and demanded Yeats receive it. He had lobbied for his choice since spring, and in June Monroe thanked him for his suggestion, but said his choice would be "unadventurous."

On 3 October, he wrote in anger: "Either [the prize] must be respectfully offered to Mr Yeats, or the americans must admit that they are afraid of foreign competition." So, despite her own feelings, Yeats was given the prize. (Monroe scrambled to gather $100 to set up a special prize for Lindsay.) Whether Yeats knew of Pound's efforts is unknown—Amy Lowell suspected chicanery—but when he replied, he said he would take only £10, and suggested the remainder go to ... Ezra Pound.

Harriet Monroe to Ezra Pound   7 June 1913

Dear E. P.

This office, committee and all, is so divided about the enclosed contribution [Orrick Johns's "Song of Deliverance"] that I'd like your opinion. . . .

I find the decision difficult just now. My sister fell ill and died last month—she and her daughter and I had lived together of late. So it is hard to collect my wits and get back to work.

Yours of the 26th arrived, also the October *Poetry*s, for which *much* thanks, as we have *very* few. Thanks for your suggestions about the prize question. No doubt we us and co. are as fit to give it as anybody, but I rather wanted to avoid the Lyric Year's way of a close corporation decision. It would be a generous thing to give it to Yeats—but unadventurous; is he still poor enough so that it would count? Lindsay would suit me all right and he's American besides, even Illinois. . . .

Ezra Pound to Harriet Monroe   *London, [late June 1913]*

Dear H.M.

As for "Songs of Deliverance", of course it's dam'd he-goatish Whitman, but that's better than peptomized Keats. It would be a great mistake not to print it. . . . *I* like it better than Lindsay. Oh a lot better. It is absolutely real. . . .

Tagore is good when he talks of a bridge "arching its back like a young cat". I dont in the least mean to minimize Tagore, but there is a point where he stops being poet and becomes priest and preacher, which is all well and good, but which does not concern the artist, or the critic of letters. As mystic, Tagore is, what you like, but he must be judged as mystic not as poet. . . .

About the $250 prize. It must be offered to Yeats. If he is so dam'd opulent as not to need it, he will probably return it. As for its not being adventurous to offer it to him, I dont see that it is our job to be adventurous in this case but to be just. He has fought a long fight and had damn little reward (in the way of cash and comfort). Lindsay isn't good enough to get ALL the prizes in any case. Also there is no reasonable way of putting Yeats hors de concours. Another thing, you can't afford to spoil the esprit d'corps of your contributors by picking so questionable a winner. You can't give much weight to the award if you make it the first year to a poem that's half a blague.

If you give it Yeats, you, FIRST, make the giving of this particular prize serious, you establish a good tradition. The person who receives it after Yeats is considerably more honoured than if he received it after Lindsay, or after any other man who can not yet be taken quite seriously as artist. . . .

Ezra Pound to Harriet Monroe   *London, 12 July 1913*

Pass this on to A.C.H. if you're too tired to bother with it.

Dear H.M.

"July" arrived. On the whole I think things are looking up. . . .

Lindsay is set to follow Bret Harte and Field and all that lot. . . .

I am glad in a way that we've had a Lindsay number, but I don't yet believe that he cares a damn for the art of poetry. . . .

As to Lindsay, I think semi-serious stuff is on the whole inimical to serious work. It gets the general public so easily on first reading. Incidentally, there is NOTHING to it on second reading. And as long as the public can get it and its pleasing facilities, just so long will they avoid stuff that requires greater effort on their part. And everything except the most serious stuff is SO easy, so easy . . . .

My conception of our function is that we should print, as much as possible, what is significant. Stuff that other periodicals cant or wont handle. Stuff that IS interesting as ART. . . .

Our secondary function is to develop the market. Do as you like, but for single poems, or short things, I open this gate, for whatever it is worth. . . .

Ezra Pound to Harriet Monroe   *London, [summer 1913]*

Dear H.M.

. . . It wasn't the brute beasts of the field that I was cussing out in my gentle salutations but the bloody fools who think they know something about art. The whole rotten lot of cheats and falsifiers from "The Atlantic" down to the understrappers. . . .

I do not love my fellow man and I don't propose to pretend to. . . .

As to the jury. What's the use. You've got to give the 250 dollars to Yeats for "The Grey Rock". I think I am celebrated enough to make that decision. I dont suppose Yeats will refuse it. I dont see why a man who has been through twenty years of poverty, as he has, should be supposed to be out of the running for such a bonus merely because he is celebrated and still poor.

If he should decline it, there is Richard's "Xorikos" and the "General Booth". . . . But in any case the 250 has got to be offered to Yeats FIRST. There is no use making a splurge about the donation; it's a reward not an advertisement. Consider the long and ghastly years when he wasn't paid. The thing to do is to send him the cheque quietly with the simple statement that the 250 was provided to augment the payment for the best poem of the year.

More anon. / Yrs / E. P.

If Yeats should return the $250 I shall split it between Richard and Lindsay. . . .

Ezra Pound to Harriet Monroe   *London, [August 1913]*

Dear Harriet Monroe,

About my stuff. Of course if you wanted to use the first things sent, you ought to have done it when you first got 'em. For there is, after all, a distinction between the bad stuff of an artist and the bad stuff of an amateur.

I sent you one lot (about ten pages) and gave the rest to [Willard Huntington] Wright [editor of the *Smart Set*], who promised to select what he wanted on the steamer, and let me know at once (i.e. about two months ago). . . . I dont in the least know what he has used already and what he has set up and what is going to use. Incidentally his rate is higher than ours. ALSO he had the good sense to divide all the poets here into two classes: Yeats and I in one class, and everybody else in the other. Such illumination can not pass without reward.

Of course, it makes not the slightest difference to me what you use. It is increasingly hard to maintain an interest in "the american reader" . . . . The public is stupid and any other opening, from me, would be the rankest hypocrisy. . . .

Of course a certain amount of space has to be charged to profit and loss, running leeway etc. I know that. Still you would do better simply to jam in the best stuff as fast as you get it and trust the gods to send more. . . .

About the 250 dollars, I should offer it to Yeats privately before I printed the announcement. He will confer a deal more honour in accepting than the committee will in giving it. And that has got to be made quite clear, both to the committee and to the reader of our forlorn hope.

Yours ever, / E. Pound

Ezra Pound to Harriet Monroe   *[London, 13 August 1913]*

Dear H.M.

. . . Of your things, Kilmer seems the best. A simple Blake-esque tone, bad reasoning but poetic—can he sustain himself? or is this a lone success? . . .

I'm sending on another poem of Frost's which may be more pleasing than those sent in. I admit he's as dull as ditch water, as dull as Wordsworth. But he is trying almost the hardest job of all and he is set to be "literchure" someday. . . .

I'd have sent some more Lawrence, if I'd known you were going to get as much stuff out in the August no. but I thought you were so stuffed up that I sent it to the S.S. [*Smart Set*]. I'll provide you with some, later, dont worry, all in good time.

Guess I'd better send this before it gets mislayed [sic].

Yours ever / E.P.

Harriet Monroe to Ezra Pound   *15 September 1913*

Dear Mr. Pound,

I find a large bunch of work on my return from Panama.

Of the poets sent by you I have had time, thus far, to read only Fletcher. I shall get to Frost and Aldington soon. Is there any haste about publishing them?

Of Frost I return the enclosed. Those I keep make a very interesting bunch, I think, illustrating vividly his various moods. . . .

Have you noticed our new prize? If not, read the enclosed circular. Mr. Levinson was determined that it should go to the best *American* poem.

I had a fine time in Panama. You should all go there.

Very sincerely yours, / H.M.

Frost's first poem in *Poetry*, "The Code—Heroics," appeared in the February 1914 issue. The Levinson Prize was first awarded in 1914 and has continued since then.

Ezra Pound to Harriet Monroe   *London, 23 September 1913*

Dear H.M.:

Lawrence, as you know, gives me no particular pleasure. Nevertheless we are lucky to get him. Hueffer, as you know, thinks highly of him. I *recognize* certain qualities of his work. If I were an editor I should probably accept his work without reading it. As a prose writer I grant him first place among the younger men. . . .

Ezra Pound to Harriet Monroe   *London, [24 September 1913]*

Dear H.M.

Yours to hand re/ Fletcher. . . . I think the committee should gravely consider the question of enlarging the format, NOT in order to print more poetry but that the prose may be adequate.

An article like Hueffer's ["Impressionism," August and September 1913] is very advantageous to us. My own efforts to write inside what I think are the proper limits for the present format have distressed me a good deal. . . . We're to carry on an educational campaign. Complacency is all right in a prospectus. The magazine may be noticed a little over here but you can bet it is not the american contributions that have done it. Most of that list of contributors is beyond the pale of anything that can be taken seriously by the cognoscenti. . . .

I believe an enlargement of the format would double the circulation. . . .

I think you ought to recognize that a critical dept. simply can not
be steered from the provinces. When I say "I" should edit it, I prac-
tically say that Hueffer and I would edit it, and also that I should
consult with Yeats, and that sort of consultation has to be done viva
voce. Also nobody else will edit it for nothing. Hueffer has his record
of the first year and a half of the English Review (that now degraded
derelict) . . . .

Etc. I wish to God you'd take that advertising motto off the maga-
zine ["To have great poets there must be great audiences too"] and
substitute Dante's "Quem stulti magis odissent" [Whom the stupid hate
the most]. After all he was a better poet than Whitman and is more
qualified to speak on such a matter. . . .

Ezra Pound to Harriet Monroe   London, [3 October 1913]

Dear Miss Monroe:

With this last imbecility I will have nothing to do. Either this rotten
£50 is an honourable award for the best poem, or it is a local high
school prize for the encouragement of mediocrity. Either it must be
respectfully offered to Mr Yeats, or the americans must admit that they
are afraid of foreign competition. They must say "We produce inferior
work and can't stand our superiors."

You've got a second prize for the village choir. (Levinson.) The com-
mittee may take refuge by posing as the local board in Haytii [sic] but I
shall not. . . .

I enclose a draft of the sort of letter that should be sent. . . .

Dear Mr. Yeats,

You may have seen our announcement of an award of £50 for the
best poem sent us during the year.

This is, I think, the first award of this sort given in America, the first
attempt to treat the poet as well as the painter is treated. An attempt to
show appreciation of the finest work in contradistinction to the com-
mercial variety.

In offering this award to you, we add more dignity to the custom,
and we hope that you will consider the spirit rather than the substance
of the act.

———   ———   ———

If you will think what the magazine would have been without the
foreign contributions!!!!!! There is no american poem worth awarding,
anyhow. You CAN not divide the arts by a political line. Mother of
God!!! You accepted Yeats' stuff. You hung his pictures. You ought either

to have specified the award as local, or you ought not to have accepted his stuff.

Does £10 per annum give the right to use a patronising tone to one of the greatest artists? Does one starve half a life time to sell out and receive doles from nobodies. Either this is a serious award or it isn't, in the latter case please count me out. . . .

Harriet Monroe to Ezra Pound   *13 October 1913*

My dear E. P.,

We are obeying your orders—but I confess I do so for the same reason that I asked you to read my letter to Mr. Yeats—because I appreciate your services to the magazine and do not wish to treat Mr. Yeats, whom you first brought to us, in any way which you disapprove. We shall announce the prize, however, in the November number, and send him the check with a letter explaining the matter. I don't think he will refuse it, but if he should, it will be no disgrace to anyone else who might ultimately receive it. . . .

Now that the decision is made, there is no use in discussing the matter further. In a more general way I would say, however, that it is easy for you, living in what one of our papers calls 'the world's metropolis' to charge with imbecility us 'in the provinces'. If we are provincial, we shall always be so until we cease to take our art and art opinions ready-made from abroad, and begin to respect ourselves. This magazine is an effort to encourage the art, to work up a public for it in America. I realize perfectly, as you must when you think about it, that it will never, in any essential sense, reach England—that it would not if it were written in gold by Apollo and all the muses. . . . America takes English poetry as law and gospel, but England won't take ours; in a certain sense, the better ours might be, the more slowly and reluctantly England would take it, because of the inevitable instinct of jealousy which any mature man, or nation, feels for his aspiring and assertive offspring.

Therefore it hardly seems to me expedient that our prose section should be edited in London. The most disinterested effort there could not represent us over here, or increase the size of the magazine—I mean in thickness—as soon as we could possibly afford, which is not now, I regret to say. I am in doubt, though, about increasing the proportion of prose. There are so many magazines 'about it and about'—my idea of this one has been that it should present the best we have, including the best of the young aspirants, as an exhibition does, and keep the prose within strict limits.

You speak of having been often irritated during the past year. I might say, so have I. Irritation is inevitable in any enterprise big enough to include more than one person. I think you must admit, however, that I have played fair with you, and I hope you may never accuse me of anything else.

Before the end of this year I shall face a deficit and have to get more money, unless our circulation, and consequently our ads, increase. I don't like the prospect, as you will understand. We are sending out some thousands of circulars, but any advertising is expensive. So you see, I can hardly print more pages just now. . . .

Vachel Lindsay to Harriet Monroe   Springfield, Ill., 28 October 1913

To the Editors of Poetry:
Kind Friends:
    This is to proffer to you and the anonymous guarantors my heartfelt thanks for the one hundred dollar prize for General Booth Enters into Heaven. As O. Henry would say "I devestate [sic] myself with felicitations." Please consider me your constant admirer and well-wisher. . . . [I]t is with some hesitation that I reveal to you what I have done with this money. Please only reveal the bit of news to those in the inner circle who will still think well of me. I gave the one hundred dollars to Mama. It may mitigate the matter to add that I owed her thirty dollars anyway. You see I gave it to her because Mama is a kind woman, generally very pleasant and affable with me—and I wanted to express my appreciation. I hope this will be all right with you. I did have one grand impulse to come to Chicago and take you all to nickelodeons and things till it was used up. But then I would have had to borrow money to come home on, or something like that.
    I wish you well—one and all—I wish you well.
                    Very sincerely with thanks / Nicholas Vachel Lindsay

Ezra Pound to Harriet Monroe   London, 8 November 1913

Dear H.M.
    I saw Yeats last evening; his idea then was that he would get himself a commemorative book-plate (@ about £10) in order that he might graciously acknowledge the award & that he would return the remaining £40, to be used as the committee thought best for the encouragement of younger writers.
    Thus we have displayed the maximum courtesy all round.
    As a member of the jury, I suggest that the remaining $200 be evenly divided between Aldington (for *Korikos*) & Lindsay (for General Booth). I suppose I'll be outvoted, so will cast my whole vote for R.A. if that will help to produce a division of the award. . . .

I think I have explained my view about Lindsay's poem. (Neihardt & the rest seem to me so bad that it would be pernicious to reward them.) . . .

The d—n thing ["General Booth"] is worth £20 bonus—just that. It is *not* worth one jot more. And the "Korikos" is worth £20 bonus. I won't say that it is worth more. But it is the high intent, and that is unweighable. . . .

I suppose you'll hear from W.B.Y. by this same mail. At least I believe his mind is made up, tho' you'd better not mention the matter until you do actually hear from him.

Yours sincerely, / Ezra Pound

You get my position re/ the semi-serious effort. *All* or very nearly the popular approbation in the U.S. turns to the half-masted work. It is so *very* hard for the "*merely beautiful*" to get its due recognition. . . . Mother of God! You cut me down to seven pages [actually, five] at the hind end of a number, on top of everything else. *C'est trop fort.*

William Butler Yeats to Harriet Monroe   London, 7 November 1913

[*personal letter*]

Dear Miss Monroe,

The letter enclosed with this you can print if you like, but I want to write you privately also. I want to make a suggestion which you need not follow in any way. Why not give the £40., or a portion of it, to Ezra Pound? I suggest him to you because, though I do not really like with my whole soul the metrical experiments he has made for you, I think those experiments show a most vigorous imaginative mind. He is certainly a creative personality of some sort, though it is too soon yet to say what sort. His experiments are perhaps errors, I am not certain; but I would always sooner give the laurel to vigorous error than to any orthodoxy not inspired. I know he is one of your staff, and it has occurred to me perhaps that some words of mine, which you could quote—the above or any sentences taken out of this letter for instance—may enable you to get over that difficulty. I would like to say, however, that I have liked other work in your magazine. I remember finding one number particularly charming; but I think one is always safest if one selects a personality. Of course there may be other men equally creative, but then you see I am in ignorance, and that is precisely why I feel I can only suggest to you a little timidly not to put my judgment before yours but because I may help you out of a difficulty.

Yours, / W. B. Yeats.

[formal acceptance]

Dear Miss Monroe—

When I got the very unexpected letter with the prize of £50, my first emotion was how much it would have meant to me even ten years ago, and then I thought surely there must be some young American writer to-day to whom it would mean a great deal, not only in practical help, but in encouragement. I want you therefore not to think that I am in any way ungrateful to you, or in any way anxious to put myself into a different category to your other contributors because I send back to you £40. I will keep £10., and with that I will get Mr Sturge Moore to make me a book-plate, and so I shall have a permanent memory of your generous magazine. I vacilated [sic] a good deal until I thought of this solution, for it seemed so ungracious to refuse, but if I had accepted I should have been bothered by the image of some unknown needy young man in a garret.

                                                                Yours, / W B Yeats

Although he had won this battle, Pound apparently felt he couldn't win the war. On the same day he received Monroe's letter of 13 October, informing him that the Guarantors' Prize would go to Yeats, Pound received the October issue. When he discovered his prose had been cut—and put, as he protested, "at the hind end of a number on top of everything else"—it was too much. He wrote to Hueffer (on *Poetry* stationery) asking him to assume his position at the foreign desk, as if it were his to assign. In a quandary, Hueffer wrote H.M. on 12 November from South Lodge:

I have received the enclosed letter from Mr Ezra Pound who has gone away into the country without leaving me his address. I don't know whether he has the literary advisership of your organ to dispose of, but I am perfectly certain that I could not do his job half so well as he has done. Could you not make it up with him or reinstate him—or whatever is the correct phrase to apply to the solution of the situation whatever that may be? I really think he applied himself to your service with such abounding vigour and such very good results that it is a great pity that you should part company. Besides, if I tried to help you that energetic poet would sit on my head and hammer me till I did exactly what he wanted and the result would be exactly the same except that I should be like the green baize office door that every one kicks in going in or out. I should not seriously mind the inconvenience if it would do any good, but I think it would really be much better for you to go on with Ezra and put up with his artistic irritations; because he was really sending you jolly good stuff. That is the main thing to be considered, isn't it?

Richard Aldington had already tried to play mediator, writing H.M. on 1 November:

> Of course it's no business of mine, but you know Ezra Pound does actually know more about poetry than any person in these islands, Yeats not excepted. Of course, he will insult you; he insults everybody; most of us overlook it because he is American, & probably doesn't know any better. On the other hand he is certainly the cleverest man writing poetry to-day, so you'd better do what he says. I don't know what the row is. I only know that Ezra came along to me at an unnaturally early hour breathing grim threats against someone; & that when I saw poor Mr Hueffer at his at-home he was in a state of utter bewilderment & wondered what Ezra wanted him to do.

The situation was still unresolved at the end of the month. On 26 November, Pound wrote to Amy Lowell to tell her he wasn't sure whether he was "shed of the bloomin' paper or not" and agreeing with her that Harriet was "a bloody fool."

Such was the *Sturm und Drang*—and these were just the first fifteen months. After so much turmoil, another editor might have bid the disgruntled Foreign Correspondent farewell long before this incident. Instead, Harriet Monroe asked him back. On 8 December, he wrote her:

> All right, but I do not see that there was anything for me to have done save resign at the time I did so.
>
> I don't think you have yet tried to see the magazine from my viewpoint.
>
> I don't mind the award as it seems to be Yeats who makes it, or at least "suggests," & as you have my own contrary suggestion for the disposal of the money made before I knew Lindsay had been otherwise provided for.
>
> For the rest, if I stay on the magazine it has got to improve. It's all very well for Yeats to be ceremonious in writing to you, a stranger, and in a semi-public letter. Nobody holds *him* responsible for the rot that goes into the paper.
>
> I am willing to reconsider my resignation pending a general

improvement of the magazine, and I will not have my name associated with it unless it does improve.

And *Poetry* did improve over the next two years: 1914–15 saw first appearances by T. S. Eliot, Wallace Stevens, Robert Frost, William Carlos Williams, Marianne Moore, Carl Sandburg, and others. But Pound still found several occasions for dispute. Chiding turned to scolding, tiffs became tirades, and the (sometimes humorous) lecturing continued. Despite his outbursts, and several breaches of faith, Monroe remained faithful to her foreign editor.

CHAPTER V

Recognition and Romance

Assailed and admired, *Poetry* was attracting much wider attention by 1914. The magazine had printed a broad range of styles, but Imagism and free verse elicited the most response, usually negative. The New Poetry polarized poets and critics, and identified the journal in the mind of the public as the literary equivalent of all that was perverse in modern art. A barbed "Salutation," sent in to the Chicago *Tribune*'s "Line o' Type" column, drew a direct parallel:

> O degenerates in the art of writing,
> and fallen ones,
> I have seen Cubists splattering their paints. . . .
> You are far worse than they are,
> And they are much worse than nothing;
> And the nude descends the staircase,
> and does not even own clothing.

Monroe herself doubted the merit of some items published in the early months, although she was convinced, as she had been at the Armory Show, that the radically new deserved a showing, if only to shake the art out of its complacency. By 1914, the more experienced editorial staff could be choosier as many more and much better submissions arrived.

Indeed, over the next two years, it was *Poetry*'s great good luck to feature in almost every number poems not only superior to most offerings in other journals but strong enough to stand the test of time. Even now it is remarkable how many significant works debuted in its pages in 1914 and 1915 alone: "The Love Song of J. Alfred Prufrock," "Sunday Morning," Yeats's "The Magi," Robinson's "Eros Turannos," Sandburg's "Chicago Poems," Pound's "Near Perigord," the first journal publications of William Carlos Williams and Robert Frost, and the first American appearances of Marianne Moore, Rupert Brooke, D. H. Lawrence, and Ford Madox Hueffer.

In her first report to the Guarantors in 1913, Monroe quoted admiring

reviews in London's *Poetry and Drama* and the *Mercure de France*. Respect-
ful notices appeared in the local papers, as well as in the *Post* and the *Sun*
in New York and the New Orleans *Times-Democrat*, which found: "This
small magazine . . . seems as a tiny taper kept alive in a windy world by
hands curled carefully to guard it. And yet, its flame may grow and spread
until it becomes a beacon light seen of all men." But *Poetry* still had one
implacable foe, the *Dial*, and again the object of its scorn was a Midwest-
ern free-verse writer. Even more than Vachel Lindsay, the *Dial* found Carl
Sandburg in violation of the supposedly immutable poetic laws it set itself
to uphold.

Sandburg was a relatively obscure newspaper reporter when Alice
Henderson plucked his "Chicago Poems" from the unsolicited manu-
scripts. The group was given pride of place at the head of the March 1914
issue, and received the first Levinson Prize in November. Even Pound
sent faint compliments on 18 April: "Good luck, glad to see Sandburg. I
don't think he is very important, but that's the sort of stuff we ought
print." But to the refined editors of the *Dial*, Sandburg's rousing paean
to the "City of the Big Shoulders" provided yet another reason for
"calling out the old guard" to avert dangerous tendencies: "the fashion
with young people to reject everything that has been tested in the alembic
of reflection, and to offer in its stead all manner of raw and fantastic
imaginings."

Conservatives had leveled similar criticisms at the "raw" material of
another newspaperman-poet, Walt Whitman, and the *Dial* likewise
objected as much to Sandburg's gritty subject matter as to his style. Situ-
ated in Chicago since the boom years of the 1880s, the *Dial* considered
itself above the stockyards, steel mills, and other "husky, brawling" realities
that made the city a commercial success (and that enabled it to enjoy so
many world-class cultural institutions). In its March 16th lead editorial
the *Dial* attacked the form, or formlessness, of Sandburg's work: "The
typographical arrangement of this jargon creates a suspicion that it is
intended to be taken seriously as some form of poetry, and the suspicion
is confirmed by the fact that it stands in the forefront of the latest issue of
a futile little periodical described as a 'magazine of verse.'"

To Monroe, these were fighting words, and with a sharp editorial in
the May 1914 issue, "The Enemies We Have Made," she cut the *Dial*
down to size:

> It is possible that we have ventured rashly in "discovering" Mr. Sand-
> burg and the others, but—whom and what has *The Dial* discovered? We
> have taken chances, made room for the young and the new, tried to
> break the chains which enslave Chicago to New York, America to

Europe, and the present to the past. What chances has *The Dial* ever taken? What has it ever printed but echoes? For thirty years it has run placidly along in this turbulent city of Chicago, gently murmuring the accepted opinion of such leaders of thought as *The Athenaeum* and *The Spectator*. During all that third of a century it has borne about as much relation to the intellectual life of this vast, chaotically rich region as though it were printed in Glasgow or Caracas. Not only has it failed to grasp a great opportunity—it has been utterly blind and deaf to it, has never known the opportunity was there. Is its editor competent to define the word futile?

1. A Banquet for Yeats, a Triumph for Lindsay

If Monroe was feistier than usual now, it was not only from pent-up irritation with her critics but from justifiable pride, particularly about her latest coup, the appearance of William Butler Yeats in Chicago at a banquet sponsored by *Poetry*. The event was set for March 1st at the Cliff Dwellers' Club, but Yeats spent a week in Chicago as the guest of Monroe and her niece Polly Root at their apartment near Michigan Avenue. Monroe took Yeats shopping (and helped him elude reporters when he went to visit a psychic), and his very presence at her side indicated *Poetry*'s status. His endorsement at the dinner confirmed the faith of Monroe's backers, and further annoyed her critics at the *Dial*.

Invitations to the banquet went out in the name of the Guarantors, ensuring that "almost everybody who was anybody was there," including William Morton Payne, "my friendly enemy at *The Dial*." Besides the local poets and writers, Monroe asked selected "outside poets" to attend, "especially the author of 'General Booth Enters into Heaven.'" The thoughtful hostess made sure her guest of honor saw it, by placing the issue of *Poetry* containing the poem on his bedroom table. Lindsay accepted the Editor's invitation to give a speech, but offered an alternate plan: a reading of his newest poem. He also coached Miss Monroe on how she should introduce him.

Vachel Lindsay to Harriet Monroe   *Springfield, Ill.,*
                                                      16 February 1914

My Dear Miss Monroe:

I am certainly flattered and honored to eat with Yeats at the Cliff Dwellers and make a noise with him and delighted to meet Ficke. I am sorry you will have to pay my car-fare, but I am dead broke. Can't you advance me what the poems are worth that you have in hand, and print them in the March number. That will do just as well. I don't want to be an extra expense. My plan of life is very simple you see—to live at home—on nothing. I only notice my empty purse when people ask me to go places. I resisted all kinds of invitations to New York—mainly from being dead broke.

I want to recite for you a poem that the Metropolitan [magazine] people bought—called "The Congo." . . . It will be far more effective than any speech I can make, I am sure. General Booth finally wears out, as a recitation, but the Congo never wears out.

Very Sincerely, / Nicholas Vachel Lindsay

Vachel Lindsay to Harriet Monroe   *Springfield, Ill.,*
17 February 1914

My Dear Miss Monroe:

My letter yesterday was mailed in haste, and I am not sure that I minded my manners. I should be grateful for the chance to meet Yeats and I will be delighted to see Ficke, with whom I have corresponded a deal . . . . I will be vain as a peacock to shine by reflected light in the presence of Mr. Yeats . . . . I fully realize that he has a lifetime of good poetry and good works behind him and I am only a beginner. Also he is probably much pursued by callow youths like me. . . .

I will try to give you a little crisper idea of the Congo than my last incoherent letter. The whole piece is elaborately syncopated, and imitates Dahomey War-Drums. But I worked hard to give it a silk lining. It takes about seven minutes. . . .

The first section deals with the basic ~~barbaric~~ savagery of the negro. The Refrain is "Mumbo Jumbo Will Hoodoo You." By implication, rather than direct statement, the refrain stands for the ill fate and sinister power of Africa from the beginning. I do not say so—but the Civil War was a case of Mumbo Jumbo hoodooing America. Any Lynching is a yielding to the power of Hoodoo. Any Burning alive, or hand-cutting depredations by [King] Leopold [of Belgium], is a case of Mumbo Jumbo Hoodooing Civilization. In the second section the Irrepressible High Spirits of the negro, as set forth in a sort of Grand Opera minstrel show in a part compensates for and overcomes the Hoodoo he brings. All the ragtime elements of our minstrelsy and the Cake Walk, etc are here symbolized. The third section is an idealized Camp-meeting—transferred to the banks of the Congo, along with a prophecy of the redemption of the race through their religious instinct, and the death of Mumbo Jumbo.

I hope as toastmistress you can cover this outline or a similar one, so that when I rise I can give all my time to the *poem direct*. I will recite it to you and Henry B. Fuller or Miss Wyatt beforehand and you can amend or replace this analysis with your own impressions. There may be several points you are just squirming to make—that this extravaganza will hook onto. . . .

Vachel Lindsay, c. 1914, after his reading of "The Congo" at the *Poetry* banquet made him famous.

About 150 people attended the banquet. In the April 1914 issue, Monroe reported that Yeats addressed his remarks "to a fellow craftsman," and declared: "[S]ince coming to Chicago I have read several times a poem by Mr. Lindsay, one which will be in the anthologies, 'General Booth Enters into Heaven.' This poem is stripped bare of ornament; it has an earnest simplicity, a strange beauty, and you know Bacon said, 'There is no excellent beauty without strangeness.' " Yeats spent the rest of his speech talking about himself and Ezra Pound. Then Lindsay took the floor—and stole the show.

Lindsay's theatrics at the Cliff Dwellers' bought him national attention and started his career as America's first "performance poet." The New York *Evening Post* printed an eye-witness account of Lindsay's sensational delivery, which was picked up by papers across the country:

Mr. Yeats himself was responsible for the reading, having declared that Mr. Lindsay was the most promising poet he had discovered in the United States. . . . In acknowledgement Mr. Lindsay began "The Congo." The moment was unpropitious, for the audience was thinking of how it could manage decently to go home. But the first lines caught its flagging attention. . . . Those who had never heard Mr. Lindsay before, and they were in the majority, were a little excited and a good deal puzzled. Mr. Lindsay chanted four lines more. . . . And then, marking the rapid syncopated rhythm with swaying body and jerking arms, he beat up his first climax in the fashion common to exhorters of every sort. . . . That "BOOM" shook the room, but Mr. Lindsay chanted on, chanted of Mumbo-Jumbo and all the other gods of the Congo, of the negro fairyland, of Jacob and the golden stairs, until: "There, where the wild ghost-gods had wailed / A million boats of angels sailed . . . 'Mumbo-Jumbo is dead in the jungle. / Never again will he hoo-doo you. / Never again will he hoo-doo you.' "

When Mr. Lindsay had finished, he was surrounded by women who wished to be his hostesses at dinner. The North Shore had discovered a lion who could roar! The young man who had come up to Chicago to stay three days remained three weeks.

Recalling the evening over twenty years later, Miss Monroe wrote: "This also was one of my great days, those days which come to most of us as atonement for long periods of drab disappointment or dark despair. I drew a long breath of renewed power, and felt that my little magazine was fulfilling some of our seemingly extravagant hopes."

2. Vachel and Sara

Monroe continued to promote Lindsay, printing "The Santa Fé Trail" and "The Fireman's Ball" (July 1914) and "The Chinese Nightingale" (February 1915), which was awarded the second Levinson Prize. In 1914 she helped get *The Congo and Other Poems* accepted by her own publisher, Macmillan, and wrote a glowing introduction to the book. (Again the author offered H.M. hints for her remarks.) She gave him advances on poems and introduced him to her friends, including Mrs. William Vaughn Moody. Harriet Moody was a helpful person to know; she had a catering business and provided food and lodging during his frequent trips to Chicago.

But Monroe's efforts did not stop there. She felt Lindsay needed a helpmate, and the woman she had in mind was—Sara Teasdale. The well-bred lady from St. Louis was an improbable choice for the bluff and ever-broke troubadour from Springfield. But if Miss Monroe's experience in the field of romance was limited, her intentions were good. Lindsay seems to have brought out her maternal side, which he exploited fully. When he referred to himself as a "callow youth" in 1914, he was already thirty-four years old, although he often adopted an almost adolescent tone in his letters to Monroe. He also flattered her and praised her poems shamelessly.

From the start, Lindsay did not hesitate to ask favors. He was in fact a skilled beggar, and proud of it. Since 1906, he had been tramping about the country, and had learned to rely on the kindness of strangers. On the road, he literally sang for his supper. In the summer of 1912, he walked from Springfield to New Mexico, at which point (he later told Monroe) he had a kind of spiritual collapse. He then hopped a train to Los Angeles, where the Editor's first letter caught up with him in mid-September, as he was in the process of revising "General Booth." In a letter to Witter Bynner in February 1912, Lindsay declared he was "a natural beggar," and had made many friends that way. From his "mendicant tours" he felt he had come to know America, and he distilled his experiences in "Rules of the Road," "The Adventures of a Literary Tramp," "The Lady Poverty," "Rhymes to Be Traded for Bread." (He printed up the last piece and used it exactly as the title indicates.) They were published as *A Handy Guide for Beggars* in 1916.

It was Bynner who first alerted Lindsay to Pound's work (Bynner had been an editor at Small, Maynard & Co., E.P.'s Boston publishers), and Lindsay wrote Pound a fan letter as early as 1910. Through Bynner he also met Monroe's friend Arthur Ficke. He confessed to Ficke in November 1913, when he was in the midst of writing "The Congo," that he doubted "this stuff" was poetry. Instead of listening to his "inner voice," he just banged on the table. He told Ficke he got ideas from vaudeville shows—which he professed to abhor. The revelation says much about Lindsay's approach: often calculating and naïvely candid at the same time.

In the summer of 1913, with the support of Eunice Tietjens, Monroe suggested to Lindsay that he make the acquaintance of Sara Teasdale, and he began to write her in mid-July. He also sent his picture, which had an effect quite the opposite of what he intended. Teasdale had already fallen in love with another man, the poet and editor John Hall Wheelock, who was reserved, cultivated, tall, dark, and handsome—all that Lindsay was not. Lindsay soon was writing daily, many of the letters running to ten pages or more. But the relationship was problematic from the start, as Teasdale most certainly realized.

Monroe did not understand that Lindsay and Teasdale were *not* made for each other. In terms of social background, temperament, and artistic ambitions, they could hardly have been more incompatible. Sara was five years younger, born in 1884 to prosperous, middle-aged parents, who overprotected their shy and hypersensitive (thus obviously superior) child. As a girl, she was sickly, and throughout her life she suffered from a variety of real or psychosomatic illnesses that required frequent rest cures. By employing private tutors, maids, and nurses to tend to the invalid she created, her mother was able to keep the fragile child under her control until she was thirty.

Writing provided Teasdale an emotional and artistic outlet. It was also

Sara Teasdale as a young woman, in a photograph sent to her friend Eunice Tietjens.

her only way of making money, and thus of escaping total dependence upon her parents. Like Lindsay, Teasdale was still living at home as an adult, but loved to travel. Unlike him, she was very careful with her funds. It was her concern for security, as much as her romantic expectations, that made the notion of marrying Lindsay unappealing. Teasdale knew he would always be "a perfect child about money," as she told Monroe.

On first meeting the Editor in New York, Teasdale had the impression she was a bitter spinster. When an early love affair collapsed, Teasdale told a friend she didn't want to turn into a sour old maid like Harriet Monroe. But following H.M.'s invitation, she stopped for a brief visit in the summer of 1913. She wound up staying ten days, during which she reversed her opinion, having discovered the Editor's sensitive side. A few days into the visit, she met Tietjens, and they, too, became close. E.T. introduced her to Floyd Dell and Chicago's Bohemian set, whose outspokenness about sex rather shocked the high-minded Miss Teasdale.

Much as she liked Monroe, Teasdale did not wholly approve of *Poetry*. She had already published two books of conventional verse, *Sonnets to Duse* (1907) and *Helen of Troy* (1911). She felt that the Editor was too much in the thrall of Pound, and that much of the material in *Poetry* reflected his difficult modernist tastes. Nonetheless, she contributed to her friend's journal throughout her career. Whatever her disagreements about its contents, she approved of the fact that *Poetry* paid. (Indeed, she never appeared in a magazine that didn't pay.) She was effusive in praising Monroe's own poetry. But, then, in other matters too she had a tendency to gush. Even so, amid the heated rhetoric there can be heard the voice of reason and skepticism—the same qualities to be found in her poems, which convey a distinctly modern sensibility within their tightly structured frames.

In her letters to Monroe, Teasdale is diplomatic in speaking of their mutual friend. But the letters clearly convey her doubts about Lindsay and indicate how coolly she sized up his character and future prospects. It is curious to note that in almost all his letters to H.M. during the affair, Lindsay talks about his writing or his career first, before getting around to "our mutual friend Sara."

Sara Teasdale to Harriet Monroe   *New York City, 29 October 1913*

Dearest Lady of All:

Why weren't you at The Poetry Society last night? I wanted to twinkle my eyes at somebody—and the right person was in Chicago. . . . You should have heard me telling the nominating committee of The Poetry Society of America that you were the finest and the very nicest of anybody that ever was.

Of course I want to visit you but it will be better for me to go straight home— —and besides I won't have a cent of money to take the longer route by Chicago for I am going to stay here until starvation stares me between the brows. I am writing to all the magazines that owe me money and to Putnam's and to everybody that has a soft heart and I am saying, "Do not send me like Hagar into the wilderness." I am worse in love than ever. I am really in love at last. I don't mind it except that it keeps me awake a lot at night. He is so much finer than anybody else I ever knew— —any man, I mean— — —that I can't take any interest in any of them. I wish that you knew him. . . . His new book, "Love and Liberation" is out. Happy lady to whom it was written! . . . Oh he is splendid! . . .

I haven't seen "Poetry" since the September number. It is waiting for me at home, I suppose. Vachel Lindsay sent me his picture. I can't like his looks (my own love is marvellously good looking) and he wants me to send him mine— — —but I'm too wise. I wanted him to come to N.Y. while I am here. But I guess he hasn't the money. He says that he is coming to St. Louis to see me. Is he engaged? He says: "Be careful what you do. For I am rumored to be engaged."

Much, much, much love / from / Sara.

Vachel Lindsay to Harriet Monroe   *Springfield, Ill.,*
20 February 1914

My Dear Miss Monroe:

. . . I have just had a two days visit with Sara in St. Louis. You are the first poet-lady I have ever met and Mrs. Henderson second and Sara third. She has a charming family, lovely people, Sara and I had written to each other so much and had never seen each other we were all crowded up with things to say and I don't know as we said any of them.

She is certainly a lovely lady and I am glad indeed to know her. . . .

Vachel Lindsay to Harriet Monroe   *Springfield, Ill., 4 April 1914*

My dear Miss Monroe:

I have just finished a poem I will forward to you soon, as soon as I have read it around for a week and put in the final small changes. It is "The Santa Fe Trail" and I hope is better than the Congo or the Fireman's Ball.

Now I want you to do me a very great favor, if it can be arranged with no great trouble to yourself. I want to be asked to St. Louis by some one you know, to entertain ~~somebody's~~ their friends. . . . I would like to spend about three days in the town, between Easter and May the first—enough to call on our mutual Sara about three afternoons. Now *don't* explain to my hostess my motive. I will tell her, if she is a real leddy—when the times comes. I want to be asked down on my *merits*—and my car-fare sent me by my hostess and five dollars pocket-money, $10. altogether. In return for this I will recite for any number of people (10 to 1000) if my hostess desires—any number of evenings. I will include the Santa Fe Trail in my performance. I hate a hotel—I am dead broke—I want to see Sara, and I don't want to ask the Springfield home folks to pay for my picnic. Sara lives in a lovely house—and her old folks are very sweet and kind—but they are *so* old, and they are not likely to be the sort to collect my crowd anyway, or get much fun out of the show. They are eminently dignified Baptists as I understand them. She is a lovely chick in a gilded cage. Sara don't know anything about this scheme—and I have tried so hard to think up some way of putting through some sort of visit, and it is the best that occurs to me till I make some coin. . . .

And now—curiosity box—of course you want to know what is *in* all this? a purely PLATONIC admiration. But since I have written about 'steen [sic] thousand letters to Sara—*and* have only seen her 24 hours of my life—one long rather strained day—we were so dammed up with things to say—well—I want to correct the lop-sidedness—or letter-sidedness of our acquaintance, and be able to chat at leisure.

No, I do not *belong* to anyone in the world. Never will. . . .

Vachel Lindsay to Harriet Monroe   *Springfield, Ill., 1 May 1914*

My dear Miss Monroe,

Let me express to you my great surprise and great pleasure and all the grand emotions over your getting a book for me with Macmillans. I do not know where you are, so am sending this letter to be forwarded.

The book will be ready for them in about two weeks. It is 80 poems now, and will be winnowed down a considerable. I began with 108 or thereabouts. . . .

Perhaps we can get this Chinese Nightingale ready—too—but that will be perhaps offering *too* much. Also, the object of this letter is not yet unveiled. I want you to write a preface for the Macmillan Book, stating that the Poetry magazine introduced me to the world, and, though not necessarily set terms, say your set in Chicago did much to get the Congo going. I want my work dramatized as it were, identified with the movements of your group. The book will be entitled "The Congo and Other Poems." . . .

Vachel Lindsay to Harriet Monroe   *Springfield, Ill., 12 May 1914*

My Dear Harriet: (Is that proper and permitted? Please allow it.)

I send you the table of contents of the New Book. The Congo and other poems. I think you have read at least half of them. Now fix up your introduction—and I only insist on a brief one—if it can be made to include your very kind thoughts—fix up your introduction so that the reader will be craftily and unsuspectingly led to desire to hear me *recite* these verses, but even *more* prompted to try to recite them himself. It looks to me like my only chance at an income—after while, when I *must* have one[.] (Pa is going to go broke paying for my shirts and trousers some day, and visits to St. Louis and all. And then I will *have* to recite for a living.)

But please make the point that many reciters over the country are reciting or chanting my pieces, who have never seen me—stirred to do so by the directions on the margins. Or something like that.

Next—please claim me for "Poetry's" own, and Chicago's own and Illinois' own, and Sangamon County's own—whether I am or not. And your own.

As for the rest—whatever is in your heart. The whole paragraph can be brief—but sufficient, if signed by your honorable name. *Then please forward to Macmillans and tell them to paste it in the front of the book.*

I might as well tell you that Gloriana in the back of the book is Saraphim St. Louis Teasdale. But that is in STRICT CONFIDENCE. Of course no one would know it who read the poems—except somebody who knew her, and knew she had red hair and such, and knew I'd been courting her. . . .

3. A Brief Romance

For several months, Teasdale tried to get John Hall Wheelock to declare his love. But he was not in love with her, a fact she finally came to realize in the spring of 1914. By then she also recognized that the painfully reserved Wheelock was self-centered, gloomy, poor, and otherwise not the ideal lover she hoped for. Still, she found it difficult to give him up. Meanwhile, Vachel flooded her with letters—humorous but filled with poetic observations—all of which Sara took with large pinches of salt. She had invited him to New York in the fall, but he declined. He advised Sara to abandon New York, stay home, and write about St. Louis. He was rather surprised to discover how determined Sara was to pursue her own career.

In letters to Eunice Tietjens, Teasdale told of her distress at her lack of progress with Wheelock, then sent E.T. train fare for a visit at the end of March. While in St. Louis, Eunice had lunch with an acquaintance, Ernst Filsinger, and discovered he had memorized many of Teasdale's poems, indeed fallen in love with her through her work. Tietjens was not convinced that either Vachel or Jack was right for Sara, so she arranged an introduction. Filsinger was a man of wide interests, and a successful businessman who had worked his way up to executive at a shoe manufacturing company. They met in April, and each was favorably impressed. Although he had only seen Sara once before, Vachel now found he, too, was falling in love with her, so much so that he started to give serious thought to making enough money to support her in the manner to which she was accustomed.

When Lindsay went to St. Louis in April, he took Teasdale to the movies, one of his great interests, but the visit was not a success. She told Eunice she was not convinced of his sincerity. Besides, she couldn't get Jack Wheelock out of her mind. But with her thirtieth birthday approaching in a few months, she felt she had to come to a decision. She invited Lindsay for a visit on May 6, and scheduled Ernst right after his departure. The meetings did not resolve the conflicts she felt.

Lindsay wrangled another invitation to speak in St. Louis. Teasdale and Filsinger attended his performance on June 1st, and Sara remarked to H.M. on "the added power that he seems to get from a room full." Lindsay wrote that he would make the great "sacrifice" of going to New York, provided he got some money from readings, and if Monroe offered him a $100 advance. (She gave him the money.) Sara stayed with Monroe for ten days in early June, and laid out her dilemma to Harriet and Eunice. H.M. thought Sara should feel privileged to marry a great poet like

Vachel. E.T. believed that, given Sara's emotional and financial needs, Ernst was the more practical choice. Lindsay arrived midway through her visit, with an engagement ring in his pocket. He didn't present it, but he did plan more readings to increase his earnings.

Teasdale saw Wheelock again after returning to New York on 17 June, and wrote Monroe 22 June that while she was sure he loved her, he didn't love her enough. While she loved Vachel, too, she knew that marrying him would present endless problems because of anxiety over money. Lindsay hoped she would wait while he made enough to support them, and still thought she could be lured back to the middle west. (There was a possibility that if Tietjens left *Poetry*, as she had mentioned, H.M. would invite Teasdale to join the staff.) He knew that Filsinger was also wooing her—Sara was always aboveboard—and when she asked him again to come to New York, he obeyed. As he waited to see her on 1 July, Sara wrote to Harriet about her conflicted feelings.

Monroe obviously was not pleased to learn of this turn of events and thought Vachel's affections were being toyed with. Meanwhile, Filsinger—who adored Sara but feared he didn't stand a chance with the exalted creature—was writing anxious letters to Tietjens. Sara told Eunice she wanted to be swept off her feet. E.T. in turn counseled Ernst to step up his campaign. He tried to bowl her over with special delivery letters, telegrams, and flowers. The strategy worked. Vachel continued to send love letters, too. The strain of it all drove Sara to her bed with the grippe. However, as she told Harriet, she couldn't just "sit in a corner," and early in August Ernst was invited to New York. He impressed her friends, including Wheelock, who urged Sara to marry him. Vachel made another plea that she wait for him, but her mind was made up. After Ernst visited Sara and her parents, the happy couple wired Eunice on 18 August announcing the wedding. Vachel seems to have endured the loss of his seraphic Sara with admirable equipoise.

Sara Teasdale to Harriet Monroe   *St. Louis, 13 May 1914*

Dearest Lady:

I write in a state of worry and weariness. My father has been ailing for some time and the doctor warns us of sudden death from heart failure or a stroke of apoplexy. It is really a case of general break-down from age—he is seventy-five and since I have been home from New York I have noticed his ever-growing feebleness. . . . Well—no more of my troubles. I went down to a little town 25 miles south of here in the greenest hills in the world last week and tried to forget it all. Vachel came down there on Wednesday and stayed until Friday morning, and

on Saturday Ernst Filsinger came down and stayed until Monday. All
went quite as it should under a full moon in May, and made me forget
age and mortality for a few days. Vachel is really a dear— —but I don't
exactly love him,—which is all the better. I was so glad that you gave
me your frank impressions of my darling J.H.W. They were just such as
I was sure that you could not help having from so short an acquain-
tance. He is cold and abstracted and un-get-at-able at first, and meeting
him in Scribner's [bookstore, where he worked] in all the glare and
bustle was a hard ordeal. He is the shyest person I ever knew— —so
very shy that out of the mere torture of it he has invented this seeming
calm abstraction. . . . Oh my beloved Harriet, you understand me so
perfectly— —I wish so much that you could take my word for the fact
of his niceness. Of all the men I have ever known, he has the deepest
and surest knowledge of me. I have never said anything to him in my
life that he didn't understand and treat with a sort of gentle humor and
tenderness. He covers up every real thing in himself when he is fright-
ened. He shows only a wooden gentleman with some culture. But he
has given me many of the happiest hours of my life— —a sort of
absolute freedom that I have never known with any man before— —I
can't help being grateful to him. Well, well, I guess that this all sounds
like the vaporing of a love-lorn maiden. Of course I know that he
would not be an ideal husband. He is too absurdly sensitive for one
thing, and too selfish for another. . . .

   Think of me lovingly, and pet me a little!

                                                             Sara

Sara Teasdale to Harriet Monroe   *St. Louis, 2 June 1914*

Dearest Lady:

   You are very sweet to me! I hardly know how to begin to thank
you— —so I won't try to until I see you.

   Life has been a complicated affair with sick parents, clothes to get
and loves and lovers that don't match. . . . I am so dead tired that I am
going to take a room at The Virginia [Hotel] for a few days until I am
in presentable shape to be in your house. Will you let me do that, and
will you realize that I truly want to be under the same roof with you,
but that I don't want to impose upon you when I am 2/3 a nervous
wreck? . . .

   We have had wild hot weather complicated by a Pageant (which was
really a fine thing) and Vachel Lindsay, and all these things together have
reduced me to a pulp. . . . Vachel's reading . . . was a marvelous thing. I've
never heard him read to more than half a dozen people before, and I

was thrilled by the added power that he seems to get from a room full. It was a big success.

I was sorry that you didn't meet Ernst Filsinger while he was in Chicago, and he was very sorry too. He is a fine fellow— —but my heart is as stupidly constant as the north star. I can't get Wheelock out of my head.

Much love and thanks to you and all kinds of lookings-forward to seeing you.

Sara.

Sara Teasdale to Harriet Monroe *New York City, 22 June 1914*

Dearest Sweet Lady Harriet:

I am so hopelessly upset in my mind and heart that I would give almost anything if your arms could be around me for a few minutes.

I saw Jack Thursday night and he seems so terribly [illegible] and worn that I longed to do something for him— —and instead I poured out my own perplexities. He undoubtedly loves me. I am sure of it— but he doesn't love me enough, and so I must try to forget him. . . .

In many ways he would be a really terrible husband. He is so repressed and black about things. In the meanwhile, I long for Vachel so much that I wrote him that I wanted him to come. . . . I've had such wonderful letters from Vachel that they almost make me cry. I want to marry him— —and yet I feel in my heart that both his love and mine will be terribly wried and perhaps twisted into hate almost by the material struggle. You are very hopeful of his future, but I do not see how he can hope to earn even as much as $200.00 per month regularly. And that would surely be necessary even if I had a little money of my own. He is a good deal of an idealist and he would think me mercenary and extravagant when I needed things that he could not see the necessity for.

I know how sweet he is and how loyal and fine—but a man who has been utterly free and roughed it as he has, can not hope to change himself into a husband and father by just wishing to. I don't know whether his love would stand the strain. And yet, tho' I can talk so seemingly calmly, I am more in love with him than I was when I left Chicago— —and that is a good deal. I long for him very much. If I were really strong, there'd be no question in my mind about it. As it is, I fear that if I marry him and have a lot of anxiety over money and all that, that I'll have another break-down like the one ten years ago that lasted so long. And this wouldn't be fair to him. But I love him, I love him.

I wish that I knew you were thinking of me this minute! I'd send you five kisses. Keats said four was enough for anybody, but I am spoiled by Vachel, and so I think even five rather too few.

Love, / Sara.

Sara Teasdale to Harriet Monroe   *New York City, 1 July 1914*

Dearest Harriet:

Just a line to carry my love. Vachel got here last night. I suppose that we are both mad as hatters. I still feel that our marriage would be a disastrous thing, but I love him. . . . Vachel is a dear. There is no doubt of that. And yet, in a queer way, his love does not seem to me quite like the love that I want from the man who is going to own me. I wish that I could talk about it to you. I can hardly write it. He *never* (even in his most passionate moments) makes me forget myself. And I feel that it is the same way with him. He himself never *loses* himself. It may be self-control. I have had some of the most perfect letters from him that I have ever read I am thankful for his love. . . .

Your letter was very fine. I love you.

Sara.

I have quite definitely put Jack out of my mind. But I still feel that the best thing for both Vachel and me would be for me to marry Filsinger (if he asks me!) Vachel knows that I feel this way. One can not live on love— —and yet I know it would be a miracle if I were ever loved as beautifully again as I am now. / S.

Sara Teasdale to Harriet Monroe   *New York City, [early July 1914]*

Dearest, dear Lady:

I am half-sick and sort of gone to pieces, but I must write you a word to thank you for the letter and the fine picture of Vachel.

You don't seem to see the whole situation, dearest of ladies,— —you seem to feel all sympathy for Vachel and only a mood of exhortation for me. If you knew the fearful mixture of happiness and unhappiness that has been tearing me to bits for the last six weeks, you wouldn't exhort your poor Sara in such a gently lecturing way. If you think that for one minute I have been playing with Vachel's love, you are hopelessly misunderstanding me. Every step of our love (and before that every step of our friendship) has been utterly sincere. I say this remembering God and the Angels. When I asked Vachel to come to New York, there was an absolute understanding on his side that I felt that we could never marry, but that I wanted to be with him. . . . You seem to feel, dearest lady, that I should sit in a corner by myself and decide which of two men I will marry without allowing either of them to make love to me, but I can't do that. I never had met Vachel until the middle of February, and before seeing him in Chicago, our meetings had been very fleeting. It seems to me that the joy of both of us in his coming to New York has been so glorious that neither of us needs any sympathy. But if you are going to give any, you must not give it all to him. I need it too.

Heavens, why do you ask me if I have thought of various things in connection with our love? What else do you think I am doing night and day?? I am half dead over it. But this is clear to me: it will be several years before he can make enough to support a wife and babies, and I want babies, and I can't wait several years before marriage if I am to have children. You speak of me getting help from his family and mine. I could not live in the Lindsay family home. From all that I have heard from Vachel, I see that that is about impossible. It would kill me. His parents could give us only the meagerest help aside from giving us their roof. As for my own family, I am too proud to accept help from them. They do not understand the artistic attitude anyway, and they would feel terribly abused to have to help support me and a man who (according to them) would not earn a living. And Vachel will not take a position drawing a regular salary— —not that I want him to, but I have sounded him and I see that he feels that he cannot. My darling lady, I don't see what we can do but let it all go as a beautiful dream. Neither one of us are going to break our hearts. Everything has been open and above board every minute. Both of us would drag our love in the dust if we tried to marry as things are now. He is a perfect child about money. He would be disappointed in it all when he saw how marriage involved an endless scramble for money.

Don't blame me, only love me. If I find after a few months that I can't stand to live without him, I suppose that I'll marry him. Oh he is so fine, so gloriously good to the very bottom, and such a gentleman! And he knows of every bit of my love for him. This uncertainty is nearly killing me— —and yet, in my heart I know that it isn't really uncertainty, for I feel sure that I will have to give him up. For both his sake and mine, whatever is done had best be done at once. If we wait for a year or two or three for him to earn something and then have to give it up, it will be all the harder for us, and for me it will mean that I shall never marry. And I must marry, for at the bottom I am a mother more intensely than I am a lover. My love to you.

Sara.

Vachel's trip to New York has been a tremendous success so far as meeting people and being given ovations goes. I know that it will be a lasting good to him.

Sara Teasdale to Harriet Monroe   *New York City, 14 July 1914*

Dearest Harriet:

Just a line (tho' you owe me a letter, I think) to give you my love and to tell you that I am living under such an avalanche of love that I am ground to bits, and went to bed sick this afternoon.

My St. Louis man, Ernst Filsinger, is sending me a flood of special delivery letters and telegrams imploring me to marry him. He has it hard [underlined eight times]. And at this end Vachel is on his head, and I am tired to death. Everybody is wild about Vachel here. He is an angel. I am very much in love, but I literally don't see how I can marry him. He will never be happy if he has to neglect his poetry, and he can not make money and make poetry too. Even the lecturing-reciting will take up so much of his time that will not have much for his art. And money never troubles him. He would be endlessly upset with me because I would never be able to "rise above it". I want babies, and babies are expensive. And besides all this, Vachel's love and mine has been so wonderful . . . that I hate to mix it all up with dollars and cents. I feel honestly that I am not strong enough physically to go thro' the years of poverty that would be ahead of us, and secondly I want him to be free to follow his art. I am living in terror for fear that Filsinger will descend upon us. . . . His letters are mad as hatters, and he is sending me such quantities of flowers that the market for roses, orchids and carnations must have gone up in consequence. If Filsinger comes, I will just have to pick up and go to Charlevoix [the Teasdales' summer home in Michigan]. I can't stand the strain of "the both of them" as our Irish girl says. I've about made up my mind that I'll have to let Vachel go unless a miracle happens. . . .

With love / your very upset and very tired / Sara.

Vachel Lindsay to Harriet Monroe   *New York City, 27 July 1914*

My Dear Harriet:

Thank you for taking so much pains with the new preface [to *The Congo and Other Poems*]. On the whole it was well worth it to me, since I presume many reviewers will read the preface and *quote it* in parts and the longer the preface, the more variety in the discussion, and quotation, and the more richness one may say, and more people will quote your opinions as their own. . . .

Poor dear Sara is a monument of indecision so far as the *future* goes. As for the *present* there is no indecision about her. She is worth coming to New York to visit. Yes indeedy. And yes, again. And I am so happy with her I can't worry about losing her till I am dead sure I will. This has been a great month for yours truly. . . .

Vachel Lindsay to Harriet Monroe   Springfield, Ill., 24 August 1914

My Dear Harriet:

I send you the Red Gods [retitled "The Ghosts of the Buffaloes"]. This is not the final form but rather the first sketch. I want your most relentless criticism at this particular stage, and hope to take it so completely you will be altogether charmed thereafter. And I hope to get this into the Poetry magazine before the year's competition closes. . . .

I have wanted to see you very very much the past week since Sara told me of her sudden engagement to the other man. I suppose it would have been sudden to me, if she had waited several years. I have one thing above all else to be thankful for—that is that she has kept my deep respect and love and did not think it necessary to heap scorn and abuse on my head to turn me away. It is really one of the glories of life to keep the image of her dignity and ladyhood intact, and I must not forget that. But it is a mixed consolation—it is very very hard to give her up—and the harder the more seriously I take matters of the soul, for certainly her truth-speaking and her thoroughbredness were great tonics for my spirit, and I can say in my coldest hour she was a staff and a help to my best self—aside from the glories that come and go. . . .

Really, I am so afraid for my soul—I do not want to lose any of the spirit she gave me because I have to give her up for a sweetheart. The idea of woman being a staff and a prop is pretty largely an intoxication and a fiction, though intoxication has its place. But Sara *was* a staff and a prop to the spirit, and I do not want her replaced by any mere intoxication. I want to be true to that fine self she gave me—that fine "myself" that I find in me when I look at her picture, and I am so afraid the picture will dim. I *cannot* think of her as being mine and another man's—

Well, if I wrote more, I would rewrite the same thing, so I close right here.

With love / Vachel

Sara Teasdale to Harriet Monroe   St. Louis, 18 November 1914

Dearest of all Ladies,
     dear Harriet:

A month from to-morrow, that is, on the 19th of December, if all goes well, I shall be Mrs. Ernst Filsinger. The whole thing is full of joy to me. There is no part of it that I dread, and I thank heaven for that. Ernst has been the tenderest and finest of lovers and I feel sure that he will be equally fine as a husband. Do you know that if it had not been for you, I should never be marrying him? For if you hadn't invited me to Chicago a year ago in June, I'd never have met Eunice, and if I hadn't met Eunice, I'd never have met Ernst. Oh Harriet, it is all so beautiful! It seems such a shame that I didn't begin being loved ten years ago! I could almost cry sometimes when I think of the loneliness that Ernst and I have both gone thro'—and here we were in the same city all the time and yet as utterly separated as if we had been at opposite ends of the earth. . . .

I had a fine and noble letter from Vachel to-day, the first in weeks. I am happy for all the honor that is coming to him. He is beyond doubt the most real of all the men writing poetry in America and I could almost say America or England. Do you not think "The Chinese Nightingale" a glorious piece of color and music? And of Vachel's best work has the quality of a vision. It seems to me that "Visions" would be a wonderful title for a book of his. . . .

Dearest lady of my heart, I have many kisses for you and far more love than can be sent in a letter. I love you, I love you, and thanks for the book!

Sara.

Vachel Lindsay to Harriet Monroe *Springfield, Ill.,*
12 December 1914

My Dear Harriet:

Please hand whatever you owe me for the Chinese Nightingale, at the proper time, to Margaret Anderson, as a perpetual endowment for the Little Review. I am broke, but want to boost that magazine. Why the Sam Hill doesn't the beautiful Polly Root write to me? I wrote her a most respectful and I thought inciting letter. I suppose I am not provocative the way I think I am, sometimes. . . .

And while we are on the subject of the ladies, dedicate the Chinese Nightengale [sic] to the initials S.T.F. . . .

4. The Later Careers of Teasdale and Lindsay

Sara Teasdale became one of the most popular female poets of the twenties and early thirties by continuing to write the lyrics on love and longing that were her forte. Unlike Edna St. Vincent Millay, her chief rival for top woman poet, she did not burn *her* candle at both ends. Teasdale was always shrewd in managing her career, and in getting others, particularly older women, to promote her. When her *Love Songs* (1917) won the Columbia Poetry Prize, precursor to the Pulitzer, Monroe pointed out in an editorial on "Sara Teasdale's Prize" (August 1918) that among the judges was the winner's good friend Jessie Rittenhouse, who raised the $500 award through the Poetry Society of America.

Like many another "helpless" person, Teasdale knew how to get what she wanted. In her discreet fashion, she went so far as to suggest to critics what they might say in commenting on her poetry. In his biography, *Sara Teasdale: Woman & Poet* (1979), William Drake notes that she once sent Rittenhouse a check to "supplement" the low fee the New York *Times* was paying for a review of one of her books. Sara had no hesitation in voicing her displeasure, either, even to Harriet, that Dearest of all Ladies. In a letter of 6 June 1917, she was "much het up" over a misprint that mixed a line from a poem by Jack Wheelock (of all people) with her own "Barter": "I am all the sorrier this should have occurred," she wrote, "since these poems are eligible for a Poetry Society prize of $125.00 and these mistakes will go a good way toward turning the poems down, since a lyric of this sort must be clear— —or nothing. I shall expect a reprint with an explanation in the July number." The misprint was duly noted and apologized for in the July issue.

Although she told Monroe she was a mother more than a lover, Teasdale proved to be neither. Aptly named and utterly devoted, Ernst Filsinger catered to her every wish. But Ernst was frequently away on business trips—his stays in South America and Europe could be extensive—so Sara was often alone in their fine apartment in the San Remo on Central Park West. Even when Ernst was in the States, they were much apart, because Sara found herself unwell and sought respite in resorts. Finally, in 1929, she got a Reno divorce and received a large settlement. Through good times and bad, she corresponded with Miss Monroe, and in a letter of 13 March 1931, she expressed her admiration:

> Vachel had lunch with me day before yesterday. You would have liked what we said of you. I have often wanted to tell you— —but have been shy about it— —that I consider you one of the three straightest people I have known in my life. I prefer that quality, straightness, to any other, but if I were to add one to it for you, it would be valor.

As Teasdale aged, her illnesses and groundless financial fears increased and she became increasingly isolated, even as her popularity grew. In 1920, she published *Flame and Shadow* and, in 1926, *Dark of the Moon*. Death, which looms as an obsession in much of Teasdale's verse, came through an overdose of sleeping pills on 29 January 1933. Her last poems were published later that year in *Strange Victory*. Admiring to the end, Harriet Monroe wrote her notice for the *Dictionary of American Biography*.

For Vachel Lindsay the future proved more complicated but extremely bittersweet, as well. His triumph at the *Poetry* banquet for Yeats launched him on a career that would make him one of the most popular poets of the teens and early twenties, and one of the most successful poetry reciters in American history. But Lindsay had grave misgivings even before the start of the enterprise. Reared in a family of devout fundamentalists, he always had strong religious compunctions concerning worldly success, and truly feared for his soul. But the lure of fame was irresistible.

At first Lindsay was exhilarated, and he reported his remarkable rise to Monroe with childlike glee. In 1915 he gave a command performance for President Wilson's cabinet and was invited to recite at several Eastern universities. Now in very great demand, he began the first of many tours around the country. In 1916 and 1920, he traveled to England and recited at Oxford and Cambridge. At hundreds of appearances in schools, clubs, and meeting halls of every description, Lindsay attracted the kind of truly popular audience not seen since the days of Longfellow. The crowds were entranced by his presentations—and were encouraged to join in—as Lindsay chanted, shouted, and whispered with dramatic effect.

In 1915, he published *The Art of the Moving Picture*, which established him as one of the first serious analysts of the medium. On 11 October 1916, he wrote Miss Monroe: "Did you know that the great [director D. W.] Griffith telegraphed for me to go to New York and return at his expense to witness the performance of Intolerance! I boast of it blatantly. It means that I am getting somewhere as a Motion Picture critic." Lindsay tried repeatedly to get Monroe interested in the cinema, even suggesting she'd make a good movie critic. She was content to leave the field to him and Carl Sandburg.

By 1917, Lindsay was being panned regularly, and he anticipated more of the same. On 9 December 1916, he wrote H.M.: "I feel it coming. Many people who misapprehended me vaguely, but in a friendly way, will begin to realize I am but mortal, and jump me hard. See if they don't. And please counsel me to take my skinning like a man when it comes, and not get sore and hit back." For all his popularity, and probably because of it, high-minded poets and critics viewed him with condescension. Pound, of course, had regarded Lindsay's work with skepticism from the beginning and predicted: "Lindsay is set to follow Bret Harte and Field and all that lot." In her highly biased *Tendencies in Modern American Poetry* (1917), Lowell lumped Lindsay with Masters and Sandburg (an association he felt honored to claim), then brushed him aside as "a middle

westerner of the middle class"—whatever that meant. Besides the snob-
bery it betrayed, Lowell's short shrift was doubtless rooted in envy over
Lindsay's success, a goal she herself worked assiduously to attain.

For the cerebral and restrictive Modernists, it was Lindsay's very pop-
ulist sensibilities and democratic idealism, strongly endorsed by Monroe,
that made him suspect. To them and Lindsay's other detractors, he would
always remain simply an entertainer with a new kind of vaudeville rou-
tine. But in direct contrast to Pound and the elite theorists, Lindsay had
an idea of poetry that was very broad, embracing the most common ele-
ments of American speech and popular culture.

Making it up as he went along, Lindsay adopted the sights and sounds
of the United States—folk songs, revival-tent preaching, political oratory,
jazz—and devised what he called "The Higher Vaudeville." This hybrid
was both familiar and novel, and had none of the forbidding aura usually
associated with the Art of Poetry. Rather than stand back in awe, he
invited listeners to participate. To the high-brow critics, the theatrics
seemed very low-brow indeed. The public loved the show.

Lindsay loved putting it on, too, at least for the first few years. By 1920,
the hectic touring began to take its toll. As Teasdale had foreseen, it
became increasingly difficult for Lindsay to concentrate on his art; the
poet didn't develop so much as repeat himself. Not that his audiences
minded. Like many another popular performer, he became typecast in
the first role that made him famous. Writing to Monroe on 15 December
1920, he complained of weariness: "I would give almost anything to
escape forever the reciting and chanting Vachel. . . . I set Jan 1, 1921 as the
quitting time. . . . I do not want to be the slave of past performances or
habits, I cannot endure to be such a slave . . . . I am a dead man in my
own eyes, and the only resurrection is in the new vista."

In 1921, he tried to make good on his pledge to stop by sending out a
form letter advising that he would be unavailable for two years. On 17
May 1921, he wrote H.M. a rambling, twelve-page letter that indicated
signs of deterioration: "I have tried several times to quit reciting . . . . But
just financially, I cannot afford to quit entirely, so I recite from hand-to-
mouth, as one may say. My books only bring me five hundred dollars a
year, at best—that is, this last year, and up to that time one to two hun-
dred dollars a year. So I must just recite a bit now and then to keep out of
debt. . . . I know well enough *I* began by being all eagerness *to* recite . . . ."

In January 1923, he suffered a physical and mental breakdown. He
found respite teaching at a junior college in Gulfport, Mississippi. On 17
February, he wrote H.M. about his collapse, and his desire to return to his
old self. From that point on, Lindsay was in steady decline. The following
year, he was diagnosed with epilepsy. He moved to Spokane, where he

met and married Elizabeth Conner in 1925; she was twenty-three, Lindsay forty-five. By 1926, when their daughter Susan was born, they were in financial difficulty, so Lindsay was forced to tour again. His son Nicholas was born in 1927, by which time the family had even more serious money problems.

Throughout this dark period, Monroe offered encouragement and advice, as well as more tangible aid, and she and Elizabeth Lindsay became friends through lengthy correspondence. On 1 March 1928, Mrs. Lindsay wrote to thank her for sending $100:

> God bless you!—we say it with all our hearts. . . . your kindness has pulled us out of our panic-stricken paralysis, and enabled us to start forward with light hearts. Vachel particularly is simply stunned by worry; he just sits and broods and gets absolutely clammy and cold with misery, which, of course, does no-one any good—especially himself.
>
> Our hundred dollars paid the rent, the milkman, the ice man, the laundry man, Susan's shoes to be soled and sewed, Vachel's suit to be pressed and cleaned (it was a mess from helping with the babies) and there is still a little left with which to begin to demolish our four month old grocery bill. . . .

Later, in 1929, Monroe arranged a special $500 prize for Lindsay, which was awarded in November. By then, he was having trouble placing poems or freelance articles, and so he went on the road yet again. Although Lindsay continued to suffer from severe mental and physical strain, in 1931 he set out on what would be his final tours. On 1 November, he thanked H.M. for sending application forms for a Guggenheim fellowship. On 5 December, the poet who had found fame with his stentorian recitations committed suicide by swallowing a bottle of Lysol.

CHAPTER VI

American Modernism: William Carlos Williams, Wallace Stevens, Marianne Moore, and *Others*

1. "Unadulterated U.S.A."

"Williams is a suburban physician, who goes into a state of coma, but occasionally produces a good poem," Ezra Pound wrote Harriet Monroe in 1915, and the backhanded compliment indicates something of their ambivalent relationship. Born in 1883, William Carlos Williams was two years older than Pound, who nonetheless always maintained a patronizing manner from their earliest meetings in 1902 at the University of Pennsylvania. There he likewise met Hilda Doolittle, who was also impressed by Pound's apparent brilliance. Though Williams was cowed and sometimes exhausted by Pound's learned discourses, he appreciated his criticism, as well as his help in getting Elkin Mathews to publish his second book, *The Tempers*, in 1913.

Williams took his medical degree in 1906, then interned at a charity hospital in New York City's Hell's Kitchen; in 1909–1910 he spent a year training in pediatrics in Leipzig. On his return from Germany, he set up his practice in obstetrics in his hometown of Rutherford, New Jersey, where he married Florence (Flossie) Herman and remained the rest of his life. But he was hardly a simple baby doctor isolated in the provinces. He kept a journal, as he had in medical school, and jotted down notes and poems, often on prescription pads, between examinations and house calls. This habit, bred of necessity, helps as much as critical theories to explain the brevity of so many of his poems.

Whenever he could, he crossed the river to Manhattan, where, like his friend Wallace Stevens, he liked to visit art exhibits. (In his youth, Williams had hoped to become a painter himself, and kept an amateur interest all his life.) He became friends with the photographer and editor Alfred Stieglitz at his famous 291 Gallery on Fifth Avenue. And, like Harriet Monroe, he was astonished by the Armory Show in 1913. He was especially taken by Duchamp's *Nude Descending a Staircase*, and recalled in his *Autobiography* (1951), "how I laughed out loud when I saw it, happily, with relief."

William Carlos Williams in Model T, with his son Eric,
in an undated snapshot sent to H.M.

Part of Williams's "relief" came from the realization that art did not
necessarily have to deal with "exalted" subject matter: a bowl of plums
and a red wheelbarrow were equally admissible. Through the French poet
Guillaume Apollinaire's typographical experiments in his *Calligrammes*
(some of which were published in Stieglitz's journal *291*), Williams also
discovered how the placement of letters, words, and lines on a page could
produce a *visual* as well as verbal artifact. Many of his differences with
Harriet Monroe centered on just such "merely mechanical" but signifi-
cant matters of form. Like H.D. and Richard Aldington, Williams particu-
larly objected to the Editor's insistence on maintaining the irrelevant
convention of capitalizing letters at the beginning of each line in poems.
But they argued over titles, metrics, diction, phrasing, and poem lengths,
too.

"To tell the truth, I myself never quite feel that I know what I am talk-
ing about—if I did, and when I do, the thing written seems nothing to
me. . . . To me it's a matter of first understanding that which may not yet

be put to words," Williams wrote Monroe in October 1913. Brief as it is, this early statement reveals the paradox and central principle that would mark Williams's voluminous writing over the next decades. From the start, his letters reveal a mixture of candor, tentativeness, and (one might say) decisive indecisiveness that became the hallmarks of his evolving style. Though Williams could be irascible, ultimately his self-deprecatory humor made him an irresistible correspondent—indeed, Monroe was immediately won over—and his many charms, both as a poet and a person, offered a sharp contrast to the usually acidulous and always dogmatic character of his old friend Ezra.

Williams had not been invited to contribute when the Editor sent out her announcements in August 1912, and she probably wasn't aware of his first, self-published book of *Poems* (1909). It was probably just as well, since his early verse was written in a convoluted, late-Romantic style of the sort that *Poetry* was seeking to counteract. In his autobiography, *I Wanted to Write a Poem* (1958), Williams recalled his first submission was rejected outright, but the next batch, selected by his wife, pleased the women at *Poetry* more. Pound wrote Monroe in the winter of 1912-1913 to endorse his friend's work: "This I *would* print. It's unadulterated U.S.A." But his recommendation was only partially helpful. H.M. noted: "Postlude—returned for revision." The Editor would ask for many emendations in later submissions, as well, much to the author's irritation.

In offering suggestions, Monroe, like Pound, wished to help Williams improve his work, in this period still in an awkward stage of transition. Such assistance usually got him steamed up, and he vented his frustrations by return mail in impetuous (and sometimes imprudent) letters—letters that offer invaluable insights into his aesthetic theories. While he was glad to accept Pound's suggestions about simplifying his work, he did not at all like the idea of its being "hammered out," as he told the Editor. In fact, to his way of thinking, it was the very improvisational or "unfinished" quality in a poem, its seeming spontaneity, that created an immediate impression of "real" life—"always new, irregular" and unpredictable. Monroe did not subscribe to this haphazard approach, and continued to return poems for further refinements. Williams became exasperated, but after he cooled down, he generally acceded to H.M.'s suggestions, if grudgingly.

Matters of form aside, Williams focused on distinctively American subject matter, the local particulars of the United States. More than he knew when he first wrote her, Harriet Monroe was very much in sympathy with this emphasis. Williams also wrote with a directness and an openness to daily life that sharply distinguished his style of New Poetry from the "international," hypercerebral "high" Modernism espoused by Pound and T. S. Eliot. Pound and then Eliot had gone abroad to *escape* America. As they became ever more immersed in the Great Tradition, they filled their highly erudite works with allusions to old masters and obscure texts in several languages, some of them obsolete. While Pound campaigned to reform and update the *techniques* of poetry, in his choice of *subjects* he seemed more interested in the past—Greek and Roman poetry, the troubadours and Provençal literature, the culture of the Renaissance, the ancient forms of China and Japan—than with contemporary conditions.

William Carlos Williams stayed at home. Doubtful the past could be reshaped to fit current needs, he set to work on native soil, where he found in the here and now of daily life, and especially the American idiom, more than enough material to revitalize poetry. This separation, literal as well as philosophical, produced the great divide in the Modernist movement in poetry. For decades, Williams would try to get his voice heard as he tried to advance his aesthetic philosophy.

Of the divergent routes, the high road of the intellectual expatriates dominated in the first half of the century, particularly after the methods of Pound and theories of Eliot were codified in the New Criticism and adopted by the Academy between the wars. Not until after World War II—with the publication in 1948 of Book One of his epic collage, *Paterson*, and then the National Book Award in 1950—did Williams's work become widely appreciated, along with his brand of American modernism. Out of the shadow of Pound and Eliot, Williams's uniqueness could finally be recognized.

Ezra Pound to Harriet Monroe   *[London, February? 1913]*

[*Note included with Williams's ms. of "Postlude," forwarded from London*]

Williams has sent me this not in my official capacity. I think it has a good deal more fervor than F.S.F[lint]. Yes, Yes. I'll be responsible for submitting it. It's *real*.

Also I'll write to him to see if he'll emend the bad locution "breasts of Amazon" etc.—probably a misprint (or an unknown substance; he has a scientific education). This I *would* print. It's unadulterated U.S.A. He is sending you stuff 'direct.' Please give it attention.

Harriet Monroe to William Carlos Williams   *3 March 1913*

My dear Mr. Williams:
    I like best your Sicilian Emigrant's Song, but I am keeping also Peace on Earth and Immortality. Postlude seems to me to need revision. I find it does not appeal so much to me as Mr. Pound, but his word goes a

long way and I should like to see the poem again when you have given it your last touch.

Would it be banal to give a more explanatory title to Peace on Earth. Something that will give the reader a hint that you are talking about constellations. Perhaps it would be sufficient to capitalize their names. In Proof of Immortality you are using a fixed iambic measure to which the fourth and sixth line do not seem to me to conform. They are both a syllable short. Will you please consider this point? I do not care much either for the title of this poem. Wouldn't "The Immortal" be better, or something else which you may think of. . . .

William Carlos Williams to Harriet Monroe   *5 March 1913*

My dear Miss Monroe:-

Your courteous letter startles me—not merely because you return with it two of my poems, truly.

I shall take up the suggestions it contains, but I cannot resist the pleasure first of expostulating with you a moment.

I had looked upon "Poetry" as a forum wherein competent poets might speak freely, uncensored by any standard of rules. "Poetry" seemed to me a protest against the attitude of every other periodical American publication in this respect.

I am startled to see that you are fast gravitating to the usual editorial position and I am startled to feel that perhaps this is inevitable: that as soon as one says, "I am an editor!" he having been in the march of poets faces about upon them.

I mean that perhaps it is a law that between the producer and the exposer of verse there must inevitably exist a contest. The poet comes forward assailing the trite and the established, while the editor is to shear off all roughness and extravagance. It startled me when I realized that this is perhaps inevitable.

Now, that was not my view of the function of "Poetry" at all. My notion was dependent on this: most current verse is dead from the point of view of art. (I enclose some doggerel showing one of the reasons why.) Now life is above all things else at any moment subversive of life as it was the moment before; always new, irregular. Verse to be alive must have infused into it something of the same order, some tincture of disestablishment, something in the nature of an impalpable revolution, an etherial reversal let me say. I am speaking of modern verse.

"Poetry" I saw accepting verse of this kind, that is verse with perhaps nothing else in it but life—this alone, regardless of possible imperfections, for no new thing comes through perfect. In the same way the impressionists had to be accepted for the sake of art's very life—in spite of bad drawing.

I do not assail you because you fail to praise my exquisite productions but—in perfect good humor—I find fault with your expressed attitude toward my exquisite productions.

Perhaps I am more than ever obscure.

Why doubt that the reader will see the stars in "Peace on Earth", when you saw them? Yet to capitalize as you suggest is good: please do so.

Isn't the art of writing titles, as all art is, a matter of concrete indirections made as they are in order to leave the way clear for a distinct imaginative picture? To directly denote the content of a piece is to my mind to put an obstacle of words in the way of the picture. Isn't it better in imaginative work to imply war in Heaven, for instance, by saying, "Peace on Earth", than it would be to say it flat out, "War in Heaven?"

Your suggestion: "The Immortal" is . . . permissible in the place of "Proof of Immortality", but not so amusing. Do as you please in this case. As to the meter in the above-named piece, if you wish to judge it as a fixed iambic measure you are dogmatically right as to the disturbing fourth and sixth lines; but why not call it some other kind of a measure? . . .

As to "Postlude", it is perhaps hyper-digested to the point of unintelligibility, but to me it seems that there is so much of an escape from the tiresome rehashings of optimism, and its equivalent in rhythmics, that from pure love of humanity it might have been forgiven its few bumps and bruises.

I'm afraid I am open to the accusation of being out of touch with my public—that's isolation, and I know my trend—but if "Poetry" does not open freely to me, in my absolute egotism, how am I to grow?

It's the new seed, the one little new seed that counts in the end; that will ultimately cover fields with vigorous growth. My idea of "Poetry" was that it must find this new seed, just as Burbank seeks and finds the new seed that is to grow his thornless cactus—pardon the moral.

Anyhow, I'm a great poet, and you don't think so, and there we are and so allow me to send you a revised "Postlude" (when it is done) hoping to gain your good favor in that way—for I must succeed you know.

Faithfully yours, / William Carlos Williams

I must not forget to thank you for the acceptance of the three poems which you have accepted; I do so now and hope to have the pleasure of pleasing you again as soon as possible. W. Williams

W.C.W. sent a revision of "Postlude" on 11 March 1913.

Harriet Monroe to William Carlos Williams   7 *April 1913*

My dear Mr. Williams:

I wish I might make more criticisms, if they would call forth such pleasant expostulations. POETRY, I assure you, is as free as air and you don't need to listen to my impertinent protestations. Yet I insist that you have improved "Postlude", and I think you would improve it still further if you would leave off the last three lines, ending at the line "Blue at the prow of my desire" [*H.M. note in the margin:* "this was done"]. You see I am quite incorrigible.

Perhaps it is inevitable that the Editorial mind should grow stilted, if you see evidences of it in POETRY, "Please punch my face in order to save my soul", as Ezra says, and I am very gratefully

Yours truly, / HM

William Carlos Williams to Harriet Monroe   10 *April 1913*

My dear Miss Monroe,

After all you *are* a person of discernment. Thank you for the criticisms—one and all—though I can't see what it is that puts you so against poor Jason [in "Postlude"]. And by the way may I adopt the habit of sending anything that I do from time to time piece by piece or would you rather have me collect the things and send the gist of them to you in yearly, two yearly, or four yearly installments?

If there is not more choice even in the above please tell me that also.

Faithfully yours, / William C. Williams

It is always a delight to me to see Ezra saluted. W.

William Carlos Williams to Harriet Monroe   3 *June 1913*

My dear Miss Monroe:—

Surely no one could desire a better presentation of his work than the pages of "Poetry" give.

The spacing, type and the accuracy with which you hold to the author's desired arrangement are satisfying.

I beg to acknowledge my face as shining very delightfully in your excellent mirror.

Sincerely yours, / William C. Williams

"Peace on Earth," "Sicilian Emigrant's Song," "Postlude," and "Proof of Immortality" appeared in June 1913. In reprinting the last poem in his *Collected Earlier Poems,* W.C.W. changed the title to "Immortality," as H.M. had suggested, and retained her capitalizations.

William Carlos Williams to Harriet Monroe   *10 October 1913*

My dear Miss Monroe:—

How a thing can be hammered out before it is first perceived is beyond me—but if your editorial judgment is correct—patience.

To me, what is woefully lacking in our verse and in our criticism is not hammered out stuff, but stuff to be hammered out. A free forum, there is the need, which asks only "Is it new, interesting?"

I should think, even, that at times you would be concerned lest you get nothing but that which is hammered and worked out—except when the divine Ezra bludgeons you into it. . . .

W.C.W. had sent a second batch of poems on 19 September, and an essay, "English Speech Rhythms," on 20 August; both were returned.

William Carlos Williams to Harriet Monroe   *14 October 1913*

My dear Miss Monroe:—

To tell the truth, I myself never quite feel that I know what I am talking about—if I did, and when I do, the thing written seems nothing to me. However, what I do write and allow to survive I always feel is mighty worth while and that nobody else has ever come as near as I have to the thing I have intimated if not expressed. To me it's a matter of first understanding that which may not yet be put to words. I might add more but to no purpose. In a sense I must express myself, but always completely incomplete if that means anything.

But—by the gods of exchange—"the divine [Ezra]"—shall be greeted and the words presented to him for the acid test.

I'll surely let you know what he writes—that is provided he writes anything.

I once sent him one other epoch-making article; this in sum, was his answer: " 'It' has arrived! Here and there I *do* get a glimpse of a meaning, you do seem to have something to say, Bill, even if you don't say it."

Whether it bears you out or whether it bears me out I don't know.

May enlightenment come upon both of us in the days hereafter.

Sincerely yours, / W. C. Williams

William Carlos Williams to Harriet Monroe   *27 November 1913*

My dear Miss Monroe:—

Naturally the benefices of Ceres delight the bare earth. Thank you.

I sent the other things to Ezrie—he makes no mention of the prose but without comment tells me the verse will go into "Poetry Review" or more likely "The New Freewoman"—better take a look at it then to see what you missed. He also tells me that Yeats liked one or two things in my new born book [*The Tempers*] that I am sending under separate cover.

I certainly was furious at you for turning that long thing down so it's lucky you accepted these new pieces when you did for I had just about made up my mind never to send anything more to you—thereby wrecking your darned old magazine—of course!!

I don't mind the "Carlos" as long as it is preceded by "William" in full or "Wm." but I despise "W. Carlos"—it's a punk practice. . . .

I think—through your suggestions—that I have helped matters a little.

Sincerely yours, / William Carlos Williams

W.C.W. wrote 3 December 1913 to apologize for not acknowledging first publication in *Poetry* of some poems reprinted in *The Tempers*.

William Carlos Williams to Harriet Monroe   22 *May 1914*

My dear Miss Monroe:—

Certainly I can work for any imaginable period at the work I choose without the encouragement of recognition—but actually to have work of mine prove valuable to your purposes or to another's—doubles all my brilliances.

Not that alone—good, bad or stupid, what I have done clings to me horribly until someone relieves me by ridicule, praise or any positive action. "Poetry" cuts the rope between the ox and his dung. Pardon the coarse allusion.

As my brother once told me of Rembrandt, a saying of his I believe: "It takes two men to paint a picture: one to put on the paint and one to cut off the other's hands when it (the picture) is finished." "Poetry" accomplishes the equivalent of this when it rescues a verse from me or better—me from my verse. Etc. etc. . . .

William Carlos Williams to Harriet Monroe   13 *January 1915*

Dear Miss Monroe:

Read this of me (will you)—then if it is as rotten as I think it is—burn it for Christ's sake and never let me hear from you concerning it.

W. Williams

On eighteenth thought send "it" back if you must. / W.

2. Williams, Marianne Moore,
Alfred Kreymborg, and *Others*

In the teens, Modernism was a work in progress and all was still in flux, including Williams, as he experimented and struggled to articulate his own vision. In New York, he became friends with other iconoclastic writers and artists, including Alfred Kreymborg, Man Ray, Marcel Duchamp, Walter Conrad Arensberg, Maxwell Bodenheim, Lola Ridge, Mina Loy, and Wallace Stevens. After her move to the city in 1918, Marianne Moore joined the circle. Like Dr. Williams, she had a more scientific background than most poets (she studied botany at Bryn Mawr), was a competent artist (as the detailed nature sketches in her notebooks attest), and was equally fascinated with the arrangement of words and lines on the page. Though much admired by the cognoscenti, her highly idiosyncratic work was hard to emulate. She had no followers, unlike Williams, whose work eventually inspired and was imitated by innumerable poets during the second half of the century.

At their meetings in the city or at Kreymborg's place in New Jersey, the young "New York Poets" debated about literature and art, adopting their own original and self-consciously outré approaches to modernity. In July 1915, Kreymborg, with Arensberg's backing, started *Others* as an outlet for their work. Though it appeared irregularly, it was the first real competition *Poetry* faced. Unlike the *Egoist, Poetry and Drama*, and the *Little Review, Others* published contemporary poetry exclusively, with little or no commentary.

When Kreymborg requested information about *Poetry* for a newspaper article he was writing in 1915, H.M. wanted distinctions drawn: "*Poetry* you know tries to publish the best we can get of ALL the different schools. We have published a good deal of rather radical experiments and shall no doubt continue to do so, but I assume that 'Others' stands exclusively for the radicals and for a rather more youthful effervescence than I am quite ready to endorse publicly." Kreymborg assured her on 4 July 1915 that he had no intention of "tying" *Poetry* to *Others*: "It is good to be alive. That is all. We are not the big fishes."

Others attracted much attention with its first issue, and the newspapers took delight in quoting and parodying its quirky contents. Pound took a more jaundiced view. On 15 December 1915, he wrote Monroe: "Kreymborg gets too many new stars for them all to be real." While many of the contributors to *Others* were young and didn't go on to produce great things, the magazine did print some important works in its early issues, including Wallace Stevens's "Peter Quince at the Clavier" and T. S. Eliot's

"Portrait of a Lady" (sent by Pound). Other "*Poetry*" authors also contributed, including Pound, Amy Lowell, Carl Sandburg, Helen Hoyt (who worked in the *Poetry* office), and Marianne Moore.

Although she had just made her first American journal appearance in *Poetry* with six poems in the May 1915 issue, Moore felt that Monroe did not sufficiently appreciate her work. When some poems she sent shortly after her debut were returned with a note, she wrote tersely from Carlisle, Pennsylvania, 7 June 1915:

> Dear Miss Monroe,
> Printed slips are enigmatic things and I thank you for your criticism on my poems. I shall try to profit by it.
> Sincerely yours,
> Marianne Moore

She didn't send another poem for sixteen years. Monroe tried to renew relations in 1918, and Moore wrote her on 10 May of that year: "Poetry's approach to art is different from my own; I feel it therefore to be very good of you to imply that I am not *ipso facto* an alien." On a trip to New York City in 1919, H.M. had a friendly meeting with M.M., and the Editor reported in the April issue that "the cryptic Marianne Moore . . . seemed less cryptic than her poetry." On later trips, H.M. visited Moore several times, and eventually persuaded her to review. Responding to news that *Poetry* might end on the eve of its Twentieth Anniversary, Moore again offered poems, and "The Steeple-Jack," "The Student," and "The Hero" appeared in June 1932.

Williams himself came close to breaking his ties with *Poetry* several times. A serious breach occurred in November 1914, when Monroe rejected his poem "The Conquest." But, as usual, he sent other submissions. His second publication in *Poetry* consisted of five poems, printed in the May 1915 issue with Marianne Moore's first work. However, with the founding of *Others*

Marianne Moore as a young woman; *Poetry* gave Moore her first American publication in 1915.

(which he helped edit) Williams now had a place to publish his poems exactly as he wished, and *Poetry*'s acceptance or rejection may not have seemed so important. On 28 October, he told H.M.: "Our taste in matters of verse seems to differ hence these outbursts first of extravagant love for you then equally extravagant outbursts of indignation." He returned to Monroe's pages again in November, with "Love Song," "Naked," "Marriage," "Apology," "Summer Song," and "The Old Worshipper."

After May 1916, *Others* began to appear at ever wider intervals: three numbers in 1916, two in 1917, only one issue in 1918, and finally three in 1919. Because of the irregularity of the issues, in 1917 many (including Monroe) thought *Others* had shut down. But throughout its run the editors of *Poetry* and *Others* were anything but antagonistic. When W. S. Braithwaite slammed *Others* (and *Poetry*) in the Boston *Transcript*, the attack brought forth this defense from H.M. in the January 1917 issue: "No one can fail to regret the cessation of that brave little magazine, which was founded without a cent of capital, and carried on for twelve or more experimental and adventurous months through the devotion and personal sacrifice of its editor." Despite his frequent rejection notices from Chicago—which gave him even more cause than Williams to resent *Poetry*—Kreymborg was always friendly (and funny) in his letters to Miss Monroe.

In 1916, Monroe visited New York and met Dr. and Mrs. Williams for the first time; they seem to have got on well, for Williams invited her to stay at his house on her next trip East. She also saw the good-natured Kreymborg, who introduced her to "the boys" and entertained her at a large reception on 25 March. On 3 March, he told of his plans for the welcoming party: "[E]verybody is clamoring to come—artists as well as poets. . . . We're going to show you how we love you and Poetry!"

In the spring of 1916, Kreymborg brought out his first *Others* anthology (new editions followed in 1917 and 1919). Mrs. Henderson was assigned the review, and couldn't help but notice the number of "I"s in the poems. In the May 1916 issue, A.C.H published a piece called "A New School of Poetry," which began:

> Replacing the outworn conventions of the I-am-bic school, we have now the I-am-it school of poetry. (NOTE: *Les I-am-its* are not to be confused with *Les I'm-a-gists*, who are already out-classed and *démodé*.) The following synopsis, telescoped from the new *Others* anthology, gives the salient features of the school.

The rest of the "review" consisted of two and half pages of quotations from the anthology, in which she allowed the contributors to condemn themselves out of their own months. The piece concluded: "We regret to say the printer announces that there are no more I's in the font."

Learning from Kreymborg that he was offended and had asked Monroe to return some recent submissions, Williams wrote to mend fences. His diplomacy was successful. On 15 May Kreymborg wrote Monroe: "At first, I took ACH's stunt as a joke—later—after seeing some of the boys—there were reactions of sorrow, spleen, fun again, and one or another of confused emotions. Since then, I've learned . . . that the thing was intended in fun. So we'll let it go at that as far as I'm concerned." After Kreymborg moved to Chicago in 1917 (and *Others* with him), the two became good friends. In June 1917 he published a special "Chicago" issue.

Williams also tried to act as peacemaker when Maxwell Bodenheim became angry with Harriet Monroe in late 1916. What Williams did not know was that Bodenheim was perpetually angry at Miss Monroe. He had already written two letters, in May and June, protesting the review of the *Others* anthology, and again in November, because he wasn't invited to speak in a lecture series featuring *Poetry* authors organized by Eunice Tietjens. He eventually turned into one of the most troublesome authors Monroe ever had to deal with. She had encouraged Bodenheim, who grew up in Chicago, and had given him a generous first presentation in *Poetry* with five poems in August 1914. She also invited him to *Poetry* gatherings, lent or gave him money, and did other favors. But he was never satisfied, and started to take offense at imagined slights.

In 1916, Bodenheim moved to New York, became friends with Kreymborg (who put him up and later had to put up with him), Lola Ridge, and the rest of the *Others* set, but gradually developed a dubious reputation there, as well. Over the years, through the post and occasionally in person, he continued to show up at *Poetry*'s doorstep, usually when he wanted something. In long, rambling letters, he reiterated accusations that Monroe was neglecting him, attacking him, or sabotaging his career.

In later years, as he deteriorated, Bodenheim eventually became one of Greenwich Village's more colorful "characters," and notorious as a leech and a drunk. Having lost what jobs he could find, he tried to start afresh and made a disastrous trip to England in 1920. When Monroe traveled to England three years later, she found the episode was still not forgotten. She wrote to Chicago, 27 May 1923: "According to Conrad Aiken, M.B.'s brief visit to London made him, and American poets in general, so unpopular as to put back the cause for twenty years." Despite his haranguing letters and the general nuisance he became, Monroe kept in contact with Bodenheim. Some of his outrageous letters she didn't answer—it would have been pointless—but more often than not she did reply. And over the next twenty years he continued to send poems and she continued to print him and to offer him hospitality when he was in Chicago. Her successors did the same, right up to his death—he and his wife were murdered near the Bowery—in 1954.

Though not as extreme as Bodenheim, several others who wrote to complain during her editorship doubtless tried Monroe's patience. Her suggestions and rejections enraged any number of authors, and several told her they would never send work to *Poetry* again. Surprisingly few kept their word. Even after castigating her judgment, more often than not they sent more poems, sometimes only weeks later.

In Williams's case, the arguments ran crankily, humorously, and continuously for over two decades, during which Monroe was faced with what must have seemed at times like a split personality. As their friendship grew, Williams freely offered her advice, even if it was contradictory. (In March 1916, for example, he suggested both a "loose" and "a more defined" policy in succeeding paragraphs.) From month to month, the poet's artistic stance and manner of writing often shifted. His moods could swing even more frequently—from exasperation to resignation and, on rarer occasions, to exuberance. On 18 June 1917, as *Al Que Quiere!*, his second American book, was going to press, Williams wrote to thank her for printing his poems immediately, and added: "My wife says you have been 'very decent' with me, 'far more decent that I would have been.' " Through the course of their long correspondence, the fact that he and Monroe could be so frank with each other gives a fair measure of the character of both the Editor and the poet.

Alfred Kreymborg to Harriet Monroe   Others, *Grantwood, N.J.,*
6 June 1915

Dear Harriet Monroe,

Will you exchange with OTHERS? And announce same in POETRY? First issue, next week, three or more pages devoted separately to Mary Carolyn Davies, Mina Loy, Orrick Johns, Horace Holley and Alfred Kreymborg, alias me. Second issue will include William Carlos Williams, Skipwith Cannell, Wallace Stevens, Robert Carlton Brown, Amy Lowell and Alanson Hartpence. Just an attempt, on a small scale to start with, to do something with New York.

The boys have weekly Dutch Treats for the purpose of working together and of condemning the world at large. 'Tis a happy pastime, albeit no more. If you are ever in town, come in and see us.

Cordially, / Alfred Kreymborg

William Carlos Williams to Harriet Monroe   *Rutherford, N.J.,*
                                                    25 February 1916

Dear Miss Monroe:—

Use capitals if you wish to; I think they are redundant and confusing to the sense.

End "Morning" at the line you suggest. If I wish to add the rest at some other time I can always do so—and if I should die first—why, I'll rely on my fame to make the additions necessary—if any is necessary....

May I suggest that you are a little too epicurean. Have not the hundred and one surpassing poets of America sent you enough pleasing verse that you must still insist and insist that I shall please you before you print me? I am glad to please you and yet a little less pure beauty and a little roughness of contour added would improve "Poetry" to my mind. You are—if I may say so—closed to rugged beginnings. Perhaps I wrong you. You seem to me to be just back of the lead. "The Egoist" keeps a freer outlook.

Yours, / W. C. Williams

William Carlos Williams to Harriet Monroe   *Rutherford, N.J.,*
                                                    1 March 1916

March 1. (Thank God) 1916

Dear Miss Monroe:—

It would be a long story to tell you how I came to change the version of the rotten "Love Song" to what it was in my last. For the present suffice it to say that whichever version you like best will satisfy me also....

Mrs. Williams is a sincere believer in your openmindedness even in spite of my occasional ravings against you, however I still believe that if I were in your place I would be still more marvelous than you in the looseness of my policy.

My frank opinion is that "Poetry" pays too much for its verse and that it is too anxious to be inclusive.

Less money and a more defined policy would keep away many a foolish rhymester. Of course you want them all "to come unto" you but if the policy of a periodical of poetry is of any less steely fiber than that of the best verse, the result will be disastrous.

Ah how pleasant it is to give advice!

Thanking you for your unfailing kindness, I am

Yours, / W. C. Williams

William Carlos Williams to Harriet Monroe   Rutherford, N.J.,
11 April 1916

Dear Harriet Monroe:

Come again and stay longer. I have a fine bed waiting for you in my tumble down spare room. As soon as I get the time I'm going to write you a real love letter—tell you your faults etc.

Two things I want to say to you now however: 1. Verse don't *pay* and no boosting by "Poetry" will ever make it pay—quit trying or you'll strangle yourself. 2. Print the better folk oftener and quicker.

Why so much Christliness? Why try to keep the poor artist—what keep can you give the poor artist (the poor, poor artist) other than Harriet Monroe's personal understanding of him?

If "Poetry" were printed free in a garret on toilet paper—it couldn't help but have a meaning. Now it has none.

The sad thing is that with Harriet back of it, it only needs to be let loose to get a meaning.

Is "Poetry" a poetic stock yard? For God's sake let's have more Harriet and less "Poetry." I despise "Poetry." There never was a more stupid commercial magazine than "Poetry"—come to life, let's have what Harriet likes (if she likes anything) and not what she thinks helpful for us. Good night if you don't listen to me.

Yours, / Williams

William Carlos Williams to Harriet Monroe   Rutherford, N.J.,
3 May 1916

Dear Harriet Monroe:

Alfred [Kreymborg] tells me he has asked you to send his stuff back to him because of that foolish review by A.C.H. [of the *Others* anthology, May 1916].

For the sake of humor give him the ha, ha! Take a chance on it please for it means a lot to me. Tell him he is a simp and that I say so. Send this letter to him if you want to.

Please do this for me if you love me for I refuse to see Alfred cut his throat and not go with him. If you allow him to take back his things, back come mine too and that would break me all up.

The review is to my mind trivial. Valueless as the Others anthology may or may not be it is a fine thrust out into the dark. It has at least been a free running sewer and for A.C.H. to ignore its positive qualities for the mere accident of its contents is too bad. . . .

Well, enough of foolish controversy. Tell Alfred to wake up and grin. I suppose he was tired when he wrote you.

I'll really answer your last letter in detail soon but to tell the truth I have been crushed under the strains of my profession for months past.

Yours, / William C. Williams

William Carlos Williams to Harriet Monroe   *Rutherford, N.J.,*
[mid-October 1916]

Dear Miss Monroe:—

What's the good of trembling when the damage is done? Anyhow, thanks for eliminating that other thing ["Morning"].

I cannot understand the feeling that wants to change and rearrange according to some yard-stick which has not the slightest application in the matter of work of some person who has spent time and attention and even more important substances to bring that piece of work into the exact mould in which it is presented. What can it matter to you what my theory of line construction happens to be? In any case it has nothing to do with articles, nouns, verbs or adjectives. . . .

As long as the poem in question is read aloud as intended it makes no difference how it is written but it will be physically impossible for anyone to guess how I intended it to be read the way you have rearranged matters.

Let it go. No one will notice anything wrong and as long as nothing is noted to disturb the gently flowing accord of the magazine from Vol. I, number I until the year of Grace which is to see its end I suppose the major part of its mission is accomplished.

I sincerely regret giving that ten dollars to "Poetry" for I believe with my whole soul that the policy you have evidenced even in such a slight matter as the elimination of my small letters at the beginning of lines and this last matter also is of the stuff that more than anything eats the heart out of honest expression.

God help me. I seem destined to offend you, a thing which is as far from my heart as anything I can imagine for I wish you well in your work but I heartily object to your old fashioned and therefore vicious methods.

Sincerely yours, / W. C. Williams

William Carlos Williams to Harriet Monroe   *Rutherford, N.J.,*
28 October 1916

Dear Miss Monroe:

I think it best that I use that money for my own schemes rather than to attempt to force it on you now.

In any case I thank you for your unfailing courtesy—I wish mine were as sure—and for the unexpectedly large check.

Our taste in matters of verse seems to differ hence these occasional outbursts first of extravagant love for you then equally extravagant outbursts of indignation.

I am only able to move myself by great effort—take that as my excuse and accept if you please my highest regards for you & yours.

Be assured the check you sent me will all be spent for poetry, if not "Poetry".

Sincerely yours, / W. C. Williams

[P.S., *written at top of page*] I especially thank you for taking trouble with my unreasonable request for that last minute change which I still feel, however, has been a great improvement to the group.

Maxwell Bodenheim to Harriet Monroe   *Chicago, 4 December 1916*

Dear Miss Monroe—

When writing of the Play, "Brown," in the last number of Poetry, you did not include Mr. [William] Saphier's name in addition to mine. I told you clearly that the idea of the play was entirely his, and his name was on the manuscript submitted to you. You are guilty, as far as I can see, of an utterly unjust action. I shall not return the play and do not wish you to print the poems of mine you have. You can, of course, keep the poems as security until I pay the money borrowed from you, but after that, I should like their return. I do not care to appear again in your magazine.

I shall tell you clearly and without rancor, my opinion of you and the group surrounding you. You are an intangible coward. You will not advance a poet whose work you respect, beyond the mere printing of him, until that poet has become "safe",—until his work is widely mentioned. Sometimes you will aid a poet who has won favor with one of the influential members of the magazine-staff. That is your only deviation. The championing of any poet who is a bit ahead of his time and therefor unpopular, is impossible to you, even though you may greatly admire his work. The scarecrow of material failure always stalks at your side and often counsels you to veil your actual opinions. One Alfred Kreymborg, who bravely shouts his youthful challenge to the philistine and pompous literary-arbiters of this country and then dies as many others have died, is worth ten timid editors like you—editors who blow their careful challenge through a muffled trumpet. . . .

I intend to quit the DIRTY GAME of "pulling strings" and salaaming to people whose influence alone will aid my work. . . . If it fails, in a material way, I shall not care over-much. I shall at least, retain the praise of my soul—something that you and most of those around you lost so long ago, that you cannot recognize it when you see it in another.

Sincerely, / Maxwell Bodenheim.

Harriet Monroe to Maxwell Bodenheim   *[draft]* 6 December 1916

My dear Mr. Bodenheim:

I enclose your poems, since you wish to withdraw them. The money I lent you may be repaid at your convenience. Perhaps sometime you will feel like telling me you regret your rather absurd letter. ~~I shall not lay it up against you~~.

William Carlos Williams to Harriet Monroe   *Rutherford, N.J.,*
18 December 1916

Dear Miss Monroe:

I appeal to you for Bodenheim. I do not know that he will accept my mediation but should I be able to get him to reconsider his withdrawal of the verse and play you had accepted would you print them for him?

It seems to me that a man so young as Bodenheim, as wilfully [sic] unattractive as he is and as unfortunate—physically, not spiritually—being the artist he is, should be forgiven much—one might even be exceptionally generous with him at no great loss.

I await your answer with keen interest.

Yours, / W. C. Williams

Alfred Kreymborg to Harriet Monroe   *[New York City],*
2 January 1917

My dear Miss Monroe—

Just a word of thanks for the note in January Poetry. It isn't my custom—as you know—to be dragged into controversy. I had no intention of answering [William Stanley] Braithwaite's lamentable twaddle—but I am, nevertheless, sensible of words written for or against my efforts and those of the many folk I believe in. Too, I have been enjoying, silently as usual, the many obituary notes written over the imaginary demise of Others. The sheet will continue to live as long as Williams and I continue to live. . . . No, Others is not dead. . . .

William Carlos Williams to Harriet Monroe   *Rutherford, N.J.,*
                                                   25 April 1917

Dear Miss Monroe:—

I cannot resist you. Resist me if you find it amusing.

Here are two excellent pieces of work of mine. As my book [*Al Que Quiere!*] will be out in a few weeks—so they say—perhaps you will want to have these put ahead of someone else's work—such as Masters'—which you were thinking of putting forward.

Well, God bless you—even though you may be annoyed at my humor to the extent of rejecting everything I send you.

Here's to success—for everybody!

Yours / W. C. Williams

W.C.W. enclosed "Smell" and "History." On 22 May, H.M. accepted them—"History" provisionally, "if certain lines on pages 1 & 2 are omitted."

William Carlos Williams to Harriet Monroe   *Rutherford, N.J.,*
                                                   25 May 1917

Dear Miss Monroe:

First of all I express my deep personal sympathy for you in your illness [the flu]—happily passed. I did not know that you had been ill. I hope you are completely recovered. Next I pay tribute to your extraordinary gentleness with me which I have always treasured for its great value. I recognise both the difficulties of a practical kind that you are facing as well as certain habitual reactions of your own sensibilities which you cannot overcome and I think I have not been slow to express how unfortunate these are in my opinion but I cannot stop for these in writing what I find should be written.

It offends my sense of completeness to have you wish to remove parts of poems for reasons that are to me so trivial that they are positively ridiculous yet beggars must not be choosers: I have few opportunities to print my work—the truth is out!

Appreciating your good feeling for me as well as what you have done for me in the past I will make concessions to you that I would make to no one else. If you do not think them worth anything I cannot help that.

In regard to the poem 'History' I wish you would delete the objectionable *words* replacing the letters of those words with full stop points. The lines are to remain the same and all words not objectionable are to remain in position. If you decide to use the poem under those circumstances I would like to see a proof. And please understand that in having poems published I have but one object: to say something that must be said, neither money nor anything else as far as I know—unless it be personal vanity—influences me much so if expense in publishing the long poem is an item dispense with that item at once. . . .

William Carlos Williams to Harriet Monroe   *Rutherford, N.J.,*   *31 May 1917*

Dear Harriet Monroe:—

My book will probably be out before you have a chance to print either of the poems. I received the proofs after writing you my last letter.

If however you have a chance to publish the poems first—do what you please in the matter of omissions only please indicate the omissions in some way.

I am glad Sandburg liked my piece. It amused me to have him count it better than Pound's latest. Pound and I have carried on a deep rivalry as to methods for many a year: it is strange to have arrived by opposite routes at a momentarily identical point. My regards to Sandburg. . . .

William Carlos Williams to Harriet Monroe   *Rutherford, N.J.,*   *17 July 1917*

Dear Miss Monroe:—

You fail to grasp the point: to confess that the check you sent me strains your treasury and at the same time to insist—in effect—on paying me that check in full is evidence of wrongheadedness run to pure whimsicality. No poet expects to earn money by his verse. If he does he is a fool and had better be disillusioned at the start. To compare him, the poet, to the painter is idle for the painter produces a single piece incapable of reproduction whereas the poet produces nothing more tangible than the paper which anyone can purchase for a cent and a few dabs of ink which cost still less.

What you are doing by paying what you do for poems is this: you are jeopardising the existence of your magazine in the mistaken notion that what poets want is money when in reality—though money is sorely needed also—they need space, an opportunity to gain print often and at will. This lack of space, this lack of opportunity to appear is hell. And you will add to this by going bankrupt! . . .

Before you go out of business, please cut your rates in half and I venture to say you will print better stuff within the month.

Sandburg's "In the cool tombs" is a splendid thing. I hope with all my power to hope that I may meet Sandburg soon. He is, if I am not mistaken, really studying his form. Few men are making any progress in

their art. They are adding new decoration or repeating the old stuff but
Sandburg is really thinking like an artist. He seems to me to know his
America and to be getting it in. Give him my best wishes.

Sincerely yours, / W. C. Williams

If we were all great artists you might try to pay us well but we are
mainly clod hoppers in verse.

William Carlos Williams to Harriet Monroe   *Rutherford, N.J.,*
12 March 1918

Dear Harriet Monroe:—

   Your recent issue of Poetry is quite interesting. The first poem of that
young Italian chap [Emanuel Carnevali] is very good, the rest—unsuc-
cessful. You are certainly the clearinghouse for a lot of mediocre stuff—
so you should be: very democratic—keep up the good work.

Yours, / Williams

Carnevali had debuted in the March issue; he joined the *Poetry* staff in 1919. See
Chapter XI.

William Carlos Williams to Harriet Monroe   *Rutherford, N.J.,*
11 April 1918

Dear Harriet Monroe:—

   Two groups inclosed. Use either but not both—at least not together.
I cannot return Crystal Garden, it'll have to lie in the hospital awhile.

Best wishes, / yours / W. C. Williams

PPPPPP   SSSSSS !!!!!!

   The review Dorothy D[udley] gave me and which you printed is a
piece of good work—judging from inside out. She was keen in her
analysis of my mood—my habitual ground mood—as far as she went.
Thank God someone criticised the book without mentioning the tech-
nique. . . . The foreword on the cover is an atrocious piece of work but
for that very reason it tickled me. I care for no reader who does not go
direct to the matter of the poem, for that reason I find a mistaken joy,
we'll say, in driving off just the plain gentle souls. I deserve very few
readers. Dorothy seems to be one. . . .

Dudley's long review of *Al Que Quiere!* appeared in the April issue. The cover blurb
on the book informs the "gentle reader" that Williams "doesn't give a damn for
your opinion" and that "his opinion of you is more important than your opinion of
him."

William Carlos Williams to Harriet Monroe   *Rutherford, N.J.,*
9 September 1918

Dear Harriet Monroe:—

Some of the enclosed poems you have already seen. Where that is the case there has been a revision.

As to the capitals: do as you please but by putting a capital at the beginning of each line against the plain rules of grammar you will always mar the effect of the poems.

At present I have a book of improvisations on hand [*Kora in Hell*] that I will have published soon. As no one will accept it—tho' I have tried no one as yet—without a cash bonus on my part I have set myself the task of earning enough money by my writing in the next six months to get my book out. I must admit that the lure of the dollar is a potent force in art.

Best wishes, / Yours, / W. Williams

William Carlos Williams to Harriet Monroe   *Rutherford, N.J.,*
10 February 1919

Dear Harriet Monroe:—

Neither in my house nor out of it must I ever speak my mind—it seems. If I said anything that seemed to injure you set it down for the true utterance of a damned fool.

As far as the poems are concerned I think some of them are the best short things I have ever done—some I do not like so well, —but to intimate that I have condemned them beforehand is to have been a crooked listener, to say the least.

I am glad you are bringing these out now as I hope to talk in Chicago on March 4th.

As far as the Little Review is concerned: it has given me the kind of an entré I have lacked everywhere else. I like the attitude Jane Heap has taken toward the American Issues and I feel that her work is to that extent important. I do not approve of Pound, nor of the English hero-worship of M.A. [Margaret Anderson]—

Do you realize the narrowness of the opening through which I must crawl?

By all means use *The Poor* [March 1919]. I like it among the first of all. Do not fail to use that poem ever.

I will see you in Chicago—I Parsival.

Yrs. / W. Williams

William Carlos Williams to Harriet Monroe   *Rutherford, N.J.,*
28 April 1919

Dear Harriet,

I return your extract from my spiel [his Chicago lecture, published as "Notes from a Talk on Poetry," July 1919]. I think you have done well in getting out the substance of what I had to say and arranging the thing as a unit. If you want to print it I am satisfied to have you go ahead exactly as you have the thing now. Your grammar is, I think, uniformly better than mine though of course a talk and an article are different in texture. I suppose I will get paid something. I hope so as I am planning to take over Others for a couple of months this summer: July and August. Send me some work of yours. I'll tell you where you get off! REVENGE! Also tell Helen Hoyt to fix her eye on the inkwell and write me off a verse or two.

I thank you for your great kindness to me while I was in Chicago. I feel a little unhappy over my own lack of graciousness in that I did not find an opportunity to reciprocate in some way, by at least keeping my appointments. I was insane while I was in Chicago. I flung myself about like a silly wave. I do not forget your kind dinner to us when you were in New York.

I cannot say that I shall ever recover from that rain sodden but vicariously sunshiney week! It was as if, or rather it was actually—I had never in my life before had an opportunity to be just a poet, the one thing I want to be. I was, to the vulgar eye at least, a poet! I was at least as near to being a poet as I had ever been and it was as if new bones had been put into me. Etc. etc. etc. We are only beginning. I feel that barring death I shall see some work done in the next five years that will be unrivalled anywhere at any time. We are at the opening of a golden age of poetry HERE.

Yours, / W. C. Williams

3. Wallace Stevens

In late October 1914, Harriet Monroe was alone in the office, going through the mail and taking a last look at November's special War Issue, when she made the greatest "discovery" of her long tenure. Among the unsolicited manuscripts was a group of short poems called "Phases." She sent the author a telegram, accepting two sections of the sequence. Although the issue was about to go to press, she recalled in her autobiography, she took it apart and reassembled "the page proofs to make room for two pages—all I could squeeze in—by this master of strange and beautiful rhythms." The poet had sent no biographical information, so in the notes on contributors H.M. wrote that Mr. Wallace Stevens was "unknown as yet to the editor." At the time, Stevens was a thirty-five-year-old lawyer working in New York City for the Equitable Surety Company, and "Phases" was his first important professional publication. Thus began Stevens's long association with *Poetry* and his friendship with Monroe, maintained through his amusing letters and several visits to the office when he was passing through Chicago on business.

Like William Carlos Williams, Stevens was not a full-time poet but a busy professional man. And like Dr. Williams, he had the misfortune of being overshadowed by T. S. Eliot (another professional, first in banking then publishing), but lived long enough to be widely recognized as one of the great masters to emerge during early days of Modernism. Like Eliot, Stevens was the most philosophical of poets. As aspiring writers, both studied with the same professors at Harvard, Eliot arriving five years after Stevens had departed. Stevens entered in 1897 as a special student, and worked as the editor and then the president of the *Harvard Advocate*.

One of the staff members he hired was Witter Bynner, a budding poet and bon vivant who was also published early in *Poetry*. In later years, though they remained friends, Bynner's more conservative tastes put him at odds with Stevens aesthetically. But like Bynner and his friend Arthur Davison Ficke, Stevens was drawn to Far Eastern art by visits to Ernest Fenollosa's Chinese collections at Harvard. This shared interest would be a factor in his friendship with Monroe. Aware that he was a connoisseur of things Oriental, she arranged for her sister, Lucy Calhoun, to shop on his behalf in Peking. Over the years, he received a number of objets d'art and shipments of the jasmine tea he particularly fancied.

Stevens's tastes were refined, and expensive. Although he was attracted to the artist's life as a young man, he did not relish the prospect of poverty that pursuing a writing career might entail. In 1900, he left Harvard, without a degree, and worked on the night desk of the *New-York Tribune*. Following his businessman father's advice, he then studied law. He was admitted to the New York bar in 1904 and started practicing insurance law. In 1909 he married Elsie Moll, the most beautiful girl in his native Reading, Pennsylvania, and Saint-Gaudens's model for the Liberty dime and half-dollar. Stevens realized Elsie was intellectually "unformed," but believed he would shape her. They soon found they were disastrously incompatible.

While Stevens was establishing his business career, they made their first home in the Chelsea district of Manhattan. Stevens enjoyed contact with the Bohemian life of nearby Greenwich Village and loved exploring the art galleries. Again like Williams, he was fascinated by the revolutionary works exhibited at New York Armory Show of 1913. During his years in New York, Stevens became friends with Williams, Marianne Moore, Marcel Duchamp, Walter Arensberg (who owned *Nude Descending a Staircase*), Kreymborg, and the rest of the poets and artists associated with *Others*. Then and afterward, however, Stevens deliberately kept his business and artistic lives separate.

In 1916 he joined the home office of the Hartford Accident and Indemnity Company and he began his extensive travels about the country, handling its surety bond business. Although he worked for the Hartford for thirty-nine years, rising to vice president in 1934, Stevens preferred his associates didn't know he wrote poetry. "They don't seem to get over it," he said. In an interview in *Parts of a World: Wallace Stevens Remembered* (1985), one of his colleagues confessed that he had tried to read Stevens's poetry, but to him it was "the biggest bunch of gobbledygook." By way of explanation he added, "Wallace was a helluva kidder . . . and I've often wondered if he didn't write a lot of these things with his tongue in cheek." But in their field of business, Stevens was acknowledged as "the dean of surety-claims men" of his day. The mundane world of bonds and the more ethereal realm of verse might seem incompatible, but Stevens didn't see a necessary conflict. He once said, "Poetry and surety claims aren't as unlikely a combination as they may seem. There is nothing perfunctory about them."

For all the comedy in his work, particularly the early poems, Stevens was always at heart a serious thinker. At Harvard, he became friends with the poet-philosopher George Santayana, who encouraged him in his writing. He also studied with the psychologist and pragmatic philosopher William James, brother of Henry and author of *The Varieties of Religious Experience*. James's explorations of mankind's need to believe in a higher order—a problem that had become acute following Nietzsche's recent declaration that, in the post-Darwinian universe, God was dead—would have a profound impact upon Stevens's own views. His approach to the modern dilemma of finding meaning in a world now bereft of the old beliefs was subtly expressed in his second and greatest contribution to *Poetry*.

When Stevens submitted "Sunday Morning" in 1915 it was not, of course, the canonical text it has since become, and the poet was still virtually unknown. Although the Editor sometimes took it upon herself to make changes on manuscripts, in this case she exercised now-unthinkable liberties. She accepted "Sunday Morning" on the condition that Stevens drop three of the original eight sections and allow her to rearrange the order of the sequence to I, VIII, IV, V, and VII. She also asked Stevens to rephrase an oblique passage. Unlike Pound, Lowell, and most of the other prima donnas the Editor dealt with, Stevens was self-effacing and exceedingly modest about his work, and he agreed to the changes. The altered version of the poem ran in the November 1915 number. Kreymborg and other friends in New York, and a few perceptive readers elsewhere like Arthur Ficke, responded positively. When Stevens published it in his first collection, *Harmonium*, in 1923, he quietly restored his original version of the poem.

Monroe became a great champion of Stevens's work, often taking the poet by surprise with her praise. She published his verse dramas, *Three Travelers Watch a Sunrise* and *Carlos Among the Candles*, even though neither play succeeded on stage. Stevens sent *Three Travelers* in anonymously, and *Poetry* printed the piece in July 1916. The Editor awarded it the $100 first prize in a one-act play contest that brought in nearly a hundred entries. The verse tragedy was produced in Greenwich Village, but even though "Edna [actually, Kathleen] Millay played the heroine exquisitely," according to H.M., the show was not a success. However, after reading the play in *Poetry*, Laura Sherry, director of the Wisconsin Players, commissioned *Carlos Among the Candles*. It was produced in the fall of 1917, first in Milwaukee and then at the Neighborhood Playhouse in New York, where it closed after one performance. H.M. thought highly enough of the "whimsical monologue with action" that she gave it top billing in the December 1917 issue. An anonymous reviewer in the Chicago *Herald* begged to differ with Miss Monroe's judgment:

> We cannot help being pleased that Chicago has, so to speak, been sponsor for Carlos. He is so much more symbolic than the symbolists, and so much more mystic than the mysticists, that one feels sure he is a forerunner of a new school of literature. There is about him here and there, it is true, a touch of GERTRUDE STEIN, the futurist. But he surpasses GERTRUDE STEIN as far as she surpassed her contemporaries. For at her best GERTRUDE was merely incomprehensible, whereas at his best Carlos is dumfounding.

Though others also found Stevens sometimes hard to fathom, the Editor published a large group of his poems under the title "Pecksniffiana" in October 1919 and awarded him the $200 Levinson Prize for 1920.

For years, Monroe pestered Stevens, sometimes in the pages of *Poetry*, to bring out a book. He was a month short of his forty-fourth birthday when *Harmonium* was published by Alfred A. Knopf. The collection, like Williams's *Spring and All* (also issued in 1923), had the misfortune of following in the wake of Eliot's *The Waste Land*, printed in the first issue of

Eliot's new journal, the *Criterion*, in October 1922. Stevens gave Alice Henderson his opinion on 27 November: "Eliot's poem is, of course, the rage. As poetry it is surely negligible. What it may be in other respects is a large subject on which one could talk for a month. . . . Personally, I think it's a bore." Although *Harmonium* was a truly brilliant first collection—besides "Sunday Morning," it contained "Peter Quince at the Clavier," "The Snow Man," "The Comedian as the Letter C," "The Emperor of Ice-Cream," "Thirteen Ways of Looking at a Blackbird," and several other now-classic poems—the book got little attention and sold poorly. (Stevens reported on his paltry royalties to H.M.)

When his second collection, *Ideas of Order*, appeared in 1935, H.M. gave it a glowing review in the magazine. Stevens remained grateful for *Poetry*'s early faith in his work and was always generous to the magazine, not only with his poems, but also with financial support. He turned back his contributor's payments and later became an anonymous Guarantor. Once he had "arrived," he asked that his poems not be considered for the magazine's prizes.

Stevens first visited the *Poetry* offices when he was in Chicago in 1918, and Miss Monroe was likewise his guest in Hartford—a rare privilege—on several occasions. She sent him letters and postcards during her extensive travels and he, in turn, corresponded when he vacationed, particularly in Florida. When the Stevenses' daughter Holly was born in 1924, "Aunt Harriet" presented a silver spoon, and continued to send the child Christmas and birthday gifts over the years. As the letters below indicate, Stevens and Monroe developed a relationship that transcended typical editor-and-author protocol.

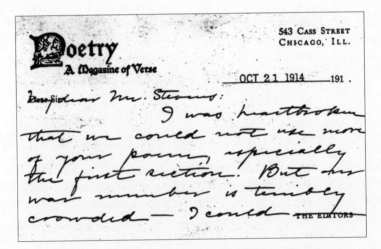

H.M.'s first, "heartbroken" letter to Wallace Stevens,
21 October 1914.

Harriet Monroe to Wallace Stevens   *21 October 1914*

My dear Mr. Stevens:

I was heartbroken that we could not use more of your poems, espe-
cially the first section [of "Phases"]. But our number is terribly
crowded—I could give you only two pages—and II-V seemed to me
about the best of it. Also it stands well without the next.

Section VI seems to me the weakest, and I don't feel that you quite
got what you wanted out of VIII and IX. With many thanks for your
telegram, which I told you not to pay for, I am yours sincerely,

Harriet Monroe

Wallace Stevens to Harriet Monroe   *New York City,*
6 November 1914

Dear Miss Monroe:

My biography is, necessarily, very brief; for I have published nothing.
I am grateful to you for your notes and, of course, for the check.

Very truly yours, / Wallace Stevens

Harriet Monroe to Wallace Stevens   *27 January 1915*

My dear Mr. Stevens:

I don't know when any poems [unidentified] have "intrigued" me so
much as these. They are recondite, erudite, provocatively obscure, with a
kind of modern-gargoyle genius in them—Aubrey-Beardsleyish in the
making. They are weirder than your war series and I don't like them
and I'll be blamed if I print them; but their author will surely catch me
the next time if he will only uncurl and uncoil a little—condescend to
change his mystically wistful and mournful muse out of the utter dark-
ness. In other words, please send more.

Yours sincerely and admiringly, / Harriet Monroe

Wallace Stevens to Harriet Monroe   *New York City, 6 June 1915*

Dear Miss Monroe:

Provided your selection of the number of *Sunday Morning* is printed
in the following order: I, VIII, IV, V, I see no objection to cutting down.
The order is necessary to the idea.

I was born in Reading, Pennsylvania, am thirty-five years old, a
lawyer, reside in New York and have published no books.

Very truly yours, / Wallace Stevens

Wallace Stevens to Harriet Monroe   *New York City, 23 June 1915*

Dear Miss Monroe:

No. 7 of *Sunday Morning* is, as you suggest, of a different tone, but it does not seem to me to be too detached to conclude with.

The words "On disregarded plate" in No. 5 [l. 8] are, apparently, obscure. Plate is used in the sense of so-called family plate. Disregarded refers to the disuse into which things fall that have been possessed for a long time. I mean, therefore, that death releases and renews. What the old have come to disregard, the young inherit and make use of. Used in these senses, the words have a value in the lines which I find it difficult to retain in any change. Does this explanation help? Or can you make any suggestion? I ask this because your criticism is clearly well-founded.

The lines might read,

> She causes boys to bring sweet-smelling pears,
> And plums in ponderous piles. The maidens taste
> And stray etc.

But such a change is somewhat pointless. I should prefer to keep the lines unchanged, although, if you like the variation proposed, for the sake of clearness, I should be satisfied.

The order is satisfactory. Thanks for your very friendly interest.

Yours sincerely, / Wallace Stevens

H.M. printed the revised lines; W.S. restored "On disregarded plate" in *Harmonium*.

Arthur D. Ficke to Harriet Monroe   *[Davenport, Iowa],*
14 November 1915

Dear Miss Monroe—

A great idea strikes me! At the end of "Poetry's" five years, why not startle the universe by publishing "The Chicago Anthology"—containing the fifty top-notch poems which you've printed? *I'm* startled to realize that you really *have* printed fifty fine poems. Salt this idea away in your brain for future consideration.

Non R.S.V.P! / A.D.F.

"Sunday Morning" tantalizes me with the sense that perhaps it's the most beautiful poem ever written and that perhaps it's just an incompetent obscurity. Let's talk about it sometime. Such restraint! Such delicate dignity! And such ambiguity! Have you known Stevens? He's a big, slightly fat, awfully competent-looking man—you expect him to roar, but when he speaks there emerges the gravest, softest, most subtly modulated voice I've ever heard—a voice on tiptoe at dawn! A personality beside which all the nice little Skipwith Cannells in the world shrink to cheese-mites! . . . .

Wallace Stevens to Harriet Monroe   *[Hartford], 8 October 1919*

Dear Miss Monroe:

During the last few days I have made three trips to Washington, making Paul Revere seem like a do-nothing, and that has kept me at a pitch where the October *Poetry* was only one leaf in a storm. But an evening or two at home have let me down, now, and I must confess, or boast, that that one leaf doesn't look so rotten, when examined with care. . . . Let me thank you also for the check. Very respectable, it seems to me—*damned* so, compared with those of your contemporaries. I wonder you can do it. Have you seen this month's *Little Review* with the quotations from the Chinese? Miss Anderson!

Very truly yours, / Wallace Stevens

Salut à Sandburg

Fourteen of W.S.'s poems were printed in October 1919 as "Pecksniffiana." The group included "Fabliau of Florida," "The Weeping Burgher," "Ploughing on Sunday," "Anecdote of the Jar," "Of the Surface of Things," "Exposition of the Contents of a Cab," and "The Curtains in the House of the Metaphysician."

Wallace Stevens to Harriet Monroe   *[Hartford], 20 October 1919*

Chère Alma Mater:

. . . I have read C. Sandburg's book [*Cornhuskers*] with sincere pleasure. So much fresh air, fresh feeling, simple thinking, delightful expression: delight*ed* expression, does one good. I cannot say that the larger pieces stir me, but one comes on the most excellent raisins everywhere. . . . At the present time, I am mortally engaged in Washington and have no plans involving Chicago; although I expect sooner or later to make a further study of your lions and their dens.

Very truly yrs, / Wallace Stevens

CHAPTER VII

Amy Lowell, Ezra Pound, and "Amygisme"

1. Amy Lowell, Poet and Politician

Amy Lowell was a large woman with large ambitions. She was a member of a famous Boston family, a cousin of the poet James Russell Lowell and sister of the astronomer Percival Lowell and Abbott Lawrence Lowell, the president of Harvard. She was also related to generals and judges, and shared the attributes of their professions. Like others of her class, she had a sense of noblesse oblige, but it often came off as patronizing and pushy. She knew how to throw her weight around.

When Lowell visited the *Poetry* office in 1914, Alice Henderson was impressed, but took an instant dislike to her. In March 1916, Ezra Pound reminded Alice that she had said Amy was "300 pounds and a charmer." He agreed: "She has charm. She is a delightful acquaintance, or would be if one were a civil engineer." After Lowell began her promotional campaign for the second *Some Imagist Poets* anthology in April 1916, A.C.H. wrote H.M. that Amy was "a pompous old fool and she wouldn't know an Imagist if she saw one. . . . [A]nd the worst thing Ezra Pound ever did was to spill her on the world. Amy *über alles*! and her place in the sun."

Imagist or not, Amy Lowell was no fool, and she did not require Ezra Pound to work her will. She had more than enough energy, political skill, and capital to make her own figure in the world. And she could be quite unpleasant if she didn't get her way. Beneath her largesse, there lurked more than a hint of quid pro quo. With strained jocularity, she wrote H.M., 15 May 1916, asking Monroe herself to review the new *Imagist* anthology, in which *Poetry* was fulsomely praised: "You see, it is tit for tat, my dear. But titting without tatting is no fun."

Like Pound, Lowell responded quickly to Monroe's first call for poems in 1912, and tried to sway the Editor through torrents of letters. The voluminous Lowell-Monroe correspondence—between 1912 and 1925 they exchanged over 580 letters—provides one of the most detailed accounts of the personalities involved in Imagism and their controversies. Lowell had plenty of time and secretarial help to send Monroe as many as

Amy Lowell: Edgar Lee Masters referred to her in 1917 as "the tremendous Amazon who for the time being is rampaging through the flower gardens of America."

five or more missives a week, in which she lobbied, flattered, and nagged endlessly for advancement. Unlike the tactless E.P., she was a shrewd tactician, and far more successful.

Though fourteen years younger than Monroe, Lowell addressed her on occasion as "my Child," and her condescension (couched in the most gracious terms, to be sure) must have been grating. The Editor was unfailingly polite with irritating authors, but in Lowell's case she was unusually deferential. In part, she was responding in the socially prescribed manner they both knew so well. But she genuinely admired Lowell's nerve and independence. She also appreciated Lowell as a benefactor. Besides giving annual $200 donations, Lowell took out ads for her books, and for the pedigreed English sheepdogs she bred. "Dear Amy" was not above reminding "Dear Harriet" of her bounty when she felt the pages of *Poetry* did not adequately reflect her several gifts.

As their friendship grew, it became harder for Monroe to deny Lowell's requests; but when Amy went too far, she didn't hesitate to set her (and the record) straight. Lowell was at least big enough to admit when she was in error. Proving Amy wrong was no easy task, however, as she was punctilious to a maddening degree. Despite A.L.'s driven behavior, Monroe could appreciate her eccentricities, among them cigar smoking. Recalling a three-day visit in 1914 to Lowell's "dog-guarded Brookline castle," Monroe presented in *A Poet's Life* a bemused portrait, and a final assessment that is surprisingly generous, considering Amy's incessant importuning:

> Imperious and meticulous, sometimes exasperatingly critical of one's literary offenses—things said or omitted in the magazine—she was yet wholeheartedly loyal in friendship. . . . But temperamental outbursts were part of her excitable make-up, and I did not take her too seriously. . . . I still think she had "everything but genius"—but whether a great poet or not, she was a great woman.

Lowell did, however, have "a genius for publicity" (as Monroe said of Frank Lloyd Wright), and when the Editor balked at letting *Poetry* become a part of her promotional machinery—by printing and placing her poems just so, publishing her literary essays, and reviewing her books with *enthusiasm*—chiding letters and recriminations ensued. When Monroe tried to make amends, her efforts often went awry. In any case, it is doubtful that Lowell could ever have been completely satisfied. Pound put the question neatly in a letter to H.M. in January 1914: "Too bad about Amy—why can't she conceive of herself as a renaissance figure instead of a spiritual chief, which she ain't?"

Lowell's first book, *A Dome of Many-Coloured Glass* (1912), was conventional, but she wanted very much to be up-to-date and experimented constantly, coming up with what she styled "polyphonic prose." Then, after reading H.D.'s first work in *Poetry* in 1913, she had her great epiphany—"Why, I too am an Imagiste!"—and she decided to go straight to the source. She asked Monroe for a letter of introduction to Ezra Pound and set sail for England in early July, with her maids, limousine, and chauffeur in tow. Once installed in her suite at the Berkeley Hotel, she summoned Pound and favored him with a recitation of her verse. He criticized it, but very gently (he knew a potential patron when he heard one), and accepted one of her poems for the *New Freewoman*. Soon after, both wrote to H.M. expressing mutual admiration.

In the beginning, the "pleasingly intelligent" Miss Lowell must have seemed an apt pupil, and so Pound decided to help modernize her. He admitted her to the Imagist group and introduced her to Yeats, Hueffer, and John Gould Fletcher. Lowell and Fletcher soon became close, and from then on assiduously promoted each other's work. Lowell gave Monroe a glowing report on E.P., concluding: "His taste is too fine to confine itself within the walls of any school, even his own. He is so young that all sorts of developments may be expected. I think the chip-on-the-shoulder attitude will disappear in time." Lowell's prophecy proved only half right.

Upon her return in September, Lowell wrote H.M. that she had "learned many things." She visited Chicago in February 1914, and in the March issue H.M. published Lowell's article on "Vers Libre and Metrical Prose." In mid-February, Lowell wrote: "I wish you could have heard me boom your magazine to all the people I met in New York." But when she read her essay in print a month later, she fired off a sharp letter accusing the Editor of altering her sentences and "changing the fine shade of my meaning." After lecturing H.M. on how she should run her journal, Lowell issued a warning: "should such a thing ever happen again," she would send no more of her work, "either prose or verse." So much for sweetness and light.

But worse was to befall. On 9 April Lowell sent a telegram, followed by a letter, demanding the new issue be suppressed. Through a printer's error, a line in her poem "The Forsaken" was dropped, which made her say "the most vulgar impossible thing." After much back and forth, and a hint of legal action, H.M. agreed to paste the correct text into every issue not already circulated. But all turned out for the best: the April issue sold briskly, as people wanted to see the poem "and be horrified, shocked." There would be many other mishaps and conflicts in the future, but differences always were smoothed over. Lowell continued to publish in *Poetry* right up to her death, in 1925.

Amy Lowell to Harriet Monroe   *Brookline, Mass., 12 January 1913*

My dear Miss Monroe:

Thank you very much for your letter. I return "Apology" because you are so good as to say that you can use it.

I do like criticism, but I am afraid I am less likely to take it than most people are. I keep my poems a long time before I send them anywhere, and go over and over them to get just the shade of meaning which I want, and just the consonant and vowel sounds. So that by the time the poems reach an editor I am hardened in crime, and only once have I changed a word at editorial suggestion. So will you pardon me if I cling to my original version . . . .

A.L. sent her first submission 27 December 1912; H.M. responded 10 January 1913 with detailed queries and suggestions but said, "whether you make the changes or not I should like to use the poem."

Amy Lowell to Harriet Monroe   *Brookline, Mass., 19 May 1913*

My dear Miss Munroe [sic];

. . . I have an article on "Vers Libre," which I will send you as soon as it is done, and you can print it or not, as you see fit. Also, have you seen a book called "Love Poems and Others" by D. H. Lawrence . . . . [A]lthough in some ways immature, it is so full of vigor and originality, that it seems to me that it would be worthy of a review in your pages . . . .

Amy Lowell to Harriet Monroe   Brookline, Mass., *27 May 1913*

My dear Miss Munroe; [sic]

. . . Let me thank you for the nice things you say about my work, in your letter. It warmed the cockles of my heart. I think you make no mistake in keeping "Apology", for it seems to me one of the best things I have done.

I enclose a short review of the Lawrence book. Will you please sign my initials at the bottom of it if you see fit to print it? I do not know whether you pay anything for reviews, but whether you do or not, please let me say that I should be very glad indeed to give you my services for this sort of thing, if you care for them, because it is such excellent practice for me. . . .

Harriet Monroe to Amy Lowell   *16 June 1913*

My dear Miss Lowell:

I am in terrible trouble. I told you to write that review of Lawrence and now Ezra Pound has sent in one; without, of course, knowing anything about yours. I am afraid I shall have to use his, as it really is his preserve. Long ago I asked him to take care of England for us, and he has sent this review in response to that agreement. . . . We usually pay for prose about $5.00 a page, which amounts to 2 cents a word, but of course I would not be mean enough to refuse to let you practice on us for nothing if you want to. . . .

Amy Lowell to Harriet Monroe   Brookline, Mass., *19 June 1913*

My dear Miss Munroe; [sic]

Your letter of June 16th has arrived. Oh, dear! Oh, dear! These editors! What we do have to suffer from them! Not—all the time I spent in writing that review, (perish the thought) but—like the cow in the nursery rhyme, "considering" how to write it! . . .

Let me hastily say that my offer to write prose, for nothing, was not prompted by a desire to "practice" upon you, as you say, because I have written a great deal of prose in my life, and fear I have got past the practicing stage. My idea was that, as you were taking so many of my poems, it was rather nice to consider these little short reviews as thrown-in, but I believe very firmly that the "laborer is worthy of his hire", and I am anxious to scrap in the arena with the crowd. . . .

If it is not asking too much, would you be so kind as to pay for these two poems, which you are publishing in July, before I go to Europe? I remember your saying that you pay on publication and I sail on July 8th., so if the pay comes afterward, your cheque will kick round till I get home to cash it, which will put your accounts out; and also, every little bit helps on a journey. . . .

Will Mr. Pound be in London when I get there? If so, won't you give me a letter to him, or does he hate to meet people in that way?

Very sincerely yours, / Amy Lowell

Harriet Monroe to Amy Lowell   *24 June 1913*

My dear Miss Lowell:

. . . Believe me, I did not mean to hint that you were practicing on us—that was an unfortunate phrase—but merely that we would not presume to pay for prose if anyone was willing to write it for nothing. However, it shall be as you please. . . .

I enclose a check at our usual rate of $10 a page for your two poems. Also a card of introduction to Mr. Pound, who I think will be in London when you are there. In that case you must take it out on him—in the matter of the Lawrence review. . . .

Amy Lowell to Harriet Monroe   *Brookline, Mass., 26 June 1913*

My dear Miss Monroe:

Thank you very much for your letter of June 24th. . . .

As to your paying, I did not mean to imply, in my letter, that having offered to do these things for you for nothing, I should now claim payment. I only did not want you to think that I was putting off anything upon you, which I considered to have no value. . . . [W]hen I get home from Europe, we can decide whether you had better pay me or not for any future things I may do. I will do just what most of your contributors do, in that line.

Thank you very much for your cheque, and also for the letter of introduction to Mr. Pound. I shall present that immediately upon my arrival, and I know I shall enjoy seeing him. It is very good indeed of you to do this for me. . . .

Amy Lowell to Harriet Monroe   The Berkeley Hotel, London,
                                                    28 July 1913

My dear Miss Monroe:

Thank you very much for the copy of "Poetry", which came last week. I was much pleased at the appearance of those things of mine. . . .

I also have to thank you for your letter of introduction to Ezra Pound. I don't know whether you have heard from him, yet; or, if you have, whether he has told you of all his efforts in my behalf. I sent him your note, and after some correspondence, he came here to dinner. We had a most delightful evening, and it ended in his taking one of my poems to print in a group of "Imagistes" in the mid-August number of "The New Free Woman," and in his advising me to send another to "The English Review," and saying that if they would not print it, he would. He has also arranged for me to meet Yeats this week, and is also to take me to tea at the Ford Maddox [sic] Hueffers'. That he has done more than justice to your letter of introduction, you see, and what especially pleases me is his evident interest in my work. Mr. Pound is no flatterer, but his reticent praise is good to hear, and his occasional criticisms very much to the point. He is reading me the ms. of his new book some day this week.

He tells me that he and you have never met. That is a pity, for he would have added to your gallery of personalities. Figure to yourself a young man, arrayed as "poet," and yet making the costume agreeable by his personal charm. Figure again a seep of conversation and youthful enthusiasm, which keeps him talking, and talking delightfully, as many hours as you choose. The violence of his writings giving way to show a very thin-skinned and sensitive personality. Opening out like a flower in sympathetic circle, and I should imagine shutting up like a clam in an alien atmosphere. A most delightful companion, and in personal conversation, not in the least didactic, rather dreading the attitude, in fact. That he will outgrow some of his theories, I feel sure. His taste is too fine to confine itself within the walls of any school, even his own. He is so young that all sorts of developments may be expected, I think the chip-on-the-shoulder attitude will disappear in time, it ought to.

Altogether you see what a pleasant road your letter has opened to me. . . .

Pound wrote H.M. 13 August: "Miss Lowell having been ill in Paris has just returned. Thanks for sending her. She is a joy and delight, and everybody is forsaking this city. I'm glad she has abandoned Paris."

Amy Lowell to Harriet Monroe   Brookline, Mass.,
                                                       18 September 1913

My dear Miss Monroe:

I have come back to my native land, having had a most interesting
summer, and having learned many things. Mr. Pound has more than
lived up to his kindness when I first arrived. He has printed a poem of
mine in the last number of the "New Freewoman" and has promised to
put in a page of my things in the middle of the winter. I see that you
put my review of Miss [Fannie Stearns] Davis's poems [*Myself and I*] in
your September number, and this emboldens me to ask if you are going
to print my article on "Vers Libre and Metrical Prose" sometime. The
reason I ask is because Mr. Pound and I had so many discussions on the
subject, and I always referred him to this article . . . .

Have you any more reviewing you would like to have me do? I
would suggest, perhaps, Mr. Fletcher's recent poems, as I do not think
that Mr. Pound intends to review them. I know he has sent you a num-
ber of Mr. Fletcher's later poems in manuscript, which, queer as they
are, seem to me to show great originality. . . .

Again let me thank you for the letter you gave me to Mr. Pound. I
feel that in him I have not only gained a personal friend, but through
his kindness, a little wedge into the heart of English letters.

                                    Very sincerely, / Amy Lowell

Harriet Monroe to Amy Lowell   19 September 1913

Dear Miss Lowell:

I was charmed to find your delightful letter on returning from
Panama. So glad you had a good time with Ezra, Hueffer et al. I wish
you were here to tell me all about it. You seem to have impressed E.P.—
I see you are an Imagiste.

The papers say you are at home again. I hope you will come this way
soon again.

                                    Yours cordially, / Harriet Monroe

Amy Lowell to Harriet Monroe   Brookline, Mass., 14 March 1914

My dear Miss Monroe:

. . . I have received my number of the March "Poetry," and, as I
telegraphed you, I should like six more copies. I enclose a check in this
letter to pay for them.

But there is one thing about that article ["Vers Libre and Metrical
Prose"] which displeases me very much. I see that in several places you
have changed my sentences, thereby spoiling my cadence, and, in some

cases, changing the fine shade of my meaning. Really and truly, dear
Miss Monroe, this is "the unpardonable sin" for an editor to commit.
One has no business to send out things signed by a person, unless the
person who wrote it is responsible for every word and for the position
of every word. . . .

You know how great my interest in "Poetry" is, and you know how
loyal I am to it, but I expect to be treated with the same loyalty and
simple fairness, in return. I must therefore ask you, if you wish me to
remain in connection with you, to leave my things, either prose or
verse, exactly as they stand. . . . It is one of the hall-marks of a first-class
magazine that the editor makes no changes, unauthorized by the
author, and indeed, without meaning to sound threatening, I feel
obliged to say that, should such a thing ever happen again, I shall feel
justified (and very sorry I should be to do so) in abstaining from send-
ing you any contributions, either prose or verse, in the future. . . .

Harriet Monroe to Amy Lowell   17 March 1914

My dear Miss Lowell:

We are giving you the lead in the April number. Proof will be sent to
you—I trust in time. I have made no changes in your copy except to
take out two or three commas, which I hope you will approve. Punctu-
ation, I think, should follow a certain system. Sandburg got the last look
at his proof last month, and made an awful mess of it, I thought. Not
that this applies to you.

In regard to your prose article, your letter surprised me, because—
though you may not believe it—I could not, and still can not, remem-
ber making any changes in your text. Most contributors, including
ourselves, send in prose rather roughly, and are glad of a few slight
changes when it is prepared for the printer. But I assure you I had no
intention of committing the "unpardonable sin," or in any way offend-
ing you. . . .

Harriet Monroe to Amy Lowell   4 April 1914

Dear Miss Lowell:

In enclosing this check, I confess that it will be a great favor to *Poetry*
if you can conveniently send it back, and deduct the amount from the
$200 which you so generously offered to send us in August. This
because *Poetry* is very poor now, and in August will be much richer
with the beginning of the third year's fund. And also because I want to
send Ezra an advance, as a hint in one of his letters shows he needs it.

Yours— / H.M.

Amy Lowell to Harriet Monroe   *Brookline, Mass., 7 April 1914*

My dear Miss Monroe:

Let me thank you very much for this cheque of $100, and for your two notes, all of which came this morning. I am afraid you will think me a great pig not to return this cheque as you suggest, but the truth is that I like to keep my earnings and my donations separate, and also I am a little stuck this month myself, and have unfortunately arranged to spend your cheque, knowing it was coming, before I received it. . . .

I am sending Ezra a small sum as a wedding present, so that will help along, if you want to send him anything before receiving my cheque on the first of May. I will send it to you on the very first day, so that won't, I hope, put you out very much. . . .

Pound married Dorothy Shakespear 20 April. E.P. also sent H.M. a wedding announcement.

Amy Lowell to Harriet Monroe   *Brookline, Mass., 9 April 1914*

My dear Miss Monroe:

I am perfectly horrified at the blunder which your printer has made in the first page of my poem, "The Forsaken," in which he has left out a whole line. The line should read, "The priest would have me repent, and have the rest of my life spent in a convent." Whereas he makes me say, "My mother would call me 'whore,' and spit upon me; the priest would vent." This is a most disgusting allusion, and I am afraid will do me a great deal of harm, particularly as this is a serious poem, and treated in a modern fashion, and coming immediately after the word "whore," nothing could have created a worse impression. I am afraid it will brand me a vulgar Rabelaisian author, which I certainly am not. . . .

I am sorry to trouble you, but I really feel so strongly about this that I must ask you to suppress immediately, as far as possible, this edition, and reissue another. . . .

Were the blunder merely an ordinary one, which only affected my artistic reputation, I should merely ask you to put an errata slip in the next number, but in this case, I feel that my reputation as a poet, and as a woman, is very seriously injured by such apparent coarseness . . . .

I really think, dear Miss Monroe, that it would be well to be a little more business-like in your conduct of the magazine, and either employ some trusty person to see, or see yourself, that each number as finally issued is correct.

Sincerely yours, / Amy Lowell

P.S. No cost should accrue to you from a reissue of the number, as it is clearly the printer's blunder, and you can force him to make good at his expense.

A.L. also sent a telegram about the error that afternoon. H.M. replied by wire: "Printing is agony. I read your proof four times myself. It went perfectly. Will make correction in every way possible but can't reissue as type is distributed. . . . Your telegram is my first information. Imagine how I feel."

Amy Lowell to Harriet Monroe   Brookline, Mass., 10 April 1914

Dear Miss Monroe:

I telephoned you last night, in the vague hope that I could hear something, and so relieve my agitated mind, and I could hear how kind and sympathetic you were, but no definite sense came over the telephone. . . .

In order to be sure that I was not demanding too much, more than I was legally entitled to, I consulted my lawyer, and find that in a case of this sort, one has a right to forbid the circulation of the magazine, and to claim damages. I tell you this with no intention whatever of invoking the law, but merely to show you how serious the situation is, and to show you that I am quite within my rights . . . .

Thinking, however, that you may have a little difficulty with your printer, and that the settlement may require some time, and it is most important to you that your magazine come out without much delay, I should be very glad to pay for the extra work involved, temporarily, it being understood that money is refunded to me at your convenience. . . .

I am thinking a little bit of advertising my dogs in your columns, as just the dog to make a companion to poets and other literary workers. Will you be so kind as to send your charges for advertising, per page? . . .

Harriet Monroe to Amy Lowell   [telegram] 10 April 1914

APRIL NUMBER IS MOSTLY DISTRIBUTED WILL INSERT CORRECTION IN THOSE LEFT NO ONE HERE CAN SEE ANY VULGAR MEANING MERELY MANIFEST ERROR WILL INFORM YOU OF DETAILS OF PLAN LATER

In May, H.M. also ran an apology and reprinted the first pages of the poem, advising readers to substitute them for the misprinted leaf. All told, they exchanged a dozen letters, calls, and telegrams over the misprint.

Amy Lowell to Harriet Monroe   Brookline, Mass., 22 May 1914

My dear Harriet,

. . . I am having a rather humorous time here, with some disagreeable elements in it. Boston is certainly an almost impossible place to work in, owing to the narrow-mindedness, unimaginativeness, and ignorance of practically everybody. They have undertaken to consider my "Forsaken" as fearfully exciting and irreligious, not to say sacrilegious, and it is supposed to attack the doctrine of the Immaculate Conception. Why such an attack in the mouth of a peasant woman should disturb them I cannot understand, but apparently it does. Also how it happens that in this Unitarian community so many people are found to believe in the Immaculate Conception I cannot conceive, but the fact remains the same, that people are buying the April number like mad, in order to read that poem and be horrified, shocked . . . .

2. From Imagism to "Amygisme"

Cheered by her stately progress in England in 1913, Lowell made another trip the following summer. But now circumstances were greatly altered in London. Pound was busy with a new "movement," Vorticism. In his letter to Monroe in August 1913, Fletcher had objected to the static quality of Imagism and pointed out the difficulty of applying Imagist principles to longer works. Pound apparently had come to the same conclusions. Using a confusing mixture of ideas about energy and theories from Cubism and Futurism, he proposed the "vortex" as a solution. In the *Fortnightly* for September 1914, Pound wrote that the Vorticist used the image "to record the precise instant when a thing outward and objective transforms itself, or darts into a thing inward and subjective." "It is a radiant node or cluster . . . a VORTEX, from which, and through which, and into which, ideas are constantly rushing."

What exactly he meant by this is hard to tell. In any case, Vorticism was very short lived, though it did produce the radically bombastic *Blast*—or BLAST, as proclaimed in huge letters on its lurid cover. The magazine, little noted at the time but much remarked on since in literary histories, was edited by Pound and Wyndham Lewis, with contributions by Hueffer, the novelist Rebecca West, and E.P.'s favorite sculptors, Henri Gaudier-Brzeska and Jacob Epstein. The few who saw the two issues in June 1914 and July 1915 were confused by the strange typography or put off by the anarchistic tone. Pound seems to have been trying too hard to be provocative in skewering the Establishment, and the result was more than he bargained for. The mainstream press virtually wrote him off.

Since Lowell had last seen him, Pound had also managed to offend many in his circle of friends. The disparate poets he had gathered as a matter of convenience under the name "Imagiste" felt uncomfortable with the label and were drifting away. Richard Aldington and H.D. had distanced themselves as early as the summer of 1913. Pound was quarreling with several of the others, and in September 1914 he told Monroe he was "no longer on intimate terms" even with Hueffer.

In February 1914, Pound had gathered "his" group into an anthology, *Des Imagistes*. To Monroe's great irritation, although two-thirds of the poems first appeared in *Poetry*, Pound didn't give it credit in either the English edition or the U.S. versions (as a book and as an issue of Kreymborg's journal the *Globe*). *Des Imagistes* received bad notices and didn't sell, either in England or in the States. Some who bought it at the Poetry Bookshop demanded their money back. Aldington wrote H.M. on 25 May: "The Morning Post, The Westminster Gazette, and the New Weekly all had long reviews. The Evening Standard was short and sweet:- 'Affectation is the note of this book from the title to F.M.H.'s poem in Greek characters at the end; some of the poems are not without merit; the book is sixty pages long, we think it sixty pages too many.' "

Such was the poisonous atmosphere when Lowell arrived in London, and perhaps she sensed the climate was right for a change, if not a coup. Lowell was invited to a celebration for *Blast*, and reciprocated with her own dinner party a few days later. Ezra and Dorothy Pound, H.D. and Aldington, F. S. Flint, Allen Upward, and Fletcher were invited, and were later joined by D. H. Lawrence, who announced that war was imminent. At the moment, however, a literary battle was brewing. After dinner, Upward, in an effort to discomfit Lowell's Boston-Puritan sensibilities, declaimed her poem "The Bath." Then Pound came in with a tub, placed it before the author, and declared *Les Imagistes* would now be *Les Nagistes*.

Writing to H.M. shortly afterward, Lowell neglected to mention this awkward incident, but did suggest reasons for Pound's unexpected hostility: "Ezra is very unhappy because he is so unsuccessful." After both his anthology and *Blast* fizzled, Pound's "movement" seemed to be "petering out." Then Pound proposed starting yet another journal, with backing from Amy, who was not about to put up $5,000 and allow Ezra to edit it "his way." She had other plans: assembling a new, improved Imagist anthology. Unlike Pound's collection, Amy's would have no controlling editor; the contents would be selected by the poets themselves. After *Some Imagist Poets* came out in March 1915, Aldington wrote Monroe to explain how it was compiled, and to assure her Pound would be most welcome in the next anthology, "provided he can satisfy our standard of work and will submit himself to the conditions we have imposed upon ourselves."

Pound had no intention of "submitting" to Lowell. Or to Aldington, for that matter, since he felt R.A., in the *Egoist* and in the Preface to *Some Imagist Poets*, had already watered down the stringent standards of the original Imagist doctrine: "To use absolutely no word that did not contribute to the presentation." E.P. wrote H.M. in disgust on 5 January 1915: "A.L. comes over here, gets kudos out of association. She returns and wants to weaken the whole use of the term imagist, by making it mean *any* writing of vers libre." He elaborated on 31 January: "If I had acceded to A.L.'s proposal to turn 'Imagism' into a democratic bear-garden, I should have undone what little good I had managed to do by setting up a critical standard." "Imagisme consists in presentation of the Image," he reminded H.M., "it certainly does not consist in talking about abstractions like 'Finite infinity'." This vulgarization Pound dubbed and dismissed as "Amygisme."

To his chagrin, "Amy's" anthology was a bestseller. Lowell promoted it with gusto on extensive reading tours, and *Some Imagist Poets* went into two more editions, in 1916 and 1917. In 1917, Lowell also published *Tendencies in Modern American Poetry*, in which she further diluted the meaning of Imagism. In the meantime, Pound had fallen upon hard times, because of the war and his restricted access to publications. He also grew ever more isolated after Aldington, Hueffer, and Hulme went off to the trenches.

Lowell used all her wiles to try to get a favorable review of *Some Imagist Poets* in *Poetry*. Even by Amy's standards, her letters to the Editor are remarkable performances in wheedling and calculated adulation, culminating in her letter of 18 April 1915. But Lowell's tactics backfired. For all her praise of the magazine, in the anthology itself she didn't give credit to Pound or to *Poetry*—always a big mistake. In reviewing the book in June 1915, Monroe not only corrected these omissions, but compared A.L. unfavorably with H.D. and E.P. Miss Lowell was not amused, and wrote Miss Monroe on 23 June: "Would it have been disloyal to Ezra . . . had you confined your remarks to the things which were in the book . . . ?" H.M. would have none of it, and pointed out on 1 July: "Of course, as your preface did not speak of us, we had to make some claim."

In *Tendencies in Modern American Poetry*, Lowell again left Pound out of the story of Imagism. Monroe explained this omission in *A Poet's Life* as "a 'Hamlet-without-Hamlet' complex caused manifestly by her quarrel with the founder of the group who had personally initiated her in its tenets." Reviewing the book in December 1917, H.M. took Lowell to task for her distortions and omissions, particularly of Lindsay, Stevens, Williams, and Eliot. Zeroing in on Lowell's biases, she found: "Miss Lowell is caught unaware by her Puritan inheritance—we have once more orthodoxy and heresy, once more a laying-down of the law. But the trouble is, the law won't stay laid."

Edgar Lee Masters was greatly offended by Lowell's assertions about his family, and wrote H.M. that Amy was "the tremendous Amazon who for the time being is rampaging through the flower gardens of America." He noted Lowell's hypocrisy: while she praised them in print, in private she disparaged Frost as "a hay-seed" and called Sandburg "just a cobbler."

In her letters to Monroe during this period, Lowell had many unkind (but true) things to say about Pound, too. In expressing her ire to H.M., Lowell said she wanted to protect her. Pound was outraged when an ad for Lowell's *Sword Blades and Poppy Seed* in the October 1914 issue of *Poetry* declared her to be "The foremost member of the 'Imagists.' " He wrote a scathing attack on Lowell and her (and Monroe's) publisher, Macmillan, which Aldington refused to print in the *Egoist*. In January 1915, Lowell warned H.M. that Ezra had written the possibly libelous piece, "dragging you and me into it." She continued her case against him by saying *Poetry* had suffered by championing Pound, and voiced her suspicion that he had tricked Monroe to get the money from Yeats's prize in 1913. "I only wanted to show you what kind of person he is," she wrote.

H.M. continued to stand by E.P., and to resist Amy's efforts at preferment. Alice Henderson took a very dim view of Lowell's machinations. After W. S. Braithwaite made snide remarks about Sandburg, Pound, and *Poetry* in the Boston *Transcript*, A.C.H. wrote H.M. 1 December 1916, trying in her own way to "protect" her:

> Braithwaite is [Lowell's] tool. Amy can't dictate to *Poetry*. Amy will raise herself by any means, whether it is a rotten prop like B. or a sound prop like Pound or Fletcher; and once up she will kick the prop aside. I can't help but suspect Amy of being secretly pleased by having it stated that the radical influence of *Poetry* has waned. She could never bear to have Boston's supremacy supplanted by Chicago.

Alice's suspicions about Amy's duplicity and self-serving motives are amply confirmed in Lowell's other correspondence. On 8 February 1916, for example, A.L. wrote to H.D. that she was "not altogether pleased with [H.M.'s] attitude just now," since it reflected Pound's ideas. She also told H.D. she was making another trip to Chicago in hopes of "managing" Harriet. Then, on 28 June 1916, she advised Aldington to send his work to Braithwaite, before submitting it to *Poetry*, since his *Poetry Review* had much larger sales. On 3 February 1920, she wrote H.D. that *Poetry* had "no influence whatever outside of a small group." She said she found it "exceedingly funny" that Monroe could run her magazine for six years without increasing its circulation, and added: "It would horrify her if she knew this was the case, but it is, and it is surprising and shows Harriet's glorious ineptness better than anything else could possibly do."

After 1917, by which time Lowell had found fame and several other outlets more receptive to her work, her correspondence with Monroe decreased. When the third *Imagist* anthology came out early in 1918, Alice told Harriet quite bluntly: "There is only one way to handle Amy, and that is with a pair of tongs." Monroe preferred to treat Lowell with kid gloves, though her grip was firm. In contrast to the Editor's characteristic forthrightness, Lowell's letters appear all the more devious, though still engrossing, as they offer an extensive catalogue of maneuvers a maniacally ambitious author was willing to deploy to further a career.

Amy Lowell to Harriet Monroe   *The Berkeley Hotel, London,*
20 July 1914

Dear Harriet,

. . . I have a lot to say to you about the situation here, but it is a little difficult to write it. I don't want to tell tales out of school, but it does seem as though you ought to know how things stand. I find our little group more or less disintegrated and broken up. Violent jealousy has broken out, whether because of the "Imagiste Anthology" and its reviews, I cannot say. Poor old Ezra has got himself into a most silly movement [Vorticism], of which "Blast" is the organ. I will send you a copy tomorrow. He is annoyed with me because I will not finance a review for him to run. My feeling is that his slanging of the public, and his indecent poems, have flattened out his reputation, even Hueffer tells me that Ezra is very unhappy because he is so unsuccessful. The opinion of everyone is that he has nothing more to say. This would tally with your remarks to me about the last batch of his poems. Poor old Ezra, I am awfully sorry for him, but he is like a prickly pear to touch. My impression is that Hueffer is also in a gloomy way. . . .

The craze for advertisement has swept Ezra off his feet. His Imagiste movement is petering out because of the lack of vigor in his poets, and the complete indifference of the public. Only one hundred copies of the "Imagiste" Anthology have been sold in England! Much less than in America. It seems now as though it were simply a flair of young men with nothing more in them. Barring Fletcher who still promises, and possibly the Aldingtons, she in her beautiful, delicate tenuousness, and he rather as a good, adequate prose writer, I think there does not seem much to look for. The jealousy and the mercenary point of view, disgust me rather. And I am thankful that I live in America where the poets seem to be generous and large minded, even if not up to this group technically. . . .

Amy Lowell to Harriet Monroe   Brookline, Mass., 10 September 1914

Dear Harriet:

I enclose a check for $60 to pay for my advertisement [for her dogs] in your magazine. It brought me one answer which did not materialize, so that it hardly seems worth while to pursue advertising. . . .

I enclose a poem on the war ["The Allies"] which I wrote while I was in London. I do not include it in the war contest poems, because I know that it has no chance whatever of getting a prize. . . . I feel certain that your vaunted democracy is not so democratic as to give me a prize if you thought I did not need it, when other more deserving people would lose thereby. This is not democracy, but it is what most people call democracy, and I fear it is your kind. Therefore I spare you the horrid necessity of a choice. . . .

Please let me hear from you as soon as possible about the article ["Nationalism in Art," printed in the October issue]. By the way, have you heard from Richard Aldington about the new "Imagiste Anthology" which we are bringing out, and which we are to bring out every year for five years? Ezra has left us, or we have left him for the moment. All the rest of us are in it, and it is only Ezra's intense desire to always run everything entirely himself which has caused him to leave our quite democratic association. . . .

Aldington had written H.M. on 16 August about the anthology, adding that *Poetry and Drama* would probably cease. On 12 September he advised: "Try and get Amy Lowell's war-poem 'The Allies'; it is extraordinarily good, beats everything else I've seen to smithers."

Harriet Monroe to Amy Lowell   12 September 1914

Dear Amy:

It's a relief to know you are home again—I hope you didn't have to come in the steerage! . . .

Your letter from London was very exciting—how I would like to talk with you! What's the trouble between Ezra and the other Imagistes?—now that you can dictate, can't you tell me all about it? Or is it just jealousy and bitterness, with no definite cause? The war should help them to kiss and make up—times are hard enough for poets without quarrels. You say "Now is emphatically your chance," yet our subscribers increased less that 10% between Aug. 1, 1913 and 1914, and now, at the beginning of the third year, the renewals come in too slowly, and already we have spent $1500 of our fund, and paid for only two numbers besides a mill-run of paper, enough for about ten. Our problem is—how can we get 10,000 subscribers or more when we can't spend money for ads?

Well, anyway, a thousand thanks for your hundred, which your brother forwarded, and for this $60 for the advertising—I am sorry it brought no returns. . . .

H.M. enclosed her annual report, indicating *Poetry* now had 1,102 paid subscriptions, about three-fourths of them renewals; advertising rose, but bookstand sales had "hardly increased."

Amy Lowell to Harriet Monroe   *Brookline, Mass.,*
                                                  15 September 1914

My dear Harriet:

. . . I am awfully sorry you do not get "The Allies." Richard Aldington says it grows on him with every reading, so I hope that it will on you. . . . [A] man, a great lover of poetry, to whom I read it on the steamer, burst into tears on hearing it. He told me that even if I had never written anything but that poem, my reputation would be made. . . .

I want to ask you what you think of "The Little Review." I am afraid it strikes me as rather amateurish and effervescent, but the Editor [Margaret Anderson] is so fearfully enthusiastic about me that I have given her some things of mine. However, I am afraid her magazine does not stand much chance of making any real place for itself.

You ask about the quarrel between Ezra and the rest of us. It is not a quarrel now, it is a schism. It is a very long story, and I do not know quite how to tell you all of it by letter.

Do you remember, Ezra was very anxious for me to run an international review, something on the lines of the "Mércure de France?" He came to me at once as soon as I got to London, and it then transpired that he expected to become editor of said "review" with a salary. I was to guarantee all the money, and put in what I pleased, and he was to run the magazine his way. We talked over the cost of expenses, and we both thought that $5,000 a year was the least that such a magazine could be run on. As I have not $5,000 a year that I can afford to put into it, I based my refusal upon that fact, and it was most unfortunate that Ezra apparently did not believe it. Like many people of no incomes, Ezra does not know the difference between thousands and millions, and thinks that any one who knows where to look for next week's dinners, is a millionaire, and therefore lost his temper with me completely, although he never told me why; and he accused me of being unwilling to give any money toward art.

In thinking over what I could do to help the poets less fortunate than myself, and also to help myself in somewhat the same manner that a Review would do, it seemed to me that to re-publish the "Imagiste Anthology" with the same group of people, year after year, for a period of five years, would enable us, by constant iteration, to make some impression upon the reading public. . . . I mentioned this first to the Aldingtons because I saw them first after I conceived the idea. I suggested that the last little book was too monotonous, and too undemocratic, in that certain poets were allowed much more space than others, and I suggested that in the "New Anthology" we should allow approximately the same space to each poet, and that we should get a publisher of reputable standing, and I offered, in case we could not get any publisher to take the risk of the volume itself, to pay for its publication.

The Aldingtons were exceedingly enthusiastic over the idea, as have been the other poets we have asked to join us. Only Ezra was annoyed. He accused me of trying to make myself editor instead of him, and finally tried a little blackmail by telling me that he would only join us on condition that I would pledge myself to give $200 a year to some indigent poet. I told him that the $200 a year might be managed should any one in stress of circumstances need such a sum, but that I absolutely refused to be intimidated into doing anything, or to buy his poems at the expense of my self-respect. . . .

He was perfectly furious for some time, and sent for the Aldingtons, and told them they must choose between him and me, which was awful for them, as he is a very old friend, and has done much for them, and I was only a new friend. They behaved with the utmost honour in the matter. They told Ezra it was not a question of me at all, but a question of the principle, that they felt it only fair to let the poets choose their own contributions, and to give each poet an equal space. He then tried to bribe them, by asking them to get up an anthology with him and leave me out. This they absolutely refused to do.

We had many consultations on the subject, in which Flint, Lawrence, and Ford Maffox [sic] Hueffer joined us, and we all agreed that Ezra could not expect to run us all his own way forever, and that if he chose to separate himself from us, we should be obliged, although most regretfully, to let him. . . .

The truth is, Ezra has ducked and draked his reputation with his last work. His poetry is too indecent to be poetical, and even when it is not indecent, it is too often merely vituperative. Please do not tell any one that I said so, but I think that he is in a very bad way as far as his work is concerned. Mr. Prothero, the editor of "The Quarterly," who has just accepted from him some of the Fenellosa [sic] manuscript, told me that the trouble with Ezra was that he had nothing to say, and I am afraid that is really true. "Blast" will give you a good idea of what Ezra has been obliged to descend to in order to keep his name before the public, and he admitted in a speech at the Imagiste Dinner, that it was nothing but advertising.

He looks very ill, and has a bad cough, and I am afraid that he is tuberculous. It has even been hinted that this may have attacked his brain. No one knows anything about it, and this is merely surmise. The fact remains that where his work is concerned he is failing every day, and except for "Poetry" and "The Egoist" there are no magazines that will take his poetry, if I except an occasional contribution to "Poetry and Drama," and he has only sold two prose articles this year. . . .

Ezra has always thought of life as a grand game of bluff. He never has learned the wisdom of Lincoln's famous adage about not being able to fool all the people all the time. Advertising is all very well but one must have some goods to deliver, and the goods must be up to the advertising of them. Now that Ezra has ceased to be a youthful phenomenon he must take his place in the steady march by which young men of talent gain to a real reputation, and he finds himself falling back at every step, and this naturally makes him exceedingly bitter. He is very brilliant, but he does not work enough, and his work lacks the quality of soul, which, I am more and more fain to believe, no great work can ever be without. At any rate, that is the situation about the Imagistes. It is not a quarrel, in one sense it never was. I have spared no efforts to keep them all on good terms with each other, even offering to leave "the anthology" myself, if it would heal the breach. Ezra and his wife dined with me a few days before I left, and we had a very pleasant and perfectly amicable evening, and it would not surprise me if he came into one of our Anthologies later on, but of course, I have not suggested this possibility to him. . . .

. . . Is there any truth in the fact which Ezra told me, that you are no longer Art Editor of "The Tribune"? . . .

The Preface to *Some Imagist Poets* (1915) stated: "Differences of taste and judgment . . . have arisen among the contributors to [*Des Imagistes*]; growing tendencies are forcing them along different paths."

Harriet Monroe to Amy Lowell   *Brookline, Mass.,*
                                                  23 September 1914

Dear Amy:

No doubt I am an idiot to return this ["The Bombardment"], but as I can't agree with Aldington and the rest it would be mere affectation for me to pretend to. And Alice is with me this time. . . .

P.S. You ask about the *Little Review*. It is amateurish, I suppose, but that is better than the dull professional tone of—*The Dial*, for instance. I like Margaret Anderson; she is a fine courageous spirit. I don't know what her financial backing is, or how long she can run, but I, for one, wish her paper long life. . . .

Yes, it is true that I am no longer on *The Tribune*, and that I greatly miss the salary. Between you and me, I was fired, the reason being, quite frankly, that the art department had brought no advertising and therefore did not pay.

H.M. drew no salary from *Poetry* until she left the *Tribune*; thereafter she allowed herself $50 a month, later $75, and finally $100.

Amy Lowell to Harriet Monroe   *Brookline, Mass., 15 October 1914*

My dear Harriet:

You surprise and distress me very much by refusing to take "The Bombardment," particularly at this time when the fall of Antwerp makes it so very apposite. . . . I was on the point of sending them ["The Bombardment" and "The Allies"] to Margaret Anderson, who has so kind an idea of my merits as never to refuse what I send her, when your letter and telegram came, and my loyalty to "Poetry" made me decide to give you the preference.

A disagreeable thought has come into my mind, and I think it always better to say things right out when you feel them, so you will pardon me if I tell you that I fear it is because of the number of pages which the two poems would take, and the consequent size of the check which you would have to pay me, which has determined your decision. I need not point out to you how manifestly unfair such a course would be, nor it seems to me, should I be obliged to suggest that I have already paid to your magazine in gifts and advertisements more than I have ever earned from it.

Surely a labourer is worthy of his hire. It may be a sad fact that I have so much, and others whom you think as worthy, so little. Life is not fair, and neither are editors. Yours will not be the first magazine which has tried to dock my pay. . . .

On 16 October, H.M. informed A.L. that no poet had more than one poem in the War issue. On 18 October, H.M. wrote: "In response to your wish we are using *Bombardment* instead of *Allies.*" H.M.'s sister Lucy stayed with A.L. in September; on her return, she urged H.M. to keep "The Bombardment."

Harriet Monroe to Amy Lowell   18 October 1914

Dear Amy:

. . . I have not answered your letter of the 15th. Your "disagreeable thought" was unjust—I have given you the same rates and treatment as everybody else, except that I have taken advantage of your offer to contribute prose for nothing. Indeed, last April I sent you full page rates, when usually, in the case of so long a group, a considerable reduction is made. From this time, however, the rates will have to be reduced from $10 to $8 a page in order to make ends meet; and we are not giving this year the $250 [Guarantors'] prize which went last year to Yeats— although it makes my heart ache to drop it—because we simply don't dare in the face of the hard times. . . .

No doubt you have your troubles in securing just treatment. But you need not fear any unfair discrimination from me.

Yours affectionately, / Harriet Monroe

Amy Lowell to Harriet Monroe   Brookline, Mass., 2 November 1914

My dear Harriet:

. . . I have been having an awful time with Ezra on account of a serious blunder of Macmillan's in the advertisement of my book. As soon as I saw it I knew what trouble it would cause and cabled my regrets, but Ezra has taken it as a personal insult and has written a most abominable letter to Macmillan and a most disagreeable one to me. . . .

Amy Lowell to Harriet Monroe   Brookline, Mass., 5 November 1914

My dear Harriet:

. . . I am very much afraid that Ezra may try his best to injure me owing to his fury at that unfortunate advertisement. It would therefore be a great kindness to me if you could review my book somewhat at length as all his friends in England see "Poetry" and a few nice words will do a great deal toward allaying the impression which he is trying to give. Not only do his letters to me show his state of mind, but Richard Aldington writes me that he is being very nasty.

Funnily enough I do not feel angry with him, merely very sad and rather disillusioned. I thought him a different man. But I do want to obviate as much as possible the effects of his venomous pen and his still

more venomous tongue on my poor little book. I am unpopular
enough and misunderstood enough by the poets of other schools with-
out having this one turn and rend me. . . .

In her December review of A.L.'s *Sword Blades and Poppy Seed*, H.M. wrote: "[O]ne
must admire her learning and artistry. She is a good workman, even though at times
the mere workmanship is a bit too apparent." A.L. wrote 9 December: "I am kind of
sorry that you put in that about learning, as above all things I don't want people to
get into their heads that I am academic and dry."

Amy Lowell to Harriet Monroe   Brookline, Mass., 15 January 1915

Dear Harriet,

I think you ought to know that Ezra has just written a long libelous
article for "The Egoist" on Macmillan's, dragging you and me into it.
Richard Aldington had to tell the head editor, Miss Weaver, that he
would resign his editorship if it appeared. So it was suppressed. Richard
says that he has now sent it to Macmillan's, and I am warning them
about it. That he should have done such a thing to you, who have
shown him nothing but kindness is outrageous. . . . I felt you ought to
know this, as "Poetry" has championed him so much. . . .

H.M. replied 20 January 1915 that she couldn't "do anything about the matter with-
out seeing the article." She also told A.L. that R.A. had given Monroe's new collec-
tion, *You and I*, a "slam" in the *Egoist*, and said: "If we ran our review from such a
narrow point of view, I wonder what some of the poets would think."

Amy Lowell to Harriet Monroe   Brookline, Mass., 23 January 1915

Dear Harriet:

I sent you a telegram yesterday, because I thought it only fair to
Richard Aldington to disabuse your mind of his ever having done any-
thing so underhand as to send Ezra's article to Macmillan. It was Ezra
himself, if it was ever done, for it may have been a huge bluff to
frighten Richard Aldington . . . .

Of course I never expected you to do anything about the article, and
it would be the greatest mistake in the world for you to quarrel with
Ezra and lose either his contributions, his contributors, or his interest. I
merely wanted to warn you to keep your eyes open. You remember he
"did" you a year ago about the prize, and got the money himself by
what I cannot help thinking was a trick; and I only wanted to show
you what kind of person he is and that, while keeping on good terms
with him professionally, you should be always on the lookout to be sure
that he is not up to something prejudicial to your interests. But, as I said

before, I ought not to have done it at all. You naturally put it down to my jealousy, which I assure you it is not. . . .

H.M. decided not to include this information in *A Poet's Life*; in the margin, she notes: "biog?—probably not". Writing to A.L. 25 January, she said she doubted E.P. sent the letter to Macmillan.

Amy Lowell to Harriet Monroe [telegram] 23 February 1915

. . . HAVE DONE EVERYTHING POSSIBLE TO SHOW MY LOYALTY AND APPRECIATION OF POETRY AND EXCEPT FOR REVIEWS OF MY BOOKS NO PLEASANT ENCOURAGING WORD ABOUT ME HAS EVER BEEN PRINTED IN ITS PAGES WHILE MANY OTHER PEOPLE ARE CONSTANTLY BOOKED   MUST SAY I AM DISTINCTLY HURT ABOUT THIS   YOU ARE ALWAYS WRITING AND HELPING EZRA   NOW THAT AM HAVING A HARD TIME WITH HIM WOULD IT NOT BE NEUTRAL AND LOYAL TO HELP ME TOO?   DID YOU SEE THE BOMBARDMENT WAS QUOTED IN LONDON SUNDAY PAPER WITH A NOTE SAYING PROBABLY BEST THING YET WRITTEN ABOUT WAR MENTIONING YOU AS HAVING PUBLISHED IT

Harriet Monroe to Amy Lowell 23 February 1915

My dear Amy:

. . . I am surprised that you feel hurt, or that you can possibly think *Poetry* has done more for anyone than for you. Except for E.P., who was on the staff from the first, I fail to see it. . . .

I find that you have had fifteen pages of verse in *Poetry*, which is more than I have had, or anyone except Yeats, Tagore, E.P. and Lindsay. And you have been in three times, which is more than almost anyone, while only two or three persons have appeared four times. And your appearance next month will put you near the head of the column. So you see you have no reason to feel that we are not backing you to the best of our ability. . . .

Actually, at this point A.L. had poems printed in *Poetry* four times, for a total of 19 pages; Lindsay had 40 pages, Yeats 28. In a telegram to H.M. the same day, A.L. apologized "if I seemed a little sore."

Amy Lowell to Harriet Monroe Brookline, Mass., 18 April 1915

Dear Harriet,

I am delighted with what you have done for me in the April number. Many thanks! Fletcher's article is certainly most handsome, and I think my poems look very well. It is a good number. Rupert Brooke's sonnets are high-minded, and serious, and thoroughly English. I think the dignity and sorrow of a real experience may make an excellent poet of him. Technique he always had, but he needed reality. . . .

I am sending you a presentation copy of our Anthology. . . . In reviewing it, please don't lay stress on the schism with Ezra. I don't want to make the row important. Rows are a mistake, and their perpetuation shall be none of my doing. Do you know, my Dear, I have had occasion to go over all the numbers of "Poetry" since its beginning, in connection with a talk on "The New Manner in Modern Poetry" I gave at the [New York] "Round Table Club," and I was immensely struck by the fact that there is not a single poet of distinction among the younger generation whom you have not printed. Go on, my Child, never mind any of us when we criticise. Taken in its entirety your review is a magnificent achievement. And the impartiality with which you represent all schools is fine. Now I have a suggestion to make. You will remember that you still have six little poems of mine, and that you were going to lead off with me sometime. Now those six are not enough, either in size or importance to go alone. Will you take "Lead Soldiers" to precede them? It is the best thing I have done, I am sure. . . .

Brooke died on 23 April. In "Miss Lowell's Discovery: Polyphonic Prose" (April 1915), Fletcher claimed Lowell's "discovery" was as important to poetry as the discovery of radium was to science. "Lead Soldiers" headed the group, which led off the September issue.

Amy Lowell to Harriet Monroe   *Brookline, Mass., 23 June 1915*

Dear Harriet:

. . . It seems to me that in your review [of *Some Imagist Poets*, June 1915] you were a little unkind to us. You laid a great deal of stress upon the fact that we did not acknowledge our debt to you. You referred constantly to the people who are not in the Anthology. Would it have been disloyal to Ezra, and would not it have been graceful to me, had you confined your remarks to the things which were in the book and not referred to so many of the things which were not? It seems to me that my constant loyalty to you, my sincere interest in the magazine, and my desire to always identify myself with it as much as possible, might have led you to assume the dignified attitude of silence, which we have taken, in regard to our schism with Ezra. If I chose to come out with the whole story, Ezra would not be left in a very pleasant position. . . . How loyal I am to you, Harriet, you will never know. I wrote and remonstrated with Richard for his method of reviewing your book and, although I am not my brother's keeper, I have done my best. Don't you want to cease referring to the break between Ezra and the rest of us? If I am willing to be silent, you, as Ezra's friend, should be thankful.

Affectionately yours, / Amy Lowell

Amy Lowell to Harriet Monroe   *Brookline, Mass., 15 May 1916*

Dear Harriet:

. . . I am sending you the new "Imagist Anthology." I suppose you will get an official copy from the publishers, but this is a personal copy. Do review it yourself. I would much rather hear what you have to say about it than what anybody else, whom you might ask to do it, would say. You will see that we have given you a handsome little tribute in the "Acknowledgements", which I had printed in large print on purpose, to make it more noticeable. You see, it is tit for tat, my dear. But titting without tatting is no fun. . . .

The acknowledgement reads: "To *Poetry* belongs the credit of having introduced Imagism to the world; it seems fitting, therefore, that the authors should record their thanks in this place for the constant interest and encouragement shown them by its editor, Miss Harriet Monroe."

Alice Corbin Henderson to Harriet Monroe   *Santa Fe,*
8 October 1916

Dear H.M.

A thought has struck me: you say *nothing* in regard to the nuptials of J. G. Fletcher. Now is it possible that he went and got himself clandestinely married to Amy Lowell—? I say *clandestinely*—for otherwise the papers would have been full of it— . . . One can hardly imagine Amy doing anything that she would not make copy of—she doesn't even take a bath without advertising it— But if anything of the sort has happened, of course we shall know ALL about it in time. And so will the Associated News and the United Press—the Kaiser and the Tsar—. . .

Edgar Lee Masters to Harriet Monroe   *Chicago, 3 December 1917*

Dear Miss Monroe:

I feel impelled to write you this letter because of the very generous friendship which you maintain for me against the critics, including the tremendous Amazon who for the time being is rampaging through the flower gardens of America. In reading your criticism of A. Lowell's book [*Tendencies in Modern American Poetry*, reviewed in December], I somehow get the impression that you did not feel free to go at the book as thoroughly and critically as you inwardly desired to. . . . I cannot detach the book from the woman, or from what she has said to me in conversation respecting some of the subjects discussed. For example, I hardly know how to take her estimate of Frost, namely that he is an immortal equal to Burns and Synge, in view of her remark to me that he was "just a hay-seed"; nor do I know what to make of her eulogy of Sandburg as a lyricist when I remember that she said Sandburg was "just a cobbler."

My explanation of her leaving out Lindsay . . . is this: that she really wished to leave out both Sandburg and Lindsay but could not ignore them both without giving you offense. She desired to retain your friendship and the favor of your magazine both for this book and for her future and past work . . . she knew [her opinions] would pass where she hopes the book will circulate; namely, the women's clubs and half literary circles where they take their opinions second-hand, sexology included. . . .

In a personal letter to H.M. 27 October 1917, A.C.H. wrote: "Amy sent me Six Amur'k'n Potes. What can one do about such a thing? Good in spots, the whole tone of it is unspeakably banal!—In the world of poetry, Amy has no idea how middle-class she is!—". When H.M. objected, on proofs, to the harshness of A.C.H.'s review, "Of Puritans, Philistines and Pessimists" (July 1918), A.C.H. replied 19 May: "Honestly, why should there be this 'Hands-off' attitude about Amy? She ain't the Kaiser—even if she is a relative of James Russell, sister of the President of Harvard, etc. etc. . . . I'm not a-skeered of Amy!"

Amy Lowell to Harriet Monroe   Brookline, Mass., 9 December 1919

Dear Harriet:

I have just received a letter from Grace Conkling telling me that you have refused to publish the review which she wrote of my book, "Pictures of the Floating World." She says quite frankly that it is evident that you will publish nothing that is complimentary to me . . . . As my reputation grows, you become more denunciatory. . . .

This is not the first time that my attention has been called to your refusal of things written in my favour. You have told me of several yourself. I never answer criticisms, but surely an editor of a magazine should be above party politics and should permit an author the expression of both sides of any question. It is true that your paper has a very small circulation and practically no influence, as, in spite of your constant pronouncements in the papers, you know very well. What I object to, therefore, is not any harm it may do me personally, because that is impossible, but to the unfairness of the constant cosseting of poets you happen to like, and the complete suppression of everything in my favour. . . .

You owe it to me to express a different opinion from the one you have been giving lately *ad nauseam.* You have allowed Kreymborg to pitch into me, you have allowed Alice Henderson to pitch into me in no unmeasured terms, but you will allow no one to say a word in my favour....

In his July 1918 review of *The New Poetry,* Kreymborg wrote: "The Lowell following is to me one of the mysteries of this planet: she is facile, prolific, a reader of good books, a genius as a propagandist, and a scintillating lady; but she has contributed absolutely nothing which is new to poetry."

Harriet Monroe to Amy Lowell   *15 December 1919*

My dear Amy:

I return from Moline and find your surprising letter. I ought not to be obliged to tell you that I returned Mrs. Conkling's review not because of the opinions it expressed but because of its utterly childish way of expressing them....

However, I have arranged for a review of your book by a poet who likes it and thinks it contains your best work, and whose word will count more and go further, I fancy, than Mrs. Conkling's. At any rate, the review will be more adult.... I need not say that I shall not mention your letter to this reviewer, who took your book some time ago.

Of course I think *Poetry* has treated you fairly, but discussion would lead nowhere. I am sorry you don't think so.

Yours faithfully, / Harriet Monroe

Marjorie Allen Seiffert's review of *Pictures of the Floating World* (March 1920) was mostly favorable. She found description was A.L.'s forte, but added: "She glitters, splashes, dazzles, assumes veils of mist . . . yet what, after all, do we know of 'the real' Amy Lowell? Is there one?"

CHAPTER VIII

Poetry on the Ascendant, Pound in Decline

1. Anni Mirabiles: 1914–1915

While Lowell kept up her barrages from Brookline, Pound continued his lectures from London. He was still quick to point out the errors of Monroe's ways, although now his tone was, for him, quite civil. As usual, he prodded H.M. to get his authors into print faster, and in March 1914 he repeated a frequent theme: "Hang it all the only way to sell a specialized magazine like Poetry is to pack it full FULL of good stuff."

In fact, H.M.'s in-basket was filling quite nicely with "good stuff." While they continued to differ, both could truthfully say that the results of their collaboration were worth their efforts. Month after month in 1914 and 1915 Poetry presented strong work, a stream of "discoveries"— Monroe's and Pound's—representing virtually every significant poet or trend. The Editor never surpassed the record of those glory days.

Turning the pages of Volumes IV through VIII, one finds these highlights in 1914: January, eight poems by D. H. Lawrence; February, Frost's "The Code—Heroics"; March, Sandburg's "Chicago Poems," Sara Teasdale's "Love Songs," and E. A. Robinson's "Eros Turannos"; a large group from Yeats in May; Hueffer's "On Heaven" in June; July, Lindsay's "Poems to be Chanted"; August, another large group by Pound and Amy Lowell's "The Coal Picker"; September, John Gould Fletcher's "The Blue Symphony"; October, Rupert Brooke's "Retrospect"; November, Wallace Stevens's first professional publication, "Phases"; and in December, another group by Lawrence. January 1915 presented translations of Rémy de Gourmont's "Epigrammes"; February, Lindsay's "The Chinese Nightingale"; March, another large group by Pound, including his rendition of Li Po's "Exile's Letter," and a group by H.D.; April, Rupert Brooke's "Nineteen-Fourteen."

May 1915 held a group of poems by Williams and the first appearances in America by Marianne Moore, including "That Harp You Play So Well," "To an Intra-Mural Rat," and "The Wizard in Words." June marked T. S. Eliot's first publication, "The Love Song of J. Alfred Prufrock." September had more work by Lowell and Conrad Aiken's "Discordants"; November, Frost's long poem "Snow" and six pieces by Williams; December, Isaac Rosenberg's poems from the battlefield, "Marching" and "Break of Day in the Trenches." Issue by issue, the back of the book was also distinguished by lively debates on competing theories and movements, strong critical pieces, and reviews of virtually all poetry books worthy of notice.

2. T. S. Eliot

T. S. Eliot: *Poetry* gave him his first publication in 1915.

From the day they met in 1914, Pound treated Eliot as *the* major new talent. In amazement, he wrote H.M. 30 September: "He has actually trained himself AND modernized himself ON HIS OWN." Eliot was then a doctoral student in philosophy at Harvard and had been studying in Germany. When war broke out, he was forced to London, where his Harvard friend Conrad Aiken had preceded him. Aiken had seen early drafts of Eliot's work, showed the revised version of "Prufrock" to Pound, and gave Eliot an introduction.

Over the next months, E.P. urged H.M. to print "Prufrock," but she hesitated. She didn't care for Eliot's generally morbid tone— her own temperament was far more optimistic—and felt that "Prufrock" seemed to "go off at the end." Pound himself admitted there were parts he did not find wholly satisfactory, but in his first letter of 31 January 1915, he testily replied to her reservations: "It is a portrait of failure, or of a character which fails, and it would be false art to make it end on a note of triumph."

Monroe was not the only one who had a less than enthusiastic response on first reading "Prufrock." Aiken had shown it to Harold Monro, the editor of *Poetry and Drama*, who threw it back at him saying it was "absolutely insane." Although in later years Pound asserted, repeatedly, he had to "hammer" the poem into *Poetry*, it appeared in June 1915,

about eight months after it arrived at the office: not an unusual interval,
particularly since H.M. had plenty of strong work in the "Accepted" files
awaiting publication. Even Yeats and Williams had work on hold for a
similar period or longer.

Response to "Prufrock" was negative, or at least puzzled. Louis Unter-
meyer wrote the Editor on 13 August:

> To come back to Eliot for a moment, I confess that his "Love Song"
> is the first piece of the English language that utterly stumped me. As a
> post-impression, the effect was that of the Muse in a psychopathic
> ward—drinking the stale dregs of revolt. The other Sunday night there
> was a group at the house—one of those not-too-'arts & crafty'
> mélanges—a few poets, a lawyer, a couple of musicians & one psycho-
> analyst. I read it to them quite seriously—& no one, not even James
> Oppenheim [poet and later editor of *Seven Arts*], who is the most seri-
> ous person in this thickly populated universe—no one could keep a
> straight face. No one, that is, except the psychoanalyst who said, "An
> extremely interesting case. I think a lot could be done for him. It's a
> muddled case of infantile repressions and inhibitions." Which, as you
> can imagine, did not clear the air to any perceptible degree. Well, I sup-
> pose since it takes all sorts of people to make a world, it takes all sorts of
> poems to make a magazine of poetry. As a varietist [sic] in the arts even
> an editor sometimes must wander from the sane & narrow paths into
> the dark alleys of the pathological. . . .

Conrad Aiken, never kindly disposed toward *Poetry*, wrote quickly to
claim major credit for "Prufrock." He had recently attacked the Imagists
in the *New Republic* and the *Poetry Journal* for their "super-refinement"
and lack of emotional force. H.M. responded with a defense of Imagist
methods in "Its Inner Meaning," in the September *Poetry*—an issue that
included a long poem by Aiken. H.M. pointed out that Aiken himself had
benefited from Imagism, judging by the improvements in his most recent
work, such as that in her pages. He immediately tried to set her straight,
at tedious length, on 4 September 1915. After protesting he had nothing
against experiments, he presented this as evidence:

> If proof is needed that I am not so provincial a Victorian as you say, I
> may add that I was indirectly, and largely, responsible for the publication
> of Eliot's "Love Song of J. Alfred Prufrock" in your June issue. That
> poem was written, if I remember rightly, nearly four years ago, and I
> had a copy of it from the first; and as Eliot himself was heartlessly indif-
> ferent to its fate, it was I who sought publication for it. Four years ago!

So you see, if I am suffering from a "culture" of radicalism—and I am sure you did not consider Eliot's poem precisely old-fashioned—I have been suffering from it rather longer than most of the Imagists.

Whatever the truth of the assertions that Monroe had to be prodded to print "Prufrock," the fact remains she *did* print it, and at a time when Eliot was still unknown and probably no other editor would have done so. She wanted to include the poem in her anthology, *The New Poetry*, but Eliot declined in a gracious letter, 7 June 1916:

> As for the Prufrock: you see, I shall probably have a small volume coming out just about the same time as your anthology, in the autumn, in New York. If it were much before or much after I should probably be quite glad to enter Prufrock in both, but it seems to me that to syn-chronise would be inadvisable. It is so much longer, and confessedly so much better, than anything else I have done, that I cannot afford (or so I think) to scatter my forces. If there is anything else that would do, I hope you will accept a substitute: the Portrait, or perhaps the Figlia che piange which I believe Pound has sent you. Will you forgive me?

When he put the book together, Eliot paid H.M. a compliment by titling it *Prufrock and Other Observations*, using the group title she supplied for his third appearance, in September 1916: "Conversation Galante," "La Figlia che Piange," "Mr. Apollinax," and "Morning at the Window." Unfortu-nately, Eliot misaddressed his proofs and the staff did not catch a most embarrassing error. Eliot wrote again on 7 September, when the issue was already off-press: "Many thanks for your kind letter. The title you have given will do excellently. The proof is alright except that I am T.S., not T.R. There is only one 'T.R.' [Teddy Roosevelt] I hope! . . . I am glad that you have taken the Portrait. All success to your anthology!"

Much more serious than the inadvertent misidentification of the author, however, was a change Monroe made to "Mr. Apollinax," without consulting Eliot. Apparently at the last moment, the Editor deleted a line containing the harmless word "foetus"—an unwise decision perhaps made in haste or panic, but one that had severe consequences. For her anthology, Eliot let H.M. reprint "Portrait of a Lady" (which Pound later regretted sending to *Others*). But he never contributed another poem to *Poetry*.

In the same issue, Monroe also made an unauthorized change to Pound's poem "Phyllidula," removing the word "bloody." She had already written E.P. on 14 May, objecting to various phrases in some of his recent pieces. He responded on 24 May: "Cut out any of my poems that would be likely to get you suppressed but don't make it into a flabby little Sunday school lot like the bunch in the November number. Now WHO could blush at Lesbia Illa??????? *WHO*???" Apparently Elkin Mathews was one who could, for he also excluded the poems H.M. rejected when he published *Lustra* in 1916.

In 1917, Dr. Williams likewise complained about the Editor's blue pencil. On 23 May, he requested: "In regard to the poem 'History' I wish you would delete the objectionable *words* replacing the letters of those words with full stop points." After much discussion, in May 1916 H.M. rejected Pound's "To a Friend Writing on Cabaret Dancers," a rather rambling affair containing the words "bitch" and "whore." On 5 June he wrote: "So long as you put the 'Cabaret' question on the grounds of expediency and the assininity [sic] of your guarantors . . . I suppose I must submit."

From today's vantage point, Monroe's qualms about vulgar but innocuous words may seem overcautious, even Victorian. But in 1914 the threat of censorship by the Post Office was quite serious. Magazines containing "obscene" material were impounded or confiscated—a fact H.M. discovered when an "ironically realistic detail" in John Russell McCarthy's "The Hero" in the War Issue (November 1914) "endangered the issue with the censor," as she recalled in *A Poet's Life*.

Pound could mock the putative Sunday-school sensibilities of Monroe's supporters; he didn't have to worry about legal and financial problems that might jeopardize the existence of the magazine. Perhaps Monroe did not realize how offensive her bowdlerizing was to authors. Certainly, editorial practices in her time were far more cavalier than today. But she did know very well that without the backing of the Guarantors *Poetry* would fold. Her budget was barely adequate to get out the monthly issues; she did not have pockets deep enough to carry on court battles or to withstand the financial pressures that mounting a defense of free speech would entail.

3. Schism and Shame

In several letters to Monroe, Amy Lowell provided her own reports on the "Status Rerum" in London during the summers of 1913 and 1914. The cordial relationship she established with Pound on her first trip soon deteriorated on the second, for the several reasons A.L. described to H.M. in detail in her letters of 20 July and 15 September 1914. In *his* letters to Monroe, Pound's versions of events were much vaguer, and curiously upbeat. He described the dinner celebrating the launch of *Blast* as "stately," and told H.M., "BLAST has relieved me," even though the magazine was a disaster for Pound professionally. He told her that

"Upward made a fine speech" at Lowell's "Imagiste dinner," but didn't mention the cruel fun they had made of their hostess. "The lot of 'em are now after my blood," he wrote, but did not offer a fuller explanation until January 1915. By then, his break with Amy was complete and "his" poets had "crossed over" to her in *Some Imagist Poets*.

Describing the breakup to Monroe, Pound placed the stress not so much on animosities toward Amy as on the violations of the strict, original Imagist ideals that "Amygisme" had wrought: "She returns and wants to weaken the whole use of the term imagist, by making it mean ANY writing of vers libre." At the end of the January, he wrote: "I think she perhaps cares more for her own publicity than for the art as such." In May, after the anthology came out, Pound told Monroe with understandable resentment: "Having provided 'em with the weapons, i.e. the greater part of the publicity they have, I certainly should not complain if they use it, their editorial jobs etc., to attack me."

Though he tried to put the best face on the situation, the truth was that by the summer of 1915 Pound was in serious trouble. His *Des Imagistes* anthology of 1914 had sold fewer than a hundred copies in England, so Lowell reported. Now he felt almost all of his original group had abandoned him for Amy, whose promotional skills made the new *Some Imagist Poets* a great success. In her long letter of 14 September 1914, Lowell explained the "schism" as Pound's doing when he forced his friends to choose between him and her.

Lowell also filled in the details of Pound's attempt to have her bankroll a magazine for him. When Amy proved no angel, Pound's attitude toward her changed drastically. Lowell said that Pound admitted that he hoped "to keep his name before the public" through *Blast* and that "it was nothing but advertising." From Lowell's description of his consumptive appearance, Pound was evidently under great stress. She told Monroe that about the only magazines that would take his poetry now were the *Egoist* and *Poetry*—which may explain the noticeably mellower tone in Pound's missives to Chicago. In his letter of 28 June 1915, E.P. himself admitted: "it is a lamentable fact that you and A.C.H. . . . are all that stands between me and a life of shame."

Ezra Pound to Harriet Monroe   *London, 28 March 1914*

Dear Miss Monroe,

    . . . No, the Fenollosa play [*Nishikigi*, May 1914] can't wait. It won't do any harm to print it with the Yeats stuff in May. Every number ought to be at least as "sublimated" as such a number will be. If we can't stay that good we ought to quit. . . .

Hang it all the only way to sell a specialized magazine like Poetry is to pack it full FULL of good stuff. You sent up the sale with the number containing Yeats and myself a year or more ago; it ought to have kept on going up at a steady rate. . . . How can the bloomin provincial poet be expected to keep a pace unless we set it. . . .

Ernest Fenollosa died in 1908, leaving masses of Japanese and Chinese manuscripts, translations, and notes on Noh drama. His widow Mary gave Pound these materials and made him literary executor in October 1913, after reading "Contemporania" in *Poetry*. E.P. adapted Fenollosa's versions in *Certain Noble Plays of Japan* and *'Noh' or Accomplishment* (both 1916). E.P. had written 23 March: "If that Nishikigi don't appear in April I shall starve in the gutter & then you *will* have to find a new thorn in the flesh."

Ezra Pound to Harriet Monroe   [London, 18? April 1914]

Dear H.M.

Here is the big fat review of Hueffer's "Collected Poems" to go in the June number along with his poem "On Heaven". I dare say it is high time I printed something peaceful. . . .

I'm sending you a wedding announcement under separate cover, or rather under this, as you can see for yourself. I've done an epithalamium but I'm afraid it wont pass in a Christian country.

Good luck. Glad to see Sandburg. I don't think he is very important but that's the sort of stuff we ought to print. . . .

Pound married Dorothy Shakespear on 20 April, at St. Mary Abbots, despite the groom's anti-Christian sentiments but at the bride's father's insistence. E.P. would have preferred the Kensington Registry Office, where Frieda and D. H. Lawrence, Nora and James Joyce, and H.D. and Richard Aldington were married. Part of the honeymoon was spent at Yeats's Stone Cottage, where E.P. worked on Noh dramas.

Harriet Monroe to Ezra Pound   12 May 1914

[*Draft in pencil; passages in* { } *brackets indicate passages H. M. struck out.*]

My dear E. P.,

A volume is due to you by this time. I was east a fortnight—three days with Amy Lowell in her dog-guarded Brookline castle!—and things were delayed. . . .

First, your poems, which arrived while I was away. {We think—don't you?—they are hardly up to your usual form—at least not up to the April group of a year ago. However, that's your look out.} Some of this group you must know we can't print {you should know that without being told}, viz:- The Temperaments, Emma, Phyllidula, The Father, and Lesbia Illa we would rather not. {Oh little indoor England and its tiresome little adulteries! For the love of heaven, get out doors!} And I am dead against Valediction—what is the use of calling names! {In this particular case your country has employed you. Why waste your time on cussing?} Does a poet in that slam-bang attitude convince anybody? . . .

About dates—we do our best to meet your wishes. But please give us as much leeway as possible, and let us know as long beforehand as you can. If a date is absolute, tell us why—that helps. Remember that people are clamoring also at this end.

The only trouble with our living up to your standard is that you like nothing but importations—an ideal which, whether true or false, is impossible for an Am. mag. However, I need scarcely repeat that we deeply appreciate what you have done for us. Moreover, we hope to keep on climbing.* . . .

{*? You say we sent up the sale with the number containing Yeats and you (and incidentally me). Maybe in England, but not especially here.}

Ezra Pound to Harriet Monroe   *London, 23 May 1914*

Dear H.M.

. . . Cut out any of my poems that would be likely to get you suppressed but don't make it into a flabby little Sunday school lot like the bunch in the November number. Now WHO could blush at Lesbia Illa??????? *WHO???* . . .

As for my only liking importations, that's sheer nonsense. Fletcher, Frost, Williams, H.D., Cannell and yrs. v.t. are all American. You know perfectly well that american painting is recognizable because painters from the very beginning have kept in touch with europe and dared to study abroad. Are you going to call people foreigners the minute they care enough about their art to travel in order to perfect it? Are the only american poets to be those who are too lazy to study or travel, or too cowardly to learn what perfection means? . . .

Ezra Pound to Harriet Monroe   *London, [July? 1914]*

Dear H.M.

Your editorial ["The Enemies We Have Made"] (May number) is very encouraging. I am glad you commence to enjoy the fair pleasure. Now when you see that the Century and Harpers AND the Atlantic and Scribners are all on the side of the Dial, all against life, all of 'em opposed to germination. NOT one of 'em who'd do a hands turn for any active artist. . . .

I'm glad the Small [Little] Review has started. All the best sellers, all the popular cries. Almost up to date. A jolly place for people who aren't quite up to our level. You should find it a great comfort and relief to have a place where the meritorious *A2* writers can go and console each other....

Personally I favour the assassination of all Americans over fifty, with the sole exception of Henry James....

Ezra Pound to Harriet Monroe　　　　　*London, 17 August 1914*

Dear H.M.

　. . . Be comforted, I have probably finished my series of satires. BLAST has relieved me. BLAST is comfort and cooling water. Even Bill Williams felt the gracious relief. With Blast to keep going one will have only one's most gracious mood for the Muses.

　I am both sorry and glad that you have quarreled with the Tribune. Will you ever get vacation enough to come to these parts?

　The BLAST dinner was stately. The "imagiste dinner" sat down thirteen to table. Upward made a fine speech. The lot of 'em are now after my blood. However I expect to survive it....

Ezra Pound to Harriet Monroe　　　　*London, [15 September 1914]*

Dear H.M.

　I am no longer on intimate terms with Hueffer but I think there is no question of his poem's being far and away the best thing we have printed this year. I think we should be open to ridicule if we awarded the guarantor's prize to any one else....

　If divided, I vote for Fletcher and Frost. I think Frost is equally deserving of the prize on his published work, but the prize is given for stuff that has appeared in Poetry. Frost is peculiar to himself & particularly American....

Ezra Pound to Harriet Monroe　　　　*London, [22 September 1914]*

Dear H.M.

　. . . An American called Eliot called this P.M. I think he has some sense tho' he has not yet sent me any verse....

Ezra Pound to Harriet Monroe　　　　*[London], 30 September [1914]*

Dear H.M.

　. . . I was jolly well right about Eliot. He has sent in the best poem I have yet had or seen from an American. PRAY GOD IT BE NOT A

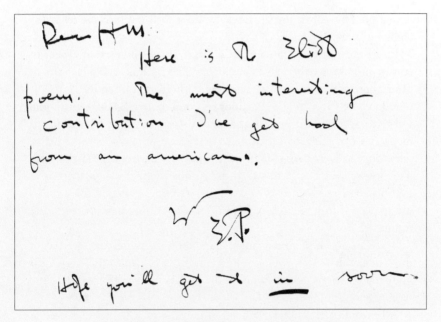

Note from Pound, October 1914, accompanying
"The Love Song of J. Alfred Prufrock."

SINGLE AND UNIQUE SUCCESS. He has taken it back to get it
ready for the press and you shall have it in a few days.

He is the only American I know of who has made what I can call
adequate preparation for writing. He has actually trained himself AND
modernized himself ON HIS OWN. The rest of the *promising* young
have done one or the other but never both (most of the swine have
done neither). It is such a comfort to meet a man and not have to tell
him to wash his face, wipe his feet, and remember the date (1914) on
the calendar.

yours ever / E.P.

E.P. sent "Prufrock" with a note: "Here is the Eliot poem. The most interesting con-
tribution I've yet had from an american. . . . Hope you'll get it *in* soon."

Ezra Pound to Harriet Monroe　　　　*London, [5? January 1915]*

Dear H.M.

Can nothing pursuade [sic] people to let the word Imagiste keep the
meaning of my first definitions.

The very root of my irritation with Lowellisme [sic] is that A.L.
deliberately tries to dilute the meaning. Granted that she writes or very
nearly writes Imagisme on rare occasions, she constantly gives way to

dilutation. The very thing she does not do is to "submit to the stark discipline of the Imagistes".

Imagisme consists in presentation of the Image, it certainly does not consist in talking about abstractions like "Finite infinity". That sort of thing is precisely what we are avoiding with greatest intensity. . . .

A.L. comes over here, gets kudos out of association. She returns and wants to weaken the whole use of the term imagist, by making it mean ANY writing of vers libre. Why if they want to be vers librists, why can't they say so. But no, she wants in Lawrence, Fletcher, her own looser work. And the very discrimination, the whole core of a significance I've taken twelve years of discipline to get at, she expects me to accord to people who have taken fifteen minutes' survey of my results.

They are more than welcome to any advantage they can get out of the name, only I wish, rather against hope, that the critical idea of clear presentation might not be wholly lost in the mix-up. The whole sense of concentration. . . .

A.L. would cheerfully have been impressionist or fantasiste as well as anything else. . . .

Your publisher Macmillan is a burning liar. Inter alia. Here's luck,

yours ever, / E. P

Macmillan's full-page ad in October for Lowell's *Sword Blades and Poppy Seed* named her "The foremost member of the 'Imagists'." On 19 October, E.P. wrote A.L. asking her to refrain from referring to herself as an Imagist and suggesting she stop the ad; it did not run again.

Ezra Pound to Harriet Monroe   *Stone Cottage, Coleman's Hatch,*
                                        Sussex, 31 January 1915

Dear H.M.

. . . Now as to Eliot. Mr Prufrock does not "go off at the end". It is a portrait of failure, or of a character which fails, and it would be false art to make it end on a note of triumph. I dislike the paragraph about Hamlet, but it is an early and cherished bit and T.E. wont give it up, and as it is the only portion of the poem that most readers will like at first reading, I don't see that it will do much harm.

For the rest: a portrait satire on futility cant end by turning that quintessence of futility Mr. P. into a reformed character breathing out fire and ozone. . . .

I will let the unfortunate [Arthur Davison] Ficke pass without complaint if you get on with "Mr. Prufrock," in a nice quiet and orderly manner. I assure you it is better, "more unique," than the other poems of Eliot which I have seen. Also that he is quite *intelligent* (an adjective which is seldom in my mouth). . . .

Ezra Pound to Harriet Monroe   *31 January 1915*

    Second Letter—to be read at *leisure* after the other.

Dear H.M.

    To this Imagiste matter, once again. . . .

    The problem is HOW, how in hell to exist without over-production. In the Imagist book [*Des Imagistes*] I made it possible for a few poets who were not over-producing to reach an audience. That delicate operation was managed by the most rigorous suppression of what I considered faults.

    Obviously such a method and movement are incompatible with effusion, with flooding magazines with all sorts of wish-wash and imitation and the near-good, with yards and pages of "application". If I had acceded to A.L.'s proposal to turn "Imagisme" into a democratic beargarden, I should have undone what little good I had managed to do by setting up a critical standard.

[*In quoting in* A Poet's Life, *H.M. inserted here parts of E.P.'s letter of 5 January, above.*]

    My problem is to keep alive a certain group of advancing poets. I was willing to weaken my position, even so, IF she were willing to make an equivalent sacrifice. She thought my idea of an equivalent sacrifice exorbitant. Voila! Or rather she chose to call it "bribing me" or something of that sort. Macmillan's ad [for Lowell's *Sword Blades and Poppy Seed*] was unfortunate to say the least. Beyond that, I have nothing to do with her later squabbles with her own faction of Imagistes, nor do I know exactly what it is about.

    As to her own over-production, it has not the justification of starvation threatening and pushing her on to publish. I am quite willing to believe the best of her, but I think she perhaps cares more for her own publicity than for the art as such. . . .

    Poetry must be *as well written as prose*. Its language must be a fine language, departing in no way from speech save by a heightened intensity (i.e. simplicity). There must be no book words, no periphrases, no inversions. It must be as simple as De Maupassant's best prose, and as hard as Stendhal's.

There must be no interjections. No words flying off to nothing. Granted one can't get perfection every shot, this must be one's INTENTION.

Rhythm MUST have meaning. It can't be merely a careless dash off, with no grip and no real hold to the words and sense, a tumty rum tumty rum tum ta.

There must be no clichés, set phrases, stereotyped journalese. The only escape from such is by precision, a result of concentrated attention to what is writing. The test of a writer is his ability for such concentration AND for his power to stay concentrated till he gets to the end of his poem, whether it is two lines or four hundred. . . .

[*A long passage follows briefly criticizing several of E.P.'s former protégés and H.M.'s favorites, repeating points made often elsewhere.*]

. . . Too bad about Amy—why can't she conceive of herself as a renaissance figure instead of a spiritual chief, which she aint? . . .

E.P. gave short critiques of eleven poets. In *A Poet's Life*, Chapter 31, H.M. printed the passage, with deletions or "improvements." Some of E.P.'s comments, uncensored: "Aldington is a pig-headed fool"; "Fletcher is sputter, bright flash, sputter"; "Masters hits rock bottom now and again"; "Has Bynner acquired any guts yet?"; "Eliot is intelligent, very, but I don't know him well enough to make predictions."

Ezra Pound to Harriet Monroe   *[London, May 1915]*

Dear H.M.

No. I dislike your "Turbine" intensely. I hate a lot of talk *about* something. "Listen my children and you shall hear", all that sort of thing bores me. I want direct presentation. Statement. Uninterrupted by exclamations, "whew!" etc. . . .

Objectivity and objectivity and again objectivity, and NO expression, NO hind-side-beforeness, No Tennysonianness of speech, nothing, *nothing*, NOTHING that you couldn't in some circumstance, in the stress of some emotion, ACTUALLY say. . . . Every literaryism, every book word, fritters away a scrap of the reader's patience, a scrap of his sense of your sincerity. When one really feels and thinks one stammers with simple speech; it is only in the flurry, the shallow frothy excitement of writing, or the inebriety of a metre, that one falls into the easy, easy—oh so easy—speech of books and poems that one has read. . . .

Language is made out of concrete things; you make thought out of an arrangement of concrete things. General expressions in non-concrete terms are a laziness, they are talk, not art, not creation. They are the reactions of things on the writer, not a creative act *by* the writer. . . .

"Epithets" are usually abstractions. I mean what they call "epithets" in the books about poetry. The only adjective that is worth using is the adjective that is essential to the sense of the passage, NOT the decorative frill adjective.

Well, I ought to have been grinding out an article or *qualche cosa vendibile* [something sellable]. . . .

Fletcher is not worth replying to, besides he did not interfere with me in any way. His supposition that "polyphonic prose" is new, is erroneous, but the matter isn't worth going into. In the Egoist he cries in passionate hope for Amy that she wants "a little more bredth [sic]". I wonder she allows him to go on so; "figure" was bad enough, but whom the gods will destroy they first deprive of a sense of humour.

Besides I have nursed a lot of 'em in my bosom and they know it . . . the whole lot of them are irritated, because having said they had certain poetic promise I later refused to accord them a mature and judicious critical faculty.

Having provided 'em with the weapons, i.e. the greater part of the publicity they have, I certainly should not complain if they use it, their editorial jobs etc., to attack me. I have only myself to thank for it. Of course, Amy would have had her position largely without me, wholly, almost wholly without me, even though she has bagged what she considered a good business asset. . . .

In his article, "Miss Lowell's Discovery: Polyphonic Prose" (April 1915), Fletcher claimed A.L's "discovery" was as important to poetry as the discovery of radium was to science.

Ezra Pound to Harriet Monroe   London, *[10 May 1915]*

Dear H.M.

. . . Now about Lindsey [sic], rubbish. Masters expresses America, and without letting all his steam off at the whistle, and besides he knows something; it isn't all froth and damn little beer. Effervescence is not vitality nor yet validity. All luck to Lindsey [sic] but there is no weight on his safety value and he don't get up enough pressure. . . .

Masters' [*Spoon River*] Anthology here today. It is a good job, the best native american job since Whitman, I should think. No beastly feathers. . . .

Ezra Pound to Harriet Monroe   London, *[17 May 1915]*

MY GAWDDD! THIS *IS* A <u>ROTTEN</u> NUMBER OF POETRY.

Dear H.M.

It is, honestly, pretty bad. MaryAnne's [Marianne Moore's] titles are nice. . . .

Is literature limited to Christianity?

Above subject for chaste debate in the american parliament.

Oh well, it's a hell of a thing to be an editor or to be in any way responsible for the prog. of letters.

yours in sympathy / E.P.

Moore's poems in the May issue, her first publication in the United States, were "That Harp You Play So Well," "To an Intra-Mural Rat," "Counseil to a Bachelor," "Appellate Jurisdiction," and "The Wizard in Words."

Ezra Pound to Harriet Monroe   London, *15 June 1915*

Dear H.M.

"June", a good number, though I dread to say so, for whenever I compliment you on a number you rush out and plunge into a career of *Crime*. Still the June number could be read with pleasure in intelligent circles. The prose is uniformly good. . . .

In being the first American magazine to print Eliot you have scored again, though you may not yet think so. He has intelligence and wont get stuck in one hole, like [Skipwith] Cannell, who has no business to be shoving off on you stuff I turned down three years ago . . . .

Ezra Pound to Harriet Monroe   London, *28 June 1915*

Dear H.M.

Here is my little lot. . . . As to date of printing, it is a lamentable fact that you and A.C.H. (and her noble efforts on *Drama* etc.) are all that stands between me and a life of shame. . . .

I rec'd a copy of "The Poetry Journal" [edited in Boston by W. S. Braithwaite] a few days ago, a very limp rag. What and who are good enough for them ought for the sake of our prestige to be rather rigorously excluded from "Poetry".

I have sent a longish poem of Eliot's ["Portrait of a Lady"] to Kreymborg [at *Others*], partly because you dont like him, and partly because I want his next batch of stuff in Poetry to be made up exclusively of his newest work. You mark my blossoming word, that young chap will go quite a long way. He and Masters are the best of the b'ilin'.

If you think he lacks vigour merely because he happens to have portrayed Mr Prufrock the unvigorous, vous vous trompez [you deceive yourself]. His poem of Christopher Columbus is vigorous, and male, not to say coarse. I think however he may produce something both modest and virile before the end of the chapter. . . .

A.C.H. acted as E.P.'s agent with *Drama*, a Chicago quarterly, which published his Fenollosa translations.

Ezra Pound to Harriet Monroe   *[London, July 1915]*

Dear H.M.

Hueffer having seen "Prufrock" came in the other day to find out if Eliot had published a book, as he wanted to write about him. WHICH shows that you cant do a good thing without its being took note of. F.M.H. was just as quick as I to see that Eliot mattered.

Whereanent I want you to hold two or three pages open for Eliot in either Sept. or Oct. First because I want the stuff out in time for my anthology [*Catholic Anthology*]. Second because he has just married percipitately [sic] and cant afford not to be paid for his best things. He has done three small (half page) jems and will have enough for three pages I should think. . . .

Eliot and Vivien Haigh-Wood married on 26 June, without telling their parents.

Ezra Pound to Harriet Monroe   *[London, 1 December 1915]*

Dear H.M.

. . . Yes, the prizes were peculiarly filthy and disgusting, the £10 to H.D. being a sop to the intelligent. However, I knew it would happen. I know just what your damn committee *wants*.

As to T.S.E. the "Prufrock" IS more individual and unusual than the Portrait of a Lady! I chose it of the two as I wanted his first poem to be published to be a poem that would at once differentiate him from everyone else, in the public mind.

I am sending on some more of his stuff in a few days, I want to see him and talk it over first. . . .

Little Bill (i.e. W.C.W. as distinct from Big Bill, W.B.Y.) writes that Amy is roaring around a good deal. He also says that she and Fletcher are to be united in wedlock, but this seems too perfect a consummation for me to believe it without further testimony.

Well, I must dust out of this. Keep on moving, remember that poetry is more important than verse free or otherwise. Be glad you have a reckless competitor in N.Y. ("Others") to keep you from believing that scenery alone and unsupported is more interesting than humanity. Really geography IS NOT the source of inspiration. . . .

I really must stop. Am arranging new channel of communication with Paris, etc. etc. etc.

Yours ever   E.P.

The Levinson Prize of $200 was awarded, not to Eliot, but to Lindsay, for "The Chinese Nightingale"; the Guarantors' Prize of $100 was awarded to Constance Lindsay Skinner, for "Songs of the Coastdwellers."

CHAPTER IX

Departures, 1916–1919

"Poetry" has, I suppose, done a good deal of what it set out to do. . . .
We *have* started a new period in American poetry, which was I
believe what was intended.

—Ezra Pound to Harriet Monroe, January 1916

1. Competition

Within a remarkably short time *Poetry* had not only accomplished most
of the goals set forth in the first prospectus but succeeded beyond all
expectation. By 1916 even the diehards at the *Dial* and in the Eastern
Establishment had to admit the "Poetry Renaissance" Pound had pre-
dicted in 1912 was a reality. *Poetry's* early picks were finding audiences
beyond the avant-garde realm of the little magazine, and the more accessi-
ble poets—Frost, Masters, Sandburg, Lindsay—were already becoming
household names.

Unfortunately, literary success did not translate into financial prosper-
ity. Pound urged H.M. to raise her rate to a "reasonable" $25 a page. He
presumed subscriptions paid for production costs, but that income never
covered expenses. In 1914 the Editor had actually been forced to reduce
the rates. In 1916 she had to scrape up $500 in emergency funds to make
ends meet. When she formulated her first financial plan, Monroe believed
that, after five years, *Poetry* would be self-sustaining. She learned the hard
way that the arts do not pay for their upkeep, let alone yield surpluses.
Like the modern politician, she now faced the prospect of the perpetual
campaign.

With the first Guarantors Fund ending in the fall of 1917, she had to
go back to her original sponsors and ask them to sign up for another
five-year plan. Perhaps out of embarrassment, she did not tell them how
precarious the magazine's situation actually was; but she knew that spon-
sors do not like to throw good donations after bad. At the end of her
campaign, Monroe had a smaller endowment to cover increased costs. In

1918 her fund fell from $5,990 to $4,605, almost a 25 percent drop in support.

In addition to money problems, the Editor now found a new and potentially debilitating phenomenon: competition. Following her pioneering work, and perhaps inspired by *Poetry's* success, several other little magazines devoted to contemporary poetry, at least in part, entered the market: the *Little Review* (founded 1915), *Others* (1915), and—all in 1916— the revamped *Egoist*, the *Seven Arts*, *Contemporary Verse*, and the *Poetry Review of America*. Ironically, the big journals—*Harper's*, the *Atlantic*, *Scribner's*, the *Century*, *Lippincott's*—which had shunned the kind of avant-garde work *Poetry* had gambled on, were now welcoming it in their pages. And since they paid better, Monroe stood to lose poems by now-acceptable authors that earlier would have been hers.

Initially, Monroe welcomed the new journals and didn't see them as much of a threat. While she did not wish to be lumped with *Others*, H.M. maintained friendly relations with Alfred Kreymborg and nearly all the members of his New York group. Monroe greeted Braithwaite's *Poetry Review of America* with good humor. Complimenting its second issue in a July 1916 editorial, she wrote: "The path of progress, like that of true love, never did run smooth for either poet or editor, but we may wish for Mr. Braithwaite the minimum of rocks and brambles."

E.P. and A.C.H. viewed him far less favorably. The *Review* was put out by the Poetry Society of America, a group supported by hefty donations from Amy Lowell, who was quick to tell Harriet that Braithwaite was eager to have her material, including pieces H.M. rejected. If not completely in her pocket, W.S.B. was very susceptible to Lowell's charms. The *Poetry Review* featured her work prominently and reviewed it favorably— so much so, A.C.H. told H.M. that Braithwaite was merely Amy's "tool."

Braithwaite was the reason Monroe had been forced to rush her very first issue to press. Since then, he had singled out authors first printed in *Poetry* and made comments about Imagism in the Boston *Evening Transcript*, but failed to give the magazine credit. Braithwaite now did something more serious and possibly damaging. After ignoring *Poetry's* existence in the *Transcript* and in his annual *Anthology of Magazine Verse*, in the preface to the 1916 edition he finally acknowledged its role in the Poetry Renaissance—by dismissing the magazine as perverse and passé. He found "the point of departure from conservatism may be dated from the establishment of *Poetry: A Magazine of Verse*, the instrument of Ezra Pound's radicalism." He then slammed Sandburg and insulted Pound: "Mr. Sandburg, a much-heralded innovator, has not lived up to prophecy; the radical influence of *Poetry* itself has waned, the collected poems of

Pound . . . find it difficult to obtain an American publisher." He repeated the charges in the *Transcript* on 28 October.

Henderson was livid, and suggested Sandburg sue the *Transcript* for libel. A.C.H. suspected that Lowell was behind the attacks, using her good friend at the *Poetry Review* to undermine *Poetry*, out of jealousy. She also noted that Braithwaite had reprinted several poems from *Poetry*, without permission. A.C.H. sent H.M. a copy of a sharp letter she sent to the *Transcript*, along with an editorial, "Criticism or Slander," intended for *Poetry*. She also sent copies to Pound, who wrote back to say the slams were "of no importance."

Although H.M. did not use Alice's hard-hitting piece, she incorporated some of her ideas in her January 1917 rebuttal, "Sir Oracle." Among other things, the Editor pointed out Braithwaite's hypocrisy: "If POETRY's influence has 'waned,' we may still rejoice that it seems to retain full power over Mr. Braithwaite himself: for in his list of the year's 'poems of distinction' he mentions sixty-five from POETRY, against thirty-five from *Others*, and thirty-three from the *Century*, the two magazines next in favor."

Poetry's influence had not "waned" but was in fact so pervasive now that it was less noticeable, almost taken for granted. In her letter to the editor of the Boston *Transcript*, dated 6 November, A.C.H. put the matter neatly:

If the radical influence of "Poetry" seems to have waned, it is simply because its radicalism has been absorbed by the other magazines and the public generally—by no means excepting the critics. In other words, the influence of "Poetry" has been so widespread and important that the 'record of its administration' may be found not only in its own pages, but in the pages of the poetry magazines founded subsequently and in the older established magazines as well.

But while the experimental techniques displayed in *Poetry*'s early years were becoming common practice, the truth was that much of the *recent* work in its pages was not very adventurous. Miss Monroe's magazine was noticeably weaker and more conventional after 1916. Issues were becoming uneven, as more space was occupied by minor voices, many of them from the Middle West, especially people closely associated with the Editor.

Henderson, Pound, Williams, and others offered advice, much of it conflicting. They repeatedly urged Monroe to forget the small fry and fill every issue with strong material. But even Pound admitted there was "an

awful slump in England." And he made it even more difficult to follow
his directions when he diverted important poems to *other* journals.

Having read the Editor's appeal for funds, in October 1916 John
Gould Fletcher weighed in with a preposterous proposal—print no new
people. His motive was snobbish (he didn't want to appear with people
he hadn't been introduced to), but his logic was stunning. *Poetry* should
make a list of *"permanent contributors"* and guarantee them two appear-
ances annually. "Limit yourself!" he warned, for if she didn't stop playing
"fairy godmother" to newcomers, "the whole 'movement' [would] col-
lapse very shortly." H.M. responded by reaffirming her original "Open
Door" policy.

2. Mrs. Henderson and Mr. Pound

Another major factor in *Poetry's* decline was the loss of its first Associate
Editor. Early in 1916 Alice Henderson was diagnosed with tuberculosis,
and in March she went to Santa Fe in hopes of a cure. During her four
years as first reader, A.C.H. had identified some of *Poetry's* best early con-
tributors and probably dissuaded H.M. from accepting more of the "sen-
sitive" lyrical effusions for which she had a propensity. Eunice Tietjens,
who had started as an office clerk, assumed her position. Though well-
intentioned, E.T. was given to enthusiasms and had neither the fine dis-
crimination nor the kind of authority that Henderson enjoyed (and
didn't hesitate to bring to bear) when she differed with Monroe.

During her "leave of absence," A.C.H. helped as much as she could
through the mails. From Sunmount Sanatorium, she consulted on manu-
scripts and scouted new material, including work by Sherwood Ander-
son. She also offered detailed advice, with unvarnished assessments of the
current offerings in *Poetry.* On 8 August 1916, for example, she wrote
H.M. that she found the August issue "pretty sad, honestly." She also tried
to curb Monroe's promotional tendencies. During the fund-raising effort
of fall 1916, she told the Editor: "And oh, Harriet, whatever you do—
don't speak of '*boosting the art.*' It is dreadful. You can *boost* a magazine—but
art is above and apart from all *boosting.*" In a letter of 7 June 1916, she
echoed Pound in urging the Editor to be more selective:

> I very much fear at times that "Cinderella" is going back to her ashes,
> and that she may feel more comfortable there than in her automobile—
> that this supposed popularity of the art is a good deal of dust, or, rather,
> that when the dust clears away, not much may remain. By that I mean
> especially that one sees so much stuff passing itself off as poetry that is

A. C. H. in her studio. In 1916 she moved to Santa Fe,
where she became a leader of the artists' colony.

nothing of the sort. The need for a perfectly high standard was never
greater than it is at this moment. What we need to do is to forget
schools, forget Imagism, forget vers libre (now that that's back history)
and talk poetry.

Poetry and *Poetry* were in a period of transition. Henderson was more
astute perhaps than she knew when she said the first phase of Modernism
was "back history." One sign that the "movement" had matured was the
appearance of so many anthologies. In 1916, Harriet Monroe was herself
compiling an anthology, *The New Poetry*. A.C.H. had agreed to co-edit
the collection, but when she was taken ill, H.M. was left with a great deal

of the work, much of it very tedious, such as obtaining permissions and compiling the bibliography. She and A.C.H. later had lengthy disputes over the proper division of the royalties, which made the distance between them not one simply of geography.

Though she had hoped to return to Chicago, Henderson decided to stay in New Mexico. Like H.M., A.C.H. was drawn to the western landscape; looking back in the 10th Anniversary Issue, she wrote she had become "as firmly rooted as a pinyon tree." She became immersed in the indigenous culture—Navajo art, Native American myths, New Mexico folk songs—and prompted the Editor to print several "Indian Songs" and cowboy ballads. By 1920, when Alice published *Red Earth: Poems of New Mexico*, the Hendersons had established themselves as leaders of the cultural life in what became the Santa Fe artist colony. They organized the first "Poet's Round Up," and Will designed the Museum for Navajo Ceremonial Arts. Their daughter, Alice Olive, married John Evans, the son of their art impresario "competitor" in Taos, Mabel Dodge Luhan.

Although Pound adopted a more measured tone in his letters to Monroe in 1915 and 1916, he never developed a warm bond with her. Despite many provocations, she remained the soul of reasonableness and conciliation, and seldom offered more than a mild reproof. But her even temper itself, and refusal to rise to his bait, only seemed to infuriate Pound the more. In frustration or confusion, he turned to Alice.

Henderson discovered Pound's work independently, then learned of him firsthand on her own trip to Europe in 1910 through a mutual friend, the pianist Margaret Cravens. Between 1912 and 1918, Pound wrote A.C.H. at least seventy letters. (They have been edited by Ira B. Nadel: *The Letters of Ezra Pound to Alice Corbin Henderson*; University of Texas Press, 1993.) A.C.H. came to act as an intermediary and an advocate for his positions. It was to her that Pound first sent "A Few Don'ts by an Imagiste" and the three Ur-Cantos, which she forwarded from Santa Fe with an enthusiastic recommendation.

Henderson's own poetry and critical sense were closer to Pound's than to Monroe's, and because they shared the same high standards, E.P. respected A.C.H. as a peer. The tone of his letters to her is genuinely friendly, and often funny, in contrast to his missives to Monroe, which are all business even when he's in a jocular mood. When he thought he had perhaps gone too far in browbeating her, Pound turned to A.C.H. for reassurance. In a letter of 23 January 1917, for example, he wondered whether Harriet was still "grumped" with him. Alice told him not to worry. A.C.H. showed some of his letters to the Editor, but many she couldn't share: Pound could be cruelly frank. But even with Henderson acting as intermediary—as an advocate/proxy for Pound's point of view or as an interpreter for him of Monroe's position—smooth relations between Editor and Foreign Correspondent were simply not possible. For most of 1916, however, Pound did not add appreciably to Monroe's burdens. The next year would be quite another matter.

Ezra Pound to Harriet Monroe   *Stone Cottage, Coleman's Hatch,*
Sussex, 23 January 1916

Dear H.M.

... "Poetry" has, I suppose, done a good deal of what it set out to do. At least I don't think the guarantors can complain that the writers have not responded to the offer made three years ago. We *have* started a new period in American poetry, which was I believe what was intended. . . .

A multitude of magazines is good in one way, but if it encourages diffuseness it is bad. And anything which tends to concentrate the force is much better. If there is too great a flood of loose verse, we shall kill the enthusiasm, the present enthusiasm, bore everyone, and lose all we have gained. . . . We all want the concentrated good in one place, not scattered in 10 little magazines.

At present I am one of the chief beneficiaries, I am aware of the fact. I get about £50 per annum. Few if any of the other poets do so well. BUT Poetry should keep up Eliot, Sandburg, Lindsey [sic] at £100 a year (since your people admire him). . . . . Masters is I suppose too far committed to family and affairs, but he, even he, might get enough to afford more time on his work. . . .

Frost should be kept up. It is ridiculous that at least the best dozen shouldn't be free to write without an eye on the gas-metre and the tick at the corner shop. . . .

Ezra Pound to Harriet Monroe   *Stone Cottage, Coleman's Hatch,*
Sussex, 29 January 1916

Dear H.M.

Here are the rest of the Joyce poems. I think you had better print all five. They are quite good in their way. It is not greatly my way, still the five of them together will convey their own atmosphere and they have a certain distinction, though it would perhaps be difficult to say why. At any rate Joyce's name on [the] list of contents will be an excellent thing in saeculum saeculorum.

Contemporary Verse has come. I had hopes from their ad. that they were going to make some sort of stand for style and finish, as a counter-weight to Kreymborg's habble-scrabble [*Others*]. Alas, they are dull and unreadable. I dont see how they can last six months, unless they've money, or buck up. There is more in two lines of Joyce than in their whole number, at any rate. . . .

Joyce made his first appearance with "Simples," "Tutto è Sciolto," "Flood," "A Flower Given to My Daughter," and "Night Piece." H.M. paid for the poems upon acceptance; they were printed May 1917. Edited in Philadelphia, *Contemporary Verse* was committed to traditional verse; it found "no point in the use of *vers libre*," and printed safe second-stringers.

Ezra Pound to Harriet Monroe   *London, 5 March 1916*

Dear H.M.

I had a long letter from [T. Sturge] Moore which I have destroyed. I have to some extent pacified him as you see by this card. BUT I wish you could realize the uncomfortable position you place me in by reducing the rates of payment without ~~consulting~~ informing me. I am not intimate with Moore and therefore it is all the worse. . . .

As to rates, less than ten dollars per page is *not* a good rate. One gets ten or fifteen dollars in plenty of places . . . .

Still: either "Poetry" IS Maecenas, upholding a principle that poetry ought to be decently paid, or else it is a sheet begging for favours . . . [sic] which last it of course is not. BUT nothing is more enraging to a writer than to receive less than he has been led to expect (even if it is only ten cents less) for a job. . . .

Being the best magazine in America is NOT good enough (that you know perfectly well). . . .

Yours ever   E.P.

The fact that there's an awful slump in Eng. poetry just at this moment is all the more reason why we should go on trying to maintain our contention that we print the best of it. . . .

Monroe was still paying Pound at the old rate, and he was unaware of the reduction until Moore and Hueffer complained to him about the size of their checks.

Ezra Pound to Harriet Monroe   *[London], 21 April 1916*

Dear H.M.

April number depressing. . . .

. . . It would be a good thing to reprint my original "DONTS", with the addition of a few notes, emendations or additions. An 8 or 10 or 12 page pamphlet for ten cents. It would certainly pay its expenses, and it could be more widely dispersed than a bound vol. of Poetry @ 1.50 would likely to be [sic]. It would be much better than my writing new articles pointing out the various sorts of silliness into which neo-imagism or neogism [sic] is perambulating, which latter could with difficulty escape allusions to Amy and Fletcher etc. etc. . . .

You will remember that the DONTS were originally intended as a slip to be sent with returned mss. so the idea of a pamphlet is not so far off the original intention. . . .

Ezra Pound to Harriet Monroe   *[London, 3 May 1916]*

Dear H.M.

This is very serious hideous news about Alice Henderson. . . . She is one of the few people who are the slightest use, so I suppose something of this sort was bound to happen. Why couldn't it be Sara Teasdale, or any one of the 9000! . . .

Now, now, I know well enough that it's not your fault that you don't give £60 a page, and also that you've worked yourself nigh to death keeping the magazine going, and I don't (I DO NOT) forget it. But you live in a desert of people always talking about "things paying" etc. etc. and it is just as well to remember our original thesis that poetry ought to be paid as well as the other arts. No not paid, but that poets should be fed. . . . The makers of pork, damn it all, they can't do anything but pay, they can't *make* stuff to go in a magazine. They *ought* to pay. The Medici and a lot of other objectionable people did it before 'em. . . .

Ezra Pound to Harriet Monroe   *[London], 5 June 1916*

Dear H.M.

So long as you put the "Cabaret" question on the grounds of expediency and the assininity [sic] of your guarantors, or in fact on any ground save the desire of the editor for the candy box, I suppose I must submit. I enclose the only other poem I have ready, to go with the inoffensive selection you already have. FOR GOD'S SAKE print 'em at once.

My next contribution will probably be a 40 page fragment from a more important Opus [the first Cantos]. . . .

Alice Corbin Henderson to Harriet Monroe   Santa Fe,
                                                                8 August 1916

Dear Harriet:-

I was much pleased to get a real letter from you! . . .

The August number came yesterday—and it is pretty sad, honestly. . . .

Amy— well Amy is not so bad—although *tinny*—but the rest is *triste* [sad]. . . .

I am beginning to believe that, if I were you, I would *concentrate* in the first place, on *getting* and *keeping* and publishing all the *first rate* poets—at least have something of each one or two of them in each month. There is *absolutely* no use in encouraging the poet who has *one* passable poem in a lot of bad ones, and who hasn't the *germ* of development, who will never—(so far as we can see)—*get* anywhere. Encourage him to *keep on trying all* you want to. But let him try outside the magazine. Now concentrate on Masters, Lindsay, Sandburg, Ficke, Fletcher, Frost, Pound, the English ones—W.B.Y.—Hueffer, Manning, etc. when you can get them. Also of course *Wallace Stevens*—and get something from Arensberg—also *Wm. Carlos Williams.* . . . But try not to let any number go out without some outstanding contribution. *This is all important.* (Amy of course doesn't count in this respect—Amy is as common as the Boston Gardens—and as well advertized—by Amy.) . . .

John Gould Fletcher to Harriet Monroe   [*n. p.*] 25 October 1916

Dear Harriet Monroe:-

. . . In your October number, I see you make an appeal for funds to carry on the paper. . . .

Poetry has undoubtedly done more than any other factor to revive the interest in the art in the U.S. This I admit. But to revive an interest is not enough. . . . If you look about you, you see The Poetry Review, Contemporary Verse, Others, The Poetry Journal—all more or less trying to do what you set out to do five years ago—to create the great audience. Well, the great audience is created, it is expectant, all it wants to know is—where is poetry tending? . . .

I will make you a sporting offer. I will personally subscribe ten dollars a year to your paper, and will send you, besides, my very best work to be printed (and you need not pay me for it) *provided that you and Alice Henderson sit down and make out a list of contributors who will be permanent contributors*—exclusive to your paper—each guaranteed two appearances a year at least—*and also, provided that you notify the world at large that you will not accept or print any new people.* This will put the onus of discovering new people on the other papers—and as the new people acquire reputations, you can add them to your list by invitation. . . .

Unless you do something of this sort, I have decided to withdraw myself altogether from "Poetry's" pages in the future. I may be an extremely bad poet, but at least I have too much self-respect for myself and the labour I have accomplished to put myself any longer on the level of quality with Gretchen Warren, Lilly A. Long, Lulu W. Knight, Peter Norden, Lyman Bryson, John Regnault Ellyson, Iris Barry, etc.— *to take only a single number* [July 1916]. If "Poetry" is going to be a "free-for-all" of this sort, then no more "Poetry" for me. I am not a "free-for-all" sort of person. . . .

. . . Limit yourself! If you don't stop this business of being a fairy godmother to everybody who sends you a MS., the whole "move-ment" will collapse very shortly. Believe me, I ask it not for myself, but for the sake of the art, and your own future. . . .

Harriet Monroe to John Gould Fletcher   *22 November 1916*

My dear Mr. Fletcher:

Your last letter must have crossed mine, in which I sent you a check for $100.00 for the *Poetry* prize . . . .

In regard to what you say about the management of the magazine, I think a little reflection will convince you that it would be impossible to run it on that basis. The magazine was started and guarantors were secured primarily to give the young poets a chance to be heard. If we should change it to be an organ of a special group it would lose its use, and the guarantors would, I am sure, one and all, discontinue. As for my part in it, I should become merely a kind of register, and all the pleasure of gambling on the young and unknown would be gone. If that had been the policy of the magazine from the beginning think how many of your friends would never have been in it at all. You tell me to stop asking people for poems. The truth is that I have never asked anybody; before the magazine started, I issued circulars generally, asking for the cooperation of poets, but since then I have not asked more than three persons to contribute, and those requests were a kind of courtesy extended when I asked for the loan of poems for an anthology. It is an awkward thing to ask for contributions, because an editor might not like them when they came. . . .

J.G.F. wrote 25 November rejecting the prize, and suggested H.M. put it in the *Poetry* fund. He wrote again 27 November to say he had been hasty and now would accept the money "for friendship's sake."

3. Cantos and More Conflicts

Nineteen-seventeen was not a very good year for Harriet Monroe. In the early months, she was working on both the new endowment and *The New Poetry*. In mid-February, she caught the flu and was ill for several

"A Lowbrow Blinks at Literary Lights": Eunice Tietjens and Harriet Monroe
lampooned in the Chicago *Daily News*, 13 June 1917.
Cartoon by Morey Schwartz.

weeks. Eunice Tietjens was proving no replacement for Alice Henderson.
A.C.H. herself had had reservations about E.T.'s qualifications, and wrote
E.P. in January that she had "raptures & impulses and no discretion." (E.P.
replied that he was all too familiar with the type—"OH HELL YES"—
and later referred to her as a "flapper.") Eunice did tend to gush, and
seems to have reinforced some of Miss Monroe's softer tendencies.

H.M. may not have appreciated A.C.H.'s advice and faultfinding, as she
reiterated points E.P. was continually making about the "pathetic" state of
Poetry. The number of the Editor's missives to them both dropped. On 6

June 1917, A.C.H. chided her for not writing. But Monroe was ill and overworked, and perhaps simply weary from the criticism on all sides. After a six-month hiatus, Pound wrote H.M. a note on 18 April 1917, to acknowledge a check and to complain about his pay, which he took as a sign the advisory board wanted him out. On 24 April, he complained he now felt "cut off," but discussed terms for "A Draft of Three Cantos."

E.P. had done his best to prepare the way, by sending the "Draft" first to A.C.H. early in February 1917. On 6 February, Alice wrote Harriet: "Of course it will be caviar to the general, but I like it." Alice was in fact delighted, and wrote E.P. on 17 February that she longed for more. (Little did she know that these so-called Ur-Cantos would be the start of what became Pound's lifelong project.) She also reassured Ezra that, whatever Braithwaite said, Harriet herself did not feel that his influence had "waned." She professed great confidence in H.M., and told E.P. that Monroe was more "elastic" than anyone of her generation.

But the Editor stiffened when she saw the Cantos. A month later, she wrote A.C.H. that after reading a few pages she took sick—and they were the cause. (It is not clear whether she was being facetious.) She hesitated turning over twenty-four pages to "that sort of thing" and didn't know what to do. As it happened, Robert Frost was passing through Chicago, and she asked him to take the poems home for examination. Asking Frost to offer an opinion was a curious decision, as he was not very fond of Pound or particularly close to the magazine. (He warmed up when H.M. gave him a prize later in 1917.) Frost replied on 24 March with a tepid endorsement of the Cantos, and told H.M. to print them, "and let the public be damned."

After pondering further, on 9 April H.M. wrote A.C.H. again. She found the Cantos more "diluted than usual" and confessed she didn't like the turn Pound's work was taking. She felt it would be "suicidal" to print all three at once, and decided to run them in consecutive issues. She also asked A.C.H. whether E.P. was "petering out." Henderson responded on 16 April, reaffirming her faith in the work. Monroe spread the three parts over the June, July, and August issues, and paid Pound £21.

Money was much more on his mind since his several reversals of fortune in 1915. Pound always harbored resentment about the tangible rewards for his labors, a feeling now exacerbated by his slim earnings in England. His basic differences with Monroe over editorial direction had led him to complain in February 1914: "I think I should have opportunity of dissociating myself from certain policies of the magazine." Now he concluded the financial situation at *Poetry* would not improve, and decided to look elsewhere for support.

In his very first letter to Monroe, Pound said he had wanted to found his own magazine. He never abandoned the idea. He wasn't satisfied promulgating his views in other journals, for few editors were as tolerant as Monroe in allowing him to air his opinions. In June 1913, he had joined the *Egoist* as literary editor (and got Aldington a job as subeditor), but he soon had a falling out with Harriet Weaver and Dora Marsden. After *Blast* ended with a whimper, he was shut out of most of the other journals in England, and *Poetry*'s £50 a year became one of his few secure sources of income.

Though he complained about his shrinking salary, what he didn't tell Harriet (or Alice) was that early in 1917 his financial situation began to look up, thanks to John Quinn. A New York lawyer, arts patron, and avid collector of manuscripts, Quinn had been a fan of Pound's for some time. On 21 April 1915, he wrote H.M. to order copies of the *Poetry* issue with Pound's first articles on Imagism, and said in closing: "You can't have too much Ezra Pound for me. He is the livest of the live ones. I read everything he writes and admire all of it even when I don't agree with all of it." Quinn had helped organize the Armory Show in 1913, and in 1917 he paid for an exhibition of Vorticist art to be shipped to New York City. He also arranged for a private edition of *Lustra* in the United States.

At E.P.'s prompting, Quinn considered acquiring various journals for him to edit, then proposed underwriting Pound's salary as literary editor for the *Egoist*, but Aldington wouldn't stand for it. Attention turned to the *Little Review*. The magazine settled in New York City in late 1916, but had fallen on hard times. Quinn made Margaret Anderson and Jane Heap an offer they couldn't refuse. For two years he would subsidize Pound as foreign editor, at $750 annually, of which $450 was to be used to pay for material he chose. E.P. began negotiating with Anderson in January 1917.

Although he was still *Poetry*'s Foreign Correspondent—and supposedly its agent for gathering material—Pound took up his new position as Foreign Editor of the *Little Review* in March. He did not inform Monroe, although he hinted at a break in his note of 18 April: "I may very possibly have outlived my utility so far as [*Poetry*] is concerned." The *Little Review* announced his appointment the same month. Then Pound did the unforgivable. In the opening pages of the May 1917 issue of the *Little Review*, he offered the following explanation for his new association:

> My connections with the *Little Review* does not imply a severance of my relations with *Poetry*, for which I still remain Foreign Correspondent and in which my poems will appear until its guarantors revolt.
>
> I would say, however, in justification both of *Poetry* and myself, that *Poetry* has never been "the instrument" of my "radicalism." I respect Miss Monroe for all that she has done for the support of American

poetry, but in the conduct of her magazine my voice and vote have always been the vote and voice of a minority.

. . . *Poetry* has done numerous things to which I could never have given my personal sanction, and which could not have occurred in any magazine which had constituted my "instrument." *Poetry* has shown an unflagging courtesy to a lot of old fools and fogies whom I would have told to go to hell tout pleinment and bonnement. . . .

Alice Henderson, who forgave Pound most of his sins, was furious. She wrote Monroe 9 June: "I suppose the real trouble is that Ezra *has no sense of values.*" The Editor had very good reasons to take offense at Pound's breach of trust. She had printed him and the poets he promoted, given him a pulpit from which to spread his aesthetic doctrines, defended him from his many critics, and stood by him when even his closest associates had written him off. All the while, she put up with his harangues about her editorial management. Just before his *Little Review* editorial appeared, she had given his work the largest representation of anyone's in her upcoming anthology. Instead of asking Pound to resign, she paid him for the Cantos—and apologized that she couldn't offer more.

At the time, she was in the midst of the second endowment campaign, and must have realized that Pound's slam could only make her efforts more difficult. On 3 July she drafted a letter expressing her surprise at his "taking up" with the *Little Review* without telling her, and distorting the facts about his relationship with *Poetry*. Finally, after years of abuse, she gave him a good dressing down, including a long-overdue lecture on his slapdash prose. Instead of airing personal grievances, she pointed out how damaging Pound's attitude was for his career: "My very respect for your work makes me wish you would not plant yourself so violently in front of it." Monroe then went on to discuss the possibility of Pound's doing articles on French poetry, leaving the door open to him.

Pound seemed oblivious to the negative impact of his brash words, or he didn't care. As Monroe's reprimand was sailing toward London, a garrulous letter he wrote on 2 July was crossing in the mail to Chicago; as though nothing were amiss, he rambled in his usual fashion about recent issues of *Poetry*. He asked H.M. to return his unwanted mss. quickly; he could be more outspoken in the *Little Review*, and since he had few friends in America, he didn't have to spare "imbeciles." After receiving H.M.'s letter of 3 July, he responded with a very long, disorganized, and repetitious "defense" on 23 July. Again he complained about low pay. As for giving *Poetry* preference with new work, he assured her he would continue to "bull the market." If her supporters wanted "the swank" of being the literary center, they could "fork up." At several points, Pound was quite confusing (or confused) about who was to get what, and on what basis.

Unrepentant, Pound continued to correspond, at times with a jaunty manner that suggested the late unpleasantness was just another one of their dust-ups. But Pound's belligerent reaction effectively marked the end of his work as Foreign Correspondent, although the official break did not come until two years later. After the summer of 1917, E.P.'s letters became fewer, but longer and more disorganized than ever. After January 1918, Monroe heard nothing of Pound, until a curious note arrived from the U.S. Mint, Philadelphia, in November. The sender was none other than Homer L. Pound, wondering if he might forward some of Ezra's mss. With almost too perfect symmetry, the end was drawing near. It was c/o his father that Monroe had sent her first letter soliciting work from Ezra Pound.

Alice Corbin Henderson to Harriet Monroe   *[Santa Fe,*
                                                 7? February 1917]

Dear H.M. Here are Ezra's Cantos. I really hate to let them go. I really like them tremendously. Another hard answer that could be made to idiots like Braithwaite. Of course they are erudite—but there is life— and a poet's life—in it & through it all—considerable vision and depth—and beauty of style. You need to read it several times—at least I did—to get the full value. In fact, it can be read *indefinitely*—& give up new meanings—which is a *good* deal to say—I am sending the mss. to your house, so you can read it away from "official" distractions. Let me know what you think about it. It was nice of E.P. to send it through me so I could read it & I am sorry I kept it longer than I meant!—
                                                 Yours, / A.C.H.

Robert Frost to Harriet Monroe   *Amherst, Mass., 24 March 1917*

Dear Miss Monroe:

I'm not so much ashamed of having kept this ["A Draft of Three Cantos"] as of having kept it too long to no purpose. I don't really feel as if I had got anywhere with it even helped as I have been by wifely counsel. There's stir in the poem of the Poundian kind and I can't say that I don't like it. But it leaves me partly baffled. I suppose that is the Sordello of it: I grant him the Sordello form. I suppose the meaning is meant just to elude you going out as you come in. That kind of meaning that won't pin down is one of the resources of poetry, or so I have always held. I could name poems I love for it. And yet, and yet—

the public be damned. Them's my sentiments. But you know better than I just how well your magazine can stand the strain.

Asking your forgiveness for the time I have taken for this little result I'm

Always sincerely yours
Robert Frost

Get better but don't get out. March air is good to keep in out of.

H.M. asked Frost for his opinion of Pound's first Cantos; part of his response, 24 March 1917.

You're not asking me whether you ought to publish it, are you? All you want is my impression of the poem as a poem and not as a magazine availability [sic]. I'm weak on the availabilities. I more than half like the poem: I trust I make that clear. I'd be half inclined to publish it and let the public be damned. Them's my sentiments. But you know better than I just how well your magazine can stand the strain.

Asking your forgiveness for the time I have taken for this little result I'm

Always sincerely yours / Robert Frost
Get better but don't get out. March air is good to keep in out of.

Alice Corbin Henderson to Harriet Monroe   Santa Fe, 16 April 1917

Dear Harriet—I am so glad you are feeling better. . . .

I liked Ezra's poem—in spite of its being a tuning up of fiddles, it seemed to have some body of its own. Of course if nothing crystalized further on, I can't see that it would be sufficient excuse for itself, except in method and quality. It is a preparation, and a linking up of times and classics, etc. preparatory, let us hope, to an individual vision. Of course as far as popularity is concerned, that's different. I don't think that's your prime concern after all—it never has been, and that's why Poetry has been worth something. . . .

Ezra Pound to Harriet Monroe   *[London], 18 April 1917*

Dear H.M.

I enclose reply, in due form, to the last communication from the Editors of Poetry.

I dont know what you think a foreign correspondent is worth, but the present rating does not seem very high.

yrs / E.P.

P.S. The receipts for the full year before the six months mentioned, had dwindled to £17. I recognized that after my connection with the magazine from the start, it would be hard for you or the Advisory Committee to ask me to quit. The proportion of my poems in your anthology would not lead one to suppose that you had decided to give up my kind of work. Still you arranged the anthology some time ago, and you may have changed your mind since. A great many people would be very glad to have me off the magazine. I may very possibly have outlived my utility so far as it is concerned. At any rate a clean break would be better than [$]7.68 and being where I'm not wanted.

Ezra Pound / 18/4/1917

Ezra Pound to Harriet Monroe   *[London], 24 April 1917*

Dear H.M.

At last a letter from you. I am sorry you have been laid up, glad you are through with it. Glad to hear A.C.H. is better and also that something was done for her last autumn.

As to poem ["A Draft of Three Cantos"], string it out into three numbers if that's the best you can do. Price named for magazine rights is satisfactory. Only fer gawd's sake send it along as soon as possible.

Let us hope you may get over your dislike of the poem by the time the last of it is printed; you disliked "Contemporania" and even the first of Frost himself, and you loathed and detested Eliot. Contemporania didn't exactly wreck the magazine. You have even put some of them into the anthology [*The New Poetry*]. . . .

Alice Corbin Henderson to Harriet Monroe   *[Santa Fe], 9 June 1917*

Confidential

Dear Harriet:—

I'm awfully sorry that you took what I meant to be a *plaintive* tone as a knock. I've been past "knocks" for a very long time indeed . . . . —
Lately it has seemed to me that there were too many *remnants* of imagism . . . . . .

Confidential

What I indicated in my last letter as having on my chest, was Ezra Pound in the last Little Review. I am utterly disgusted, and am writing him to say so. I mean particularly his opening contribution. The rest of the stuff seems to me poor enough. I wrote and told him when I read the announcement of his connection with that journal that I thought he was a fool, but I wasn't prepared for this indication of it! . . .

As you know, I have always been a staunch advocate of E.P. and I would hate now to do anything to cut off his income or anything of that sort. But obviously we have different ideals of conduct. I can not understand why he should so calmly assume that he was at liberty to be foreign correspondent of The Little Review *and* Poetry, unless he had made arrangements with you in advance? It isn't as if the L.R. were paying him handsomely. . . . I suppose the real trouble is that Ezra *has no sense of values*. To connect oneself with the L.R. as it has been for the last two or three months is perhaps suicidal enough to be sufficient punishment in itself! .... Isn't he a great idiot? . . .

Harriet Monroe to Ezra Pound   *11 June 1917*
[*Note on receipt form for payment of £21 for "Three Cantos"*]

I have much to say, but no time to say it now, so I won't delay this draft. This is the best I can possibly do for the poem—just now anyway. Poetry is strapped—and terrible bills coming in for paper etc. H.M.

Alice Corbin Henderson to Harriet Monroe   Santa Fe, 15 June 1917

Dear Harriet:

. . . About Ezra, I think I would simply write him a letter and say that you were surprised that he should assume, without saying anything to you, that he could continue as F.C. for Poetry and for the L.R. as well, and that his policy of washing linen in public is not exactly in good taste, nor gentlemanly, etc. Whatever else you care to say of course I can't dictate. At first I was simply furious, but I am honestly too sorry for E.P. to continue mad. He ruins his own case continually and perpetually. I told him he was an idiot to tie up with the L.R. before I saw this last no. Haven't written since. . . .

Harriet Monroe to Ezra Pound   *3 July 1917*

Dear E.P.

I have been somewhat surprised at your taking up with the Little Review without saying a word to me about it; still more at your airing public matters which I should have thought anyone would have held confidential—and in a misrepresenting sort of way, moreover, for there has been no spirit of compromise in POETRY. I never pretended to hand over the Editorship and make it your "organ." Also I have marvelled somewhat over the bad taste, and, I must confess, the dumbness of your slam at Tagore, whom you once admired. And, though Eliot is clever, I am not overwhelmed by your first numbers. But all this may be according to your ideas of good faith. — —I could, with some effort perhaps, try to understand them. The item which strains most severely the belief I have always had in your fundamental loyalty is the Little Review's printing of the poems by Yeats in July and August—poems, which, apparently, if you are still acting for us, should have been sent to me. This, taken in conjunction with the fact that Mr. Yeats has recently refused, for another poem, the highest rate per page we ever offered him, would seem to indicate that your influence with him of late has not been in our favor. So I should like to know what is your idea of our present relation—are you still expecting to send us the best verse you can get hold of, and to confine your Little Review activities to prose?

I am more sensitive than you seem to be over any connection with such a magazine as the Little Review has been during the last year or so, when I have thought even its Editor—in fact, everyone except its creditors—was losing faith in it. Perhaps you can pull it up—doubtless you would not try unless someone (perhaps Mr. John Quinn?) were giving it more solid financing than it has ever had. Its promise of forty pages in the next number convinces me that there must be money behind it. . . .

Your prose, when you take the trouble, is good hard stuff, done with style. But some that you send us, like one or two editorials now in the office, may be called "slop" with probably more justice than anything which troubles you in our prose section—loose, shapeless, full of repetitions, etc. And when it is slop thrown in other people's faces that antagonizes without other result, I have to draw the line. . . . And your violence against all things American doesn't strike home as it would if you used a more Gallic stroke; also, of course, the effect is left-handed, because you are expatriate. You are your own worst enemy, alas! Something in you fails to realize that a little rudimentary tact is not compromise; that anyone who carries a bludgeon for friend and foe finds himself before long, butting the empty air. My very respect for your work makes me wish you would not plant yourself so violently in front of it. . . .

"Lustra" arrived at last. Not having it hitherto, I didn't know you had changed certain poems quoted in THE NEW POETRY. Glad you like the collection, on the whole. It has many faults, no doubt, but Alice dropped out of the work early, and I had much too much to do. . . . No more Anthologies for me! . . .   •

I guess this is enough for to-day.

My illness interrupted my campaign for refinancing POETRY, but I hope to finish next Autumn, though the war makes everything uncertain.

H.M.

In its June issue, the *Little Review* had printed Yeats's "The Wild Swans at Coole," "Presences," "A Deep Sworn Vow," and "In Memory of William Pollexfen." In August, *L.R.* presented Yeats's "Upon a Dying Lady," for which H.M. had offered his agent $11 a page, which was declined.

Ezra Pound to Harriet Monroe   *[London], 23 July 1917*

Dear H. M.

Re/ yours of July 3. Among the main points of your original program was the statement that "Poetry" aimed to secure for the poet a cash reward (or comparable) to that given to sculptors and painters for work requiring equivalent time and skill.

I have seen little or no mention of this aim for some time.

When I had been reduced to two cheques of 15/ shillings each for a period of six months, it looked rather like a freeze-out, and I do not blame myself for looking elsewhere for my rent and victuals. . . .

I shall certainly bull the market on Yeats' and Eliot's stuff. If the guarantors want the swank of making Chicago THE centre, they can fork up. . . .

Returning to your opening paragraph. I can't see that I in the L.R. imply that you pretended to hand over the editorship of Poetry to me. I specifically mention attacks or an attack on Poetry made by calling it my "instrument" or some such word. A.C.H. had made one reply in the Transcript, and I certainly had as much right to make my own correction, saying it was more than my instrument. I have mentioned all the points to you privately and often during the past five years, and no notices taken of them.

Re/ my prose. When you don't want it, all I ask is that you send it back at once, so that I can use it elsewhere before it is too late. . . .

The implication for some time has been that I am a dead weight about your neck, and that your Chicago Committee was always wanting me got rid of. . . .

My conception of loyalty does not include staying behind your entrenchment in perpetuum. I shall use the L.R. to carry things as far forward as possible. It is mainly a prose organ, and one for projection of things outside the scope of the prose section of Poetry.

I dont see that my position is a bit weaker for being expatriate. It would be untenable if, knowing the life of the arts is more vital on this side of the Atlantic, I continued to live in a suburb.

The best artists come over here. Masters has relapsed into his surroundings, given way to them. Sandburg alone is keeping his flag up. . . .

Chicago, America in general, has got nothing but money. If they want to be an art centre they must at least contribute *that*, they must at least give what they've got. . . .

Robert Frost to Harriet Monroe   *[telegram] Amherst, Mass.,*
2 November 1917

DEAR MISS MONROE:
MY CONGRATULATIONS TO YOU AND YOUR FELLOW EDITORS OF POETRY ON WHAT IS BOUND TO PROVE A VERY POPULAR AWARD IN THIS FAMILY [a $100 prize for "Snow"]. I WAS FEELING BLUE WHEN LIKE A BOLT FROM THE BLUE CAME SO MUCH WEALTH AND GLORY. I AM THE MORE SENSIBLE OF IT ALL THAT IT IS MY FIRST REAL PRIZE IN A LONG LIFE. HITHERTO MY UTMOST HAD BEEN A FEW DOLLARS FOR RUNNING AT A CALEDONIA CLUB PICNIC, A PART INTEREST IN A PAIR OF EAR-RINGS, AND A PART INTEREST IN A GOLD-HEADED CANE FOR IMPERSONATIONS AT A MASQUERADE, A GOLD MEDAL FOR SHEER GOODNESS IN HIGH SCHOOL, AND A DETUR FOR SCHOLARSHIP AT HARVARD. ALWAYS SINCERELY YOURS

ROBERT FROST

Homer L. Pound to Harriet Monroe   *U.S. Mint, Philadelphia, Pa.,*
5 November 1918

Miss Monroe.
    Poetry.
    My Dear Miss Monroe. I have Mss. of Ezra's on New poetry—and he wishes me to ask you if you "Does she want it"[sic] Payment to be made to him.—

    Why do I have it? Well, I made a sort of muddle over this Mss. thinking I was doing him a favor. Before sending it to you I thought best to hear from you. I have not seen anything of his in Poetry for some time, I suppose "there's a reason".

    I am enjoying the Nov. Poetry—especially the Chippewa Songs. In my early days I saw much of the life of the Chippewa Indians in

Northern Wisconsin, so I may say I am a Chippewa—as I was born in
Chippewa Falls Wis....

4. "Homage to Sextus Propertius"

Homer Pound's timing was awkward, to say the least. Ezra had just given
Poetry another gratuitous slam in the September 1918 issue of the *Little
Review*, through a snide but hopelessly misinformed article on American
poetry by the English novelist Edgar Jepson that had first appeared, to
scant notice, in the *English Review*. Based on selective misreading, Jepson
claimed *Poetry* to be the center of a western school of writing notable for
its ugly American speech and cultural content. While praising T. S. Eliot,
he classed Frost, Lindsay, Masters, and Sandburg as types of the primitive
"plopp-eyed bungaroo." Anyone familiar with *Poetry*'s actual publishing
history could see how weirdly distorted the article was. Aside from get-
ting in another dig, why Pound would bother using Quinn's money to
reprint a piece he knew to be quite worthless is a mystery.

Again, Monroe did not seem to be angry at Pound for his attack by
proxy. On 25 November, she sent him a letter of acceptance for four sec-
tions from "Homage to Sextus Propertius," and offered Pound a generous
£10/10. She showed the manuscript or perhaps the page proofs to
William Gardner Hale, a distinguished classicist at the University of
Chicago, who was appalled and counseled her not to publish it. Even so,
parts I, II, III, and VI from the sequence appeared in the March 1919 issue.
The next month the Editor published Hale's scathing critique, "Pegasus
Impounded."

Eliot, in his introduction to Pound's 1928 *Selected Poems*, defended
"Propertius" as a "persona" or "paraphrase." A noble gesture, but Hale's
citations of numerous errors in elementary Latin grammar and mistrans-
lations—which served no purpose as *poetry*—were hard evidence that
Pound had misread the original. As Hale put it: "Mr. Pound is incredibly
ignorant of Latin. He has of course a perfect right to be, but not if he
translates from it. The result of his ignorance is that much of what he
makes his author say is unintelligible." Hale said he found "about three
score errors," but kindly limited his remarks to the more egregious ones,
and their sometimes hilarious consequences. His conclusion:

If Mr. Pound were a professor of Latin, there would be nothing left for
him but suicide. I do not counsel this. But I beg him to lay aside the
mask of erudition. And, if he must deal in Latin, I suggest that he para-

phrase some accurate translation, and then employ some respectable student of the language to save him from blunders.

With another writer, "liberties" in translation might have been chalked up to poetic license. But Pound had presented himself as a great expert in foreign tongues, and as a poet-critic he had demanded "precision" as the first principle of his artistic creed.

Pound responded with a short letter of protest on 14 April 1919, and signed off: "In final commiseration," which H.M. took as his resignation. She discussed the position of Foreign Correspondent with Richard Aldington, and he agreed to come on in October, but only if he had firm assurances that Pound was out. On 1 November, H.M. wrote E.P. formally, accepting the obvious. Pound did not contribute poems again until 1933.

Alice Corbin Henderson to Harriet Monroe   *Santa Fe,*
                                                              7 November 1918

Dear Harriet:

I was about to write to you this morning at eleven, when all the whistles started blowing down town and the bells ringing—the reports of the signing of the armistice, perhaps premature, but I hope true. . . .

Another thing, Harriet. What precisely are your present relations with Ezra? Does he do anything at all for you? If he doesn't, after the French leave he took of you in his first issue of The Little Review, I see no reason for keeping him on. . . . He has his own *organ* now—and *leave him have it*!

Ezra Pound to Harriet Monroe   *London, 14 April 1919*

Editor,
Poetry.

Cat-pisss and porcupines!! The thing ["Propertius"] is no more a translation than my "Altaforte" is a translation, or than Fitzgerald's Omar is a translation.

Poor brute [Professor Hale] naturally cant make much of the fragment of the poem you have used; but he misses a number of avoidances of literal meaning, including that unfortunate (from his presumable? point of view) mis-statement about Thebes.

                                        in final commiseration / E. Pound

5, HOLLAND PLACE CHAMBERS

Editor,
Poetry.

Cat-pisss and porcupines !! The thing is
no more a translation than my " Altaforte " is a translation,
or than Fitzgerald's Omar is a translation.

Poor brute naturally cant make much of the
fragment of the poem you have used ; but he misses a
number of avoidances of literal meaning, including that
presumable ?
unfortunate (from his point of view)   mis-statement about
Thebes.

in final commiseration

E. Pound

14-4°19

H.M. took this letter of 14 April 1919 as E.P.'s resignation
as Foreign Correspondent.

Harriet Monroe to Ezra Pound   *1 November 1919*

My dear Mr. Pound:

Your last letter to me, received in May, was signed under the words,
"in final commiseration."

I have taken this, as you doubtless intended, as a resignation from the
staff of POETRY, a resignation emphasized by your subsequent silence.
But as I am about to make an arrangement for a London correspon-
dent, it may be as well for me to say this word in formal acceptance of
the situation.

I feel unfailing gratitude for all that you did to help the magazine

along during those difficult first years, and deep regret that we have had
to come to a parting of the ways. I cordially hope that you will con-
tinue to contribute to POETRY, and that poems finer than you have
ever written—which is saying a great deal—may be yours next year
and the years after.

With all good wishes, I am / Yours sincerely, / Harriet Monroe

5. An Afterword

Commenting on the split in her autobiography, Monroe observed that
Pound continued to prod in the years following. "And if his stings and
stabs should cease," she wrote in 1935, "it would mean for me the loss of
life's most deliciously acrid flavor." But from his earliest correspondence,
Pound's attitude was clear. He was the Idea Man, Miss Monroe and her
staff handmaidens, as it were, who could attend to the menial chores of
proofreading, production, distribution, subscriptions, routine correspon-
dence, record keeping. And, of course, raising the funds to pay him and
the poets. (He adopted the same manner in his dealings with Harriet
Weaver at the *Egoist* and Margaret Anderson and Jane Heap at the *Little
Review*.) When sorely tried, Monroe did assert her authority, but more
often than not she gave in to E.P. because of his badgering.

With the passing years, Pound repeatedly charged that he had to "ham-
mer" in Frost, Eliot, H.D., and others, leaving the lasting impression that
Monroe had to be coerced into printing them. But the facts do not sup-
port this claim. Whatever her reservations, or the pressures on her pro-
duction schedule, she did print most of Pound's recommendations within
three or four months, sometimes sooner: this, in the days of transatlantic
mail by slow steamer. A very few, like Eliot, "waited" for perhaps eight
months between manuscript arrival and appearance in print—which a
poet today would consider very speedy service indeed. The truth remains
that *Poetry* received most of its bad press and harshest reactions from
readers when Monroe presented poems sent in by the Foreign Corre-
spondent. Despite his adverse effects, she consistently stood up for him.

Always adept at myth, Pound was a prodigious propagandist for
authors he believed in, and for himself. When he presented a revisionist
account of "Little Magazines" and his years at *Poetry* in the *English Journal*
in 1930, Monroe offered a rebuttal, which probably few saw. But Monroe
abetted Pound's mythologizing (and did herself a disservice) in *A Poet's
Life*, by putting a positive spin on their many conflicts. She was very
selective in the Pound letters she presented, each carefully edited to
smooth over the rough spots. (Pound's *Selected Letters* [1950] was well

edited, too, and arranged to magnify his participation, as Monroe's successor, Morton Dauwen Zabel, pointed out in his memoir of H.M. in *Poetry* in January 1961.) But, as the original texts indicate, Pound was a far more dodgy collaborator than the heroic figure he and some historians have portrayed.

What is very clear in their exchanges is that both poets were idealists, but a basic conflict in motives made it hard for them to cooperate. Both wanted to advance the art and improve the lot of poets. Each bore resentment toward keepers of the status quo in the literary establishment and the academy. Monroe's response was to create her own venture and to put it on a firm footing. Pound was a poet-critic of intense but constantly shifting enthusiasms, a man of concepts and causes fervently proclaimed but sometimes quickly abandoned, a generous supporter of fellow artists whose mercurial personality made it difficult for him to sustain friendships.

Pound considered publishers and editors charlatans (with the possible exception of those who printed him), and the public they catered to philistines. He espoused the elitist premise of Art for Art's Sake and its corollary, that only other poets—and then but a select few—could judge and appreciate poetry. As early as December 1912, he told Monroe: "so far as I personally am concerned the public can go to the devil." But the Editor's express purpose in founding *Poetry* was to create a larger audience. As she reminded him during their first big crisis in October 1913, "This magazine is an effort to encourage the art, to work up a public for it in America."

To Pound, Art arose from those aspiring to the highest standards and using the most rigorous techniques—necessarily a small and very exclusive group. Monroe wanted to be *inclusive*, welcoming innovators while respecting those who practiced the craft along traditional lines, including the "minor" voices. (After all, she knew she was one of them.) In August 1912, she wrote Arthur Davison Ficke, with typically vague high-mindedness: "I must lead my subscribers gently to the appreciation of poetry of that lofty kind." But she was particularly proud of her own relatively down-to-earth poems on "modern" subjects, "The Hotel" and "The Turbine." Pound was far less interested in subject matter. Manner of presentation, level of technical skill, made the true measure of an artist's worth.

Given their differences, the wonder is that their relationship lasted as long as it did. But if they disagreed on many points, they were not alone. Editors, authors, and critics have been taking sides and arguing over the same questions about the nature of the art and the best way to advance it in hundreds of little magazines founded since *Poetry* began.

CHAPTER X

World War I and the Aftermath

Poets have made more wars than kings, and war will not cease until
they remove its glamour from the imaginations of men.
—Harriet Monroe, *Poetry*, September 1914

1. Poets and *Poetry* in Wartime

After the banquet for Yeats in March 1914, Monroe recalled in *A Poet's Life*, "the world seemed at peace and intent upon progress toward a new and more friendly internationalism. Neither he nor I realized that we had reached the end of an epoch." A few weeks later, Rupert Brooke arrived in Chicago, on his way home to England from Tahiti. He saw Maurice Browne, who was producing his play, *Lithuania*, at the Little Theatre, then stopped by 543 Cass Street. The Editor was alone in the office when the poet Yeats described as "the most beautiful man in England" arrived unannounced. She invited him home for dinner, and they talked about poetry and their "Far Eastern adventures," his in the South Sea Islands, hers in China and Japan. She also had a photographer friend take his portrait. The picture was framed, with a letter Brooke sent her in October, shortly after he entered training at the Royal Naval Barracks; it still hangs in the *Poetry* office. In July Brooke sent "Retrospect," which was printed in the October 1914 issue. By then most of Europe was at war.

On 28 June, the Archduke Francis Ferdinand, heir to throne of Austria-Hungary, and his wife were assassinated at Sarajevo, Bosnia, and Austria-Hungary declared war on Serbia. On 4 August, Germany invaded Belgium, and Great Britain declared war on Germany. "It was a sudden shattering of hope, a brutal denial of progress, a bloody anachronism," Monroe wrote in her autobiography. In August she traveled to Colorado for a long-planned camping trip with her brother Will. When she returned, she found that Mrs. Henderson had announced that *Poetry* was conducting a contest for the best poem "based on the present European situation." The Editor went along with A.C.H.'s plan, although in the

September issue she published an editorial, "The Poetry of War," which placed a good deal of blame for wars on the collaboration of artists, who through battle hymns, epics, and statues abetted kings, "to give war its glamour, to transmute into . . . forms of beauty its savagery and horror, to give heroic appeal to its unreason, a heroic excuse to its rage and lust."

Pound wrote 15 September, strenuously objecting to the contest, but it was too late. No less than 738 entries arrived— "good, bad, and indifferent, but mostly very bad"—but they agreed with the Editor's position: "All these war poems of our contest were protests." Fourteen were selected for the November 1914 "War" (or antiwar) number; Louise Driscoll's "The Metal Checks" won the

Rupert Brooke in a photograph H.M. had taken when he visited her in April 1914. It hangs in the *Poetry* office, framed with the letter he sent in October 1914 from the Royal Naval Barracks.

$100 prize. Other contributors included Henderson herself, Sandburg, Lowell, Bodenheim, Stevens, and Aldington. Aldington was already sending reports on the situation in England and Europe.

At the beginning of the war, there was optimism, as many felt it would all be over within months—a year or two at most—and the armed forces were filled by volunteers. Aldington wrote that by mid-August almost 100,000 had enlisted. He and Pound tried to sign up but were rejected. E.P. wrote in August 1914 that "the War is eating up all everybody's subconscious energy." Another of Monroe's correspondents about the war was D. H. Lawrence, who was found unfit for service because of his frail health. On 1 October 1914, he wrote from Buckinghamshire: "In this god-forsaken little hole I sit like a wise rabbit with my pen behind my ear, and listen to distant noises. I am not in the war zone." The War Issue made him livid:

It put me in such a rage—how dare Amy talk about Bohemian glass and stalks of flame!—that in a real fury I had to write my war poem,

because it breaks my heart, this war. I hate, and hate, and hate, the glib
irreverence of some of your contributors. . . .

The War is dreadful. It is the business of the artist to follow it home
to the heart of the individual fighter—not to talk in armies and nations
and numbers, but to track it home, home, this war. And it's at the bot-
tom of almost every Englishman's heart—the War, the desire of War,
the will to War—and at the bottom of every German's.

In December 1914, Monroe printed an editorial suggesting war as
catharsis: "the world must get what comfort it can out of the heroic self-
sacrifice, and the purging and cleansing effect of war." Such delusions did
not last. As the months dragged on, the realities of mechanized warfare
sank in—the agonies of the trenches, the poison gas attacks, and the enor-
mous carnage ending in stalemate. Over the course of the war, England
had over 8.9 million in uniform, and suffered over 3.1 million casualties.

Rupert Brooke was one of the early fatalities, and to Monroe a per-
sonal loss as well as "a symbol of the waste of war." He had written her
about the siege at Antwerp in 1914, and sent a group of his war sonnets in
January 1915—"Peace," "The Dead," and "The Soldier," with its famous
opening lines: "If I should die, think only this of me: / That there's some
corner of a foreign field / That is for ever England." With the manuscript
he enclosed a note: "I doubt if I have time to write any more before I go
out again." The poems were scheduled for April.

Shortly after the issue came off the press, Brooke was gone; he died of
blood poisoning (some said sunstroke) on 23 April in the Dardanelles.
Monroe's draft in payment, with a note wishing "good luck to you," was
returned with "deceased" scrawled on the envelope. She eventually was
able to get the check to the poet's mother. Pound notified H.M. immedi-
ately on hearing of his death. Pound did not really like Brooke's work,
and could only bring himself to write a short tribute, "Whom the Gods
Love," which she did not print. The Editor's own memorial notice to the
"lyric Apollo" appeared in June 1915. Her eulogy concluded: "He is
archetypal of the millions upon millions of proud young men who have
gone singing to their death on the world's battlefields, obscure pawns in
mighty games played for ends they never questioned."

By fall 1914, the war had escalated drastically. Paris was under a state of
siege, and the Battle of the Marne took place on 6–10 September. Early
in October, Antwerp surrendered to the Germans, who started bombing
cities along the east coast of England in December. In early 1915, German
submarines started to blockade the British Isles, and on 7 May the
Cunard liner *Lusitania* was sunk off the Irish coast, claiming 1,152 people,
over one hundred of them Americans. Zeppelins began bombing the

London suburbs; in June several other English towns were hit. As casual-
ties rose, volunteers were not sufficient; in February 1916, Britain started
conscripting troops.

Aldington was among those drafted, and served on the Western Front
from 1916 to 1918, until he was gassed. In *Death of a Hero* (1929), he
recounted in graphic detail the savage conditions at the Front. Among
the notable English poets and writers who served was Robert Graves,
who told of his experiences in *Goodbye to All That* (also 1929). Siegfried
Sassoon enlisted in 1914 in the Royal Welch Fusiliers, where he met
Graves. Recovering from shell shock, he became friends with Wilfred
Owen, who was being treated in the same hospital. Regarded as one of
the greatest of all war poets, Owen died one week before the Armistice.

Ford Madox Hueffer served in the Welch Regiment, as well. He suf-
fered nervous collapse following ten days under fire during the Battle of
the Somme. (In that month-long battle alone, 400,000 English troops
were killed.) After inhaling poison gas, he was invalided home in 1917.
After convalescing near Dieppe, Pound's friend and collaborator Wynd-
ham Lewis was returned to the Front near Dunkirk in 1917. He told E.P.
of being gassed and shelled all night; but he survived the war. T. E.
Hulme, Pound's mentor and the chief theorist for Imagism, was not so
lucky. Stationed less than a mile away from Lewis, he was blown to bits
by a direct hit.

In 1916, *Poetry* printed one of the strongest poems to come out of the
war, "Break of Day in the Trenches," by Isaac Rosenberg. In contrast to
Brooke's conventionally patriotic verses, it gave an unvarnished view of
battle-line experience. He enlisted in October 1915 and served in the
Royal Lancaster Regiment, never rising above the rank of private. He
was sent to the Western Front in 1916 and stayed there, first in the
trenches at the Somme. In September 1916, Rosenberg sent Monroe
"Break of Day," which, she recalled, was written "on ragged scraps of
dirty paper." She printed it, along with his poem "Marching," in Decem-
ber 1916. Even after several hospitalizations, Rosenberg was sent back to
the trenches. He was shot to death at dawn on 1 April 1918.

The United States did not sever relations with Germany until Febru-
ary 1917. War was finally declared on 6 April, and President Wilson signed
the conscription bill on 18 May. Eventually over 4.3 million U.S. forces
were mobilized; almost 365,000 became casualties. When the United
States joined the Allies, Monroe observed, "the American public became
impatient for war poems, martial masterpieces." In a July 1917 editorial,
she found, "As yet poets writing in English have but touched the edges of
this awful subject."

Many Americans had already gone Over There to fight or to serve in the auxiliaries. Polly Root, Monroe's niece, went to France as early as 1915, to work for the Fund for the French Wounded. The following year, Monroe's recently widowed sister, Lucy Calhoun, became the chief recorder of cases in the Red Cross hospital at Neuilly. Monroe commended a number of other women who served, including the poet Eloise Robinson, who ran a "rolling canteen" at the Front. While serving hot chocolate one day, Robinson wrote H.M., she tried to recite "a beautiful poem on trees by Joyce Kilmer," but couldn't remember the words. "One of the soldiers thereupon recited it—it was Sergeant Kilmer himself! This was only a few weeks before he was killed."

Writing from the battlefields on 5 August 1918, Robinson described the physical and psychological conditions of both troops and volunteers. In the October 1918 issue, H.M. printed Robinson's poem "War," and a portion of her letter:

> I wish I might tell you of my visit to the French Front, and how for two nights I slept in a "cave" with seven Frenchmen and had a hundred bombs dropped on top of me. Not directly on top, of course. The nearest hit just in front of the house, and for five days and nights after that I was taking chocolate to advance batteries of men who can never leave their guns, even to come to the *Foyer du Soldat*. The Foyer was only a dug-out, and the air was so thick with flies and smoke that it looked like jam. Every morning when I got up I literally had to pry myself out of the mud—of course there were no beds. . . .
>
> I cannot count the officers who have told me that if they have someone to entertain the boys just before they go into the trenches they go in laughing and singing and apparently happy, but if they do not have anything of the sort the men are very different—quiet and thinking all kinds of mournful things. And the need is even greater when they come out. Our boys haven't been used to killing and seeing other men killed, and it is pretty hard for them.

Other women volunteers tried to cheer up the troops with various kinds of entertainment. Laura Sherry, the manager of a little theater in Milwaukee, went to France and set up dramatic troupes that put on plays with and for soldiers. Eunice Tietjens went to Paris in the fall of 1917 as a reporter for the Chicago *Daily News*; she helped distribute toys to children, and sent back word of H.M.'s relatives and gossip. (Alice Henderson wrote H.M. 7 November 1918, with annoyance: "And what the devil is Eunice doing in Paris that she doesn't send you any news of French poets?") For some of the volunteers, the strains of war service were overwhelming. Gladys Cromwell, whose work *Poetry* published in 1917 and 1918, ran a canteen service in France with her twin sister early in 1918. "Delicately reared" in a wealthy New York family, H.M. recalled, the women found the grim realities of war too great a "nervous strain": they leapt from the ship that was to take them home and drowned in the Seine.

Many copies of *Poetry* were sent to men at the Front. Throughout the war and in the months following the Armistice, letters from American soldier-poets arrived at the office, some of which Monroe printed. Writing from the Front, Paul B. Sifton reflected: "At the time of taking the soldier's oath I thought to gain color for future writings. Now that I am here, close to the quivering wide-gaping wound of War, I have put the thought from me, for a time at least—perhaps for good, if my life is necessary in the caging of the imperialists. If I come out—pathos, hate, lust, abnegation, I shall have known them all." Malcolm W. Vaughn, another infantryman who saw action on the front line, reported:

> We were nearly a dozen in a foul dugout one night (though its foulness was sweet for the safety it offered). A pretty heavy bombardment was going on above and most of us were not without fear. We jerked out an occasional sentence and smoked heavily, and altogether wished we might be some miles back; when some fellow from the west, quite simply—naturally it seemed then—began Aldington's "Choricos." We listened; fell upon it eagerly; were thankful. As he came to the invocation to Death he stood up full length, his head at the roof of the *abri*, and recited those splendid lines with an aristocracy of accent which gave them sympathy and understanding. I tell you, those lines are immortal; more than that, they offered us immortality to share in.

From the trenches an unidentified soldier also touched upon poetry: "To read poetry in the midst of these naked circumstances out here is a pretty mean test; but I have found that some of Miss Lowell, Masters, Sandburg and Lindsay have survived where several of my old favorites have died in the shuffle." The doughboy's succinct observation was a harbinger of the final passing, for many, of the older styles of poetry, and the collapse of the philosophical sentiments expressed therein. Platitudinous verses seemed increasingly irrelevant in the face of brutal modern realities. Through the last months of the war, *Poetry* reported on the whereabouts of American soldier-poets in the various branches of the service. By Armistice Day, 11 November 1918, the magazine had printed thirty-two of them.

Richard Aldington to Harriet Monroe   The Egoist, *London,*
                                                    7 August 1914

Dear Miss Monroe,

Thanks for yr cheque & for the paper received. We are having moderate hell here. The country is practically under martial law. Every hour brings some fresh news of fighting. Everything is disorganized, and most of our sources of income are cut off. Your paper was the first American mail we have had for a week.

I went the other day to join the Honourable Artillery Company and thanks to my peculiar appearance was temporarily arrested as a spy! To-day I went with Hueffer to see [C. F.] Masterman [member of the British Cabinet] and Ezra & I have put ourselves at the disposal of the government. Don't expect we can do much.

This is going to be the biggest thing in history—you Americans must stand by us, especially the artists, because we're all done for, at least for a decade.

The Belgian defence of Liege has given England & France enough time, I hope. The North Sea is sown with mines, so the British Fleet is useless except for defence. But you'll know all this from the papers; but we can't talk of anything else.

Miss Lowell is safe in London; Fletcher is lost in Switzerland; Cannell in Paris. Conrad is in Hamburg. There is no communication with Germany. The Embassies & the [American] Express Co. are doing all they can for Americans; I don't think they'll suffer. It's queer to hear Americans fleeing from the Continent talking of England as "home"!

I think we'll win through.

                                    Yrs in great haste, / Richard Aldington

Ezra Pound to Harriet Monroe   London, *15 September 1914*

Dear H.M.

. . . I am VERY glad that you had nothing to do with that "War Poem" prize offer. After trying for two years to make the point that poetry is an art, it is rather disheartening to have the magazine burst out with a high school folly . . . .

I can see no chance of making that War Prize anything but ridiculous unless you defer it at least a year. I suppose it can't in honour be withdrawn. UNLESS there is positively no response before Oct. 15. . . . Some ass is sure to do something, but if there is any excuse for not doing it I should certainly drop the matter at once. . . .

Rupert Brooke to Harriet Monroe Royal Naval Barracks, Chatham, 28 October 1914

Dear Miss Monroe,

I received the cheque for £1-10 (also your note from a few weeks ago). Many thanks. It's very acceptable money—in these indigent days.

I'm afraid I shan't do anything more while the war lasts: and we expect it to go on at least a year more, probably two. Afterwards, I hope to start again: I've been having a great time (& a terrible one, in a way). We, the Naval Brigades, went to Antwerp for the last part of the siege. I'll never forget the sight of hundreds of thousands of refugees, white desperate stunned creatures. There can never have been a nation so amazed and tortured in European memory. For me who liked Germany as much as I did, it is incredibly painful.

She'll pay the penalty in the end, whatever it costs. I hope the world'll be better afterward.

Shelter the refugee Muses for a time. Europe is no place for them.

Good luck to you. / Rupert Brooke

Ezra Pound to Harriet Monroe London, 9 November 1914

Dear H.M.:

... There is an exhibit of Rodin at the South Kensington museum, good of its kind but it does look like muck after one has got one's eye in on [Jacob] Epstein's Babylonian austerity. And [Henri Gaudier-] Brzeska's work, for all that he is only 22, is much more interesting. ...

Brzeska by the way is at the front, French army. 7 out of his squad of 12 were killed off a few weeks ago, when scouting. He has killed two "boches." The dullness in the trenches for the last weeks has bored him so that he is doing an essay on sculpture for the next number of *BLAST.* Also he has done a figure, working with his jacknife and an entrenching tool. ...

Richard Aldington to Harriet Monroe London, 13 January 1915

Dear miss Monroe,

... M. [Rémy] de Gourmont wrote me the other [day] that you had sent him a cheque, which was "fort bien". I am so sorry that you were disappointed with the article. It seemed reasonably good to me, but then it is natural to be very indulgent toward the work of a friend. If you are disappointed I can only ask you to remember that M. de Gourmont has in his time done a great deal for European literature. He is

now old and very ill and grief-stricken over the war; he has lost very
dear friends and young men in whose future he had great hopes; and
his young brother has just been mobilised. Therefore I am not alto-
gether surprised to find him writing badly; the wonder to me is that he
can write at all. . . .
    I enclose [a] list of French writers killed & wounded & prisoners.

                                        Yours very sincerely / Richard Aldington

R.A. had sent an article by Gourmont 14 November; H.M. sent advance payment,
but it was not printed. On 1 October 1915, Aldington wrote that Gourmont had
just died, at age fifty-seven: "He had been ill for a long time, and the anxiety of the
war killed him. It is a great loss to literature."

Rupert Brooke to Harriet Monroe   *The Hood Battalion, Royal*
                    Naval Division, Blandford, Dorset,
                                    26 January 1915

Dear Miss Monroe,
    Military training and life haven't left me much time or energy for
studying. But I ground out these five [War Sonnets], to appear in the
next and (for the time) final New Numbers, sometime, I think, toward
the end of next month. So if they seem to you worth printing—there
they are, one or all. One, perhaps two, are goodish, I think. I doubt if I
have time to write any more before I go out again.
    Chicago seems very remote from the good and evil of Europe. . . .

Ezra Pound to Harriet Monroe   *London, [28 April 1915]*

Dear H.M.
    I had intended to do a longish appreciation and threnody on
Brooke, but I have got his book [*Poems*, 1911] and reread or at least read
it, and if I appraise it sincerely the article will develop into an attack on
his pestiferous group, his English niceness, his stomach for what is worst
in mod. eng. poetry, etc. etc., all of which would be untimely. He is not
as good as [Ernest] Dowson. . . .
    Brooke has been, undoubtedly *taken* by some belated goddess with a
taste for beautiful semi-conscious youth. He was the type of the "young
Lovell" but if I develop that theme I shall sentimentalize and also I
should be impertinent and intrude rather on the privacy of his death,
for I had only met him twice and have no right to a public lament.
    His association with the dullest of english writers was unfortunate,
but still he was of their class, he agreed with them, though he was a
damd sight better poet than any of them. . . .

WHOM THE GODS LOVE

Rupert Brooke who had sailed with the British expeditionary force to the Dardanelles is reported dead at Lemnos. The accounts give a rather confused statement of the cause, ascribing it to sunstroke and septic poisoning. He was, with Walter de la Mare and D.H. Lawrence, the best of the poets of the Georgian Anthology group and will be widely regretted....

There is in his work a fine *élan* and many who could not agree with his tendencies as an artist will mourn the loss of a very good poet *sub flore juventutis* [in the flower of youth]. He was twenty-seven on the third of August last, the day of the declaration of war.

(Ezra Pound)

Arthur Aldis to Harriet Monroe [April 1915]

Dear Miss Munroe [sic]—I wonder if this, from Cathleen Nesbitt, might not properly be published in *Poetry* [July 1915]—and would it not interest readers. Yrs—Arthur Aldis

Upon hearing of the death of Rupert Brooke, Winston Churchill telegraphed to his own brother, then in the Dardanelles, asking him to be his representative at the funeral. This short but very beautiful description of a romantic and fitting funeral was telegraphed back and a copy of it has been received by one of the subscribers to "*Poetry*"; we believe that it will be of interest to Rupert Brooke's many friends and admirers in this country:

"I received your wire about poor Rupert Brooke, but he was already buried. He had a most romantic funeral. French and English officers carried the coffin about two miles up a beautiful gully in Scyros Island, and he was buried at a spot he had admired a few days previously. The difficulties of carrying him were great as there was no road, and it was a long climb over very rough ground. He was buried at midnight, and as soon as the officers returned on board the transports weighed anchor and left for their rendezvous."

Richard Aldington to Harriet Monroe London, 10 May 1915

Dear Miss Monroe,

The effect of the war & the Lusitania [sunk on 7 May] has wrecked my nerves &, like the Belgian refugees, I am losing my memory! I had forgotten all about those verses, & for the life of me I cannot remember which you have, or how many....

Apparently, a good deal is expected from the latest attack of the

Allies. I am told that practically we can win the war, if England will sac-
rifice a million men. A heavy price for a war which was none of our
seeking.

Yours sincerely, / Richard Aldington

Richard Aldington to Harriet Monroe   The Egoist, *London,*
7 June 1915

Dear Miss Monro [sic],
. . . If you could see the men hobbling about without legs, without
arms, the blind soldiers & sailors being piloted along the streets by
nurses, you would cry against it even more. And England has suffered
less than any other of the belligerents!

You ought to be in Europe. The crash & overthrow of morals, insti-
tutions, nations, cities, of every decency & kindliness are comparable
nearly to the desolations of the fall of the Roman Empire. There is so
much more I would like to say on this subject, for I am utterly sickened
with this shambles; mais j'ai peur du censeur [but I fear the censor]! . . .

Ezra Pound to Harriet Monroe   London, *28 June 1915*

Dear H.M.
. . . I went out this A.M. and all that offers is the chance of a ghoul's
article on Brzeska. He was killed at Neuville St Vaast, early this month,
but the news is just in.

This is the heaviest loss in personnel the arts have suffered by the
war; it is not the case of a beautiful youth who had perhaps done his
best work. Brzeska was five years younger than Brooke, but he was a
man of full vigorous genius, and there is no one to replace him. Also he
had seen months of fighting and had been twice promoted for daring.
There is probably no artist fighting with any of the armies who might
not have been better spared.

Finis.

D. H. Lawrence to Harriet Monroe   London, *15 September 1915*

Dear Harriet Monroe,
How is poetry going in America? There is none in England: the
muse has gone, like the swallows in winter.

This is the real winter of the spirit in England. We are just preparing
to come to fast grips with the War. At last we are going to give our-
selves up to it—and everything else we are letting go. I thought we
should never come to this: but we are. And the war will go on for a
very long time. I knew it when I watched the Zeppelin the other

pure reality, the reality of the clear, eternal spirit. One must speak for life & growth, amid all this mass of destruction & disintegration.

So I bring out this little paper. And will you take it too, & get one or two friends to take it — not for the money's sake, but for the spirit which is struggling in it.

Pray to heaven to keep America always out of the war. God knows what will be the end of Europe. Yours D. H. Lawrence

1, BYRON VILLAS,
VALE-OF-HEALTH,
HAMPSTEAD,
LONDON.

15 Sept 1915

Dear Harriet Monroe,

How is poetry going in America? There is none in England: the muse has gone, like the swallows in winter. This is the real winter of the spirit in England. We are just

Despondent over the war, D. H. Lawrence wrote to H.M.,
15 September 1915.

night, gleaming like a new great sign in the heavens, a new, supreme celestial body. I knew by the spirit of London—game for fight, all consideration gone—and I knew by the look of the Zeppelin, which had assumed the heavens as its own. God knows now what the end will be.

Only I feel, that even if we are all going to be rushed down to extinction, one must hold up the other, living truth, of Right and pure reality, the reality of the clear, eternal spirit. One must speak for life & growth, amid all this mass of destruction & disintegration. . . .

Pray to heaven to keep America always out of the war. God knows what will be the end of Europe.

Yours / D. H. Lawrence

Richard Aldington to Harriet Monroe London, *29 November 1915*

Dear Miss Monroe,

I ought to have written you earlier, but Miss Weaver has gone away & left the whole of the Egoist in my care—& I have the translation series & a job of translating a novel as well!

H.D. was very glad to get the prize [$50, for five poems in March] &

asks me to thank you very heartily for it. Certainly among all the gloom & horror of this ghastly year, it comes as a most welcome reminder of the fact—which everyone here tries to make one forget— that the arts still go on & still have appreciators. The immense increase in the cost of living makes the money itself most welcome, & H.D., & I too, both want to thank you kind Americans for it, and more too for the spiritual boost!

I express myself badly. But you, who live in and long at peace, can have no idea of the extraordinary depression, the concentrated gloom of the countries at war. London is really fortunate—that little strip of sea means so much, but Paris! When the Parisians come to London now they call us frivolous—I'm afraid the Americans must find us funereal. . . .

After the first rage of sentimental patriotism had evaporated, I decided to keep out of this horror as long as possible. The accounts the returning soldiers give would freeze anybody off. I believe I can do more good by trying to keep a little wee corner for the arts than by peeling potatoes for ex-navies, blacking the boots of "temporary gentlemen" or by getting pneumonia in the trenches. Do you think so? I have made up my mind that in the event of my being conscripted I won't kill anyone—but there isn't much chance of that as most artists & highly sensitised people go mad in the first week! Jolly look out, isn't it? Do you know there are 153 names of dead writers in the Bulletin des Ecrivains? Over _10,000_ French schoolmasters have been killed. If the war goes on much longer there won't be any Europe left. Germany & Austria are bankrupt, so is Russia; France is on the edge; England within a year of it. And they say the war will last two years more. Without any metaphorical exaggeration, the nations are mad. Heaven knows what will come of it all.

But I mustn't depress you, especially as you will get this letter about Xmas time. I dare say we shall get through.

Thanks once more from us both. / R.A.

1 LCpl. Richard Aldington to Harriet Monroe   London,
21 December 1916

Dear Miss Monroe,

I'm just off to France, this afternoon as a matter of fact, so send you this little note of farewell. I haven't seen H.D., which is perhaps as well, for it might have worried her.

I hope Poetry will continue a success, and become financially as well as intellectually independent. Whatever happens, don't forget my interest in your paper & in American poetry. . . .

Well, as this may be the last time, good luck to you. Be nice to H.D.

> yours / Richard Aldington.

William Rose Benét to Harriet Monroe   The Century, *NewYork,*
11 June 1916

Dear Miss Monroe:

. . . Now that it's "Johnny get your gun" my mind is full of France day & night—but it seems I can't go yet. My eyesight has kept me out of Plattsburgh, though the rest of my physical exam. was satisfactory. . . . I know the best way I could help would be as an officer, if they'd only give me a chance. I have to be content so far as a Lieutenant in the Home Guard. I can't write of the war—except for one thing not yet published. The thing's out of all whooping now. Anything may eventuate. My own faith is that great big things are in the making—a new world. . . .

Well, we live day by day, now. Nothing is the same. I don't think it ever will be the same again. I don't see how it possibly can be.

> Sincerely, / Wm Rose Benét

Edgar Lee Masters to Harriet Monroe   Chicago, 29 May 1918

Dear Harriet

I want to withdraw "Spoon River Revisited." In a time like this when the nation is rising to such spiritual heights, this poem is out of key—is an affront to the America which is living so heroically. I feel you must agree with me.

> Truly, / E.L.M.

Richard Aldington to Harriet Monroe   [France], 21 June 1918

Dear Miss Monroe,

Your letter, after going all round England, was sent to me by H.D. for me to read, & then proceeded to go half round France before it reached me.

Thank you very much for the notice of "Reverie"; it is so much greater praise than the little book deserves. I only had a few copies printed for H.D. But I am chiefly happy to think that anything I have written ["Choricos"] has helped a soldier in France. It would take too long to explain just how much I am touched to think that any young men "remembered me in hell". This is really the first justification of my work that has ever reached me. . . .

William Rose Benét to Harriet Monroe   *[n. p.] 1 November [1918]*

My dear Miss Monroe:

Thanks. Hooray!

I'm due *something*, even if it sounds pathetic—for—but I should only break into awful & unhelpful cursing. And I said it in "Bomb-proof". There, as Robinson hath it, "is nothing more to say."

William Rose Benét, 1 November 1918. He had hoped to serve abroad; note that Poetry is shooting down Verse.

Germany looks to be licked. I guess it's over. I doubt if anybody will try ever to put anything over on the world again, not to mention America. They'll be rather foolish if they do. The latent energy in this country is something I never realized before this war. It can do anything it wants to.

I've put a new engine in my ship & am sending it back. Its rpm doesn't make the Liberty blush, but I guess it's about 2 lbs. per h.p. & that's the norm.

My ambition was to use the binoculars from a sausage on the bombing of Berlin. Too late now.

Love to you all, / Wm. R. Benét

[*P.S. in left margin:*] Oh, as to the poem to Vachel, just "can" it.

Richard Aldington to Harriet Monroe   *London, 17 February 1919*

My Dear Miss Monroe,

I am much obliged for your letter and for taking the poems. With this I am including the last poem I wrote on active service: if you included it with the others it would give them more weight. . . .

It is wonderful to be back again. I'm still a little dazed & uncertain, but am slowly getting back a grip on things. I think I may have some years of work and comparative happiness now. But I've only been back four days, so I can't say how things will turn out. . . . I am living in a Soho café, while I am looking for a flat. H.D. has to live in the country now as her health is very poor.

Yes, Poetry must carry on. We've got a big job before us & we can all help. *Order* is the great urgent necessity now; I am doing a little anonymous political writing here, urging the absolute necessity of social order. It would be too tragic to lose in disturbances all we have gained by those long years of struggle.

Well, au revoir, / Yours very sincerely, / Richard Aldington.

R.A.'s "Prayers and Fantasies" appeared in November 1918; four poems, "In France (1916–1918)," were printed in July 1919. He and H.D. separated after the war.

Richard Aldington to Harriet Monroe   *London, 14 October 1919*

Dear Miss Monroe,

. . . I feel very discouraged about literature & things in general. Europe is in an appalling state. And my own condition is difficult. There are no houses or flats for soldiers, no anything. I haven't been able to afford a holiday as I had to start work at once to live. They have broken up our lives without any effort at compensation.

Excuse the grouse. But it is hard to see those who didn't fight pros-
perous & happy & to see the soldiers coolly kicked out to struggle for
themselves.

Sincerely yours, / Richard Aldington

2. The Postwar Slump

By war's end, nearly all the verse magazines founded after *Poetry* had
folded, or were on their last legs. *Others* limped to its final issue in July
1919. Complimenting *Others* in a February 1921 editorial, Monroe wrote:
"We have deeply regretted that no enlightened New Yorker offered to
serve the art by financing the magazine . . . . One organ, whether perfect
or imperfect, is not enough—there should be *Others*." Alfred Kreymborg
didn't need convincing; in the fall of 1921 he went to Rome and started
Broom.

Though *Poetry* was still standing, its finances remained shaky. The orig-
inal list of Guarantors dropped from 108 to 75; by 1920, their contribu-
tions ($3,825) covered only a third of the budget. Circulation also fell
during and after the war. Costs for paper, printing, and almost everything
else had risen 75 to 90 percent. In October 1920, Monroe was forced to
raise annual subscriptions from $2.00 to $3.00. (Miraculously, or foolishly,
the rate stayed there for the next twenty-six years.) John Hall Wheelock,
who worked at Scribner's, suggested tapping the library market, and
offered to tuck in *Poetry* subscription blanks with the publisher's mass
mailings. In October 1921, H.M. announced subscriptions now totaled
just over 1,700, including 400 from libraries.

Issues now ran to sixty pages, allowing more space for prose. The old-
fashioned, impressionistic reviews of the first years were gradually
replaced with sterner stuff. Pound could take satisfaction at least that part
of his advice was being followed. Alice Henderson continued her witty
dissections, and when Marion Strobel joined the staff as Associate Editor
in 1920, she carried on in A.C.H.'s incisive style. During the twenties sev-
eral younger poet-critics joined the stable; their no-nonsense attitude
toward poetic claptrap tested the limits of Monroe's editorial tolerance.
Longtime contributors were disconcerted when the policy of "no fear,
no favor" resulted in unflattering notices. After H.M. refused to print a
glowing review of Lowell's *Pictures of the Floating World*, Amy informed
Harriet: "[Y]our paper has a very small circulation and practically no
influence." Curiously, Lowell continued to send her work.

Pound from the start and Henderson from the late teens had com-
plained about the amount of mediocre material in *Poetry*. In the postwar

period, the situation worsened. Lindsay and Masters were in steep decline by the late teens. Yvor Winters wrote H.M. in early 1920 that Sandburg's poems in the January issue were "very sad. Very dull echoes of himself." And he worried that, if the slide continued, *Poetry* would be "among the dogs." Monroe continued to allow too many "genteel" poets to take up space with the verse equivalents of wallpaper, usually in moody pastels and delicate floral patterns.

Soldier-poets who made it through the war were slow to resume writing. After three years at the Western Front, Aldington returned embittered, and never again produced work equal to "Choricos." Politically, he became increasingly reactionary; artistically, he turned ever more conservative. In the spring of 1920, he signed on as the magazine's new Foreign Correspondent. He had little direct contact with the current scene, and what he did see, did not impress him. (He found Apollinaire "trivial," mocked Dadaism, and dismissed Jean Cocteau and Tristan Tzara as pranksters.) The few young writers Aldington could recommend were Aldous Huxley, Herbert Read, and the Sitwells—Osbert, Edith, and Sacheverell—to him, "the most vivid literary personalities which emerged in England during the war." R.A. soon realized he was unsuited for the job of correspondent, and resigned in March 1921.

Pound shared Aldington's pessimism about literary life in postwar England. In April 1921, *Poetry* published his article, "Thames Morass," which condemned the British for their general apathy concerning the arts. In the teens, he had urged enterprising young American writers to come to London. Now he advised them to stay home, for nothing of any importance was happening in England. He himself had already left for France early in 1920. Soon many of the so-called "Lost Generation" also crossed the Channel to find artistic and other adventures in Paris, where the living was cheap and far more exciting than in censorious, Prohibition-era America.

3. Changing Directions

Although *Poetry* printed a fair number of contributions from expatriates in the twenties, Monroe depended increasingly on domestic productions, which reinforced the impression that *Poetry* was becoming, if not parochial, provincial. As early as September 1918, H.M. printed an editorial called "The Great Renewal," which urged poets to turn (or return) to Nature to revive their art. Downplaying modernist theory and the "super-civilized past," she suggested American writers look to the tradition of Whitman, Emerson, Thoreau, and Longfellow for their inspiration.

In "A Century in Illinois" (November 1918), she boasted of the original accomplishments and independent spirit of the Middle West, and warned: "the dangerous enemy of this spirit is self-distrust—a certain colonialism which leans upon London, Paris, New York." As a prime example, she cited the attitude of the *Little Review*, which had become "the organ of a choice little London group of super-intellectualized ultimates and expatriates." In the September 1919 issue, Monroe was again harping on the subject of "Back to Nature," asking: "Will not the spiritual renewal of the race, especially of this rainbow-hearted race of ours which is forming . . . come rather through a more direct appeal to more original sources—through the immediate contact of our people with nature in her sacred and intimate reserves?" It was a theme Monroe never tired of repeating, though her idealism (and florid rhetoric) must have seemed increasingly outdated as the twenties roared in.

Standard-issue "nature" and "travel" poems were always liberally sprinkled through *Poetry*, as in most journals. But now Monroe allotted more and more pages to those subjects. Several issues between 1918 and 1922 featured regional poetry. The April 1922 number was devoted to Southern Poetry, edited by Hervey Allen and DuBose Heyward, librettist of *Porgy and Bess*, with the contents provided by staid members of the Poetry Society of South Carolina. Coincidentally, the same month saw the inaugural issue of the *Fugitive*, whose editors, Donald Davidson and Allen Tate, took a dim view of the special issue's rehashings of Old South stereotypes. (Tate later apologized to H.M. for the slam, and edited a far superior Southern Number for *Poetry* in May 1932.)

After her move to Santa Fe in 1916, Alice Henderson became enamored of the Spanish and Indian culture of the Southwest, and in 1917 *Poetry* printed her first "New Mexico Songs." In 1919 several poems later printed in her collection *Red Earth* appeared. In the twenties she also became interested in cowboy ballads. Cowboy songs and "Western poems" appeared in August 1920, which also featured A.C.H.'s "New Mexico Folk-songs" and her article on "The Folk Poetry of These States." In the same number, Helen Hoyt wrote on "Negro Poets." Other issues presented Fenton Johnson's "Negro Spirituals" (June 1918) and Janet Lewis's renderings of Ojibway songs (January 1923).

Monroe was a multiculturalist long before the word was coined, and anxious to save not only the landscapes but the original cultures of the places she visited. She spent many summers in Northern Wisconsin, and particularly admired Native American arts and traditions. She printed Lew Sarett's transcriptions of a Chippewa Medicine Dance ("The Blue Duck," November 1918) and his Chippewa "Council Talks" (October 1919); the January 1920 issue included a Mes-qua-kie ceremony. In a long article on Native American cultures in the Southwest, printed September 1920, Monroe worried that many would be destroyed by "Indian schools," and remarked that at least the Franciscan missionaries had respected a great deal of the indigenous arts.

These excursions may have come as a relief to that part of her readership that had grown weary of the intellectual rigors of high modernism and its ascetic tone. Reviewing *Poetry*'s accomplishments in the 10th Anniversary Issue (October 1922), Monroe noted the magazine's far-flung audience, but she rejected foreign avant-gardes and theoretical movements. She suggested that the poetry of the future would be found close to home: "If America is ever to have a rich spiritual life and to express that life in art, this art must come, not from super-civilized coteries, but from the vital strength of the nation."

Poetry for August 1922 was an all-women issue, though inadvertently. But a quick perusal of many other issues could leave the impression that female authors predominated, because of the frequent appearances of

H.M. shoeing Pegasus: cartoon from the Philadelphia *Public Ledger*, 30 January 1921. The headline to Walter Yust's accompanying article read: "How Would You Like a Job Such As This Woman's? Nothing To Do All Day But Interview Poets and Give Advice to Young Authors—But She's a Factor in Modern Literature."

Marjorie Allen Seiffert, Agnes Lee Freer, Helen Birch–Bartlett, Jessica
Nelson North, and other friends of the Editor. In "Men or Women?"
(June 1920), she quoted the Philadelphia *Record*, which found: "The vig-
orous male note [is] now seldom heard in the land, and almost never at all
in the pages of POETRY"—and the reason was obvious: the editor and
her staff were women "with radical and perverse notions."

H.M. looked up the facts: from April 1919 through March 1920 she
had printed sixty-four men and forty-one women; in total pages, the
ratio of work by men to that by women was "almost exactly two to one."
Marion Strobel observed, however, that of the 3,000 or so "real or alleged
poems which reach us by mail each month, men and women are about
equally guilty." She added that "more rotten verse comes from women
than from men." H.M. concluded: "Perhaps women are just beginning
their work in the arts, and this twentieth century may witness an extraor-
dinary development."

Against the dreariness of many issues during the twenties, H.M.'s dis-
plays of truly first-rate art shone all the more brightly, particularly poems
from Frost, Yeats, Robert Graves, Teasdale, Williams, and, above all, Wallace
Stevens. In the December 1920 issue, the Editor chided Stevens because
he "refuse[d] to print a book and thereby prove himself the peer of any
poet now living, and of many a famous one now dead and enshrined."
Monroe remained faithful to Lindsay and Masters, as well, and her
extravagant reviews may have bucked up their spirits during the periods
of self-doubt that followed their first successes. In the long run, however,
their reputations weren't helped by the scores of pages she devoted to
their later work. Since almost all these writers could easily get printed
elsewhere, and at better pay, gratitude doubtless prompted their loyalty to
Poetry.

CHAPTER XI

Another New Generation, 1918–1922

I shall be glad to have you make any changes you wish in my poems, as I know that if anyone wishes to be a recognized poet, one must at least get one poem published in "Poetry".
—Marya Zaturensky, July 1919

For the generation born on the cusp and in the early years of the century, *Poetry*'s reputation made it *the* place to be seen in print. Many student-poets got their education in contemporary writing from *Poetry* and the other little magazines. *The New Poetry* also became, in effect, their textbook. The first edition was issued in 1917, and by 1919 the anthology had been reprinted eight times. Marya Zaturensky, a Russian immigrant who began sending poems when she was seventeen, wrote to H.M. in 1921: "I can't ever forget what your anthology on the New Poetry did to me and a lot of other young people in introducing the best in American and English modern poetry."

To these aspiring writers, the heated debates over free and formal verse were history; the principles of Modernism were now simply givens. They didn't have to take sides in the old battles, but felt at liberty to write sonnets or *vers libre*. Most visible among them was Edna St. Vincent Millay, a glamorous reader whose conventional lyrics and unconventional love life personified the liberated new era. Millay burst upon the scene in 1912, at age twenty, with "Renascence." She entered the poem in a contest; when it didn't win first prize, readers protested and columnists made her a celebrity. She first appeared in *Poetry* in 1917, and in 1918 the magazine printed her "First Fig," a poem that came to symbolize the Jazz Age.

Like the previous generation, the new poets were often isolated until they found themselves in the pages of *Poetry*. Appearances led to friendships, literary collaborations, and sometimes romance. Besides a place of publication, "Aunt Harriet" offered the uncertain and struggling a sympathetic ear, professional and personal advice, and cash during crises. Students were welcome at the office, and many dropped in at Cass Street

Edna St.Vincent Millay in a
photograph sent to Floyd Dell,
an early lover.

and, after the move in 1922, to 232 Erie Street.

Most precocious of these visitors was Yvor Winters. Still in his teens and a first-year student at Chicago, Winters was known to Miss Monroe, Miss Strobel, and Miss Hoyt by his first name, Arthur, when they met around 1918. In 1919, he contracted tuberculosis and went to Santa Fe, carrying H.M.'s letter of introduction to Mrs. Henderson. Winters and A.C.H. shared similar interests and became good friends. Winters's earliest poems were written in the Imagist mode. As he aged, he grew much more conservative, espousing formalism and the values of versification. But from the beginning, he was nothing if not sure of himself, and his earliest letters to Monroe are filled with shrewd observations and pungent remarks about noted practitioners, and *Poetry*. The amusing character revealed during this period presents a marked contrast to the dour image he projected as a Stanford English professor.

Janet Lewis grew up in the Chicago suburb of Oak Park, where she was a high school classmate of Hemingway's. H.M. invited Lewis to tea when she entered the University, and she worked in the office in the summer of 1919, an experience she recalled in the 75th Anniversary Issue (October 1987):

> I remember Miss Monroe, small, dominating, obstinate, acidulous, yet warmly affectionate upon occasion and always reserved. . . . Though as opinionated young writers we quarreled sometimes with her dicta, she was for all of us encouraging. She made the writing of poetry not only respectable but admirable, and the publishing of poems an actuality. She introduced us to the Best People, either in print or in person . . . .

Lewis met Winters in 1921; she, too, caught TB and went to Sunmount, in 1922. Sixty-five years later, she recalled that Miss Monroe visited her at the sanatorium, bringing "two enormous dahlias of rich colors." Lewis and Winters corresponded when he started teaching in New Mexico and went on to graduate school at the University of Colorado; they married in 1926. Lewis and Hemingway made their first appearances in *Poetry* in the same issue, January 1923. She eventually published several poetry collections, as well as four novels, including *The Wife of Martin Guerre* (1941).

Before Winters went West in 1919, he asked H.M. for Marsden Hartley's address. Hartley was among *Poetry's* several contributors who stopped off in Santa Fe to see Mrs. Henderson and Witter Bynner, by then central figures in the growing art colony there. Hartley already had a wide reputation as an artist. Before the war, he did several striking expressionist paintings in Germany. Returning to the United States, he lived in Taos in 1918–19, creating abstract landscapes. But he had also been writing poems since his student days, and became close friends with Hart Crane. *Poetry* published groups of Hartley's poems in 1918 and 1920, as well as his tribute to his friend Joyce Kilmer in December 1919.

Hartley discovered a fellow free spirit, Robert McAlmon, through the pages of *Poetry*, and they became friends in Los Angeles. A flyer during the war, McAlmon began sending work shortly after he was demobilized; his first poems appeared in March 1919. His jaunty letters were free from cant and pretension, and Hartley assured H.M.: "McAlmon is the real thing, though I won't say as poet." He eventually made friends with Kreymborg, Williams, Stevens, and many of the brightest poets of his generation. (Stevens wrote A.C.H. in 1922 about McAlmon's poetry: "Awful stuff—but such pep!") In 1920, he co-founded *Contact* with Williams, who wanted his own showcase for "native artists."

In 1921, McAlmon married Winifred Ellerman, an heiress and writer who used the pen name Bryher. They moved to Paris, where, with his wife's money, McAlmon set up Contact Editions and published Williams's *The Great American Novel*, Gertrude Stein's *The Making of Americans*, and Hemingway's first book, *Three Stories and Ten Poems*. Bryher started submitting poems to *Poetry* in 1918, and became a close friend with H.D., who had broken up with Aldington after the war. In the early thirties, Bryher sent Monroe a number of letters after trips to Germany, describing in detail the persecutions during the rise of the Nazis.

Two other colorful characters, Emanuel Carnevali and Ernest Walsh, entered the pages of *Poetry* during this time. The Editor always had a soft spot for writers in distress, but in these hapless cases she showed the unusual lengths she would go to help—and the hazards involved. Carnevali was born in Florence in 1897, and immigrated to the United States when he was sixteen. In New York City, he lived in abject poverty, working long hours in Italian restaurants and groceries. He began sending manuscripts in 1917, with letters in which he unburdened his soul to Miss Monroe. She offered advice about the poems to her "dear boy" (as he soon was called), as well as consolation.

Poetry gave Carnevali his debut with six poems in March 1918. Monroe visited him in New York and introduced him to a number of her literary friends, including Francis Hackett, editor of *The New Republic*. He introduced himself to Waldo Frank and James Oppenheim, the editors of *Seven Arts*. He also made friends with Lola Ridge, the American editor for *Broom*, and through her Kreymborg, Williams, and the *Others* circle; Williams dedicated the last issue of *Others* to Carnevali. With his vivacious personality, he seems to have charmed all he met. He told H.M. that he could out-talk even Ezra Pound.

Monroe sent Carnevali advances for his work, and in 1918 she awarded him a special $50 prize. Instead of a thank-you note, he sent her an unpleasant letter. H.M. had begun to feel he was taking advantage of her good will, and had written him not to "expect any more money from this quarter." He was much aggrieved that she should have taken his descriptions of poverty as a call for charity. Monroe and her old advisor Henry Fuller felt Carnevali's talent was being wasted in servile labor, and helped get him a position on an Italian-language paper in Chicago in 1919. He promptly quit the job after quarreling with the editor.

Monroe tried to help him by having him write reviews. Meanwhile, Carnevali approached some of *Poetry*'s supporters for money to start up *his own* magazine. H.M. didn't hold this poaching on her territory against him. When Helen Hoyt resigned in the fall of 1919, Monroe gave Carnevali her position, though with "trepidation." He justified her fears by coming and going as he pleased, skimming the manuscripts "with violent contempt," and skipping the routine office chores so obviously beneath him. After six months of this, the Editor was relieved when he told her he was returning to New York.

But before he could leave, Carnevali came down with a mysterious illness and appeared to be going insane. He was committed to a psychiatric hospital, but the doctors were unable to find a clear source for his condition. He recovered somewhat and went to New York, where he was diagnosed with *encephalitis lethargica*, a form of sleeping sickness. He never recovered from the disease, which causes acute palsy. Carnevali returned to Europe in 1922 and was eventually placed in a charity ward in Bazzano, Italy. Though constant shaking made typing almost impossible, he contributed poems and reviews to *Poetry* at irregular intervals until 1931. He also finished a collection of prose and poetry, *A Hurried Man*, which McAlmon's Contact Editions brought out in 1925.

All but destitute, he was supported for years by regular checks from McAlmon, Williams, Kay Boyle, and others. H.M. not only sent money but asked various friends to donate. Helen Hoyt had been sending monthly checks; but by 1931, when H.M. asked her to continue, she did so reluctantly. She felt Emanuel had never shown any gratitude to either of them. Dr. Williams, too, was "sore" when he discovered so many others besides him had been supporting "Em." Carnevali is believed to have died in 1942 (there is no record), and Kay Boyle gathered various pieces of his writing into *The Autobiography of Emanuel Carnevali* (1967).

Ernest Walsh also availed himself of the largess of Monroe, and other generous souls. Walsh first wrote in the summer of 1921, from an army hospital bed. A flyer during the war, he crashed his plane (in Texas) and was severely injured; he then developed a persistent case of tuberculosis. In his isolation, he wrote poems, which he sent to H.M. She replied with comforting words, and published his first group in January 1922. Walsh also sent her a letter addressed to the President of the United States, and asked her to see that he got it. The letter explained that, although he had been pronounced permanently disabled by the army doctors, he had never received a response from the veteran's bureau and was now penniless. Miss Monroe did not know Mr. Harding, so she approached her friend Mrs. Medill McCormick, the wife of a U.S. senator, to act on Walsh's behalf. Within two weeks, he received a permanent disability allowance of over $100 a month, war insurance of $57.50, and about $3,000 in cash, to make up for his years of neglect.

Although the doctors advised him to lead a quiet life, Walsh told H.M. he would go insane if he followed orders, and decided to make the most of life, however much of it he had left. On 7 February 1922, he wrote an exuberant letter (printed in *Poetry* January 1927) warning the Editor:

> If you should see a weird-appearing affair in tweeds come dashing down Cass Street, grabbing girls and taxi-drivers and policemen, and respectable married women and stout aldermen, and embracing them—and if this same strange nuisance should dance into the office of Poetry, and circle around the editorial staff Don Quixote-wise, and then proceed to do an Irish jig, you'd know by these and other appropriate salutations that Ernest Walsh was in Chicago en route to Dublin, London, Paris, Edinburgh, Brussels. . . .

Walsh showed up in Chicago, as threatened, and visited the office, where Monroe cautioned him to conserve his resources. But he was already squandering his pension at a fast clip, and had decided to go to Paris. While in New York waiting to board ship, he was mugged and found himself in dire straits. He wired H.M. (collect) for help in raising $200. Since she didn't have that kind of ready cash, Monroe called a wealthy friend, the poet Leonora Speyer, who gave him the $200. Monroe informed Walsh that she had guaranteed the loan and that he could repay her in installments. She also promised to line up other contributions and some writing jobs. It is not clear whether he ever repaid her.

In Paris, Walsh made friends with James Joyce and many American expatriates, including Kay Boyle, McAlmon, Hemingway, and Pound. (E.P. gave him pointers, and then they feuded.) Boyle depicted him as "Martin" in her novel *Year Before Last* (1932). In *A Moveable Feast* (1964), Hemingway characterized him as "The Man Who Was Marked for Death"—a con artist who used his tubercular condition to coax sympathy and support from fellow writers. (The portrait was drawn from life. Helen Hoyt wrote H.M. in 1924, wondering if her husband would ever get back the $300 he had loaned Walsh.) In 1925, with help from McAlmon, Boyle, and Ethel Moorehead, he started a little magazine called *This Quarter* in Paris. He sent H.M. the first issue, and was very disappointed when she didn't give it a rave review. In the second issue (the last he edited), Walsh wrote "furious diatribes" against *Poetry* and Monroe, as she mentioned—along with a too-kind assessment of his work—in the obituary she ran three months after his death on 17 October 1926.

Marsden Hartley to Harriet Monroe   Brooklyn, N.Y.,
                                                     [6 March 1918]

Dear Miss Munroe [sic]:-

I am sending with this mail a set of selections . . . . Alfred Kreymborg, our mutual friend[,] has written you a letter, and has spoken to you some time ago of me . . . .

I am trying to get to the southwest this summer, for various reasons, partly for health, but chiefly to do a lot of painting and writing in peace and quiet neither of which is to be found in New York—at least I have come to that conclusion after a fifteen years trial; I want a place for escape, and the southwest offers me that—I shall have to get all the monies together that are possible, and publication of my poetry would be a superb lift in this direction; I know you will pardon the intimacies, but Alfred has made it possible for me to speak openly, and he knows me intimately for these last fifteen years, and we spent several of those trying years of poverty and struggle together in the same quarters. I shall be very happy to make my debut in Poetry, and hope you can comply with Alfred's request in sending me the check in advance. . . .

H.M. accepted four poems, which were printed under the title "Kaleidoscope" in the July 1918 issue.

Marsden Hartley to Harriet Monroe   *Taos, N.M.,*
12 September 1918

Dear Miss Munroe [sic]:-

...When we have worn away the fetich [sic] such as is so elaborately idolized and to which so much dragged out attention has been given by such as Amy Lowell and Ezra Pound, we shall it is hoped, and even expected, have a more natural type of expression in the field of poetry, and in the field of painting ... through a fusion of the modern extravagance and an honest return to nature; Cubism and futurism have shown their limitations already by a very certain factitiousness in the result, not owing to insincerities, but to false premises.... I am convinced that the thing to do [is to] get theory out of modern poetry and painting, and that the thing for poets to do is to cultivate real poetic sensibility and realize that poetry is not a rhythmic arrangement of a diary of the emotions....

Emanuel Carnevali to Harriet Monroe   *New York City,*
[October 1918]

Dear Miss Monroe;

You are so very, very good! ... you are as good a person as I had not dared to find in this country that does not know and does not want to know me.... Poetry has saved my life—with a check in time when all the rest of the world was irresponsive [sic]—and with a fine poem when all the rest of the world was dull....

I'm invited to lunch with Mr. Filsinger, to-morrow. I haven't seen him yet, tho I liked his voice on the phone. I cannot adequately thank you for this.... Not long ago I have the MUMS (is that how you write it?) Can you beat it? A man like me, who can talk Ezra Pound deaf, ignorant and quiet! ...

H.M. printed E.C.'s first group in March 1918 and his essay on Italian poetry in February 1919. On 24 October, Sara Teasdale wrote that her husband, Ernst Filsinger, was trying to find him a job in New York.

Emanuel Carnevali to Harriet Monroe   *New York City,*
[November 1918]

Dear Miss Monroe:

... Last night I slept but three hours, with my clothes on, having left off work at 4 a.m. and began it again at 7 a.m. And about 11 o'clock I went downstairs and there was that little blue envelope that I had so much desired [with a $50 prize from *Poetry*]. I was tired and sick and there was no comfort: a perspective of more work and more work and more work and that's all. I tell you: it made me mad. . . . Did you understand the descriptions of my poverty (in my letters) to be appeals? Have you accepted my poems and paid [for] them, given me that prize for charity? Then why such phrases as "don't expect any more money from this quarter"? You just take the whole joy out of my life, that's all. . . .

Don't scold me any more. It isn't that it insults me, not so much that, as that I feel too old and too sick and too miserable to be scolded. . . . It is no guilt to hate work, since I am not lazy. (I have walked as much as 20 miles to get a job as a dishwasher once and I used sometime to work from 11 a.m. to 3 a.m. uninterruptedly.) . . . I am mad and sad that the things that everybody tells me you should come and tell me too. And that the romance of our acquaintanceship has just been spoiled by this bit of despicable realism. . . .

Malcolm Cowley to Harriet Monroe   Pittsburgh, 1 November 1918

My dear Miss Monroe:

I am very pleased that you accepted my three poems. As to any changes, I give you carte blanche. . . .

I feel inclined to close the letter with some gossip. You know of course that Maxwell Bodenheim was starting a new magazine to be known as "The Looking Glass." He had discovered a coracial backer named Charles Sonnenschein. And now Sonnenschein has died of influenza, and the magazine is probably buried along with my subscription. The amusing thing is that Sonnenschein caught the disease from Max—something I call hardly grateful of the latter.

Very truly yours, / Malcolm Cowley

Cowley's "Moonrise," "Barn Dance," and "Danny" appeared in November 1919.

Marsden Hartley to Harriet Monroe   [Santa Fe, 13 November 1918]

Dear Miss Munroe [sic]:-

Your letter came down from Taos yesterday . . . I am now in Santa Fe, glad to leave the stupidest place on earth, namely Taos, glad to be in Santa Fe which is at least something of a town. I am glad also to have the associations of an attractive and intelligent woman like Mrs. Henderson, though I may say that usually intellectuals bore me; I never go where they are if I can avoid it. . . . I realized after I sent you the prose and poem on Joyce Kilmer that you would not be able to use both . . . . Joyce had a fine sense of humour, and would laugh, if he were not already beyond laughter, at the stuff that is being talked out on the dead poets . . . .

H. L. Mencken to Harriet Monroe   *Baltimore, 17 November 1918*

Dear Miss Monroe;-

. . . Chicago, I fear, will never see me. I have resolved to travel no more in the United States until Prohibition is abandoned. But may I not see you on your Eastern trip? I surely hope so.

Louis Untermeyer is here today, lecturing to some Jewish Damen-verein [women's club] on "The Poetic Principle". I shall have to waste some precious gin on him tonight.

Sincerely yours, / H. L. Mencken

Alice Corbin Henderson to Harriet Monroe   *Santa Fe, 18 November 1918*

Dear Harriet:

. . . Thank you for the check for the poems, but to tell you the truth I was surprised that it was not larger. . . . I don't know therefore that I can *afford* to be so loyal another time. . . .

I am afraid, Harriet, that you are surrounded by people who are will-ing to say the pleasant thing and the easy thing about POETRY, instead of the honest thing and the hard and possibly bitter thing. You may tell me it is none of my business, if you like, but if you are satisfied with POETRY, *I'm* not. . . .

POETRY—you, me, and all of us—have a tendency to harp back to what we've published, mostly in past tense, and too much on the corn-fed poets of the middle-states. It has got to be an obsession. But what we ought to do is look ahead. And if you don't, you'll find yourself a back-number as sure as you are born. Things are likely to start up now that the war is over, and there will surely be new magazines on the order of The Seven Arts, etc. Another thing, try to get rid of the parochial tone in the prose. I have begun to loathe the first person in reviews—sounds like The Little Review and the naked "I" comes to be almost indecent. When it doesn't sound patronizing. . . .

Edna St. Vincent Millay to Harriet Monroe   *New York City, 1 March 1919*

Dear Harriet Monroe—

This is to remind you that if you don't find a place for those poems of Edna's very soon, you gotta return 'em to her. There are two of them—Recuerdo; and She Is Overheard Singing; stunning things, both. You are committing a bitter and a presumptuous folly in thus long keeping them from the world. If you don't look out I'll just tell the world all about it, and then where will you be?

Lovingly, / Edna St.Vincent Millay

The poems were published in May 1919.

D. H. Lawrence to Harriet Monroe   Middleton-by-Wirksworth, Derby, England, 2 March 1919

Dear Harriet Monroe

. . . Excuse the pencil—I have been struggling with the Flu for a month, & am still in bed,—am getting better: a very nasty disease. —As soon as I am well & Peace will be signed we are due to go to Germany, where my dear old Frau Baronin mother-in-law sits in lament in Baden-Baden, my brother-in-law manages to weather the storms in Munich, and remain Minister of Finance to the new Bavarian republic, a cousin bobs up and down in Berlin, & so on. I want to come to America this summer, and I will if the gods are not too spiteful. At present however a voyage autour de ma chambre finishes me. —You have got a big lake in Chicago, haven't you? I should like that —I should like to see you all in Chicago very much indeed—after all poetry is a great freemasonry. . . .

The sun shines—the snowdrops are out in the garden, under the bushes. I long to begin afresh, in a new country.

mila saluté buoni / D. H. Lawrence

Yvor Winters to Harriet Monroe   Riverside, Calif., 4 March 1919

Dear Miss Monroe;

. . . I am stranded here on the edge of the world's backwaters for the next five or six weeks, but hope to get to Santa Fe again about the middle of April. This is a great town in which to rest, though, so I suppose I ought to be satisfied. . . . The town's chief attraction is an Airedale pup that lives about a block from where we are. He is the best specimen of his breed that I have ever seen—on a bench or off—this side of the Mississippi. I shall cultivate his acquaintance.

I tried my hand as a propagandist today—converted my barber to Socialism while he was cutting my hair—and was really amazed at the talent I displayed. I merely guided his flow of conversation—which started Republican, and ended redder than Max Eastman. My technique was impeccable. . . .

Winters was interested in dogs since boyhood; he eventually became a famous breeder of Airedales.

Yvor Winters to Helen Hoyt   *Riverside, Calif., 23 March 1919*

Dear Miss Hoyt:

... Ezra's translations [of Propertius] almost moved me to break forth with a triumphal chant of some sort—something beginning, say, "See, he returns," etc. The last one, especially, gave me about as big a thrill as I have gotten in some time. It is really a comfort—for one of my opinions and predilections at least—to feel that Ezra has not yet collapsed. Of course I noticed that his name was missing from the back of *Poetry*, but somehow I cannot work up any great amount of sympathy for your plight. I have a faint suspicion that *Poetry* will struggle along without him. . . .

It is unfortunate, I think, for M[argaret] A[nderson] and company, that intellect is not as contagious as are idiosyncrasies. . . .

H. L. Mencken to Harriet Monroe   *Baltimore, 7 May 1919*

Dear Miss Monroe;-

Thanks for your note. I had a notion, too, that [James Weldon] Johnson's poem was a bit too suave and sophisticated, but it seemed to me that you ought to see it. He is, by the way, a remarkable man—a good politician as well as a sound writer. The thing, of course, was not for us. We [*American Mercury*] have gone back to short lyrics, and wallow in the high respectability of it. After all, some one must do it. You have got all other magazines imitating your experiments. . . .

Sara Teasdale to Harriet Monroe   *Boonton, N.J., 13 May 1919*

Dearest Harriet: Your letter and the returned poems came this morning and I have been considering your criticisms and so on. Some of them I fully agree with—others not, as is natural. . . . You are right, "Let It Be Forgotten" [September 1919] is one of the best songs I've ever done, and comes nearer in music, and a sort of silence at the end, to what I mean by a lyric, than anything else of mine that I can think of. . . .

I'm awfully glad that Muna Lee has found happiness—at least let's hope it will be happiness. She talked a lot about wanting to find "a rock" and I told her men are never rocks. *I've* never found one. Women are less likely to turn out un-rock-like than men. Women are solider than men—less likely to get all worked up and light-headed. A man is almost always light-headed and somehow you don't mind it after

you've learned you have to put up with it. . . . Ernst, for instance, is
emotionally so far as likelihood of feeling in love with any other
woman goes, very stable, but in a general way, more excitable than I—
and that's going some. And if she has a Latin-American, heaven keep
her.

My dear love to you, Harriet, and a kiss / Sara.

Lee edited a special Latin-American Issue in June 1925; the first comprehensive
coverage of the literature in an English-language magazine, it presented poets from
every Spanish-speaking country in the Hemisphere.

Marsden Hartley to Harriet Monroe   Santa Fe, 3 July 1919

Dear Miss Munroe [sic]:-
   . . . I have just returned from California after three months of inter-
esting investigation. There is no landscape there to speak of. Mostly
scenery. It has the look of a stage set. I like what it does to the crowds
however. . . . They are for the most part intellectually vacuous, but that
was pleasant to me, and one hears little of the quack quack of the artis-
tic element so persistent in the east. . . .

Robert McAlmon to Harriet Monroe   The Ace, Los Angeles,
                                                  2 August 1919

Dear Miss Monroe:
   I intended last night to write and tell you to send back the things of
mine you have. I concluded I was no poet, had no ability to record any
esthetic perceptions I might have, and could not intelligently allow
myself to be one more of the 150 odd beings who can't write poetry,
yet try. . . .
   I'm editor of "The Ace", an aviation [magazine] which will attempt
to locate an art, a literature, and a sport of aviation. . . . Marsden Hartley
will probably give us something. If you know any writers whom the
subject interests have them send things in to us. Having granted to
myself that I'm no poet, I want to at least help others who are. . . .

McAlmon first appeared in the March 1919 issue with six poems under the heading
"Flying."

Robert McAlmon to Harriet Monroe Los Angeles, 3 September 1919

Dear Miss Monroe:
   . . . I told Hartley I had a horror of writing "pretty" stuff. He thinks I
have an 'anti-beauty complex'. I really want never to try to write beau-
tiful things just for the sake of attaining beauty. . . . I like him tremen-

dously, but we don't bother much about each other's poetry, or prose. We walk around the city streets together, or did when he was here, watch humming birds in the yuccas, rave over kid goats, and eat. There's a ripping place in Los Angeles for doughnuts; you should taste them. You're interested in eating, aren't you? . . .

It's a horrible fact, if I'm right, that the more intellectual you get the smaller your audience, and the less possibility you have of making a living. . . . I'm desperadoing into as far corners of the earth as I can get money to pay carfare, or ship fare. They won't commercialize me. They won't even make a sensible person of me. It's better to write 8 immortal lines of poetry than to have a full belly. I haven't written them yet, but then I've never thought I had either. . . .

Yvor Winters to Harriet Monroe   *Sunmount, Santa Fe,*
                                                    28 January 1920

Dear Miss Monroe:

. . . The far western number [January 1920] bored me from start to finish. There are some superb things being done by actual [cow] punchers down here. Why can't you get hold of them? Glenway [Wescott] swears that some recent things he has seen by Jack Thorpe are among the most strangely original things he has found in contemporary poetry. Badger Clark is one of our best second rate poets—much better than Lindsay, I think. People are too apt to look upon the cowboy poets as merely amusing phenomena, whereas they are really of huge importance. They are your true Anglo-Saxon-American folk-poets and are likely to have as big an influence in shaping any American tradition that may grow up as either the Indians or the negros [sic]. . . .

I have decided that professional criticism is the worst thing that can befall a young poet, and so have decided to choke my aborted critical career. In the future my criticism will be confined to correspondence and conversation. I still think H.D.'s poem ["Hymen"] an abomination. Worse than Aldington's love poems, if that is possible. Why Williams should like it is beyond me. And how H.D. could write it is beyond me. Sandburg's poems in your new number struck me as being rather sad. Very dull echoes of himself. He ought to know that the sea is allowed to do things that poets are not.

The rest of the number is worse. If you will pardon my frankness, I will say that I fear Poetry is sliding rather too rapidly, and will soon be, as the saying is, among the dogs. So far this fiscal year, and in the two preceding it, the only things I can recollect as having been at all achieved or at all important—from my standpoint—are the two groups

by Stevens, Pound's fourth Propertius poem, a couple of poems by
Williams, and a couple by Mrs. Henderson. There are always a few stray
lines that seem alive . . . . I am thinking of Glenway Wescott. And he is
not even slight, as compared to most of your stuff, has a very personal
technique, etc., etc. I am not trying to defend him as a poet. You may
even say he is damnable. All I will try to argue is that he is less
damnable than ninety five percent of the stuff you print. . . .

Harriet Monroe to Yvor Winters   *3 February 1920*

My dear Mr. Winters:
    . . . I like immensely to get your critical letters and the contrasting
opinions that come to the office are amazing. You don't like the January
and February numbers; Sandburg thinks the former about the best we
ever put out and some people whose opinions I respect greatly admire
the latter. . . .
    I am sorry you fear "Poetry is sliding rather too rapidly", sorry you
think we are making so many mistakes, but the very poems which you
scorn have been praised by others of the elect. So what am I to believe?
    As for Glenway Wescott's things . . . I don't say he is damnable but I
do think he is rather thin; I should call it very promising student's work
and I should say that if he keeps on he will accomplish something really
worthwhile before long. . . .
    In conclusion I only wish that you were in good enough health to
help us with POETRY for I should greatly value your type of mind in
the work we are trying to do; but in the meantime I am very glad to
get your letters and your critical advice.

                                        Yours very sincerely, / H.M.

Yvor Winters to Harriet Monroe   *Sunmount, Santa Fe,*
                                                    7 February 1920

Dear Miss Monroe:
    . . . I suppose a magazine justifies its existence if it prints one great
poem a year—if so you continue to justify your existence and quite a
bit beside. The slump in minor verse in the last two or three volumes—
for I still think there has been one—may well be due to the perishing
of so many of the gang you rounded up a few years back and the failure
of a new crop. Bodenheim, Aldington, H.D., [Orrick] Johns,—where
are the poets of yesteryear? Lindsay and Masters in the last stages of
decomposition, Sandburg decrepit (or such are appearances at present)
and Ezra middle-aged. . . . They, at least, have been great poets—and I
hope they still are, but . . . [sic] Stevens and Eliot seem to be holding

their ends up and Williams is only getting started, and Mrs. Henderson continues to produce fine poetry. Those four seem to me about the best we have right now. Stevens seems to me a veritable Titan. . . .

As to the puncher poets: Jack Thorpe is a discovery of Mrs. Henderson's, so you will probably see some of his work as soon as he does enough that she approves of. She is completely batty about him, and I thought she might have mentioned him to you. He is an old-timer and knows all the dead and reformed bad men, and probably a few yet in action. From what I hear of him he may well have been one himself. . . .

Hilda Doolittle to Harriet Monroe   *Territet, Switzerland,*
                                                                   1 March 1920

Dear Miss Monroe,

. . . Robert McAlmon's [Contact] press are printing a prose book of mine, "*Palimpsest*", in the early summer. I will try to get him to send it to you, but there is difficulty about the foreign post. However, you may like it. I am afraid I do rather but have been much discouraged. H.D., it seems, is not to be allowed to do anything but her early stuff. Editors ask me for poems "in the early manner." I consider it a downright insult. However, when I have been thoroughly "slam[m]ed" about the prose perhaps I will be too depressed ever to sque[a]k again. . . .

"Elmer Chubb" to Harriet Monroe   *[Chicago, March 1920]*

Dear Madam:

I have written an epic on the Mormons, treating of the tragic death of Joseph Smith, the flight from Nauvoo to Salt Lake, the practice of polygamy, and finally the punishment which overtook them at the hands of a just God in the righteous interference of our Christian government. This epic would fill your magazine for about two years, and would not only increase its circulation but would do much to uplift the spiritual sloth of our beloved country, now unhappily sunk in indifference and sin. Awaiting your favorable reply I remain

        Yours truly / Elmer Chubb LLD. PhD. [Edgar Lee Masters]

Yvor Winters to Harriet Monroe   *Sunmount, Santa Fe, 2 April 1920*

Dear Miss Monroe:

Thanks for check. . . . I am still convinced, however, that professional criticism is not for me. Not one tenth of one percent of the stuff that is printed seems to me worth a toothpick, and when I start cursing a man I usually end up by cursing him tooth and liver and getting myself into a

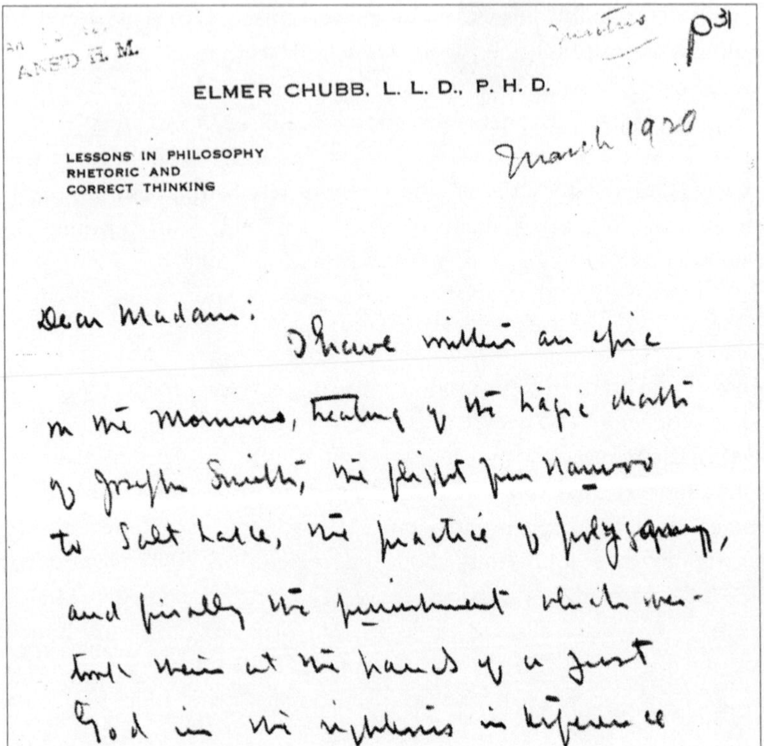

ANS'D H. M.

ELMER CHUBB, L. L. D., P. H. D.

LESSONS IN PHILOSOPHY
RHETORIC AND
CORRECT THINKING

March 1920

Dear Madam:

I have written an epic on the Mormons, treating of the tragic death of Joseph Smith, the flight from Nauvoo to Salt Lake, the practice of polygamy, and finally the punishment which overtook them at the hands of a just God in the righteous interference of our Christian government. This epic would fill your magazine for about two years, and would not only increase its circulation but would do much to uplift the spiritual state of our beloved country, now unhappily sunk in indifference and sin. Awaiting your favorable reply I remain

Yours truly
Elmer Chubb LLD. PhD.

"Elmer Chubb," aka Edgar Lee Masters, offering an epic, March 1920.

mean mood generally, and I fail to see wherein the occupation justifies itself for me. . . .

Lindsay has been here for the last week. I reread his work in honor of his coming, and then heard him read it, and found both him and his

work crude and stupid and sentimental. He knows less than almost any-
one I have ever met, and his work shows it. . . .

Y.W. also wrote Glenway Wescott 1 April that he found Sandburg "a disgusting
fake," and didn't see how they "fell" for him.

Yvor Winters to Harriet Monroe   *Sunmount, Santa Fe,*
                                          31 October 1920

Dear Miss Monroe:
     . . . I wish my signature changed to Yvor Winters, using my middle
name. As Glenway remarks, A.Y. bears a depressing resemblance to "yea,
bo". . . . (The name is pronounced Ivor.) Glenway is in Evanston at the
home of Monroe Wheeler. . . .
     Sandburg's new book [*Smoke and Steel*] is awful. Sort of plasmodial
delirium—or rather the morning after such. I hate a mess. . . .

Elinor Wylie to Harriet Monroe   New York City, 28 November 1920

Dear Madam,
     On the rejection slip sent back with my verse, "Sea Lullaby," one of
the associate editors of "Poetry" was kind enough to write some words
of praise & a suggestion that I should send you more. I do this with
hesitation, as I do not consider most of my work modern enough or
good enough for "Poetry". I enclose a few things—I suppose you hate
sonnets but I put one in, as it has just been written. What I send you has
never been sent elsewhere. I have never published anything—never
tried to, until the last few weeks. I have just had a sonnet accepted by
"Contemporary Verse" but I am as proud of my few words of praise
(though they were on a rejection slip!) from "Poetry".

                            Sincerely yours, / Elinor Wylie

Wylie first appeared in April 1921 with four poems: "Velvet Shoes," " 'Fire and Sleet
and Candle-Light,' " "Silver Filagree [sic]," and "Atavism."

Yvor Winters to Harriet Monroe   *Sunmount, Santa Fe,*
                                          3 December 1920

Dear Miss Monroe:
     I am sorry you don't like my six-syllable poems. —However, they
remain better than Sandburg. . . .
     In six months or so I shall probably print twenty or twenty-five six-
syllable poems in a booklet, and shall by then be well on my way
toward the upper ether. My next book will be in four syllables, the next
in two, and then I shall vanish. If you would only catch hold, I might be

able to take you along, but with your feet stuck so everlastingly in the prairie mud, it will require some effort from you. And then with Miss Strobel fastened around your neck . . . .

Richard Aldington to Harriet Monroe
Malthouse Cottage, Padworth, Nr. Reading, Berks., 18 January 1921

Dear Miss Monroe,

. . . I wish ardently that I could see you for an afternoon and have a long talk with you about literature. That way only could I tell you without any falsity or chance of misunderstanding just why Sandburg's poetry is so repulsive to me. . . . To me Sandburg is a man who is mistaken in his conception of literature, in his ideas of civilisation, in his "values", in his methods! I feel constantly irritated by his poems—and that which irritates you or me is not poetry for you or me. So as I said, there are "irreconcilables". . . .

R.A. formally resigned as Foreign Correspondent 19 March. He suggested H.M. find someone younger and more in contact with London, and thanked her for *Poetry's* hospitality to his work before and since the war.

William Carlos Williams to Harriet Monroe
Rutherford, N.J., 10 May 1921

Dear Miss Monroe:-

After May 1st all poems by William Carlos Williams will be $50. —a piece minimum—so get a thrill by rejecting five or six hundred dollars worth while you may.

Best wishes, / WCW

H.M.'s note: "These ac'd—if at our usual rates." "Wild Orchard," "The Lonely Street," "Spouts," and "The Widow's Lament in Springtime" appeared in January 1922. He wrote 21 June 1921: "Mrs Williams, who is your staunch champion, is always made content by my appearance in Poetry. She thanks you."

Osbert Sitwell to Harriet Monroe
London, 28 September 1921

Dear Miss Harriet Monroe,

I have the pleasure of submitting to you 3 poems by myself and 3 by my brother. We should be so delighted if you should publish them.

I hope I am not overwhelming you with my family. . . .

"Mrs. Freudenthal Consults the Witch of Endor" and "Dead Man's Wood" appeared in December 1921, "Maxixe" in June 1922; Sacheverell was not published in *Poetry*. Dame Edith was printed once, in 1955.

Ernest Walsh to Harriet Monroe   *Army Hospital #64,*
                                          Camp Kearny, Calif.,
                                          22 October 1921

Dear Miss Monroe:

O you are so good! To read your letter was like touching the fingers of Lady Graciousness. Here are the poems you chose with the revised copies attached. One of them, COLLAPSE, you did not mark. It goes back to you unchanged. Am I correct in supposing you thought it all right? I add a bundle of things for your inspection. Maybe you will find something among them you will like.

It must be fun to be YOU! bringing so much encouragement to off-tone singers like myself.

You know—my life is a sea and my poems are the waves. I must confess however, that while I could not live without writing, there are moments when I experience a kind of psychic nausea and, for the time, think it is all a lot of rot. I usually come out of it to express my mood in verse! . . .

Life is so exciting! And particularly for me as I am never quite sure just how much more of it I'm going to have the fun of living. I'm very young, you know, (25) and haven't had time to get sour on things. But I'd go mad if I couldn't write. I'm so terribly bed-bound and will be—O such a long time!

I just saw your anthology today for the first time. Because I am quite too poor at present to subscribe, a woman in San Diego loaned me twelve back

Ernest Walsh in Army Hospital #64, Camp Kearney, Calif.; snapshot sent to H.M., late 1921.

numbers of POETRY. I'd like to get famous and all that sort of thing, just so I could repay you for your heaven-sent encouragement by saying to the cussed multitude, "There she is! She did it! My friend Harriet Monroe". . . .

E.W. was first presented in January 1922, with four poems, and had groups in January and October 1924.

"Clyde Berman, Jr." to Harriet Monroe   New York City,
                                                          29 October 1921

Dear Miss Monroe,
   May I ask, with all respect, why so many of your annual prizes have been awarded to groups of Indian Poems? . . . I was truly surprised to discover that Maxwell Bodenheim had failed to receive any one of the prizes which you awarded this year. This year, perhaps more than any other, his group of poems, Sappho and Aristotle [May 1921], revealed him at his ironical best, and in addition, held a note of dramatic power which has never been fully present in his work. . . . your honorable mention list had a length that robbed it of much distinction, and was composed of newcomers, or poets whom your prize-awarding commitee [sic] had previously honored. . . .

H.M. note: "Is this Bodenheim?"

Robert Frost to Harriet Monroe   Ann Arbor, Mich.,
                                                   1 November 1921

Dear Miss Monroe:
   How'll you swap the poem you have for a long poem in blank verse called "A Witch of Coos (Circa 1921)"? Coos is the next county above where you were in the White Mountains. If you were there in August, you could probably have found us there by looking for us; and we are the boys what could tell you of pleasant places where you could stay for less than $8 a day. Well if we didn't meet in Franconia, probably we shall before long in Chicago unless you avoid me. Van Wyck Brooks has been telling me the future lies with the East in art. I don't know what he knows about it. But I thought I would look around Detroit and Chicago a little before I came to any conclusions for myself. Of course, I am hopelessly Eastern in my accent: I have half a mind to call my next book The Upper Right Hand Corner; but that's no reason why I shouldn't view the landscape o'er more or less impartially for a while yet. I'll let you know when I am ready to award the palm to any section. Well what do you say about the long poem?
                                        Sincerely yours / Robert Frost

"The Witch of Coös" was printed January 1922 and won the Levinson Prize ($200). Frost thanked H.M. on 4 November and said: "I don't care what people think of my poetry so long as they award it prizes."

Ford Madox Ford to Harriet Monroe [*Fittleworth, Sussex*],
7 *November 1921*

Dear Miss Monroe;
I am really extremely touched and pleased by the award of your prize—I don't know whether more touched or more pleased. It is the first public—or "buckshee", to use an Army adjective—recognition that my writings have ever received, except from France. . . . I thought at first of returning the cheque to you and asking you to bestow it upon someone younger. But then I said: "Hang it, no!" My need of perpetuating pleasant memories is at least as great as can be that of any youngster who will probably besides have longer years in which to accumulate them. I will buy myself an Alsatian wolf hound such as I have desired to possess for a great number of years and it shall be a reminder of the kindness from Chicago. And so I will as soon as I can find one good enough to serve as memorial.
Thanking you again for all you have done for poetry—and for me—these many years, I'm
Yours very sincerely, / Ford Madox Ford

Ford's "A House" was printed in March 1921 and won the $100 Guarantors' Prize.

William Carlos Williams to Harriet Monroe *Rutherford, N.J.*,
20 *November 1921*

Dear Miss Monroe:
. . . New York is very delightful this fall with all the neurosis in Paris. One walks the streets in quiet enjoyment knowing there is no one of importance to be met at the next corner. I have some very interesting letters from McAlmon. Kenneth Burke remains, however, in the land of the free, and him I do not avoid.
I am working at my trade in all the luxurious moments and hours of freedom from my profession that come to me. The kind and indulgent god of poets alone knows whether I am becoming a better craftsman than I was. I believe, really, that I am learning how to write at last. Perhaps I am even learning out of what to make up my pellets. This is all very uncertain.
So is THE BROOM.
I am / Your obedient servant / W. C. Williams

Kreymborg sent H.M. an advance copy of *Broom* from Rome and wrote her 15 September 1921: "If there is anything I can do for you here, don't hesitate to use me. Although I'm certain that American poetry shines by comparison with what I have seen of European."

William Carlos Williams to Monroe   *25 November 1921*

Dear Harriet Monroe:

All I meant was that since the book [*Sour Grapes*] is coming out soon you'd better know it so that you can plan accordingly. . . .

I'm very glad that you have decided to bring me forward in January. As always I wish what you have of mine were better stuff. Not that it is unrepresentative of all that I am capable of but somehow or other I do not succeed in satisfying myself. How strange you must find this!

Oh yes, there was one thing I really wanted to say: one of the pieces you have will not appear in the book, it is the one about the apples— Wild Orchard, I think the name is. In making your note please bear this in mind.

McAlmon is restless and ill at ease. I am sure by this that he is happily married.

Sincerely yours

[self-portrait of W.C.W. in pencil]

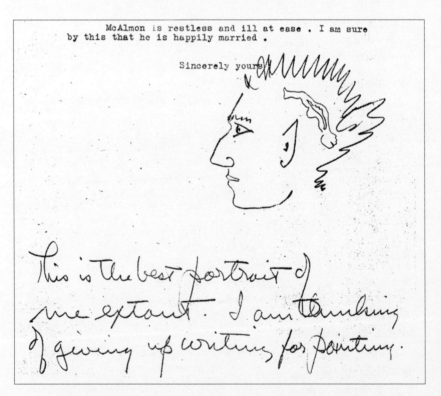

W.C.W. offers a self-portrait and reports on Robert McAlmon's marriage to Bryher, 25 November 1921.

This is the best portrait of me extant. I am thinking of giving up writing for painting.

Ernest Walsh to Harriet Monroe   *[night letter] New York City,*
13 March 1922

Robbed of over thousand dollars. Am nearly crazy. Ship sails Wednesday morning, March fifteenth, and I haven't a dollar. Owe hotel eighty-five dollars . . . . Not to sail now would take meaning from life. Do you know some rich friend to poets in Chicago who could loan me two hundred dollars, my heart for security. Can't sail unless receive money Tuesday. Terrible loss to American letters if I don't see Paris, also very dismal funeral for you to attend. Please don't tell me I'm a fool. I know it which doesn't ease my suffering. Every friend I have in world has failed me, wire immediate reply.

Walsh telegraphed again the next morning. H.M. replied: "Know nobody to ask. Can't you get passage money back and wait awhile? Are you asking personal loan from me? Can hardly manage so much." E.W. immediately wired again: "Passage not refundable Ship sails noon tomorrow." H.M. replied: "I have telegraphed Mrs. Edgar Speyer, 22 Washington Square. Telephone her."

Ernest Hemingway to Harriet Monroe   *Paris, 16 July 1922*

Dear Miss Monroe:-
    I am very glad the poems are to appear in Poetry and am sorry not to have written before.
    Enclosed are some more you might be able to use.
    With very best regards to Henry B. Fuller, and, if you see him, Sherwood Anderson.
                        Very sincerely, / Ernest M. Hemingway
P.S. I met a boy, Ernest Walsh, here who says he is a friend of yours. He has been quite ill, but is much better now. . . .

Ezra Pound to Harriet Monroe   *Paris, [March 1922]*

Dear Harriet:
    After many days. Differences of view separating us. Still you once had the same idea that american money ought to be used to keep up American literature. . . . [sic] and you have (usually misguidedly, so far as discriminating what was literature), but still you have done a certain amount toward it; the money having in about 5% of the cases gone where it should. . . .
    The point is that Eliot is going to pieces physically. He had a break down a few months ago, went to Switzerland, recovered, sufficiently to

do probably the most important modern poem of its length (19 pages) that there is [*The Waste Land*]. Returned to London too soon and is again wearing out; Lloyd's bank not being the proper place for him.

Now in my opinion, for what it is worth, Eliot is the most valuable poet we have. There is not only no one better in America, there is no one so good in France, and no one in England (save Yeats, and Hardy) who can come any where within reach of him.

If he were English he wd. be provided for; he wd. have a Cambridge fellowship, as Brooke had, or he wd. have a government sinecure.

You may accept my gratis opinion that the American plutocracy are a lot of baboons with no sense of responsibility, and try to disprove it. Given what Eliot has been through, there is nothing but a permanent job, with lighter work; or more sanely, *much* more sanely, the sort of endowment that has been given to Joyce or to Frost (Frost being about 1/27th the importance that Eliot is). . . .

Wd. it help if it were publicly announced that I am desperately jealous of Eliot, and that I wd. probably die of raging jaundice IF he received a suitable subsidy, before I had? . . .

Have you ANY idea how bloody dead "Poetry" now is, how dead the comments, how dead the contributions??? How dead the whole bloomin' sheaf of American publications? How soft and impermanent the acclaimed output of the back-patters, the stand-patters, and the people who keep on telling you that main-street is THE centre, the unique and only centre of the KAWSmoss, ("moss," is about it). . . .

Eliot in an Eng. bank. H.D. in Switzerland, and the young still flocking toward Europe. . . .

The rush to escape, on the part of the young, is more desperate, and they arrive here so callow and so unprovided that they dont know what to do when they get here. No digestions.

No, ma vieille, you ought to have one more line up before you permanently relapse into EX egzacly the tone of the Century in 1892 of the last era.

Yrs / Ezra

Wallace Stevens to Harriet Monroe   *Hartford, Conn.,*
                                                        24 August [1922]

Dear Miss Monroe:

. . . A few weeks ago I came to the substance of an agreement with Mr. Knopf for the publication of a book [*Harmonium*] in the fall of 1923. This, by the way, is confidential for the present; but I don't know of any one more entitled to first news of it than yourself. . . . Williams drove through town a few weeks ago on his way to Vermont with one of his children and a dog. It was a blessing to see him although we were both as nervous as two belles in new dresses. I hope to see him again on his return trip. I also saw Marcel Duchamp in New-York recently. He seemed like a cat that had been left behind. . . .

Wallace Stevens to Harriet Monroe　　　*[Hartford, Conn.],*
23 September 1922

Dear Miss Monroe:

. . . When I get back from the South I expect to do some short poems and then to start again on a rather longish one; so that sooner or later I shall have something for Poetry, to which I send what I like most. But it takes time and, besides, I have no desire to write a great deal. I know that people judge one by volume. However, having elected to regard poetry as a form of retreat, the judgment of people is neither here nor there. The desire to write a long poem or two is not obsequiousness to the judgment of people. On the contrary, I find that this prolonged attention to a single subject has the same result that prolonged attention to a senora has according to the authorities. All manner of favors drop from it. Only it requires a skill in the varying of the serenade that occasionally makes one feel like a Guatemalan when one particularly wants to feel like an Italian. I expect that after a while Crispin (the present title is "The Comedian as the Letter C") will become rudimentary and abhorrent.

Always sincerely yours, / Wallace Stevens

Alfred Kreymborg to Harriet Monroe　　　*London, 25 October 1922*

Dear HM:

Greetings from London. . . . I've just heard of your tenth anniversary, and I must write a line at least.

Naturally, my warmest congratulations go to you and Poetry. I believe I am in as clear a position as any other man or woman about the work you have contributed to America during that period; and I hope I am at least as grateful as my neighbors for the opportunity given to me personally in your pages, and for the incentive Poetry has generally been to me. No one can wish you a finer joy for the next decade than yours below; and I can only add that I shall always hold myself ready to provide my mite of assistance any time it is called upon—and also at times when it is not called on. Prosit! . . .

In November, A.K. won $100 for "Pianissimo" (July 1922). He wrote H.M. 9 November: "[Harold] Monro handed me Poetry for November, and I collapsed.

Fell over into Aiken's arms. I had to be dragged to the nearest pub for resuscitation." The money helped pay his passage back to the United States.

Wallace Stevens to Harriet Monroe

Hartford, Conn.,
28 October 1922

Dear Miss Monroe:

The box from Peking reached us yesterday. *Box*, I say, for lo and behold, Mrs. Calhoun sent not one or two, but five, really delightful things. Of these, the chief one is a carved wooden figure of the most benevolent old god you ever saw. . . . I have had considerable experience in buying things abroad through other people. This, however, is the first time the thing has been wholly successful . . . . Mrs. Calhoun has clearly gone to a lot of trouble. I have written to her today. But I am as much indebted to you for this blissful adventure and I must thank you too. . . .

I observe that *Poetry* honors me once more. Gathering together the things for my book has been so depressing that I wonder at *Poetry's* friendliness. All my earlier things seem like horrid cocoons from which later abortive insects have sprung. The book will amount to nothing, except that it may teach me something. I wish that I could put everything else aside and amuse myself on a large scale for a while. One never gets anywhere in writing or thinking or observing unless one can do long stretches at a time. Often I have to let go, in the most insignificant poem, which scarcely serves to remind me of it, the most skyey of skyey sheets. And often when I have a real fury for indulgence I must stint myself. Of course, we must all do the same thing. Ariosto probably felt the same thing about the solid years he spent on Orlando. . . . Pitts Sanborn brought back a copy of Ulysses for me and other things including some liqueur from Santa Maria Novella which we absorbed in his room to celebrate the death of his landlord which occurred during the summer.

Always sincerely yrs, / W. Stevens

W.S. received Honorable Mention for "Another Weeping Woman," "Tea at the Palaz of Hoon," "Of the Manner of Addressing Clouds," and "Hibiscus on the Sleeping Shores," printed in October. Joyce's *Ulysses* had recently been published in Paris by Sylvia Beach (Shakespeare and Company).

Ernest Hemingway to Harriet Monroe

Paris, 16 November 1922

Dear Miss Monroe:-

I have been wondering when you were going to use the poems, as the Three Mountains Press here, Ezra Pound editing, is bringing out a

Hartford, October 28, 1922.

Dear Miss Monroe:

The box from Peking reached me yester-
day. Bne, I say, for lo and behold, Mrs.
Calhoun sent not one or two, but fine, really
delightful things. Of these, the chief one is a
carved wooden figure of the most benevolent old
god you ever saw. He has a staff in one hand
and in the other carries a lotus bud. On the back
of his head he has a decoration of some sort with
ribbons running down into his gown. The wood
is of the color spazedon but it is neither hard
nor ugly. And there you are. But the old man,
Hem-hering, has the most amused, the nicest
and kindliest expression: quite a pope after one's
own heart or at least an invulnerable bishop
telling one how fortunate one is, after all, and
not to mind one's bad poems. It is on a little
teak stand as is, alas, each of the other things.
The other things are a small jade screen,
two black crystal lions and a small jade
figure. The jade pieces are whitish.

Thank-you letter from Wallace Stevens to H.M., 28 October 1922.

book of my stuff shortly and I want to use the poems you have if you will give me permission to republish them.

Paris seems fairly quiet now. Dave O'Neil of St. Louis, whom you know, I believe, is in town with his family and will probably stay over here a couple of years. He says indefinitely, but that usually means two years. . . .

Gertrude Stein is down in St. Remy in Provence and says she won't come back to Paris till after Christmas. We had an enormous candied casaba melon from her in the mail yesterday. It was pretty nearly as big as a pumpkin. She is doing a new book [*The Making of Americans*].

I don't know whether you ever knew Lewis Galantiere when he lived in Chicago. He has just undergone a very trying love affair with a girl from Evanston, Ill. who is over here getting cultured. She's just left town and we have all cheered up.

Hueffer is coming to town tomorrow to stay a month. He's been living on his farm in England. Joyce is sick in Nice. He has a dreadfully hard time with his eyes. Frank Harris has been trying to get Sylvia Beach, who published Ulysses, to publish his autobiography. She doesn't want to although I told her it will be the finest fiction ever written.

T. S. Eliot's new quarterly The Criterion seems to have inspired the Dial and their last issue was pretty good. But that's American gossip, not Paris. . . .

The hot rum punch and checker season has come in. It looks like a good winter. Cafes [are] much fuller in the day time now with people that have no heat in their hotel rooms.

This reads like the personal column of the Petoskey Evening Resorter [sic]. Perhaps the gossip bores you anyway.

Yours sincerely, / Ernest Hemingway

Hemingway's six poems were printed in January 1923: "Mitrailliatrice," "Oily Weather," "Roosevelt," "Riparto d'Assalto," "Champs d'Honneur," and "Chapter Heading."

Kay Boyle to Harriet Monroe   [New York City], 29 November 1922

Dear Miss Monroe—

I wonder if these later developments will interest you?

Upon reading "Monody" ["Monody to the Sound of Zithers," December 1922] I find it breaks my heart. Primarily because that phase received burial rites six months or more ago. And secondarily because I think it is characteristic of too much American poetry—I mean unutterably weak sentimentality that manages to protrude from even our most brilliant and metallic stuff. In my later things I have managed to stamp it out, I think, with some success.

Faithfully, / Kay Boyle

H.M. note: "ans'd Feb 2 1923: Retd—Cummings diluted"; Boyle was then an editor at *Broom.*

Wallace Stevens to Harriet Monroe   *Hartford, Conn.,*
21 December 1922

Dear Miss Monroe:

. . . Mrs. Stevens and I spent the last half of last week in New-York shopping, seeing friends and so on. Alfred Kreymborg had lunch with us one day. He is the greatest concocter outside of politics. I never heard so many schemes spoken of in so short a time. Evidently he plans a marvelous year, and certainly he seems fit enough to carry it through. Knopf has my book, the contract is signed and that's done. I have mixed many things, exercising the most fastidious choice, as far as that was possible among my witherlings. To pick a crisp salad from the garbage of the past is no snap. . . . Well-o, merry Xmas and happy New Year to you and to Poetry and to all friends, now and forever: e pluribus unum.

Always sincerely yours, / Wallace Stevens

CHAPTER XII

The Twenties

In the spring of 1923, with the magazine safely into its second decade, the Editor took her first long break from *Poetry*. On 2 May, she sailed for England on the SS *President Monroe*, leaving Eunice Tietjens in "absolute control." It was a decision she would come to regret. In London, Monroe saw her old friends May Sinclair, John Galsworthy, Rebecca West, and Edwin Arlington Robinson. At the Cheshire Cheese, she finally met Richard Aldington, and was surprised to find he looked "more like a football-player than a poet." She had tea with the Sitwell brothers at the Poetry Bookshop, then attended the premiere of *Façade* at Aeolian Hall, where from behind the curtain Edith Sitwell declaimed her poems through a megaphone to the music of young William Walton.

In Paris, she was delighted by the postwar artistic ferment. At Constantin Brancusi's studio she met the eloquent "father of modern music," Erik Satie. In the Boulevard Arago she found Ford Madox Ford, who had "definitely dropped the *Hueffer*," again at the center of an artistic colony. (The next year he would found *transatlantic review*.) And there, at last, she met Ezra Pound. What personal remarks they may have exchanged, she did not record. But she reported that Pound was much perturbed that writers like James Joyce and T. S. Eliot had to "bother about shillings and pence." He told H.M. he was trying to "rescue" Eliot, who was still "imprisoned in a bank." She later met Joyce through Sylvia Beach at her famous bookstore, Shakespeare and Company, which had recently issued *Ulysses*—still unavailable in the United States, Monroe noted, because of the censors. Pound told her he himself was working on an epic that would "take him forty years to complete," so that she probably would "never see the end on't."

Monroe also spent an afternoon with Paul Valéry, and was invited to dinner by Robert McAlmon and David O'Neil, a friend from St. Louis, at an artists' café in Montparnasse. Pound showed up with Jane Heap, who told H.M. she was trying to continue the *Little Review* in Paris. With them were the "quite irresistible" Mina Loy and Tristan Tzara, "the original dada-ist." Then she was off to Barcelona, Toledo, Seville, and Madrid;

paintings in the Prado inspired a group of poems she published in March 1924.

When she returned to Chicago in September, H.M. discovered the Acting Editor had fiddled with the cover design, printed one of Monroe's poems without permission, and assembled an issue devoted to "The Poetry of Youth." Then she put together an all-sonnet edition for September. With amazingly poor judgment, Tietjens led off the issue with "The Return," a thirteen-part sequence by her close friend Edgar Lee Masters detailing the poet's recent, extremely ugly reunion with his estranged wife. It created a sensation.

Edgar Lee Masters, with daughter Marcia, early twenties. When Eunice Tietjens printed his sonnet sequence "The Return" in *Poetry* in September 1923, it created a sensation.

In bitter numbers, Masters described the disrepair of his house, his wife's haggard appearance, the "spiritual torture" of living with her, and their spats, including a quarrel during which he slapped her. Masters portrayed himself as the injured party, but the public knew better. All the newspapers had been following the marital discord of Chicago's most famous author for years. In "The Return," the poet neglected to mention that his house was falling apart because he had abandoned his wife and their two minor children. Helen Masters sued for support, with Clarence Darrow as her attorney, and had the court tie up all his assets. The reason for the poet's "return" in September 1922 was he was broke, and had little choice but to go home again. Mrs. Masters obtained a divorce on the grounds of cruelty in May 1923. By then, Masters was a pariah to Chicago society. When the September 1923 *Poetry* came out, the *Tribune*, *Daily News*, and *Herald* had a field day, rehashing the slapping incident in particular. Eunice crowed to H.M. that she had had to have more copies printed. E.T. departed for France, leaving the Editor to take the heat from irate Guarantors, including Henry Fuller, her oldest advisor, who wanted to resign.

In May 1924, a more serious story grabbed the headlines, the Leopold and Loeb case. Hoping to commit the perfect crime, the brilliant teenagers kidnapped and murdered fourteen-year-old Bobby Franks, but were soon caught and confessed. Richard Loeb was the son of Albert Loeb, an executive at Sears, Roebuck, as well as one of *Poetry*'s most gen-

Eunice Tietjens, in Chinese costume,
early twenties.

erous supporters and the sponsor of several prizes for young poets. At the
first "trial of the century," Clarence Darrow saved the killers from execu-
tion with a brilliant, twelve-hour summation attacking the death penalty.
One of the more interesting letters H.M. received about the case came
from Yvor Winters.

In the winter of 1924, Harriet Monroe was struck by a car and was laid
up with a broken kneecap for six weeks. It was inevitable, as she had a
penchant for charging across busy intersections with her head down. She
didn't break the habit. As she was rushing to do a radio broadcast, she had
another run-in with a car, in almost the exact spot on Michigan Avenue,
just before Christmas in 1927. This time her leg was in a cast for two
months, and again she edited from home.

On 12 May 1925, the indomitable Amy Lowell died, at age fifty-one.
The previous fall H.M. had published a long essay on her work and had
given her the Levinson Prize, to the dismay of many who felt Amy had
already reaped rewards far beyond her merits. In her "Memories of Amy
Lowell" (July 1925), Monroe declared that she was "a true and loyal
friend," and insisted, abundant evidence to the contrary, that she was "a
good sport." In one of her last letters to H.M., Lowell voiced her disap-
pointment with the new generation and wondered whether Harriet's
helping hand hadn't "done harm."

Monroe didn't agree, and continued to welcome the young poets, even
when she didn't always understand them or accept the postwar attitudes
their work expressed. Among the dozens of new voices she presented in

the twenties, often for the first time, were Langston Hughes, Laura Riding, Countee Cullen, Richard Eberhart, Louise Bogan, R. P. Blackmur, Allen Tate, Elder Olson, and George Dillon. Dillon was still an undergraduate at Chicago when he debuted with six poems in August 1925; H.M. made him an Associate Editor the same month. In the fall, he won *Poetry's* young poet's prize and replaced Marion Strobel, who resigned to take care of her two small daughters. (The younger girl grew up to be the painter Joan Mitchell and wife of Barney Rosset, founder of Grove Press.) Dillon served for two years; a decade later he became Editor.

Among the most original of the new talents was Hart Crane. Largely self taught—he was a voracious reader of both the classics and the most avant-garde little magazines—he quit high school and moved to New York to make literary contacts. When his father, a candy manufacturer and the inventor of Life Savers, cut back his support, Crane took a number of jobs, from reporter to shipping clerk, and kept on writing. Yvor Winters admired poems of Crane's he'd seen in the *Little Review* and other magazines and became an ardent supporter.

Monroe was perplexed by Crane's highly allusive, compressed style, and in May 1926 Winters wrote to allay her misgivings. He assured the Editor that Crane ranked with the best writers of his time. When Crane submitted "At Melville's Tomb," she queried him about his puzzling metaphors. "Take me for a hard-boiled unimaginative unpoetic reader," she wrote, "and tell me how *dice can bequeath an embassy* (or anything else); and how a calyx (*of death's bounty* or anything else) can give back *a scattered chapter, livid hieroglyph*; and how, if it does, such a *portent* can be *wound in corridors* (of shells or anything else). And so on." She hastened to add:

> All this may seem impertinent, but it is not so intended. Your ideas and rhythms interest me, and I am wondering by what process of reasoning you would justify this poem's succession of champion mixed metaphors, of which you must be conscious. The packed line should pack its phrases in orderly relation, it seems to me, in a manner tending to clear confusion instead of making it worse confounded.

Crane replied that he hoped to clarify "the obscurities apparent in my Melville poem . . . . But I realize that my explanations will not be very convincing." Before his image-by-image exegesis of the poem, Crane revealed some of the theoretical concerns behind his complex technique:

> . . . as a poet I may very possibly be more interested in the so-called illogical impingements of the connotations of words on the consciousness . . . than I am interested in the preservation of their logi-

cally rigid significations at the cost of limiting my subject matter and perceptions . . . .

Much fine poetry may be completely rationalistic in its use of symbols, but there is much great poetry of another order which will yield the reader very little when inspected under the limitation of such arbitrary concerns as are manifested in your judgment of the Melville poem . . .

In the minds of people who have sensitively read, seen and experienced a great deal, isn't there a terminology something like short-hand as compared to usual description and dialectics, which the artist ought to be right in trusting as a reasonable connective agent toward fresh concepts, more inclusive evaluations?

Monroe responded, "I would not deny to the poet the right to take certain of the liberties you claim," but added: "I think that in your poem certain phrases carry to an excessive degree the 'dynamics of metaphor' —they telescope three or four images together by mental leaps (I fear my own metaphors are getting mixed!) which the poet, knowing his ground, can take safely, but which the most sympathetic reader cannot take unless the poet leads him by the hand with some such explanations as I find in your letter." Crane could not have been encouraged when Monroe concluded: "Your poem reeks with brains—it is thought out, worked out, sweated out. And the beauty which it seems entitled to is tortured and lost." Although Yvor Winters thought his "Marriage of Faustus and Helen" was equal to the best of Stevens, Pound, or Eliot, she told Crane: "Well, I cannot grant it such a rank."

Despite her reservations, Monroe published "At Melville's Tomb" and, more remarkably, their exchange about the poem—six pages in very small print—in the October 1926 issue. In 1927, *Poetry* published "O Caribe Isle!" and "Cutty Sark," the third section of *The Bridge*. But when Monroe returned "Moment Fugue" in 1928, Crane wrote to Winters "in disgust." Winters sent H.M. a sarcastic letter, out of "pure affection," diagramming the entire poem. Jessica Nelson North, her assistant, wrote him an ill-advised protest, and Winters sent a scathing riposte. Even so, Crane gave *Poetry* "Eldorado," and when Winters asked to review *The Bridge*, Monroe agreed. In "The Progress of Hart Crane" (June 1930), Winters faulted the epic for its loose structure and said it largely failed, because of its "Whitmanian inspiration." Crane thought Winters's interpretation was totally mistaken, and felt personally betrayed. The review ended their friendship.

Another Winters review in 1930 ended his relationship with Monroe, as well. Allen Tate was a great favorite of his at the time, and Winters wanted *Poetry* to publish his paean to Tate's "Ode to the Confederate Dead." When H.M. balked at his application of the word "greatest," Winters pointed out her own liberal use of the words "great" and "major." Winters had been growing ever more disillusioned with the Editor's taste in the twenties—and sounding ever more like Pound in the teens—and her editing of his piece was the last straw. With scorn, he catalogued her faults in judgment while ranking himself among the great poet-critics, including Dr. Johnson. On Winters's envelope, H.M. asked Morton Zabel, the Associate Editor, to comment on the letter, noting: "I think we shall have to give him up." Zabel replied, on the same envelope:

> This is all very sad . . . and of course Winters is tiresome. But I shall view his alienation with very great regret, for he is a critic of unquestionable distinction . . . . I wish he had a few grains of humor along with one of the few authentic brands of seriousness now visible to the naked eye. . . . But can't a tentative truce be arranged? Or is all hope of that past & gone?

Winters couldn't be pacified, and wrote H.M. a disdainful letter. He did not contribute to *Poetry* again until two years after Monroe's death.

Pound himself reestablished contact with " 'Arriet" after their meetings in Paris, chiding her as of old, but in better humor. He, too, felt the magazine had declined badly, and he urged her to get more Hemingway, Moore, Carnevali—even "the obstreperous Ernest" Walsh. He also recommended Louis Zukofsky, several times. Though Zukofsky's work was unpalatable to her, Monroe first presented him in 1923, printed an early "movement" of his *magnum opus* "*A*" in 1928, then gave him a free hand to edit an entire issue. The "Objectivist" Number (February 1931) featured Williams, Charles Reznikoff, George Oppen, Carl Rakosi, Basil Bunting, and Kenneth Rexroth. In 1928, E.P. again offered to steer authors her way, to "liven up [her] established family magazine."

Another old friend, indeed almost part of the "family," also made more frequent contact. After his triumphant tour of England in 1920, Vachel Lindsay saw his career fall into steep decline. After a nervous breakdown early in 1923, he wrote Monroe of his attempts to recover. Throughout the decade, she sent letters of support, accepted new poems, and praised his books. After his marriage in 1925 and the birth of his two children, Lindsay was often in debt. Again Monroe came to the rescue, with advances, loans, and cash, some of which she said came from unnamed "admirers." Knowing the poet's spendthrift ways, she sometimes sent money secretly to his wife.

After the stock market crash on 29 October 1929, many other struggling poets would turn to Harriet Monroe and the magazine for help in emergencies. With the onset of the Great Depression, *Poetry* was often on the brink of collapse itself. Even so, the Editor found it impossible to deny anyone, and almost always managed to send at least something, or to convince someone else, to help a poet in distress.

Vachel Lindsay to Harriet Monroe   Gulfport, Miss.,
                                                      17 February 1923

My Dearest Harriet:-

I went clear to pieces and had to stop travelling for a year, and by good luck landed into the midst of this place [Gulf-Park Junior College] amid old Hiram College Friends. . . .

Well here I am, and likely to flood you with manuscripts soon. You may have first choice of all I fix up. I have a suitcase full. Now hold me to it. . . .

Now my dear and best Harriet, let us to the fray once more. If I could get my heart and mind just where they were when I first wrote for thee about 1913, I could supply thee with epics. But I assure you I need your strong hand, and earnest expectation. . . . I would give anything to establish the old relation, the concentration and intellectual and personal devotions we had, when adventure in the Poetry Magazine was supreme adventure for me, and I first came from Springfield to thee. . . .

Vachel Lindsay to Harriet Monroe   Gulfport, Miss., 28 March 1923

My Dear Harriet Monroe:-

Believe me your letter did me worlds of good. . . . People cannot understand I have been speaking these seven years, *not* writing. They seem to think I can do both, and those who hate "Americanism" rejoice exceedingly and say I have written myself out, while I have spoken in every University in the United States and all those in West Canada. Most of the principal American Universities have recalled me two to four times. Doing all this, besides appearing at Oxford, Cambridge and The University of London England, those who wish me ill anyway say that I am *"written out."* . . .

D. H. Lawrence to Harriet Monroe   Vera Cruz, Mexico,
                                                20 November 1923

Dear Harriett [sic] Monroe

I am sailing in two days time from Vera Cruz to England. In September I was in Chicago for a day: a queer big city with a sort of palpitation I couldn't quite understand. But I hope to come again soon, & to understand a little more.

Did you [receive] *Birds, Beasts & Flowers*? I promised you a signed copy, and will send it you from London. . . .

I am still coming to Chicago— poco a poco [little by little]. Am not very keen on going to Europe, if I must confess it.

D. H. Lawrence

Witter Bynner spent several months with Frieda and D. H. Lawrence in Mexico, where he became disillusioned with D.H.L. and his theories. On 6 November 1923, W.B. wrote H.M. that Frieda was "comfortable, likable," but said: "D. H. Lawrence usually infuriated me . . . . He is the most brilliantly lost man I can imagine, fleeing always with a violent grace from his own shadow."

John Gould Fletcher to Harriet Monroe   *[n. p.] 1 May 1924*

Dear Harriet Monroe,

I enclose herewith the last poems I have written, and the last I shall ever write. As your paper was the first to pay me for my work, I am sending them to you, in the hope that you may find something of value in them. . . . Herman Melville, who was a poet, declared, "If I wrote the Gospels in this century I should die in the gutter"; I do not say I could write the Gospels, but I do say that I have spent fifteen years of my life, with no return for my investment, and at the cost of a great deal of money unwillingly spent by my relatives. In the future, I shall devote myself to prose. There is no sense in piling up manuscript for future generations to destroy. . . .

After reading H.M.'s essay on him (January 1926), J.G.F. sent more poems in July 1926.

Wallace Stevens to Harriet Monroe   *Hartford, Conn., [July?] 1924*

Dear Miss Monroe:

This is not letter-writing weather. All I want to say is that as soon as I have something that I think you will like I shall send it to you. . . . There is still a good deal to go through so that the chances are that I shall

Wallace Stevens, c. 1923, when
Harmonium was published, after
frequent urging by H.M.

continue to loaf and smoke cigars in the evenings for some time to come. We do not go away in the summer. Hartford is as good as any other place then and better than most. And somehow or other my work always seems to grow deeper and deeper then. I do not expect to be in Chicago in the near future. The truth is that I have not even been in New-York for more than two months. For that matter, post-cards indicate that everybody I know is in Europe. Mrs. Calhoun wrote to me a few weeks ago, from which it appears that *Harmonium* reached Peking. My royalties for the first half of 1924 amounted to $6.70. I shall have to charter a boat and take my friends around the world.

Always sincerely yours, / Wallace Stevens

Yvor Winters to Harriet Monroe   *Boulder, Colo., 2 August 1924*

Dear Miss Monroe:

Thank you greatly for your letter of some weeks ago and your information regarding the two boys [Leopold and Loeb] on trial in Chicago. It is a terrible thing, surely, but I cannot help thinking that the cause is more complex than you seemed to believe. I cannot imagine such a crime being committed without some sadistic or other abnormal element entering into it—and such things are of course surprisingly common and very little understood. The hysteria about the crime is nauseating. . . . The murder case is simply—or so I suspect—an example of fairly common aberrations, that because of the law of averages, happened to strike in a high place. The other is symptomatic of one hundred percent Americanism. If the boys are executed it will be criminal on more than one score. They ought to be kept and studied at least. . . .

Your editorial on Miss Millay surprises me. Her poetry has always made me suspect that she would be a very nice girl to flirt with, but has never interested me beyond that. I could name a dozen contemporary women that seem to me far her superior from every possible angle—many of them on her side of the fence for that matter. . . .

In her seven-page article, "Edna St. Vincent Millay" (August 1924), H.M. praised Millay for being a modern woman, ranked her sonnets among the best in the English language, and called her lyrics the "most precious" of any woman since Sappho.

Edgar Lee Masters to Harriet Monroe   *[New York City],*
                                                       2 September 1924

Dear Harriet:

I have been intending to write you more at length ever since your editorial in résumé of my work [July 1924]; and since that appeared I have read with care what you have to say of Millay and Sandburg, and while not agreeing with all of your conclusions I am impressed with the judicial spirit in which you approach these appraisals. . . . [Y]ou know what poetry was in 1898 and in the years that preceded it, and how difficult it was for a writer in central Illinois in the late eighties and early nineties to rise from the earth bound conditions. . . . It was a rough, ignorant town [Lewiston, Ill.], save for a few oases, and my companions were Huckleberry Finns and boys who were working, or who were the sons of lawyers and had every possible contempt for what I was doing. My own people too played a part far beyond their right; my father in particular, who thought such things were worse than a waste of time. . . .

Add to this the fact that I was immediately thrown into all sorts of life and heart experiences, in all sorts of fascinating distractions, and add to that the constant dinning of my father to drop writing and buckle down to the law and you have a further key. And I did get into the law, and I was working like a Turk; and then I was married. Well, what was Chicago then as an inspiration to the muse? There was no market for anything and no interest in it after you did it. . . . So it went until Spoon River which I printed under a pseudonym [Webster Ford] for the reasons of prudence. I couldn't write what others were writing; neither could I under the conditions write what I had in mind. . . . I was punished by getting now money and nothing else. The prose plays…all trash, save that I didn't distort my convictions. Political essays! A law book of 4,000 pages, which was never published…my God! What labors…and law, law! This is an explanation, not an apology. But if I had not had a constitution like the United States I should have gone under long ago. Finally at an age when lots of men are all in, I took hold and flung out a lot of poems. Then what happened: my law practice dwindled, as I knew it would when I remonstrated with [William Marion] Reedy about throwing off my anonymity; and later I took to novels for money. . . .

THE NEW SPOON RIVER will soon be out. I think it a richer and profounder book than the old one, not so episodical of external things, but as much so as to soul experiences. I hope you will like it. It is a longer book too. The old one had 276 epitaphs; this one about 350. I wrote it in Bill Slack's kitchen in that awful winter of 1923, having no place to sit but there, without going to a hotel. I hope all is well with you. . . . My perturbed spirit may rest even in life. But I have had a good life, wondrous fun, beauty, and many loves, and not all bad. Good luck and great affection.

Ever, / E.L.M.

My letter, Harriet, is not for use—but for you to see; though it contains a confessional that might furnish material sometime for an analysis.

H.M.'s essays on Masters, Lindsay, Lowell, Sandburg, Millay, Frost, Teasdale, Pound, H.D., and others were collected in *Poets and Their Art* (1926). Clarence Darrow was E.L.M.'s law partner 1903–1911. Slack was his divorce lawyer (Darrow represented Mrs. Masters) in 1923. *Spoon River Anthology* was published in 1915, but poems from the book were first printed in *Reedy's Mirror* beginning mid-1914.

Amy Lowell to Harriet Monroe　　Brookline, Mass., 25 October 1924

Dear Harriet:

I am astonished and very sincerely pleased. I woke up the other day to receive newspapers from Ada [Russell, A.L.'s companion], my secretaries, and my servants, all of whom had noticed your award of the Helen Haire Levinson Prize to me . . . .

I feel frightfully old this year, due, of course, to too much hard work; but, after all, one is not young any longer, though I expect to shake off a good many years when I have finally finished with the book [her two-volume biography of Keats]. . . . On the whole, I am not greatly impressed with the younger generation. I think we did better—don't you? Perhaps this is the usual myopia of age; perhaps we are not going to have any immediate successors. Look at the poetry magazines; where is the one that is half as good as yours? And how prejudiced these young things are; how unintelligent and vapid! Were we as bad as that? I do not believe it. Even those boys and girls whom I think have promise do not seem to fulfill it. . . . I am not sure that the welcoming hand extended to poets all over the country to-day, by you and all other editors, has not done harm. In the days when poets had a difficult time they seemed to write pretty well, I think. . . .

Robert Frost to Harriet Monroe Amherst, Mass., 19 December 1924

Dear Miss Monroe:

That is the question, Where am I? I now have three homes, mind you, not just summer and hunting camps—three going on four, all bought and paid for out of poetry. So that even when I may be said to be *at* home, I am nowhere in particular. . . .

Your letter need not have been so worried about your article ["Robert Frost," December]. So long as you don't give me credit for Robinson's (or Tennyson's?) Enid you may regard relations between us as unstrained. It is a good article and a real Christmas present if I may take it as such done up as it comes in red. I had been hinting round to the family for something simple to wear in my hair when I am out with the Opera Club this winter toadying to various and sundry Continental pretenders; and here I get a whole crown.

Nay but seriously I am pleased with your article especially where it warns people against taking me too seriously. My debt to you has piled up to some altitude above sea level since you first printed blank verse of mine in 1913. We have grown to be old, if not yet quite first name, friends. May we never be less.

Merry Christmas to you and a great discovery or two in poetry for 1925. And you mustn't keep getting bowled over by cars. . . .

Sara Teasdale to Harriet Monroe Lake Mahopac, N.Y., 1 February 1925

Dear Harriet:

. . . Vachel has sent an avalanche of disturbing letters recently. I don't know what should be done about him. I had talked over all possible things with Dr. Wakefield and it seemed decided that Vachel was to go to Egypt this winter. He could have made his expenses by writing newspaper or magazine articles to be used later in a book. But, as you know, he is in Spokane and underneath his thin layer of seeming to like it, is fearfully depressed and rudderless. . . . Of course if V. could find

exactly the right woman to go with him, so much the better. I some-
times think that V's bringing up and mine might both better have laid
less stress on the Galahad idea. V. would be bound to be disillusioned by
marriage (unless a miracle of a woman came along) and as for a big
family of children, nothing could be finer if there were money to sup-
port them—but Vachel's income from his books is not likely to increase
and he finds reciting deadly. What is to be done? . . .

Edgar Lee Masters to Harriet Monroe   *[New York City],*
                                                         23 June 1925

Dear Harriet:

. . . You do tackle Amy Barnum Lowell after all her treatment of
Lindsay. Well, but she was not a critic at all, nor a stylist at all . . . . she
got away with more murder than anybody in my time; she wrote stuff
so inane, so lacking in imagination, feeling and sense that it was next to
idiocy, and she printed it in the magazines. She wrote that absurd Fable
for Critics, or whatever she called it [*Tendencies in Modern American
Poetry*, 1917], and got away with that; though it was without wit and
without sense, and was malicious enough. In that book of hers she
bracketed Sandburg with me, in addition to ignoring Lindsay; and
Sandburg has as much relation to me as he has to George Santayana.
The truth is that she was not a critic at all; and the word goes around
here that her heart was broken over the British reception of [her book
on] Keats. Some professor of Massachusetts had a letter in the Post here
about a fortnight before she died in which he catalogued the grammat-
ical solecisms of her Keats. That would have killed her, as she was always
rapping other people for such things. Peace no less, and this epitaph: "A
Dome of many colored glass" [the title of A.L.'s first book, 1912]. Her
work was not of precious or semi-precious stones—but of colored
glass—American make. . . .

Ezra Pound to Harriet Monroe   *Rapallo, Italy, 13 November 1925*

Dear Harriet:

I onnerstan; i.e. have recd. warning that friend [Ernest] Walsh is
blowing our heads off for the [Ralph Cheever] Dunning award [of the
Levinson Prize for 1925].

Which has led me to look at the table of awards for the first time in
some years. Seems to me chief weakness of the ten years record is that
Lindsay is on both lists, and W. C. Williams and Eliot on neither. (Frost
on both, is also an excess) but an excess ONLY in view of the omission
of the other names.

Yr. Last two numbers seem to show tendency to liven up the old schooner once again.

Why don't you (without mentioning my name) try to get another batch of poems from Hemingway, McAlmon, Carnevali, or even the obstreperous Ernest [Walsh], the ineffable Cummings. Might bring you back onto the map. . . .

Yvor Winters to Harriet Monroe   *Moscow, Idaho, 11 May 1926*

Dear Miss Monroe:

. . . My enthusiasm for [Hart] Crane is based on a single poem, For the Marriage of Faustus and Helen, which seems to me one of the great poems of our time—as great as the best of Stevens or Pound or Eliot. . . .

Why in heaven's name don't you return everything for six months, and catch up? From the looks of most of your contents, you wouldn't be missing much. If I thought you would print me inside of two years I would send you a group of original poems, which are really excellent. But you wouldn't. . . .

[Ernest] Walsh will if I send them to him [at *This Quarter*]. He is a damn fool, with no manners and no taste and very little talent, but he is running a great magazine for the moment. And he is printing the work that might save you from the fate of the Atlantic. If he goes on for ten years he will be another American Mercury. But he won't go on, and will leave a glorious name behind him—as an editor.

Why not risk a "quibble of mixed metaphors" by Hart Crane—it can't help but be well-written, at least—instead of some silly little jingle by some school girl or club-lady from Keokuk? . . .

Malcolm Cowley to Harriet Monroe   *Gaylordsville, Conn.,*
3 June 1926

Dear Miss Monroe:

. . . I'd like to say that I was enormously pleased to hear you were publishing my poems, all of them. To publish a few verses here, a few verses there, at the foot of a page, has very little effect. Especially in the case of long-winded, unemphatic, unfigured work like mine, where several poems together are required to create an atmosphere, to cause a state of mind. Next spring I want to publish a book, and the appearance of a group of poems in Poetry is the very best introduction to that book, the best assistance to its publication. And Poetry is indeed the best read of magazines. . . .

As for the title of the group of poems, and of the first poem, I was glad to hear your suggestion. Let's say "Blue Juniata" for the group, and "Bones of a House" for the first poem. When I publish a book, I want to call it "Blue Juniata," so I'll be glad to see this group of poems carry the same title. . . .

The group, printed in November, won the Guarantors' Prize ($100). *Blue Juniata* was published in 1929. Cowley wrote H.M. 29 January 1929 that the messy ms. would have stayed in his drawer, "if Hart Crane hadn't helped me out, retyped some forty poems, and sent them out. And then, by a strange accident, the book was accepted by two publishers simultaneously. . . . I shall insist on giving you full credit for your assistance, which was invaluable."

Langston Hughes to Harriet Monroe   Fire!! *Devoted to Younger Negro Artists, New York City, 2 November 1926*

My dear Miss Monroe,

Thank you very much for my check from POETRY. Such things come in very handy when winter time's approaching and overcoats are

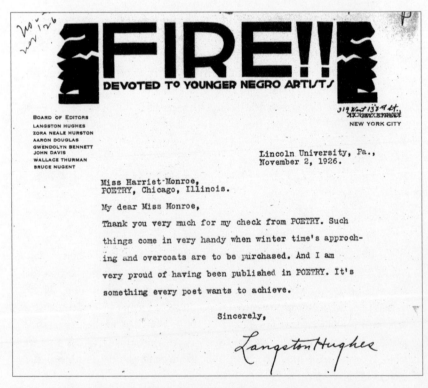

Thank-you letter from Langston Hughes, 2 November 1926.

to be purchased. And I am very proud of having been published in POETRY. It's something every poet wants to achieve.

Sincerely, / Langston Hughes

L.H. had five poems in the November issue, under the title "Blues."

Ezra Pound to Harriet Monroe   *Rapallo, Italy, 10 November 1926*

Dear Harriet—

. . . The award to Amy was an infamy, especially considering her financial rating & even not considering it at all. . . .

My Dear Harriet you are showing a liking for the chewed and the second rate; and a lot of magazines (dull ones at that) that have started behind you, have gone on and got in front.

God knows I am not supposed to have any prejudice in favour of American intelligence, but I decline, even after all these years, and from this distance to believe things in murka [America] are as dead and watery as a survey of your last five years record wd. indicate.

I admit your perseverence has been wonnerful; and your benevolence indisputable; and your vacations infrequent; but take a pill; take a week off; even read the New Masses; but do, fer Xt's sake, do SOMETHING to freshen your eye. . . .

I suppose you have by now heard of poor Walsh's death. I imagine Carnevali feels it more than anyone else. And might possibly do the best memorial notice. I found a lot of Walsh's poems here on my return from Paris (naturally unpublished). . . .

France is dead enough; england possibly worse, america still the leading firm for production of dish-water, sugar, and soft soap. . . .

Yvor Winters to Harriet Monroe   *Moscow, Idaho, 27 November 1926*

Dear Miss Monroe:

. . . Crane is writing a long poem [*The Bridge*] . . . . I have seen a couple of sections of it, and I am sending you the advance information that it is one of the supreme great poems of our time. . . .

You do not mention Williams' In the American Grain among the works in prose that you admire—and yet it is, if there is such a book, a greater book than [Elizabeth Madox Roberts's novel] The Time of Man. It and Spring and All alone would suffice to place W. as the greatest master since Hardy.

Best wishes, / Yvor Winters

Ezra Pound to Harriet Monroe   *Rapallo, Italy, 30 November 1926*

Dear Harriet—

. . . Yes I saw your article, if you mean the one that says what a delightful writer I used to be, and what a shame I have probably petered out. . . .

I personally think extremely well of Mussolini. If one compares him to american presidents (the last three) or British premiers, etc.... in fact one can NOT without insulting him.

If the intelligensia don't think well of him, it is because they know nothing about "the state", and government, and have no particularly large sense of values. Any how, WHAT intelligensia? . . .

I think Muss. has very sound ideas on how to govern Italy; and I greatly enjoy seeing a man who knows his own job . . . .

In her essay "Ezra Pound" (May 1925), H.M. praised his revolutionary early work— still fresh, she thought—but found his recent poetry "narrowed down to a merely literary inspiration."

Yvor Winters to Harriet Monroe   *Santa Fe, N. Mex., 28 June 1927*

Dear Miss Monroe:

. . . I write you thus out of pure affection: you are about three movements behind the times, and the present movement is really important. You ought to catch up. Your refusal to take risks is ridiculous. As your magazine now stands nothing could hurt it, and variety would at least be a change, and might even without your realizing it, result in something more. . . .

I shall be in Santa Fe all summer, and next year shall go to Stanford to work on a doctorate. I am contemplating a thesis . . . which will establish beyond all cavil the dynasty of Emerson, Dickinson, Williams and Crane, and simply eliminate yourself unless you get into line quick. . . .

Janet is much better and will go to California with me.

Best wishes from both of us, / Yvor Winters

Vachel Lindsay to Harriet Monroe   *Spokane, Wash.,*
11 November 1927

Dearest Harriet Monroe:-

Your beautiful letter just this day came, and I agree with you entirely, and Elizabeth and I thank you with all our hearts.

So far as I know you are the only human being on the face of the earth who wants me to write more poetry or who believes I can do it

well. I have many poems, nine-tenths written packed into 20 note-
books, I carried on the train since 1912. But no one wants me to
develop these notes. If my publisher sues me, he will have to serve the
papers where I sleep in the graveyard. I am at the top of my singing
power and creative strength, and I have been hectored into silence for
these two years. I doubt if I will ever write another poem.

With love / Vachel

H.M. wrote Elizabeth Lindsay an encouraging letter, then sent $100 on 21 February
1928, saying it was "a tribute from an admirer." She also sent V.L. a $50 advance pay-
ment for poems in the October 1928 issue. Mrs. Lindsay thanked her for the "wind-
fall" on 2 March 1928. The "admirer" was almost certainly H.M.

Yvor Winters to Harriet Monroe   *Palo Alto, Calif., 31 July 1928*

Dear Miss Monroe:

Hart Crane sends me your note regarding his Moment Fugue. Not
begging help, but in disgust. Out of admiration for Crane, however, and
pure affection for yourself, I am volunteering to parse the thing for
you. . . . I suspect Crane needs the money and you certainly need a
good poem. I have been considered competent to teach freshman com-
position at this august institution, which, I would bet a dollar none of
your staff could do, so perhaps you will feel some confidence in my
ability to dissect a sentence even though you don't always follow me.
Here goes:

First stanza. Subject: the syphilitic (adj. used as noun)
                           selling—pres. part. mod. subj.
                           violets and daisies—objects of pres. part. *selling*
                           calmly—adverb mod. pres. part. *selling*
                           by the subway newsstand—adverbial prep.
                             phrase mod. pres. part. *selling*
              Verb: knows
                             how—subord. conjunction introducing
                             adverbial clause.
                             hyacinths—object of *offers*
2nd St.   This April morning—subject of *offers* and of
                             adverbial clause introd. by *how*
[*And so on, diagramming the rest of the poem.*]

The poem, so far as I can see, offers two syntactic difficulties that
would not trouble you had you not decided early in your editorial
career that all the poetry of the past was ipso facto affected and ridicu-
lous and hence not to be read. There is one poetic inversion, the prose

order of which would be: "How this April morning offers hyacinths" etc. See any of the English classics for precedent. Or simply see any of the English classics for a few elementary notions of style in general. There is also one pivot word, *eyes*. This is not common in English but has been sanctioned by some 3 or 4 centuries or perhaps more of Japanese classical tradition, not to mention some 3 or 4 years of Mr Crane, Dr Williams, and myself. This ought to make it fairly respectable. . . .

Jessica Nelson North to Yvor Winters　　　　　　*[mid-August 1928]*

August whatever it is

Dear Arthur:

Your rather ~~impudent~~ outspoken letter was received while Miss Monroe and I were both on our vacations. She says she doesn't think she will answer, but I am going to because it makes me a little bit mad.

To begin with if I couldn't teach freshman composition in any institution I should walk into Lake Michigan until my hat floated. I just turned down an offer to teach ten hours a semester of creative writing at Manhattan Kansas, a somewhat larger school, at two thousand five hundred a year. Anybody past eighth grade could follow your analysis and I suspected that was what Mr. Crane meant, but I laughingly diagrammed the thing a la high-school grammar books to show him that it was ambiguous, and it was.

Secondly. Poets without a sense of humor have no business existing. . . .

Thirdly. I had nine years of Latin. I don't know how much Miss Monroe had. I never heard of anyone who didn't know what an objective genitive was. Don't be so proud.

Fourthly. If you had been reading Miss Monroe's editorials you would know that she had been writing an exhaustive series on poets of the past.

Fifthly. Whether or not Mr. Crane is a major poet is a moot point. Who are you to make out the list?

Yours for a reasonable tolerance, / Jessica North

Yvor Winters to Jessica Nelson North　　　　　　*Palo Alto, Calif.,*
24 August 1928

Dear Miss North:

Thanks for your detailed and crushing rejoinder. The job you turned down was precisely $1200 dollars more than I shall get here, which will doubtless comfort you. I have to teach only nine hours, however—you see my job is a sort of graduate scholarship for sub-Ph.D.'s. But even at best the difference is humiliating. When, however, you cast aspersions on Stanford University, my wrath rises. It is small purely from preference; and with nine years of Latin, an A.B., M.A., and honors, you must surely realize what the words "state college" mean, especially in Kansas. . . . We have no courses here in creative writing, and if we had and I had the kind of corn-college reputation that would get me that kind of a job, I should still prefer to keep myself clean and continue in my present humble state until I could call myself a philologist. . . .

Mr Crane's being a major poet was decided some time ago by God, as well as your being a proper associate editor of Poetry. I just happened to stumble onto the fact by accident. I have noticed Miss Monroe's exhaustive articles on the poets of the past, but no longer read Poetry notwithstanding. Your admiration for them is the funniest crack in your letter.

> Sincerely, and for putting corn colleges in their place,
> Yvor Winters
> A.B., AM, Phi Bete, and Ph. D. to be.

P.S. Janet sends love.

Ezra Pound to Harriet Monroe   *Rapallo, Italy, 10 September 1928*

Dear Harriet:

I am sending you sep. cov. registered a group of Zukofsky's poems that has just come in. I shd. think you ought to be able to get from it a group of things (say about 10–12) pages that wd. suit you. . . .

You might let me know if there are any authors whose contributions you WANT, or whose work you feel wd. liven up your established family magazine. . . .

Ezra Pound to Harriet Monroe   *Rapallo, Italy, 1 November 1928*

Dear H.M.

Very glad you have taken the Zukofsky, am forwarding the nooz to him, and spose he will communicate his desires re title to group. . . .

Do send Zukofsky his chq. as soon as convenient. I think he can use it. . . .

When is the blarsted and devastated rebooblik going to put me in charge of its eddykatn in licherchoor? When is a consortium of kawledg presidents going to ask me to debunk their present method of wasting the time of the roisin generation, by giving them the tip as to where the STUFF iz. etc. After twenty years of howling down their ear trumpets, or praps they aint gaawt no ear trumpiks, or any ears, or any optic or auditory nerves, or in fak, perhaps they don exist, but are merely a figment of imagination, like the lemon Coolidge wuz weaned on (when in reality he aint never bin weaned.)

?

William Rose Benét to Harriet Monroe   The Saturday Review of Literature, *New York City,* *12 January 1929*

Dear Miss Monroe:

I am glad you had that letter from [Elinor Wylie]. She spoke to me of how kind she thought it of you, giving her the prize. She had been here less than a week.

For years she surmounted physical handicaps that would have laid any other low. She did her beautiful work. She lived her life heroically. She still stirs us like a trumpet-call.

It came so quickly that I do not believe the utter darling could have known much pain then. She was stricken down standing, as she would have wished to die.

Always yours, / William Rose Benét

Wylie died of a stroke on 16 December, at age forty-three. She debuted in *Poetry* in April 1920 and received the Levinson Prize in November 1928. Benét helped publish her second collection, *Nets to Catch the Wind* (1921); they married in 1923.

Richard Eberhart to Harriet Monroe   *New York City,* *4 October 1929*

My dear Miss Monroe,

The friendship of your letter is good to know, and I am sorry we disagree on the poems I sent you. It is difficult under any circumstances to argue about poetry, usually futile; yet sometimes critical standards are clarified if it is done. May I make one suggestion? That the poems in Poetry tend to be too much alike, and that you might make it a more powerful organ if you had more daring? . . .

After a long-seeming time of attempt at literary jobs, I no longer clasp shadows, but pinch myself now and then to realize if it is true that I awake at 6 A.M. Monday morning to enter the Meat Packing Industry! The guts of life! To begin infernal passage down a river of blood, to the nethermost depths of common reality. Strange, the pilgrimages we make! . . .

Henry Rago to Harriet Monroe   *Chicago, 19 December 1929*

Dear Miss Monroe:

As you advised, I read some modern poetry and tried to be as candid as possible about it. I still prefer Tennyson and Poe to Millay and Masters. However, I did discover the beauty of expression in vers libre. I also found that modern poetry was written about simple things, each writer seeing the object in a different light.

I remembered what you said about self-expression. . . .

I am enclosing my first effort to write modern poetry. It is surely appropriate this morning. I hope it complies with what you suggested to me.

Respectfully Yours, / Henry W[adsworth] Rago.

H.R. enclosed a poem called "Fog." *H.M. note:* "14 years old. My protégé."

CHAPTER XIII

The Depression Years, 1930–1936

1. Near "Calamity"

While the thirties were the worst of times financially for the magazine, they were among the best of times artistically. *Poetry*'s earliest "stars" were offering H.M. some of the strongest works of their maturity. Meanwhile, another ambitious generation was emerging, and under the pressures of hard times, the poetry they were writing had new urgency and energy. The self-absorption and escapism of the previous decade were less acceptable to poets coming of age amid economic collapse and social upheaval.

Among the scores of new writers *Poetry* presented in the thirties were Theodore Roethke, Paul Engle, May Sarton, Paul Bowles, Dudley Fitts, Robert Fitzgerald, Ruth Lechlitner, J.V. Cunningham, Robert Penn Warren, Edwin Rolfe, Lorine Niedecker, Muriel Rukeyser, Kenneth Patchen, Josephine Miles, Mary Barnard, Richmond Lattimore, Delmore Schwartz, and Elizabeth Bishop. Many were still in college or recent graduates when they started to submit poems; most eventually contributed reviews, as well. Allen Tate, F. R. Leavis, Kenneth Burke, Stanley Kunitz, and Marianne Moore also joined the roster of critics. The essays *Poetry* published during the thirties reached a new level of incisiveness and stylistic brilliance, and they remain instructive seventy years on.

Major credit is due to Morton Dauwen Zabel for the marked improvements in both the front and back of the book, immediately apparent after he joined the staff. His own articles—elegant, witty, and withering when warranted—were judicious in appraising established authors and remarkably prescient in assessing new talents. Zabel had a scholarly perspective (his academic field was actually fiction), and he kept track of latest developments in virtually all the U.S. and European literary journals. His tightly printed columns on Recent Magazines marked debuts (and demises) and detailed individual issues, especially of critical-cultural journals like Eliot's *Criterion*, Lincoln Kirstein's *Hound and Horn*, and Leavis's *Scrutiny*. Few new trends escaped his attention, and M.D.Z.'s surveys provide a valuable chronicle of literary life during this turbulent period.

Zabel enjoyed entertaining writers who passed through Chicago, and he carried on a wide correspondence outside his *Poetry* duties. Like Mrs. Henderson, he exchanged letters with Ezra Pound, who questioned Zabel's taste but hoped he might influence H.M. again through her associate. But Zabel disliked Pound's protégés, thought he was becoming increasingly isolated and unsound, and referred to him as "the perpetual undergraduate of Rapallo." Still, H.M. continued to indulge Pound's rants on "one-track" university education, censorship, and "official low-brows" in high places in the United States.

But the era of good feeling, rekindled in Paris in 1923, almost came to an end when Pound published an article on "Small Magazines" in the *English Journal* for November 1930. In his survey, he stated that the "active phase" in America began with Monroe's founding of *Poetry*, and he praised the pure (i.e., non-commercial) motives of her "trade journal." Then he charged, yet again, that he had had to argue "six months" before Eliot and Frost got their first appearances, and accused Monroe of "mutilating" his "Homage to Sextus Propertius."

Monroe immediately fired off a letter to the editor in rebuttal. Up to this point, she had tolerated Pound's revisionist history. But her patience had been frayed earlier in 1930 by Margaret Anderson's autobiography, *My Thirty Years' War*, wherein the editor of the *Little Review* not only neglected to mention her predecessor—and the fact that *Poetry* published nearly all "her" authors, including Joyce and Hemingway, years before Anderson did—but even claimed to have first printed the speech Yeats delivered at the famous *Poetry* banquet in 1914.

By 1930, all of *Poetry*'s first serious competitors had gone out of business, including the erratic *Little Review*. It expired in Paris in May 1929, its glory secure for serializing large parts of *Ulysses*. Despite Marianne Moore's strong editorship during its last four years, the *Dial* died in July 1929. *Contemporary Verse* completed its thirteen-year run in December. *Poetry*'s days appeared to be numbered, too. In 1931–32, the magazine had a deficit of $502; the following fiscal year it tripled, then rose to $3,397 in 1933–34. Monroe lost half of her oldest supporters, and as the Depression deepened replacements were hard to find. The Editor began to make final arrangements.

In the spring of 1931, Monroe told a few friends she might retire. She was now seventy and believed that, even if the magazine did go on a few more years, it couldn't survive after her death. In May, she bequeathed to the University of Chicago *Poetry*'s books (most first editions), chapbooks, manuscripts, correspondence files, and extensive runs of journals. In her

Marianne Moore, Editor of the *Dial*,
photographed by Morton Dauwen
Zabel. Pound recommended her as
Monroe's successor.

October 1931 "Birthday Reflections," Monroe explained she felt "some return should be made to the city for its disinterested investment." The University promised to give the collection its own space in the new Harper Library. Harold H. Swift, a University Trustee, provided $5,000 anonymously to support the magazine as long as Monroe remained Editor, after which it would be used to enlarge "the library of modern poetry." The University got a bargain. But since the interest from the endowment amounted to only $250 a year, *Poetry*'s problems were far from over.

Before she finalized the deal, Monroe broached the subject of closure with Pound. He tried to buck up her spirits, praising her for getting the "porkpackers" to pay for poetry, and he assured her she was "good for another ten or fifteen years." But if she was determined to quit, he submitted that Marianne Moore was the only suitable replacement. By this time, Monroe and Moore had grown quite friendly, and H.M. visited the poet and her mother on her annual visits to New York. The Editor admired Moore's criticism and entrusted to her books by Eliot, Williams, Yeats, and Stevens for review. But, as E.P. said, it was unlikely that she would leave Brooklyn, or her mother.

In her October editorial, H.M. reported that several friends "reproached us for not trying to perpetuate the magazine under other management." All *Poetry* needed was 10,000 subscribers to be independent, she replied, but after "almost twenty years of struggle" she had concluded that "120 million fellow-citizens of the richest country on earth" couldn't afford even 5,000 $3 subscriptions. Therefore, she still had to depend on donors. Since most Guarantors gave because of their personal confidence in her, she feared their support would end upon her resignation.

Monroe managed to keep *Poetry* afloat through the 19th Anniversary, and in February 1932 she presented an English Number, featuring Ford Madox Ford, Michael Roberts, Julian Huxley, C. Day Lewis, and Basil

Bunting. In his survey of "English Poetry Today," Bunting noted the increasing prominence of W. H. Auden, and the growing backlash to T. S. Eliot's authority: "Mr. Eliot's *Criterion* is an international disaster, since he began to love his gloom, and regretfully, resignedly, to set about perpetuating the causes of it—kings, religion and formalism." Bunting later tried to mitigate some of his remarks about the baneful influence of *The Waste Land*.

Early in 1932, Monroe asked Allen Tate, who had been critical of *Poetry's* Southern Number of 1922, to edit an updated Southern issue for May, which included Robert Penn Warren, John Gould Fletcher, Josephine Pinckney, John Peale Bishop, and Donald Davidson. In July, *Poetry* also presented Tate's essay on "Hart Crane and the American Mind." On 28 April, sailing to New York from Vera Cruz, Crane had jumped to his death in the sea. Tate had known him almost a decade, and reported that "a year ago he told a friend in New York that his work was at an end." Crane's mother offered Monroe his last poems, which *Poetry* printed in January 1933. In July 1932, the magazine also published the last poems of Vachel Lindsay. He had committed suicide in December 1931, and in her memorial the following month, H.M. recalled their stimulating talks in 1914 over spaghetti and wine at Victor's, the café around the corner from the old office.

Reminiscences of happier days preoccupied H.M. in the spring of 1932. In "Volume Forty" (April), she wondered "whether there will be a *Volume XLI*." Every summer of the last decade, she said, "we have trembled in our boots for fear of a deficit." Now, "at an age when even the servants of government are permitted, or in some cases commanded, to retire," she, too, had reached "a day of thoughtful reckoning." But friends protested: " 'It's your duty to keep the magazine going—the poets can't get on without it!' " So she offered a compromise: she would continue "for awhile . . . if the financing is taken off my hands." All that was needed was an annual subsidy of four or five thousand dollars—better still, $100,000 for a permanent endowment. If any readers knew of a millionaire who could provide it, would they kindly inform her?

Photograph of Allen Tate inscribed to *Poetry*, 1938. Tate edited a special Southern Number for the magazine in May 1932.

Response to the editorial was immediate and outraged. Anxious letters poured in from poets, readers, and former staff members. The editor of the New York *Herald-Tribune* telegraphed that he was "greatly distressed," having read H.M.'s editorial "with mingled hope and alarm." Newspapers nationwide echoed the sentiment. A Hearst columnist declared: "If POETRY: A MAGAZINE OF VERSE perishes in Chicago, its death will be something in the nature of a national calamity. And have we not had enough calamities?" The Chicago *Tribune* decried "the threatened loss to Chicago of an institution—for such the magazine is—which, in proportion to what it costs, gives the city a loftier fame throughout the world than any other asset Chicago possesses."

The Saturday Review led off its 30 July 1932 issue with "Poetry and Miss Monroe," which praised H.M.'s "fighting spirit" and declared *Poetry*'s "discontinuance will reflect discreditably upon the American people." In its May issue, the *Wilson Bulletin for Libraries* (Stanley Kunitz, Editor) printed a two-page lament for "the impending cessation." The article pointed out: "If all the libraries that should have subscribed for POETRY had done so, there would never have been a financial problem to harass its editor." It continued:

> American letters in this generation could receive no more disastrous blow. . . . Miss Monroe has encouraged experimentation, but if a poem had merit, she did not care whether it was conservative or radical, rhymed or in free verse, modern or archaic, lyrical or metaphysical, imagistic or objectivistic. . . . Young poets owe much to her . . . and though they sometimes abused [*Poetry*] . . . like as not you would find them, at an early date, numbered among its contributors . . . it is the one magazine in English where good poetry has been consistently welcomed, published, and paid for.

Monroe herself couldn't have said it better. Despite the kudos and dire predictions, no millionaire stepped forward. Smaller donations did arrive, however, and in August the Editor wrote: "We have been more touched to the heart by a few checks which have come in than by all the protests and praises: one for $5 from a high-school teacher, to be repeated monthly; one for $25 from a young lawyer-poet; one for $15, to be repeated monthly if possible, from a western poet whose letters sound far from affluent."

Subscriptions increased, members of the Poetry Society of America and the Friends of American Literature collected for a *Poetry* fund, and a number of poets "generously requested 'no payment' for their work." In the fall, the Editor announced no *Poetry* prizes would be awarded for

1932, the only time they were suspended. Some sponsors could no longer afford to underwrite them; others asked her to put the money into the general budget. And so the magazine survived another decade.

Hart Crane to Harriet Monroe   *Brooklyn, N.Y., 3 February 1930*

Dear Miss Monroe:

I wish I hadn't had so many engagements with visiting relatives during your recent visit here. I tried, as you know, to reach you on the phone, hoping that you might take lunch with me the following day—and again, later, to thank you for your invitation to tea . . . . I hope I'll have better luck on your next visit to this new Babylon!

The Liveright edition of "The Bridge"—of which "Eldorado" is a part—won't be out until the first of April. Sometime during March the Paris edition (Black Sun Press) will probably arrive, but that is limited to so few copies that it ought not to interfere with your use of "Eldorado" in Poetry if you still want it. Review copies of both these editions will be sent to Poetry, and both can, I hope, be reviewed together. The Paris edition is certainly of sufficient beauty typographically to deserve mention.

Please convey my thanks to Mr. Zabel for his friendly letter. . . .

Yvor Winters to Harriet Monroe   *Palo Alto, Calif., 10 February 1930*

Dear Miss Monroe:

I have a complete ms. of Crane's book [*The Bridge*] here. I will do a review of it some time soon and let you see it. If you don't want it I'll send it to some one else. Crane has major faults; they are more evident in this book than in the last. But he also has major virtues, and they ought to be insisted upon in a world composed mainly of cheap journalists and scandal-mongers. I do not believe him the "whole show"; he is not as good a poet as Tate, nor, I suspect, as good a poet as Howard Baker is likely to appear within a year or so. But regardless of all that ails him, he is incomparably better than such impostors as Jeffers and such weaklings as MacLeish. . . .

Basil Bunting to Harriet Monroe   *Brooklyn, N.Y., 2 August 1930*

Dear Miss Munroe [sic]:

. . . I am now in the United States, and seeing what prices you Americans charge for eats I could very well do with the price of my "Villon". If I were likely to be in Chicago before the end of September I would collect it in person. But I am never likely to reach Chicago at all, nor to get farther than the Brooklyn cemetery unless I can collect it before that.

Besides, I have got married and my wife eats too.

Yours faithfully / Basil Bunting.

E.P. forwarded "Villon" on 30 November 1929, and recommended it for one of *Poetry*'s bigger prizes; it was published October 1930 and won the 1931 Lyric Prize ($50).

Yvor Winters to Harriet Monroe   *Palo Alto, Calif.,*
                                                23 September 1930

Dear Miss Monroe:

I said the "Ode [to the Confederate Dead]" was the greatest poem of its generation and *one of the greatest* of the century. You really misquote me. As to the use of those two adjectives being forbidden in your magazine, you are, I am sure, mistaken. You once described the egregious Edna [St. Vincent Millay] as the greatest woman poet since Sappho, and to the tune of quite a few pages. How many centuries did it take you to arrive at that conclusion? You once headed a review of Hueffer, "A Major Poet." But perhaps the adjective was entirely military. . . .

Yvor Winters, with John Crowe Ransom and Allen Tate, at Kenyon College. Winters had an angry parting from *Poetry* in 1930.

Yvor Winters to Harriet Monroe   Palo Alto, Calif., 1 October 1930

Dear Miss Monroe:

Your note received. But you fail to tell me what you are doing about the review, and I want to know.

As to Hardy on Edna, all the great critics have been great poets, but few great poets have been great critics, and H. was not one of them. He was too engrossed in his own material to be much of an observer of other writers' methods. The great critics could be counted on fewer fingers than you possess: B. Jonson, Dryden, Sam Johnson, Coleridge, Landor, Arnold, Mr Tate, and myself, and very few others in English.

Believe me, then, for I speak it as a great critic, Edna sounds like a sack full of old kitchen utensils, and Lindsay sounds worse. I can't see a jot of difference between Edna's sonnets and Dillon's in your last issue, than which nothing worse could be said of either.

As to a few of us getting together to praise each other, forget it. My review of Crane cost me his friendship, and I am hardly on more than bowing terms with Tate. I will tell you a secret, however, and it is not for publication: the best poetry of my generation has been written by Tate, Crane, Howard Baker, Janet, and myself. . . .

You sidestep Crane for years, and then print the worst thing he ever wrote or could have written; you get around to patronizing Robinson (who was a great poet when you were lifting your eyebrows at him) in his dotage. You have alienated all of the best poets of my generation and practically all of the preceding. When are you going to wake up?

And what about that review.

Yours, / Yvor Winters

H.M.'s note on letter: "Ansd Oct 7 1930 / No use in discussing our dif. points of view. Tate rev retd—wd. you care to rev. for us Robinson's *Nightingales*, or that & *Col. Poems?*" She asked Zabel for his opinion; see introduction to Chapter XII.

Yvor Winters to Harriet Monroe   Palo Alto, Calif., 10 October 1930

Dear Miss Monroe:

Your refusal of my note on Tate is, as I have already shown you, not dictated by any love of moderation on your part, but on your refusal to allow me to praise a poet whom you fail to understand. You have written much more immoderately yourself, and with much less to say. . . . You have been aware ten years that I had not one jot of respect for the poetic principles for which you stand; you allowed me in my reviews of Crane and Jeffers to expose those principles. There are only two attitudes for you to take: you may refuse to let me review for you altogether, or you may allow me to express my opinions completely and plainly. Your offer of Robinson under the circumstances is little short of an affront. There are not more than two or three writers living from whom I would even consider taking such dictation, and you are not one of them. . . .

Harriet Monroe to W. Wilbur Hatfield   *22 November 1930*

My dear Mr. Hatfield:

I have read with absorbing interest Ezra Pound's article in your November number [of *English Journal*]. True it is that its author has been stirring the rest of us up for twenty years. . . . And among the slight credit-marks due me as founder of POETRY, the most purple one, no doubt, rewards my perspicacity in asking Mr. Pound to help me.

And he *did* help most generously: indeed, probably I made the mistake of my life in not giving him complete possession of the magazine, like the Arab in the fable whose tent room was absorbed by the camel he had invited in. If I had, POETRY would perhaps have cut a wider swath through the mud and mire of the world's dullness. However, I doubt if it would have gone very long or far, because Mr. Pound, who puts his shoulder to the wheel with such dynamic energy, invariably gets tired of the job after a few turns. He wearied of POETRY, of *The Little Review*, of *Blast*, of *The Dial*, even of his own *Exile*. The wrecks of his wild runs strew the path of progress.

To take up a few of his points:

Mr. Pound's memory may be better than mine in regard to those six months of argument over the acceptance of Messrs. Frost and Eliot. Argument, as he used to carry it on, would have burned me up long before that!

But my memory would seem to be better than his in regard to the Propertius incident. For I did not "mutilate" his translation of Propertius; in fact, the four accepted sections of it were printed straight, exactly as they now stand in Mr. Pound's *Collected Poems*. . . . In fact, it was Mr. Pound who "mutilated" Propertius, for, according to the late William Gardner Hale, the distinguished University of Chicago Latinist, the translator made "excisions here and additions there." And in the next number of POETRY Mr. Hale listed certain schoolboyish errors in an urbane and unanswerable letter which Mr. Pound has never forgiven.

Mr. Pound finds that the various "small magazines" were of service to the art only if, when, and so long as he was connected with them.

However, he admits that "POETRY continues as a very meritorious trade journal". I accept this as higher praise than he may have meant to imply. To promote the poets' trade in every possible way—to fight their battles, increase their meagre pay, keep them informed of every step forward (or sideways), inspire them to self-respect and pride in their art, and show the world the best they can do—these are the functions of a "meritorious trade journal", in poetry as in plumbing, and we rejoice that Mr. Pound gives us so fine and discriminating a tribute.

Yours sincerely, / Harriet Monroe

Hatfield printed H.M.'s rejoinder in the January 1931 issue. In her first draft, H.M. wrote that when she showed Professor Hale Pound's "Propertius" he reacted "in horror, begging me not to desecrate our pages with a translation guilty of numerous school-boyish errors. Nevertheless I printed it as it stood over his protest, suggesting that Mr. Hale put his criticism in the form of a letter to the next issue of *Poetry*."

Archibald MacLeish to Harriet Monroe   Fortune/*Time, Inc., New York City, 29 November 1930*

Dear Miss Monroe:

. . . Ezra is so completely out of touch with America that he recently wrote one of the boys he supposed he would be lynched if he set foot in New York. Poor devil, not more than ten people would know who he was. And they would be more apt to hang him with laurel than with feathers. . . . Why can't he act like a poet? Why does he have to pamphleteer in the accents of an exasperated asp? I don't suppose you can answer that question any more than I can. . . .

Ezra Pound to Harriet Monroe   *Rapallo, Italy, [28 February] 1931*

Dear Harriet

. . . Re/ yrs in Eng. Journal / YOU have never answered a straight question re my Propertius: Did either you or Hale suppose that my reference to Wordsworth in my "Homage" as a mistranslation from the latin?

Hale was a god damn fool, I don't know whether that demands "forgiveness" or not. At any rate I leave both vendetta and pardon to the forces of nature. . . .

There is an unimportant error or vagueness in yr/ remarks re/ my fatigue. Not weariness but indignation (beginning with the 2nd number) and overcome time after time, divorced me from Poetry. No elephant has my patience.

The Lit. Rev. ejected me. Blast ceased through no act of mine. The Dial was always hell, or nearly always, endured on the principle "faim saillir le loup du bois" [hunger drives the wolf from the forest].

"Exile" was undertaken to print what no other mag. wd. print. As soon as there were other mags. in existence that cd. carry on I desisted. . . .

All right. Make out another list of what these reviews and any other li'l reviews published when they were trying to prove me an imbecile. . . .

Ezra Pound to Harriet Monroe   Rapallo, Italy, 27 March 1931

Dear H.M.

. . . Re/ Poetry stopping. Having performed the great feat of manipulating the god damned borzoi into spending a little money on the best poetry at yr/ disposal (given yr/ lights) it wd. be a crime to plug the hole. You ought to leave as durable and continuing a monument as possible to the fact that you extracted from among the porkpackers a few less constipated and made them PAY money for the upkeep of poesy. The five just men in Sodom were as nothing in comparison. . . .

I don't care HOW they are made to do it. If love availeth not, tell 'em ALL the young writers will go communist the moment they stop. That's NOT so far out, anyhow. Bourgeois litcherchoor is pretty well on the blink. Am a democrat myself . . . .

I still return to the fact that you ought to reprint the DONT's as a challenge to see whether the young think they have made any progress. Damn it all, spring housecleaning don't have to be wholly different every year // fact that no new method of cleaning has been invented don't liberate you from necessity of dusting and scrubbing.

yrs/ still emphatically / E.P.

Marianne Moore to Harriet Monroe   Brooklyn, N.Y., 2 June 1931

Dear Miss Monroe,

. . . As you seem willing to believe, I am drawn by instinct to books; and besides wishing very much that I might be a help to you, I should enjoy writing some reviews. The best of those I have done were, I think, "briefer mentions"—in The Dial. Should it occur to you to suggest something to me for review, do please say how long the review should be; that is to say, how many words. . . .

M.M. reviewed Eliot's *Marina* (September 1931) and Pound's *A Draft of XXX Cantos* (October 1931).

Ezra Pound to Harriet Monroe   *Rapallo, Italy, 6 October 1931*

Dear Harriet

Not being given to gloom or to worrying about calamity I have not given much thought to "Poetry" a mag for 1951. I forget how old you think you are but you are good for another ten or fifteen years anyhow. However if you insist on making a will, the coincidence etc. incites me to the obvious idea that the only person in amurikuh who cd. continue your periodical is Marianne. The necessary irreproachable respectability that against which no lousy ploot [plutocrat] can object on grounds of her not bein' a lady or bein' likely to pervert the growing school child etc.

It shd. also be possible to get a certain amount of backing for Marianne that wd. *not* be available for the wild and boisterous or cerebral younger males. . . .

I dunno 'bout the CHIcago pt/ of view. Nothing but a definite position wd. I suppose take M.M. to Chicago or move her from one side of 4th. ave to the other. But Chicago might be inspirationated [sic] to BRING one of the best contemporary amurikun minds into Chicago. After all Marianne wuz born in St. Louis, and can be claimed by the West in general. . . .

William Carlos Williams to Harriet Monroe   *Rutherford, N.J.,*
                                                     25 October 1931

My dear Miss Monroe:

Many thanks for your note informing me that I had been awarded *Poetry's* THE GUARANTOR'S PRIZE to the amount of one hundred dollars. The check too is most welcome. Let's hope the distinction thus conferred on me will help in getting a new volume of verse published. I really can't understand why so many of my friends are so much more successful in this respect than ever I have been. Here's wishing you luck! . . .

Vachel Lindsay to Monroe   *Springfield, Ill., 1 November 1931*

Dearest Harriet Monroe,

. . . Thank you indeed for the Guggenheim fellowship blanks. With the very faithful help of Elizabeth, they have this night been filled out; and I am very grateful for Elizabeth's energy and determination in keeping me at it. . . .

It seems to me that Poetry magazine has had a marvelous career, and possibly the grimmest but most convincing evidence is the long list of rivals that were born after it came into the world, and died long ago. Such an amazing list of heroic failures is the ultimate tribute to your success.

Elizabeth and I think of you with the most faithful affection. The children are already beginning to talk in poetry, and make good songs for their age and state. Come and see us whenever you can.

Yours, in Delphic bonds, / Vachel

H.M. note: "My last letter from Vachel Lindsay. He died Dec. 5."

Ezra Pound to Harriet Monroe   Rapallo, Italy, 11 November 1931

Dear Harriet

. . . Re/ Marianne. I know she has her damned old "ma" on her back. I have never met 'em. But everyone who has, seems cordially to desire the demise of the old 'un. An' anyhow she can't live forever. . . .

Of course if you are bound to shut up shop, you might end it with some sort of burst of glory. Final award to Ella Wheeler Wilcox? I spose Basil B[unting]'s 50 [dollar prize money] will be absorbed in maternity fees. Might convert remainder of guarantees into permanent pension of 600 dollars a year to Carnevali.

Award to ole Bill Walrus some compensation for the Edna. HER stuff that I saw in Poetry was the worst trype [sic] I recall reading in it since the days of Neihardt and co.

Oh well, Benedictions. Country lousy with money and can't either feed its population or do anything with its concentrations of cash. etc. . . .

Basil Bunting to Harriet Monroe   Rapallo, Italy, 21 January 1932

Dear Miss Monroe,

Enclosed a mitigatory letter, which please print if possible in the same number with my article ["English Poetry Today," February 1932], if not, in the next. I don't want to call Eliot names, as I almost appear to in the article as it stands. . . .

I have heard a rumour that POETRY was to cease publication. That would be a pity. There's nothing to take its place. I hope the rumour's untrue.

[attached letter]
Dear Miss Monroe,

I see from the proofs of my article on English poetry, which arrived at this remoteness too late for revisions, that it might appear to a rapid reader that I was making a personal attack on Mr Eliot, whereas I want to have it quite clear that it is only his influence I want to denounce;

his influence acting probably far beyond his intentions, maybe even contrary to them. So far as I am aware he has always encouraged whatever decent poetry came his way, independent of its political, religious and so forth aspects. It is the pressure of his phenomenal prestige that extinguishes the sparks, etc. It is all so much weight added to the existing inducements to retrogression in England. If the mournful cadences of The Waste Land have turned out to be as hypnotically effective as the Eat More Fruit advts., it is, of course, Mr Eliot's fault, but in a sense in which one might as justly call it his misfortune.

2. Help in Hard Times

For the Twentieth-Birthday Number (October 1932), Sandburg, Stevens, Moore, Bynner, and other early contributors sent poems, while former staff members shared stories of life with H.M. on Cass Street. Eunice Tietjens opined: "*Poetry* will die with Harriet Monroe, or under her direction. That is as it should be." M.D.Z. was sure that with the aid of "immortally valued friends" the magazine would persevere. In December H.M. told readers that "recent liberal contributions to POETRY's Fund make us quite certain of carrying on," at least through September 1933.

But in late December Monroe confided to Pound that she doubted the magazine would last beyond then. The prospect of retirement, she added, did not displease her. (She told Stevens in August she rather looked forward to being free to write her memoirs.) Pound had offered two new Cantos, and as usual was irritated that she hadn't responded quickly. She assured him she was interested in his new work, and in having him back as Foreign Correspondent—but was not inclined to print more stuff like Zukofsky's or Bunting's. After much further discussion (at one point T. S. Eliot also got involved), H.M. printed Cantos XXXIV and XXXVII, with great reluctance.

In the February 1933 issue, Monroe announced that, thanks to a $2,500 "emergency grant" from the Carnegie Corporation, *Poetry* would continue "without question." The following year, the foundation gave $5,000. Then, beyond all expectation, it promised a $10,000 grant for 1937–1938, provided new sponsors and subscribers could be found. (Between 1933 and 1935, subscriptions dropped from 1,825 to 1,678.) The awards saved the magazine.

Throughout the Depression, H.M. herself received many emergency calls for aid, and *Poetry* became an informal credit union, giving loans to poets in need. The Editor also advised, arranged book contracts, and wrote many letters of recommendation. When she complained to

Guggenheim Foundation trustees that few of her candidates got awards, they put her on the literature panel; she saw to it that Louise Bogan, Paul Engle, and George Dillon got fellowships. Many writers, among them Norman Macleod and Kenneth Patchen, were leading nomadic existences. Macleod, who had drifted around the country and Europe, sent H.M. an SOS in 1932 from Rotterdam, where he fled (and was stuck) after being expelled from Paris, he said, for singing the "Internationale."

Jobless or barely getting by, many young poets were drawn to socialist politics. H.M. did not care for protest poems—she considered Muriel Rukeyser's early submissions "propaganda"—but she did print many leftists. In his Recent Magazines columns, M.D.Z. kept track of "proletarian verse," frequently mentioning the *Left*, *Front*, the *New Masses*, the *Anvil*, the *New Republic*, *Partisan Review*, and *Dynamo* ("a journal of revolutionary poetry"). Zabel found that few communist poets were actually revolutionary: solidarity with the working class, not insurrection, was their rallying cry. For May 1936, H.M. had Horace Gregory edit a Social Poets Number, with work by Rukeyser, Edwin Rolfe, Kenneth Fearing, John Wheelwright, R. P. Blackmur, Hildegarde Flanner, Josephine Miles, Harold Rosenberg, and Delmore Schwartz.

In July 1936, Monroe voiced her own opinion of "Poetry of the Left": "We have protests, statements, exhortations, eloquence didactic or prophetic; but as yet very little poetry." She cited Patchen's *Before the Brave* to illustrate a typical approach: "a heaping-up of disconnected exclamations guiltless of bourgeois sentence-building, of punctuation, rhythm, or any kind of structure." Still, she was supportive when Patchen wrote to her about his miserable jobs. She was particularly disappointed in Paul Engle, who got his start in *Poetry* in 1930, while a student at Coe College. H.M. found his socially conscious third book, *Break the Heart's Anger*, undisciplined, melodramatic, and vulgar: a betrayal of his early promise, and of the many "boosts" she gave him.

In 1933, for example, when Monroe was invited to read her work at the Chicago "Century of Progress" exposition, she asked Engle to join her on the program. In June, H.M. led off her "Century of Progress" Number with Engle's "America Remembers," which won first prize in a contest *Poetry* sponsored to celebrate the fair. Reflecting on the mediocrity of the entries—and of most regular submissions to *Poetry*—the Editor noted how little "progress" had yet been made in poetry. Most manuscripts were "narrow," the poets "interested too exclusively in their own personal emotions, or in technical experiments . . . . Meantime the larger aspects of the modern world, the whole drama of tremendous change through which we are living today, were scarcely being recorded."

Proletarian verse, on the other hand, had wide vision, but smaller artistic accomplishment, at least to Zabel, who observed in June 1934: "The large majority of it reduces serious experience and banal sentiment to a level of equal mediocrity and slipshod craft." The situation abroad was different, if not necessarily better. In his English Letters for *Poetry* in the mid-thirties, F. R. Leavis reported Eliot's "extraordinary authority" but had mixed feelings about the conservative trend in his wake. (In contrast, he considered Pound "ridiculous.") Leavis tracked the rise of the new "social" poets—Stephen Spender, C. Day Lewis, Louis MacNeice, and W. H. Auden—who, unlike their American counterparts, tried to give intellectual depth to their poetry of "common experience."

Zabel compared Spender to Rupert Brooke (not a compliment) and thought Day Lewis wrote in the best (i.e., worst) "English public school tradition." By the late thirties, Auden had clearly emerged as the most versatile poet of his generation, and M.D.Z. asked him to edit the second English Number (January 1937). It featured Auden's "Journey to Iceland," Dylan Thomas's "We Lying by Seasand," and work by Spender, Ronald Bottrall, George Barker, Edwin Muir, and Michael Roberts, who co-edited the issue and provided an overview of English poetry, 1932—1937.

In January 1933 Monroe went to Yucatán and Mexico. In the May issue she described the ruins at Chichén Itzá and Uxmal (still being extricated from the jungle) and the Pyramid of Kukulcán (which she climbed). In August 1934, she began a six-month journey to China, where she stayed with her sister Lucy Calhoun in Peking and lectured at several universities. In the April 1935 Chinese Number, she printed translations of classic Chinese poems.

Throughout the thirties, Monroe and Zabel continued to give pride of place to Yeats and the aging Modernists, who demonstrated their fidelity to *Poetry* by contributing many poems in its hour of need. The honor of appearing in the same pages with Williams, Marianne Moore, Stevens, and the other major figures of their time was (and continues to be) one of *Poetry*'s greatest attractions for aspiring poets. The delight expressed by the teenage Elder Olson, Henry Rago, and Harry Brown was probably no greater than the Editor's pleasure in presenting them. Her kindness to Brown—advice, prize money, introductions, help getting him into college—was also rewarded with some of the most charming letters she ever received. Olson became a professor and founder of the "Chicago School" of criticism. Brown eventually became a novelist and screenwriter; he wrote the script for *Ocean's Eleven*, and his novel *A Walk in the Sun* (1947) was adapted into one of the finer films about World War II.

Marianne Moore to Harriet Monroe   Brooklyn, N.Y.,
                                                    22 February 1932

Dear Miss Monroe,
    Aware of Poetry's limited space and the wilful [sic] trend of my own
work, I'm not so much submitting these pieces to you as asking you to
look at them. I feel the hospitality shown me by you in Poetry, and the
manner of it, so deeply that I resolved, as I said to you when you were
here, to offer first to you, even on a peradventure, what I have been
working on. Should it not be what you need or like, you must have no
hesitation or regret in returning it. . . .

"The Steeple-Jack," "The Student," and "The Hero" opened the June 1932 issue.
On 14 March, she sent revisions, with a note: "I shrink from being one of that class I
came to know in my office experience, the kind of person that 'When you except
to one of his verses, tells you it cost him more labor than all the rest.' The mere
phrase, 'I am always right in my own eyes' would save an editor a good deal of tire-
some reading."

Maxwell Bodenheim to Harriet Monroe   New York City,
                                                       26 March 1932

Dear Miss Monroe:
    I have just discovered that you were on the advisory committee this
year, for the selection of applicants for Poetry Fellowships in the
Guggenheim Foundation. If I had known this before, I would not have
wasted the paper on which I wrote my application as a poet. For 16
years you have deprived my verse of all honors, awards, and sincere
encouragements, and your action in voting against a Fellowship for me
was therefore only logical. I have frequently starved and suffered to cre-
ate my 8 books of verse, and I will be only too glad to continue the
process for my verse-books still to come, if I can only continue to sup-
port Minna and my eleven-year-old son. I'll leave the rest to your con-
science, if you have one.
                                    Sincerely, / Maxwell Bodenheim

H.M. note: "Wrong, as usual."

William Carlos Williams to Harriet Monroe   Rutherford, N.J.,
                                                            1 August 1932

My dear Harriet Monroe:
    There seems to be nothing for it but for Carnevali to become a pub-
lic charge in Italy. I think he would be better off that way too. . . .

I myself have been sending the man ten dollars a month for some-thing over a year. Last month I told him I'd have to cut it down to five a month. I haven't heard a word from him since. Nor did I know that anyone else was sending him money. That makes me a little sore. Though I do not blame Em under the pathetic circumstances of his life if he has been a little fearful of telling too much sometimes. . . .

Wallace Stevens to Harriet Monroe　Hartford, Conn., *5 August 1932*

Dear Miss Monroe:

Whatever else I do, I do not write poetry nowadays.

Some time ago *Contempo* wrote to me and I looked round and found a few scraps, which I sent to it. I don't know what would happen if, shortly after telling you that I had not a thing to my name, *Contempo* should come out containing what I sent.

With that possibility in mind, I am enclosing another scrap ["Good Man, Bad Woman"], but it is the best I can do. If it is of no use, don't hesitate to say so. Of course, I shall be furious. But what of it? The ego-tism of poets is disgusting.

I wish it were possible for me to come to the aid of Poetry. But I have been most extravagant recently. Besides, I have a pretty well-devel-oped mean streak anyhow.

Yours very truly, / W. Stevens

Harriet Monroe to Wallace Stevens　　　*8 August 1932*

Dear Mr. Stevens:

Of course I want your "scrap" for October—and if you find—or write—any other scraps I beg you to send them on.

I am glad you would like to "come to the aid of *Poetry*"—but for the extravagance and the "mean streak." Shall I whisper a confidential word into your ear? If *Poetry* stops, I shan't feel so bad as some other people seem to—I shall be quite willing to retire and write my memoirs. Twenty years are a long time to stay at this job—I think I have done my share.

At least I am finally resolved not to go on raising money for it. But that's not important compared with your deserting *your* job. Is there anything—*anything*—I can do to keep you keen for it?

Don't you ever come west these days?

Yours cordially, / Harriet Monroe

I hope Holly is well, and as beautiful as ever.

Norman Macleod to Harriet Monroe   *c/o American Express,*
                                          Rotterdam, 30 August 1932

Dear Harriet Monroe—

I hope if you have published my poems yet [sic] that you can send me a little money— I know *Poetry* is hard up now & I hate to ask, but I am absolutely stranded in Rotterdam and alone.

I saw the August issue of Poetry in Brentano's . . . got in a lot of trouble in Paris—Paris seems to be a good place to get into a jam in—I never saw so many artistic & dilletante [sic] derelicts. If I ever get back to America (which depends upon whether or not I get money or a job working my passage across), I don't think I will ever leave.

America is better for Americans of moderate income & one language.

I read your editorial about Poetry continuing—I hope to gawd it does—good magazines are become more & more rare.

                              Fraternally, / Norman Macleod

H.M. sent him an advance of $30 for "Biography in Blues"; thanking her on 26 September he said: "It seems that POETRY is the best friend that a poet has." Writing from the *New Masses*, 24 January 1933, Macleod explained further: "You probably saved me from four months in a French prison, as the people I was in refuge with in Rotterdam were later arrested by the Dutch police."

Harriet Monroe to Ezra Pound   *17 December 1932*

Dear E.P.:

. . . It would please me very much to print your new *Cantos*, and to have you resume as foreign correspondent—the latter provided we are not too far apart on policies and poets. But there are certain facts to be considered.

I feel more and more that POETRY can hardly last beyond next September, the end of our 21st year. Our guarantor list is already more than half wiped out, and very few of the rest can be counted on for another year. We could not finish through September but for a windfall—an "emergency grant" of $2500 from one of the Foundations, the most surprising thing that ever happened to us . . . . The only possibility of continuance would be for that Foundation to take us on to the tune of $4500 to $5000 a year, and my sober judgment is that there is absolutely not one chance in a thousand of that . . . . I have said that I wouldn't carry the financial burden longer, and I won't—that's flat. And even if I wanted to try, I couldn't possibly get new guarantors in these times. So please don't flare up—just accept it as final that an annual subsidy from that Foundation is the only thing that could keep us going. . . .

To let you in for—say—1/3 of the space would mean more work and bother in the make-up rather than less than at present, and as long as my name is on the cover I couldn't shift all responsibility for your part of it. You think a lot of Zukofsky, for example, while I think he is no poet at all, his "objectivist" theories seem to me absurd, and his prose style abominable. Bunting's verse and prose are better, but after all he is no great shakes. If these are the best new ones in sight, the magazine may as well quit.

But it would be a great satisfaction to me, and a distinct enlivenment to the magazine, to have you as foreign correspondent for even a few months. Also it would round out our history, complete the circle, so to speak. . . .

I wish you would answer as frankly as I have. Please don't question the exact truth of every word I have said. I haven't yet decided whether I shall even *try* to move the aforesaid Foundation to subsidize us annually, by presenting a plea when I go to New York in January; but even if I do, please realize that the chance of success is as 1 to 1000. And please don't indulge in useless railing at the Foundation, or our Guarantors, or

Yours sincerely, / H.M.

Thomas Lanier Williams to Harriet Monroe   *St. Louis,*
11 March 1933

Dear Harriet Monroe,

Will you do a total stranger the kindness of reading his verse. Thank you!

Thomas Lanier Williams

The poems (unidentified) were rejected; Tennessee Williams first appeared in *Poetry* in June 1937.

Louise Bogan to Harriet Monroe   *New York City, 15 March 1933*

Dear Miss Monroe:

Mr. [Henry Allen] Moe wrote me on Saturday last that the Trustees of the [Guggenheim] Foundation had awarded me a fellowship "for creative writing, abroad,"—for one year, beginning with April 1st. —I can't tell you the happiness and enthusiasm that this news has given my heart and mind. And for your good offices in the matter, I cannot express my gratitude. I am a little abnormal, because I fear so much and expect so little, help from outside has come so infrequently to me that I have taught myself never to expect it, and never, if possible, to ask for it. So that this fellowship gives me great confidence in myself and in the possibilities of future work that I may do. Nothing like it has ever happened to me before, I can assure you. I hope that some work will come through, and that it will be worth your faith in my abilities. . . .

Bogan wrote H.M. several letters during her travels to Genoa, Siena, Florence, Venice, and Sicily.

Kenneth Patchen to Harriet Monroe   *Pauling, N.Y., 10 April 1933*

Dear Editor,

I was born in Ohio twenty one years ago. My formal education has been limited to a year in Micklejohn's Experimental College and some months in a small college in Arkansas. However in a somewhat sterner sense I have been educated. I have spent in all about eight months on "the road"; severe hardship and paralyzing disappointment have haunted my steps through the haunts of the homeless in the south and west. I am in a peculiar sense without a home. I have never had the security necessary to work.

My feeling for art has made it possible for me to endure and hope but I am growing bitter and discouraged for unless something develops soon another winter (and another) of aimless misery is before me. . . .

I write to you in the hope that you (or some member of your staff) will see fit to advise or make suggestions. It is possible that there are student scholarships, loans etc. to which you can direct me. Or perhaps you know of someone who could aid me in getting a job—I have had experience as gardener, clerk, laborer, odd-jobs-man, steel mill work and other work. I can drive a car, do landscape gardening and could do professional cooking with a little more experience. . . .

I am willing to go anywhere, live anywhere, do anything in order that I may write. Can you advise me?

Truly, / Kenneth Patchen

W. Bryher to Harriet Monroe   *London, 29 April 1933*

Dear Miss Monroe,

I am just back from a trip to central Europe where I spoke with many refugees from Germany. Unhappily things are far worse than any newspaper dare print. People who have been beaten and imprisoned are forced to send out messages that all is well, often lest worst [sic] things befall their relatives and friends. . . .

One man told me that a friend of his received a visit from the N[azi]'s. They searched his library and found a couple of books on economics; the friend pointed out that being a professor on the subject he needed some foreign books for reference. They left. The next day police seized his entire library, including Goethe & Schiller, burnt it in the street below, and forced people to witness the "destruction of a traitor's books."

I know personally a family where father and son are forbidden to exercise their profession, which is medicine, and are thus left slowly to starve to death unless we outside, can contrive to get them out of Germany. Their only crime is that they are Jews resident in north Germany for over a century. The father served during the war but that has not saved him. Another woman I know was brutally assaulted and injured, because she took in and fed a homeless child, whose parents were in prison. Again she had no political affiliations, merely has given her whole life to work with children. Another man I met, was a Jewish professor who had escaped with one hour only from a warrant for his arrest. I may not give you his name but he was well known in the States. In none of these cases known to me, were the people other than the most respectable and quietly living of citizens.

I saw also the hospital certificate and report of a young worker. In this case the man had belonged to a left organisation that was not, however, at that time unlawful. He was dragged from bed, beaten till the room ran blood, offered the choice with a revolver at his head of being shot or drinking a litre of castor oil, lost consciousness and was found lying on the sidewalk and taken by a passerby (and you cannot I fear appreciate the bravery of this passerby) to hospital. After 21 days, he was discharged not cured but because he was able to walk and they were overcrowded with cases. He was met on the steps by the warning if he returned to his home they would "finish the job." He escaped but they fear now he will lose his reason, he cannot legally obtain employment where he is, not being a citizen of the country, and he can obtain no news of his mother, whose sole support he was, left in Germany.

Please speak of these matters as you will but I must ask you not to quote nor to publish my name, because I am joined now with relief work, and if my name is known I cannot even return to central Europe. . . .

I am absolutely certain that unless there is firm and definite action from England, France, and most important of all, the United States, we shall have war within the next two or three years. Germany would like to wait while she re-trains. The whole country is governed by terrorism and nobody dare say a word, lest they be accused also of liberalism. The position of the Jews even is nothing to the punishment meted out to those liberal minded Germans who had encouraged friendship with France.

Really the situation is desperately serious, because civilization, poetry or art, cannot withstand I fear another war. . . .

Kenneth Patchen to Harriet Monroe   *New York City,*
                                                       [early May 1933]

Dear Harriet Monroe,

With its face filled with forwarding addresses, your letter has just reached me. I am now janitor of two apartment houses, one on West 13th and the other on West 12th; the pay is $25 a month with a room. I am up at 6 thirty and am kept busy until about 8 P.M.

Starting at scratch something over a week ago I will not be paid until about the 10th of May as I can assure you that the $15 will be in the nature of a life-saver. . . .

H.M. note: "Ans'd H.M. May 20 1933; new ac'd / sent $15"; K.P. first appeared with "Empty Dwelling Place," "Tristanesque," and "Parting Coney Island" in January 1934.

Kenneth Patchen to Harriet Monroe   *Hanover, N.H.,*
                                                       4 September 1933

Dear Harriet Monroe,

I lost my janitoring job some months ago; since then I have been working on a farm in upstate New York (for room and board); just now I am caretaker in a hiker's shelter on the Long Trail, here too I make nothing but my keep. The season for hiking ends with today (Labor Day) and I must move on. I am at a loss, not knowing where to go. . . .

Do you know any people in Boston? I should like to get a job there. Anywhere in New England. . . .

Paul Engle to Harriet Monroe   *Cedar Rapids, Iowa,*
                                                  6 September 1933

Dear Miss Monroe:

. . . The night of the day we read at the Fair I was walking near the University of Chicago chapel with a friend when we were "stuck up" by four of your city's dirtier gangsters and robbed of our little store of wealth. Also, I had an attack of appendicitis that night. I had to hitch

Kenneth Patchen to H.M., 4 September 1933,
asking for help after losing a job.

hike home to Iowa next day as my money was gone, and with the
attendant aggravation and discomfort I was suddenly carted off to the
hospital and my appendix jerked. . . .

It was lots of fun going to the Fair that day with you, and the whole
trip was worth the loss of my pocket book and my appendix.

You seem to have been the instrument of much good for me this

year, for I have just purchased a third class passage on the Empress of
Britain (sailing Sept. 30 from Quebec) with the prize money for the
World's Fair poem, and who knows but what your wire to Mr. Moe
was the deciding factor in my [Guggenheim] selection. . . .

Ezra Pound to Harriet Monroe   Rapallo, Italy, 14 September [1933]

Dear Arriet

I know you hate like hell to print me. And that an EPIC includes
history and history ain't all slush and babies pink toes.

I admit that economics are *in themselves* uninteresting, but heroism IS
poetic, I mean it is fit subject for poesy. . . .

Anyhow Van Buren was a national hero, and the young ought to
know it. . . .

CANT keep the VanB. out of print any longer; whoever can think,
OUGHT to be made to do it NOW. . . .

If things get any wurse I may embarrass you by offering my services
as European Correspondent// anyhow you cant say yr/ jejune jesuit
Mr ZAABULL isn't woikin.

and so on/ appy daze. / Z

Canto XXXIV appeared April 1933, Canto XXXVII ("'Thou Shalt Not,' Said
Martin Van Buren") in March 1934. In September 1933, E.P. commented on the
new magazine *Cambridge Left* and treatment of social problems in literature, and said
that most leftist writers failed "by sheer craven intellectual laziness."

W. Bryher to Harriet Monroe   Vaud, Switzerland, 27 September 1933

Dear Miss Monroe,

I was very glad to hear from you again and I am glad that *Poetry* is
able to continue for the time without too much worry. . . .

I fear that we are near war. I am not sure that in order to save peace,
we should not at once declare war. Certainly after what I have seen of
Germany, I would join to-morrow in any army that went against her,
and you know I have been for years a pacifist. But it is not merely Jews
who are suffering, hundreds of liberal north German protestants are
being exiled, imprisoned, and tortured, and this side of affairs is alas too
little known for they have no friends in other countries to speak for
them. I was at tea with H. G. Wells only a week ago, just before I left
London, and heard there some very distressing accounts of what is hap-
pening to young scientific workers, and an English acquaintance of
mine was over, who married a German professor who has been ordered
dismissed from his job, unless she can prove that her great grandparents

Pound from Rapallo, 14 September 1933:
"Dear Arriet: I know you hate like hell to print me. . . ."

were Aryan . . . everyone possible has been dismissed from the higher
jobs and replaced by Nazi troopers. . . .

England's main idea is to keep out of war at any cost. Prosperity is
returning there, but if there is a general war I think it will either come
to a struggle to the death between communism and fascism or there
will be such an economic collapse that England will be dragged down
with the rest. . . .

Muriel Rukeyser to Harriet Monroe   *New York City,*
                                                      15 January 1934

Dear Miss Monroe,

I was glad to have your letter—it was a provocation to define my
stand in answer to your charge of sermonizing instead of writing
poetry, and to find how you felt toward the poetry of which I suppose
my piece was a type.

You spoke of it [*Theory of Flight*] as 'propaganda—a kind of ser-
mon—rather than poetry,' and I hoped I might explain why I resent the
label. . . . There has been none of the obnoxious slogan-sandwiching
which has tempted a few of the most earnest away from poetry: it
seems to me that distinctions must be made between repulsion from
historic fact and resentment of the sort of hortatory poetry which
always ends, "Join the Communist Party." If political or social ideas
intrude themselves of necessity into a poem's content, there is no rea-
son to pigeonhole the poem because of the presence of one of the low-
est common denominators of modern existence, the acknowledgement
of a class division whose tokens are lynchings and the forms of power
misused by my Committee-member [in the poem].

Poetry has been for so long one of the very few, and at times the only
outlet for new departures in poetry that I hope a valid and contempo-
rary movement that is now making itself clear will not be overlooked
or ruled out. . . .

On 25 February, Rukeyser sent two other sections of *Theory of Flight*, which H.M.
also returned. The book eventually won the Yale Younger Poets Award and was pub-
lished in 1935.

Harriet Monroe to Ezra Pound   *[draft] 26 January 1934*

Dear E.P.

Your polite note, just received, seems to imply a desire for political
scoops. If your *Cantos* are not poetry but politics, I suggest that you
submit them to the N.Y. Times or the Chicago Tribune.

Yeats, Eliot, Williams—very imposing names! Have they praised or
published ~~your political~~ Cantos XXXIV and XXXVII?

I regret that the latter (to be in March) is the last of your political
manifestos which *Poetry* will care to have the honor of printing, but we
shall always be hospitable to poems less motivated by a desire to instruct
the world and the President.

                                                      Yours / H. M.

On 14 January, E.P. told H.M. even though she was "too stupid to understand the
Cantos," it was "ROTTEN EDITING" to hold back "the Van Buren."

My Dear Harriet

                    Even if you are too
stupid to understand the Cantos/ and
if you are too bull headed to believe
that it is rather unlikely that "cats' Eliot/ W.Williams/
etc/etc.etc/ shd· ALL be wrong.

                    CAN you understand that it is NOTHING
DOING , after I have delivered the Van Buren

                    TO WAIT until Roosevelt has said it
instead of printing it when I said it.

        I know the country is populated by muddleheaded mutts ,
etc/ but haven't you the courage to suppose at least 15
/// readers of knowing this or deaf and so forth.

E.P.'s "polite note" to H.M., with drawing, 14 January 1934:
"Even if you are too stupid to understand the Cantos . . . ."
Morton Zabel called Pound "the perpetual undergraduate of Rapallo."
"Anno XII" indicates the date in the "Fascist era."

Wallace Stevens to Harriet Monroe   *Hartford, Conn.,*
                                        12 February 1934

Dear Miss Monroe:
    . . . I reached Hartford in time for the opening performance of
Gertrude Stein's opera [*Four Saints in Three Acts*, with music by Virgil

Thomson]. While this is an elaborate bit of perversity in every respect: text, settings, choreography, it is most agreeable musically, so that, if one excludes aesthetic self-consciousness from one's attitude, the opera immediately becomes a delicate and joyous work all round.

There were, however, numerous asses of the first water in the audience. New York sent a train load of people of this sort to Hartford: people who walked round with cigarette holders a foot long, and so on. After all, if there is any place under the sun that needs debunking, it is the place where people of this sort come to and go to.

I make one exception: You will remember that I signed my name in your guest book close to Bryher's name. She came. . . . I was tied up with some pretty awful people. But she sent me a note which it was delightful to have. . . .

Bryher visited the United States the winter of 1933–1934 and wrote H.M. 15 February, thanking her for "look[ing] after us so well in Chicago." In New York, she met Horace and Marya [Zaturensky] Gregory and saw Marianne Moore several times.

Witter Bynner to Harriet Monroe   *Sarasota, Fla., 7 March 1934*

Dear H.M.:

" 'Thou Shalt Not' Said Martin Van Buren"!

Scrapings not from a palette but from something less nameable! Why in hell print it? Just for a name, a name with nothing left behind it? Silly woman, I'm ashamed of you.

                                        Ever yours, though / WB

Why not a few random passages from the Congressional Record?

Elder Olson to Harriet Monroe   *Chicago, 28 March 1934*

Dear H.M.:

. . . What a curious feeling to sign a book-contract! I feel as though I had pawned my grandmother or something. After that terrifying mass of clauses and provisions I wanted to ask (very timidly, in the faintest pencil, on the margin) whether they were going to let me *read* my book [*Thing of Sorrow*]. . . .

I wish I knew how to thank you. I worked awfully hard on that book, but I don't deceive myself—it would all have come to nothing without your kindness & help: and so in the end the book owes as much to you for its acceptance as for its even being at all. The debt's more than I can pay. It's hard to say how acutely aware I am of this. . . .

Harriet Monroe to T. S. Eliot   *2 April 1934*

My dear Mr. Eliot:

... I don't wonder that you find Pound's letters "mysterious" and that "little emerges in apprehensible form." Those he sends me are incredibly violent and abusive, but I am used to that and usually don't mind.

The history is briefly this: In April 1933 POETRY led off Volume XLII with *Canto XXXIV*, which was chiefly about early American politics—Adams, Jefferson, Madison, Napoleon, J. Q. Adams, etc. I can't say I was enthusiastic about its quality as poetry, and when, soon later, he sent us *Canto XXXVII*, all about Martin Van Buren and in my opinion merely choppy prose, I was in no great haste to print it. In January he wrote raging about the delay . . . . Also, he challenged my right to be less appreciative of his *Cantos* than you and two other authorities. I replied, somewhat less mildly than usual, that *Canto XXXVII* was listed for March, but that it would be the last one of that kind which we should care to print, that if he was writing politics and not poetry why didn't he send it to the N. Y. Times, and that I doubted whether you had ever read the two Cantos POETRY printed. (I guessed it right in this detail, it seems.)

Evidently you like his recent cantos better than I do if you are willing to print any or all of them in the *Criterion*. I violated my artistic conscience in giving space to *Canto XXXVII*, so I was compelled to tell him I wouldn't do it again.

His answers to my letter are unspeakable—one to Mr. Zabel, who was wholly innocent having known nothing about the incident, and missives to me which might surprise you, however accustomed you may be to his epistolary style.

Pardon this lengthy explanation, but if E. P. has slithered me to you it is only fair that I should give my side of the story. I am sending you the two numbers of POETRY containing his cantos.

Yours sincerely, / Harriet Monroe

From the *Criterion*, T.S.E. thanked H.M. for her explanation on 19 April, and said of E.P.'s letters: "I hope that you don't take the violence of his style too seriously; I am completely habituated to it myself."

Wallace Stevens to Harriet Monroe   *Hartford, Conn.,*
                                              13 March 1935

Dear Miss Monroe:

... Last autumn, when I heard that you were in Pekin I wrote to Mr. Zabel (his name sounds like an exercise in comparative philology) to

ask him your address, because, of course, the mere idea of your being in
Pekin, instead of suggesting temple roofs, suggested tea and other
things. . . .

Now, your letter makes me feel all the more interested. Do you sup-
pose your sister would care to do a little shopping? . . . say, a pound of
Mandarin Tea, a wooden carving, a piece of porcelain or one piece of
turquoise, one small landscape painting, and so on and so on. . . .

I have only recently returned to the office after a visit to Key West.
Robert Frost was spending the winter there. We had a number of pleas-
ant meetings, after which I invited him to come to dinner one evening.
. . . [I]t was nice to meet him, particularly since he was a classmate of
mine at college, although we did not know each other at Cambridge.
Key West, unfortunately, is becoming rather literary and artistic. . . .

H.M. had written W.S. 11 March, describing her trip to China; she wished he could
see Peking. On 5 April he thanked her for sending tea, and remembered earlier gifts
sent by her sister Lucy Calhoun.

Harry Brown to Harriet Monroe   *Portland, Maine, 5 May 1935*

Dear Miss Munroe [sic]:

Your note of acceptance yesterday morning nearly knocked me
down. Being accepted by POETRY after having been writing only
three months was, until yesterday, beyond my most personal dreams.
But here is your note lying on my desk. I can see the ink. I can rustle
the paper. I can feel it. I can taste it. It is real. As a result, I have been in
a major daze for 24 hours. Miss Munroe, you have made me a lost
sheep. . . .

Harry Brown to Harriet Monroe   *Portland, Maine, 23 June 1935*

Dear Miss Munroe [sic]:

Your letter came this morning as a very welcome surprise . . . . I was
seventeen at the time of your first acceptance [of three poems], but I've
been eighteen for a month now. The poems that you have were written
when I was seventeen. I am very glad that you like them.

I have read all the modern poetry that the Public Library affords. My
favorite moderns are Eliot, Pound, Aiken, MacLeish and Hart Crane.
Also Wallace Stevens. Not being able to afford their work, I usurp them
from the Library. I excuse myself on this point by saying that there are
few people in Portland with sufficient appreciation to read them and
those who can read them are more able to afford the books than I. As a
result, I usurp them. So far my library contains two books of Eliot (one
of which I bought) and books of Ernest Walsh, W. H. Auden, MacLeish,

Pound, R. T.Young, and Wall's "Anthology of theYounger Poets." I also have "Ulysses." I had to save for two months to get it.

I have written perhaps 125 poems of which I consider 100 worth keeping. They range in length from 8 lines to 500. . . . I am sending along "Mrs. McGrundy." . . .

Harriet Monroe to Harry Brown   *Travers City, Mich., 25 July 1935*

My dear Mr. Brown:

I brought Mrs. McGrundy north with me to read in the country . . . . I think you are taking too steady and exclusive a course in modernism even modernistic poetry, and my advice would be to take back to the library all those "usurped" books (apparently you mean stolen, and you are hardly competent to decide that no one else may want them or old enough to realize that that kind of crooked veering from the straight line will ultimately affect not only your mind but your art) and read for awhile only the great classics—Shakespeare, Spenser, Milton, Dante . . . . It will do you good to separate yourself entirely from those moderns until you honestly realize that ultra-sophistication is not the only mood and style for a present-day young American. . . .

Harry Brown to Harriet Monroe   *Connecticut State Farm for*
Women, Niantic, Conn.,
[late July 1935]

Dear Miss Munroe [sic]:

As you can see from the above heading, my address has been changed. I am now working on the State Farm as a hand, hoping that I shall be permitted to stay all winter. I've got to get to college and this is the only way I can do it. . . .

I am sitting here writing to you with a splitting headache. About a half hour ago we were loading logs on a truck and one of them (a very heavy one) fell on my head. . . .

Reading Mrs. McGrundy in a soft and blue place led you to rather incorrect conclusions about my reading. Although my Greek is less and my Latin is smaller than Shakespeare's, I have read every ancient author that I could. I have read, besides the moderns, Homer, fragments of Sappho, a great many things by the Greek dramatists,Virgil, Livy, Sueto-nius, Juvenal, M Aurelius Antoninus, Cicero, Horace, Dante, Shake-speare and the Elizabethan dramatists, Chaucer, Langland, Polo, Mandeville, Herrick, the English essayists, Boswell, Gibbon . . . .

The great trouble with me now is that I have read too much of Eliot. [*H.M. note in margin:*"true"]

I am sorry that you are displeased with my manner of aquiring [sic] books. I know that it was wrong and I have regretted it. As to returning the books, it is a much harder task than it was to obtain them in the first place. Also, I am away from home and there is no notice of my return. But I will take no more—I have decided that. Hereafter I shall go without or buy them myself. [*H.M. note in margin:* "good"] . . .

Harry Brown to Harriet Monroe   Niantic, Conn., 2 August 1935

Dear Miss Munroe [sic]:

. . . I hope that you will not think that I am presuming by writing incessant letters, but I am rather alone here, having few people who will talk literature save a lot of artists at Old Lyme who have long hair and screeching wives. . . .

As you asked about my schooling, I shall confess. I have graduated from high school (in 1933) and finished with very low marks. The two high spots of my high school career were on the day that my Eng. Lit. teacher called me a genius (for learning Old English) and my mathematics teacher called me a damned fool (for failing 30 consecutive tests), both with vehemence and within two hours of each other. It was nice of them.

I could not pass a college board at the present time but, by studying and reviewing this winter, I hope to overcome them this following June. College boards and dentists are the two great fears in my heart. . . .

As to my family, I have no brothers or sisters and my parents are separated, my mother being here at the Farm as third in charge. . . .

Marya Zaturensky to Harriet Monroe   New York City, 13 August 1935

Dearest Harriet Monroe,

. . . I can't resist telling you that we've heard from Louis Zukofsky who has at last (so he says) decided to cut himself off from Ezra Pound. It seems that Ezra has been sending him too many Major Douglass tracts to distribute and after so many years the worm turned. He sent an undocile letter to E.P. And Ezra amazed at the temerity of his minion, told him to go to hell. So there is poor Zukofsky, no God, no Ezra, no nothing. He is going to try communism and has gone around humbly to C. P. headquarters asking for guidance. The Cultural directors Stanley Burnshaw, Orrick Johns etc. gave him a lot of proletarian poetry, but naturally it was difficult to swallow after Ezra who is after all a craftsman. Life is very hard for those who can't face life without guidance from an inspired source. I wanted to recommend the Catholic Church to L.Z. but it isn't my affair after all.

Affectionately / Marya Z. Gregory

Harry Brown to Harriet Monroe   Niantic, Conn., 31 October 1935

Dear Miss Monroe:

The copies of Poetry arrived yesterday . . . .

Somehow, though, I can't appreciate Edna Millay. She seems artificial to me; she always has. To me even "Renascence" was a bit too exultant. But the thing I don't like about her is this: here she is, a respectable married lady, approaching or past 40, and writing passionate lyrics and sonnets that sound as though she had twenty lovers, hidden behind as many bushes. Her husband must be a very brave man. . . .

I have just discovered that Aldous Huxley is a great poet. [*H.M. in margin:*"?"]

I am now deep in Medieval History, trying to get into the college which is receding from me very fast. It's hell to be poor. . . .

In November, Brown won the $50 Young Poet's Prize for his very first work, printed in September. In December H.M. sent him an advance, so that he could see the publishers Covici-Friede in New York City.

Wallace Stevens to Harriet Monroe   *Hartford, Conn., 4 December 1935*

Dear Miss Monroe:

I am quite staggered by your notice of IDEAS OF ORDER [December 1935]. It was just as if a rich uncle had died and left me everything he had. In any case, I took it home with me last night and read it carefully. It is really very skilful, and I am grateful to you, as I have had so many occasions to be in the past. . . .

Harry Brown to Harriet Monroe   Niantic, Conn., 13 February 1936

Dear Miss Monroe:

I am sorry you still couldn't use the poem but I *am* glad to find that I have six pages coming up. Unfortunately, I have nothing that possibly could floor you. And when does a poem floor one? The only poem that ever left me gasping at the first reading was "The Waste Land," and it still leaves me gasping. I'm just an old swooner, that's all. . . .

I attended the dinner of the Poetry Society, and it was, to be a trifle uncouth, lousy. A lot of excellently paid hacks . . . . At my right sat a girl, a Bennington College sophomore, who was typical of every female

sophomore I have ever come across. She insisted on telling me about
her English instructors and how she LAHVED, simp-ly LAHVED,
poetry. I finally discouraged her by saying (she was *intense* enough to
believe me), that I would much rather have been at Minsky's Burleycue
than where I was....

I have had some correspondence with the Chairman of the Yale
Board of Admissions and he said that I might have the examination
requirements modified, but he couldn't be sure until he had seen my
high school record.

Now, if you will excuse my saying so, my high school record is a hell
of a mess. I was too young, for one thing, and was unable to study, really
study. As a result, I received low marks in nearly everything. And to a
Board of Admissions, that record means a great deal. It worries me.

Now, Harvard has a plan by which applicants who graduated in the
highest 1/7 of their class are allowed to enter without examination:
they are simply given a card of admission. I am not fool enough to
think that I could pass a College Board exam. But if I could only—
somehow, God knows how—get a card of admission to Harvard, I am
certain that I could stay there. Do very well, too....

H.M. asked the poet and Harvard professor Robert Hillyer to give Brown advice.
On 25 March Hillyer wrote that he might serve as a reference, but that H.B. would
have to get high marks on the entrance exam.

Edgar Lee Masters to Harriet Monroe   *New York City,*
24 February 1936

Dear Harriet: I am obliged to you for the March POETRY; and I have
read your review of the Lindsay book [biography] with great pleasure,
and full appreciation of the comprehending way in which you treat the
book. It is the best review of the book that has appeared....

The book has only sold 1,240,334 copies. The biography of Dwight
Morrow has already sold 2,330,654 copies; and Mrs. Astor's Horse has
reached nearly 3,000,000. Poetry is a dishonored art, and poets are nuts.
Ever Thine for Apollo, / E. L. M.

Marya Zaturensky to Harriet Monroe   *Bronxville, N.Y.,*
[early 1936?]

Dearest Harriet Monroe,
    ...The Lindsay thing was strange wasn't it? I think you told us that
there were rumors of suicide but that you didn't believe it. The newspa-
pers reported Lindsay's death as a heart attack following apoplexy. Why
was there such deliberate hiding of the facts?—and if the facts distressed

his family so much why after the elaborate lying did they spring all the detail into Masters' morbid hands? . . . Why does he hint at Lindsay's utter friendlessness in the last years. I *know* that he had a few loyal friends and that you were one of them!

But I know that any one who is fortunate enough to have gained your friendship is fortunate indeed and I know how much it has meant to me—how often the thought of it has kept me alive. There were years in my life when I had nothing but the thought that you somehow believed in me—to keep up a feeling of self-respect. This is very sincere—very inadequately expressed—and I doubt whether you ever thought of it—but it is true of others as well as myself who must have drawn the same courage from you. . . .

Thomas Lanier Williams to Harriet Monroe   *University City, Mo.,*
27 March 1936

Dear Miss Monroe:

I was surprised and delighted by your selection of "My Love Was Light" [June 1937]. It is the kind of poem which I write most naturally but am always afraid editors will find too much in the traditional style. Nearly a year? A breath-taking expanse of time! But I will try to be patient—and time punctuated by the monthly arrival of POETRY is bound to pass more quickly. The Wednesday Club's twenty-five dollar poetry prize, which I won this week with a sonnet sequence, affords me the luxury of a subscription.

Thanking you again many times,

Very truly yours, / Thomas L. Williams

Harry Brown to Harriet Monroe   *Niantic, Conn., 22 July 1936*

Dear Miss Monroe:

This is to let you know that I've just got into Harvard—received the certificate of admission yesterday. I greatly surprised myself by passing the entrance examinations, even getting honors in the English exam. So, again, I want to thank you for helping me. . . .

CHAPTER XIV

Passing the Torch, 1936–1941

1. The Death of Harriet Monroe

In the summer of 1935, the Editor began reviewing old diaries and the correspondence files, and started writing her autobiography. The following spring, she was invited to the P.E.N. International Congress in Buenos Aires. She had reached the year 1922 in *A Poet's Life* when she left Chicago on 20 August 1936. Before departing on the SS *Southern Cross*, she spent three days visiting old friends in New York. George Dillon accompanied her to Hoboken and waved her off at the pier. He was the last person from her *Poetry* "family" to see Harriet Monroe.

She arrived in Buenos Aires for the opening of the Congress on 5 September. Monroe wrote home that she enjoyed meeting the writers—Jose Ortega y Gasset, Jacques Maritain, F. T. Marinetti, Giuseppe Ungaretti, and the exiled Stefan Zweig among them—but the sessions themselves proved a disappointment. The windy speeches and quarrels gave her little chance "to tell the ignorant world about our renaissance." On 11 September, she informed the staff of a sudden change of itinerary: she was going to visit the Inca ruins at Cuzco. "I feel very adventurous in taking this trip," she said, "but it's the chief allure for me in South America and I hate to leave the continent without it."

Instead of flying, she decided to travel overland, a thirty-six-hour trip across the pampas by primitive train and car, then up the Andes via narrow-gauge railroad. The ascent on the last leg, from Mollendo to Arequipa (elev. 7,500 ft.), left her exhausted. Still, she was determined to push on to Lake Titicaca and Machu Picchu, after a pause at Arequipa (or "place of rest"). On 24 September, she felt ill, but not enough to cancel her plans. The next day she had a massive stroke, lapsed into a coma, and never regained consciousness. She died the morning of 26 September. A tourist with her at the end wrote a few days later to assure Miss Monroe's family that she was happy her last days, "doing exactly what she wished and enjoying every sight and sound and revelling in the scenery."

Cables flashed the news to Chicago, and papers across the country ran obituaries extolling Monroe's many efforts on behalf of American poets. The *Poetry* staff was in shock as condolences streamed into the office. The November issue was already at the printers, but Zabel stopped the presses and reassembled it to insert excerpts from H.M.'s first letters from South America and a eulogy. After praising the Editor's valiant character, loyalty, "energy and love of life," Zabel noted her singular achievement: "She was perhaps the first modern editor of verse to step outside personal preference and prejudices, to foster a vigorous eclecticism of choice, to take in many schools of craft, to welcome dissenters as editors and defiant talents as contributors." In a special memorial issue for December, M.D.Z. printed Monroe's late-arriving final letters, with several remembrances by poets and former staff members. Leading them was a tribute entitled "Vale":

One of the last portraits: the Editor at her desk in the Erie Street office, mid-thirties.

> The death of Harriet Monroe will be felt as a personal loss by everyone who has ever contributed to her magazine. No one in our time or in any time has ever served the cause of an art with greater devotion, patience, and unflagging kindness. The greater and more frequent one's differences of view about that art, the greater opportunity one had for weighing these qualities in her.
>
> A difference of place, a difference of twenty-five years in time, might well separate individuals altogether. Measuring by space and time, the elasticity of her perceptions and the freshness of her interest were those of a great editor, and as no one more acrimoniously differed with her in point of view than I did, so, I think, no one is better able to testify to her unfailing sincerity, to the unfailing purity of her intentions. . . .
>
> The new generation of the 1930's can not measure, offhand, the local situation of 1910. An exclusive editorial policy would not have done the work of an inclusive policy (however much the inclusiveness may have rankled one and all factions).

It is to Miss Monroe's credit that POETRY never degenerated into a factional organ. Her achievement was to set up a trade journal in the best sense of the word. You might say it preceded the guild sense—if you even now see any signs of that component of civilization emerging in the American disorder.

During the twenty-four years of her editorship perhaps three periodicals made a brilliant record, perhaps five periodicals, but they were all under the sod in the autumn of 1936, and no other publication has existed in America where any writer of poetry could more honorably place his writings. This was true in 1911. It is true as I write this.

EZRA POUND

A more personal note was struck by the poet the Editor most admired:

Her job brought Miss Monroe into contact with the most ferocious egoists. I mean poets in general. You could see her shrewd understanding adapt itself to her visitors. When they had left her office she remained just as amiable. There must be many of her contributors to whom she gave the feeling not only that she liked their poems, but that she liked them personally, as she usually did.

No one could have been more agreeable, yet she had not a trace of the busy welcomer. She wanted more time so that she might know you better. She would go along to lunch and then invite you to her house for dinner. She did the most she could for you and gave you the best she had. To cite not too exalted an instance, I remember that on one occasion she produced after dinner as a liqueur a small bottle of whiskey which she said was something like ninety years old, almost colonial, as if stored up for that particular winter's night.

We had the pleasure of seeing her on several occasions in Hartford, where again she impressed us with her sincerity and good will.

All this reflected itself in POETRY, which might so easily have become something less than it was: something less in the sense of being the organ of a group or mode .... It was notably a magazine of many people; it was the widest possible. She made it so. She liked to be among people; in a group she was always most eager. It was not merely courtesy that made her think well and speak well of others; she did it because she enjoyed doing it.

WALLACE STEVENS

Harriet Monroe was buried in the Peruvian highlands. "The hope of bringing her ashes to Chicago could not be satisfied," M.D.Z. explained in the November issue. A memorial service was held at the Fortnightly Club of Chicago on 22 November. Monroe's brother Will had a plaque made and placed on the vault in Arequipa. Edgar Lee Masters thought a bronze should be erected in Memorial Hall in the U.S. Capitol. But shortly after the Editor's death, Monroe's family, the *Poetry* staff, and many other poet-friends had already resolved to keep the magazine alive as the most fitting monument.

Zabel agreed to carry on as editor while the executors, Will Monroe and Edwin S. Fetcher, considered how to put *Poetry* on permanent footing. Zabel and Geraldine Udell, H.M.'s assistant since 1925, also took on the job of seeing Monroe's autobiography through the press. Zabel completed the narrative from 1922 to 1936 and gathered her last letters in an epilogue. Udell handled permissions and copyediting. Nearly all the poets Monroe quoted in her book allowed their letters to be used as written and without charge.

True to form, Ezra Pound had objections and demands. He complained that dates were missing (even though he himself neglected to supply them on many letters) and wanted certain passages changed to reflect his current thinking. He had told Monroe in 1935 that he would allow use, at "1000% the publishers will pay," and the question of fees remained unresolved. Harold Latham, H.M.'s longtime editor at Macmillan, said Pound was "a tough customer," and was afraid he might ask for $1,000 and sue if they did not do exactly as he said. Udell was loathe to alter the historical record. Latham wondered if perhaps it mightn't be wiser just to drop E.P.'s letters altogether: "Do you think that it would do any particular harm to omit them?" A compromise was struck: certain sentences were italicized, footnotes were inserted for E.P.'s pedantic commentary, and dates were supplied where possible. In the end, he settled for $50. *A Poet's Life: Seventy Years in a Changing World* was published to favorable notices in 1938.

Besides the special Monroe memorial and English numbers, the regular issues Zabel presented during his tenure were very strong, notably for work by Wallace Stevens ("The Man with the Blue Guitar, I–XIII," April 1937), first appearances by Elizabeth Bishop ("A Miracle for Breakfast," "Paris, 7 A.M.," and "From the Country to the City," July 1937), translations of Federico García Lorca, and essays by Allen Tate, William Empson, Kenneth Burke, Richmond Lattimore, and Ford Madox Ford. Stevens also lead off the Twenty-fifth Anniversary Issue, followed by Louise Bogan, Williams, Sandburg, Fletcher, Robert Penn Warren, Horace Gregory, and Eda Lou Walton. In "*Poetry*'s Quarter Century," M.D.Z. emphasized the future, and his hope the magazine would continue to be "sympathetic to all schools" but especially to the original talents who were bold and "refuse[d] to compromise with mere popularity and easy success."

2. George Dillon and Peter DeVries

After seeing *Poetry* through its silver jubilee, Zabel resigned. During his eight very active years, he had not only handled most of the prose and run the magazine during Monroe's four long trips abroad but also taught at Loyola University. Jessica Nelson North agreed to stay on and assist her old friend, the new Editor, George Dillon. Everyone agreed he was the ideal choice. Since his first service as Associate Editor, 1925–1927, Dillon had gained national recognition, and many critics ranked him among the best lyric poets of his generation. Dillon's first book, *Boy in the Wind*, appeared in 1927, when he was twenty-one. After graduation, he left *Poetry* and took a job in advertising.

In 1928, while she was in Chicago on a reading tour, Edna St.Vincent Millay met Dillon and instantly fell in love. He was fourteen years her junior and resembled F. Scott Fitzgerald, only better looking. Utterly besotted, Millay pursued him through the mails with extravagantly romantic letters that would have scared off men less callow. Dillon was a reluctant paramour, but "Vincent" had her way, as she had with Floyd Dell, Arthur Davison Ficke, Edmund Wilson . . . to name just a few of her earlier conquests. Their affair was the inspiration for her 1931 bestseller, *Fatal Interview*.

George Dillon, age 21, when his first book was published in 1927.

In 1932, Dillon's second collection, *Flowering Stone*, won the Pulitzer Prize. The same year, with Millay's and Monroe's endorsements, he was awarded a Guggenheim, which allowed him to study abroad. Millay followed him to Paris, leaving Eugen Boissevain, her heroically indulgent husband, in waiting at Steepletop, their farm in upstate New York. Dillon finally extricated himself, and for once, the now-fading femme fatale was herself rejected. Still, they remained friends. While freelancing in New York in 1935, Dillon began translating Baudelaire, with her encouragement. They collaborated on *Flowers of Evil*, which was published, with a preface by Millay, in 1936.

Dillon had maintained close ties with *Poetry* since 1927 as a member of the Advisory Board, so he knew what he was getting into. Upon word of Monroe's death, readers had flooded the office with expressions of sympathy, but still not enough tangible support to made up the annual $3,000 deficits. To celebrate the 25th Anniversary, Zabel had produced a glossy, oversize brochure with pictures of *Poetry*'s best-known poets and highlights from each year since 1912, which was sent to some 14,000 English teachers, in hopes of increasing classroom use. But neither this illustrious chronicle nor the recent abundant publicity translated into sustainable income. Like H.M. and M.D.Z., G.D. found himself hitting up old donors and trying to find fresh sources of revenue.

With the new regime, several former *Poetry* authors reestablished contact, not all of it enjoyable. Some, like Yvor Winters and Maxwell Bodenheim, wrote to rehash grievances. Eunice Tietjens, who should have known better, angled for special treatment. Dillon generally had less patience than Monroe with petulant poets. But, as always, there were plenty of old contributors and eager new talents sending manuscripts, including Nelson Algren, E. E. Cummings, and Weldon Kees.

Rolfe Humphries first appeared early in Dillon's tenure and later became a frequent cause of unpleasantness. In June 1939, *Poetry* printed his "Draft Ode for a Phi Beta Kappa Occasion." After the issue was distributed, it was pointed out to Dillon that the first letters of each line spelled out "Nicholas Murray Butler is a horse's ass." Butler was the President of Columbia University, and the Editor was not amused. In a tart "Statement" in August, Dillon decried the "puerile" practical joke and said the cryptogram was a serious "breach of confidence" that automatically would "debar" the author. Nonetheless, Humphries appeared again the very next year. In 1948, he attacked *Poetry* in the *Nation*, claiming that Dillon could only publish second-rate material since the magazine didn't pay "enough"—a charge he levelled at G.D.'s successors, as well.

One of the earliest submissions Dillon accepted was sent by a novice poet from the South Side of Chicago who would become indispensable for *Poetry*'s survival. Tall, nattily dressed, and exceedingly sharp witted, Peter De Vries always created a strong first impression. In 1935, the twenty-five-year-old had phoned up *Esquire* and obtained an interview with its legendary editor, Arnold Gingrich, who recognized his talent for humor at once and printed him frequently thereafter. De Vries had introduced himself succinctly: "I do nothing and writing." In truth, he was servicing a vending machine route, selling taffy apples, and helping run his ailing father's moving business. He was also on call for bit parts in dramas at a Chicago radio station, often playing gangsters. In his "spare" time, he was completing his first novel. De Vries's gift for improvisation and capacity for hard work would be put to the test at *Poetry* over the next nine years.

De Vries made his first appearance with "Late Song" in January 1938. In April Dillon hired him as a part-time first reader, much to the relief of Jessica North. De Vries assumed her title and a salary of $25 a week. Dillon was sometimes away for months at a time, looking after his aged parents in Richmond, Virginia. While he edited at long distance, De Vries and Udell ran the office. Besides sifting manuscripts and easing Dillon's burdens by handling book reviews, the outgoing De Vries was soon called upon to help the reticent Editor with fund raising. These efforts frequently meant attending parties with potential donors and talking to women's groups and literary clubs.

Sometimes situations proved awkward, including De Vries's very first public event. On 24 May 1938, a banquet was held at the University of Chicago to celebrate transfer of the *Poetry* archives. As junior member of the party, De Vries found himself "crawling on [his] hands and knees under the speakers' table looking for Ford Madox Ford's glasses." (He didn't find them.) Although he professed to loathe speech making, the Associate Editor carried off his assignments with great aplomb. Charmed by De Vries's puns and quips, the writers' groups and Society ladies were enthusiastic. The feeling wasn't always mutual. De Vries quickly realized that tea-table chats and luncheon addresses rarely resulted in subscriptions or substantial donations.

While *Poetry*'s financial situation remained shaky, on the editorial side operations ran smoothly with De Vries in the office, although the new man was more liberal than the cautious Dillon and often disagreed with G.D.'s generous assessments of certain older authors. In July 1938, with De Vries's hearty concurrence, *Poetry* published a special issue devoted to poets employed on the Federal Writers' Project, which contained, as promised, "a striking variety of style and subject-matter." Many of the poems were experimental or voiced social protest, including work from Sterling A. Brown, Kenneth Fearing, Dorothy Van Ghent, Kenneth Rexroth, and Harold Rosenberg. Alfred Kreymborg returned after a long absence with "Bread and Poetry," and Malcolm Cowley provided an essay on the federal "Poetry Project." In the mid-forties, when he was de facto editor, De Vries printed old-time leftists like Max Bodenheim and younger proletarians such as Thomas McGrath, while giving Nelson Algren, Muriel Rukeyser, Langston Hughes, and other socially committed poets frequent exposure. In an editorial for the 30th Anniversary Issue

(October 1942), De Vries asked: "How clean a bill of health . . . can we give ourselves on the count of racial prejudice?"

Although she was not credited on the masthead, Inez Cunningham Stark, a Chicago poet, first volunteered in the thirties and assisted Dillon as a reader. Among the poets she encouraged were Gwendolyn Brooks and Margaret Danner. She became a pivotal figure after she married Rudyerd Boulton in 1942 and moved to Washington, where her husband worked in the State Department. In 1940, she introduced Dillon to Julia and Augustine Bowe, who were impressed and became *Poetry's* most active supporters.

Gus Bowe was a judge and later Chief Justice of the Municipal Court in Chicago, and wrote poetry in his spare time. Judge Bowe had his nephew and law partner, John Casey, draw up papers of incorporation for the Modern Poetry Association, which was chartered and became the publisher of *Poetry* in August 1941. As a nonprofit organization, the MPA guaranteed that all gifts to *Poetry* would be tax deductible, a crucial factor in the many fund-raising campaigns ahead.

In the spring of 1942, there was considerable doubt whether *Poetry* would survive to celebrate the Thirtieth Anniversary. Dillon had tried, twice, to get the Carnegie Corporation to renew its support after its last grant in 1938. Even with supporting letters from Archibald MacLeish and Robert Maynard Hutchins, the formidable president of the University of Chicago, both requests were denied. Early in 1942, Dillon had no better luck with the Rockefeller Foundation. Rumors began circulating.

"Beginning the sixtieth volume of POETRY," News Notes for April 1942 began, "we have much the sensation of starting to walk a plank." News Notes for May announced: "This is the first issue of POETRY we have ever made up without knowing whether or not it would be published." There was only enough cash to go on for one more week. Julia Bowe formed a committee, and within six weeks they were able to get 180 supporters to donate almost $3,000 to the Emergency Fund. A series of other short-term measures were employed to staunch the red ink in the following years.

Despite the constant financial pressures, Dillon and then De Vries maintained quality, as well as *Poetry's* international perspective. They presented translations of Eugene Jolas and criticism by Edouard Roditi, the magazine's unofficial agent in Paris, who kept the Editors apprised of European writers. The March 1942 issue featured *Exil* by St.-John Perse, the French diplomat-poet Alexis Saint-Léger Léger, who eventually won the Nobel Prize in 1960. In May 1943, *Poetry* published its second Latin American issue, representing the leading poets from eleven countries, among them avant-garde and Marxist poets such as Pablo Neruda of Chile and Nicolas Guillén of Cuba. Not all readers were pleased with what they perceived as a leftist bent. But *Poetry* continued to welcome a very wide range of philosophical viewpoints and poetic styles, from the formal to the surreal.

Getting good reviews for the back of the book was more problematic than gathering interesting poems for the front. An entertaining stylist himself, De Vries was a skillful editor of prose. His strong sense of humor was also useful in dealing with "difficult" authors. Dillon was blunter, as with cases like Oscar Williams, a writer better known for his many *Immortal Poems* anthologies who became a perennial pest with his wildly uneven manuscripts. De Vries displayed Monroe's eclectic tastes and adhered to the founder's "Open Door" policy. While *Poetry* continued to print the older luminaries and the newer stars of the day, including W. H. Auden, Elizabeth Bishop, Delmore Schwartz, and Dylan Thomas, De Vries recommended to Dillon several emerging talents. After war was declared, many were writing from military installations.

Among those who found very early (and sometimes very first) publication under Dillon and De Vries were John Ashbery, John Ciardi, Robert Duncan, Randall Jarrell, Kenneth Koch, Robert Lowell, James Merrill, Howard Moss, Howard Nemerov, John Frederick Nims, and Karl Shapiro. From the start of their careers, De Vries was particularly helpful in publishing and later promoting Shapiro and Nims, both recipients of several *Poetry* prizes, as well as future Editors at the magazine—in Nims's case, at three different periods. In his extensive correspondence through the forties, Shapiro shared his opinions about contemporary poetry with De Vries, who was not always in agreement.

Edgar Lee Masters to George Dillon   New York City, 9 March 1938

Dear Mr. Dillon:

Yesterday's Herald Tribune had a very friendly review of *A Poet's Life*, Harriet Monroe's autobiography. I sent to Macmillan's for the book and have mostly gone through it—and with a pain in my heart, you may believe, both for memories of those rich days of 1914 and after, and for the figure of Harriet Monroe as she emerges from these pages. When I think about her spare living, her battles there in the Hittite capital of Chicago, against all those hard forces, battle for architecture, for poetry, for pictures, for beauty in everything, I am free to say that Harriet is Chicago's most notable and ever memorable woman. . . .

I don't know Will Monroe's address—but anyway I write this letter to you as the head of the magazine, and her successor, to make the suggestion that a start be made now to put a bronze of Harriet Monroe in Memorial Hall in the Capitol at Washington. How much more fitting that she should be there as the voice of poetry than Frances Willard who fought booze. Something should be done by way of a memorial to her and to the art in the state capitol at Springfield. Take this up with your group and with Will Monroe, and if you want me for anything in furthering it let me know.

Cordially yours, / E. L. Masters

William S. Monroe wrote Masters 15 March, thanking him for his "fine tribute of Sister Harriet" and his idea for a bronze statue, but told him: "Poetry could hardly undertake to promote a memorial such as you have in mind, as George Dillon and his staff have enough to do to promote the interests of the magazine and they seem to be doing a good job of that."

Yvor Winters to George Dillon   *Los Altos, Calif., 31 May 1938*

Dear Mr. Dillon:

I will pass on your letters to Miss [Beth] Allen. Your first letter, however, expressed no hopes whatever that you would be able to make up a group of her poems. . . .

I realize perfectly that I am supposed to be an arrogant and irritating person, and that it has long been one of the many minor traditions of the Poetry office to endeavor to keep me in my place. One is irritating, however, when one has for years been irritated. Let me tell you a story or two, of which you are probably not cognizant.

As early as 1923 or thereabouts I began making efforts to convince H.M. that she ought to publish Hart Crane. About 1926 I began trying to persuade her to publish Tate. I finally severed my last slender ties with her as a result of her refusal. She finally published both, years after I had been trying to persuade her, and she got inferior work from both . . . . I reviewed Crane's first book in Poetry. I began the review with a brief and impressionistic summary of his faults; I then praised him in terms so high that H.M. published a note of protest at the end of the review. Yet in the critical note on Crane in the last edition of the New Poetry, the first sentence of my review was quoted as my opinion of Mr. Crane, and a fulsome and rhetorical eulogy quoted from Mr. Zabel followed. This was, I believe, downright dishonest. . . .

Now had H.M. taken my advice in regard to the few people in connection with whom I gave it to her, it would have saved her a little subsequent embarrassment and the need—or what apparently she regarded as the need—of a little subsequent prevarication. I am telling you now that Miss Allen will be among the half dozen real poets of her generation. You may take this statement anyway you like it, but in any event I take my poetry very seriously. It is no parlor game with me, and I play for keeps.

Sincerely, / Yvor Winters

George Dillon to Yvor Winters 4 *June 1938*

Dear Mr. Winters:

You are at liberty to send us the three poems again, and we shall be glad to give them another reading. However, our first choice was made after careful consideration, and it is not likely that we can give a different report unless some of the weaknesses in the three poems have been remedied.

When we invite a poet to submit further poems, it is usually with the hope of making up a group. And when the poems of a young writer interest us as much as your pupil's, we feel that it is particularly wrong to rush matters; we prefer to wait until the poet can be represented with a selection of what we consider to be his strongest work. I think you are wrong, however, in saying that an unknown writer has nothing to gain by publishing a single poem in *Poetry*. That depends entirely on the poem.

As for the rest of your letter of May 31, I can only assume that you were ill when you wrote it. Even so, I must register disappointment at your slur on Harriet Monroe's integrity. Surely the fact of changing one's mind about certain writers and being honest enough to admit one's previous errors of judgment should not be called "prevarication." The note on Hart Crane which you referred to was written by Mr. Zabel. In any case, it is not pleasant to hear Miss Monroe attacked by one whom she admired and befriended.

Sincerely yours, / George Dillon

Yvor Winters to George Dillon *Los Altos, Calif., 19 June 1938*

Dear Mr Dillon:

. . . Since you are unable to use Miss Allen's poems without their being revised, I shall not trouble you with them, for we are not able as things stand to discern where the revision should take place. Considering the crass amateurism of most of the stuff in Poetry, I confess that I find this demand perplexing.

As to my other remarks, I accused the Poetry Office of some 10 years back . . . of dishonesty, not because it changed its mind, but because it expressed its irritation at having to change to a position which I had pled for it to take for years by deliberately misrepresenting my own position and by indulging pretty consistently over a period of years in sneaking and underhand thrusts of a variety of kinds at myself. I gave you a few specimens; you can check the accuracy of my statements in ten minutes. I could extend the list at great length if I felt sufficient interest. Under the circumstances, your not finding it pleasant to hear me mention the fact, strikes me as a piece of extraordinary insolence, as is also your statement that H.M. befriended me. I asked her no personal favors and she did me none. She published me, and thought well enough of the bargain to advertise the fact. The kindness was mutual.

The really irritating thing about Poetry, however, is something that is not morally reprehensible: it is the brute stupidity of the journal. I had hoped that you might set about mitigating this situation, but I gather that you have no such intentions. For this reason, I shall trouble you no further. I have it in my power to send a good deal of first rate work your way, but you have little desire, I take it, for first rate work, and I have insufficient time for extensive argument about it.

Sincerely, / Yvor Winters

Beth Allen's "Psyche" was published in November 1939; it was her only appearance in *Poetry*.

Dylan Thomas to George Dillon

Carmarthenshire, S. Wales, 8 July 1938

Dear Mr. Dillon:

Early in April, or perhaps late in March, you accepted four poems of mine, and said that you thought they would appear in your May number. Have they appeared yet? Or, are they going to be printed in 'Poetry' sometime in the near future? I am anxious to know because, if you have now decided *not* to use them, I should like to have them printed in England so that I can get a little money for them. I am very poor.

Yours sincerely, / Dylan Thomas.

"When all my five and country senses see," "O make me a mask and a wall," "Not from this anger," and "The spire cranes" were published in August, and were awarded the Blumenthal Prize for 1938.

Edna St. Vincent Millay to George Dillon

Steepletop, Austerlitz, N.Y., 22 September 1938

Dear George,

The proofs will reach you in a separate envelope. . . .

I hope you will like the photograph I am sending. If not, just ship it

Gosport
Laugharne
Carmarthenshire
S. Wales.
8ᵗʰ July 1938

Dear Mr. Dillon,

Early in April, or perhaps late in March, you accepted four poems of mine, and said that you thought they would appear in your May number. Have they appeared yet? Or, are they going to be printed in 'Poetry' some time in the near future? I am anxious to know because, if you have now decided not to use them, I should like to have them printed in ~~America~~ England so that I can get a little money for them. I am very poor.

Yours sincerely,
Dylan Thomas.

Dylan Thomas to George Dillon, 8 July 1938: "I am very poor."

back to me and I will try to find something else for your Poetry Gallery. . . .

You are probably amused by the stern orders on all my envelopes to you: "Private: To Be Opened by Mr. Dillon Only" but I have never discussed with the editor of any magazine a phrase, a word or even a comma in any of my poems as to whether or not it might better be changed and, of course, you know that I do this with you not because you are the editor of *Poetry* but just as I always did and loved to do because I so deeply respect your judgment in such matters and am so grateful to you personally for any advice you may give me—even though I don't always follow it! ...

Millay adopted a few of Dillon's suggestions, but was reluctant to accept others; "Inert Perfection," "Song for Young Lovers in a City," "Sonnet in Tetrameter," and five other poems opened the October 1938 issue. Dillon led off the May 1939 issue with another eight poems by Millay, her last in *Poetry*.

Theodore Roethke to George Dillon   *State College, Pa., 16 October 1938*

Dear Mr. Dillon:

Thank you for the suggestion about the last poem. I hope you think that the change I have made is an improvement....

My job up here has been inaccurately reported in the past because there are two departments. I'm an instructor in the department of English composition (not English department). And it's *The* Pennsylvania State College. Not, of course, that this matters to me, but there are always local boys who brood about such matters.

I teach courses in verse writing and argumentation, incidentally.

My longwindedness is no doubt due to the fact that your acceptance of this group constitutes the most important recognition I've ever had.

Sincerely yours, / Theodore Roethke

On 30 November Roethke asked Udell to send copies of the December 1938 issue, containing his poems, to thirty-five people, including heads of English departments and university presidents. On 17 December, he wrote Udell: "I hope this method of casting bread upon the water will help, eventually, in getting me out of the academic coolie category. (A mixed figure, perhaps, but I think you know what I mean.)"

E. E. Cummings to George Dillon   *New York City, 8 November 1938*

Dear Mr. Dillon:

a chap aptly named Pound recently suggested you'd like to print something of mine: if so, will you most kindly send me a printer's verdict on the enclosed; if un-, please return which?

in either case, if not both, I give myself the more than pleasure of remarking that a generously i.e. seriously contrived illumination by a gentleman psych with a Japanese name went to the right spot

—sincerely / Cummings

S. I. Hayakawa reviewed Cummings's *Collected Poems* in the August 1938 issue. E.E.C. had seven poems in January 1939 and five in August 1940, including "anyone lived in a pretty how town." Hayakawa taught semantics at the Illinois Institute of Technology 1939–1947; he was the husband of Associate Editor Margedant Peters and served on the *Poetry* Advisory Board in the late forties. He later became President of San Francisco State University (1968–1973) and a U.S. senator (R.-Calif., 1976–1982).

Eunice Tietjens to George Dillon   Coconut Grove, Fla.,
                                            3 December 1938

Dear George:

But, my dear, you can't send me back like that! Others yes, but not me. I am not outside of "us," I am inside. And moreover I am inside in a quite particular fashion. . . .

So far as I know—though of course I have been absent for long spaces—there have been only two people in the history of the magazine who had earned the right to publish in it occasionally what they wished to publish. One was Ezra Pound in the old days. Harriet had made an agreement with him that in exchange for being London correspondent he was to have the lead twice a year with whatever he chose to send. And no matter what she thought of the poems she printed them without question. . . . The other is me. (French emphasis.) I earned the right by so many years of standing by—twenty-five years now. With me it gradually grew up. For a long time it was tacit agreement but about five or six years ago she put it into words. To my surprise she sent me back a long poem I had sent with pencil marks in various places and asked me to revise it. I didn't return it and the next time I saw her she said, with one of those moments of humility that made H. M. so charming: "See here, Eunice, I don't know why I sent your poem back. After all I trust your judgment as I trust my own. If you were willing to accept it I would leave the editorship to you in my will. So why should I edit your stuff? Send me whatever you think best and I'll print it." So I imagine I am just one of those things editors inherit—and if I'm the only one you're lucky. . . .

Since, however, you don't altogether like the ones I sent I am sending you everything at all decent I have on hand for you to choose from. Take what you prefer. Only please, George, keep the double sonnet "Creation." I am dead set on that one.

And now it's my turn to hope you "won't be too cross" with me.

                                            Cordially, / Eunice

G.D. returned all the poems and wrote E.T. 13 January 1939, suggesting she hold them for six months: "It may be that my own reaction will then be different, I being a so much older and more experienced editor. There is even the happy possibility that I may be relieved of the job, by that time." There is no evidence that H.M. made the special arrangements Tietjens alleges, with either her or Pound; H.M. in fact rejected several of E.P.'s submissions.

Arthur Davison Ficke to George Dillon   *New York City,*
                                           10 January 1939

George!
   Honestly!
      If M.
        r.
                   EE
     cuMM
         ink
          s
    is
     le
       ss
    thaN
     a horses ass,
  THEN I AM MILTON.
     Nuf Sed,
        Arcturus
    Sage of Seventh Ave.

What does Vincent think about such rot as that? Surely she doesn't like
it, does she?

Maxwell Bodenheim to George Dillon   *Chicago, 1 March 1939*

Dear George Dillon:
   I'm in a terrific jam through no fault of my own. Last January, I
dropped out of the Communist Party, because of certain disagreements
with its present tactics and aims. At the time, I also obtained a job on a
WPA Bibliography Project in New York City. I won promotion to the
office force and was about to be elevated to assistant supervisor, when I
was abruptly fired on the ground that I had committed perjury in stat-
ing that I was not a Communist.
   My fellow-workers protested, and outsiders protested, but all in vain,
and the New York newspapers raised a red cry against me, thus closing
all private avenues of gain, employment. I was even denied temporary
Home Relief, and even my last two-weeks salary was withheld on the
ground that I had earned it under false pretences! So, I came here
because the situation in New York made me "Mr. Robinson Crusoe"—
disliked by Communists and *doubted* by other people. If you could
advance me five dollars now, you could take it out of my next poem or

poems of mine you accept, since it is certainly probable that you will take at least two more poems of mine before I die! *Please write to me immediately*, as I'm in danger of *walking the pavement here*, a martyr to a former, mistaken surge of idealism. . . . I'm leaving a new sonnet.

As ever, / Maxwell Bodenheim

P.S. I'll be in Thursday at 6 p.m. if I haven't heard from you.

W. H. Auden to George Dillon   New York City, 1 April 1939

Dear Mr. Dillon,

Thank you so much for your letter. My difficulties at the moment are that I am trying to collect the various possibilities so as to see how many places I can get in. Could you tell me

(a) The dates of the various terms.

(b) If you think 3 is possible as it is what I should prefer. Entre nous I am rather frightened of Universities . . . (1) because I don't know anything (2) because the kind of student one is likely to talk to is too interested in LITERATURE. Thanks so much for taking all this trouble.

Yours very sincerely / W. H. Auden

Auden had immigrated to the United States in January 1939, and was looking for a teaching position. With Richard Eberhart's help, he got a job at St. Mark's School; he then went to Michigan in 1941.

Thornton Wilder to George Dillon   New Haven, Conn., July 1939

Dear Mr. Dillon:

That's fine. I'm fully empowered to give the permission [to print Gertrude Stein's "Stanzas in Meditation," February 1940]. In fact, Gertrude will be very pleased. . . .

As to the Note to accompany them, the reason I don't feel I can do it is, *au fond*, that I don't really understand them. I've already been to the bat with two prefaces for her, and am often approached as an expert, and gradually I feel more and more hypocritical. I often told G. that I don't understand her extreme style, but she forgets that I've said so and starts talking to me about some of it as tho' I were an initiate. . . .

I'm very glad you're doing this; her verses tho' "unintelligible" to me, nevertheless have that air of unmistakable authority. . . .

Oscar Williams to George Dillon   New York City, 9 September 1939

Dear Mr. Dillon:

Don't you think somebody in America or even in England should make some heroic and gigantic efforts to save poets like Auden,

Spender, MacNeice, Dylan Thomas and George Barker from getting killed in the war? It seems to me that one of the great tragedies of the last was the death of Wilfred Owen and Rupert Brooke. Surely the lives of the five poets here mentioned could not help the war, and their death would be a colossal crime against civilization. I know that the poets themselves would not consider being exempt, but couldn't a poetry propaganda board be arranged by the English government which would conscript the service of these poets for the duration of the war *away from danger and the front line?* And wouldn't they be of greater service this way to England in any case? Why move the art treasures into a place of safety? Aren't these makers of present day literature as important? . . . Couldn't a group of American poets sign a petition, or something? I'd be glad to do everything in my power.

Sincerely, / Oscar Williams

George Dillon to Oscar Williams   *15 September 1939*

Dear Mr. Williams:

I can sympathize with your desire to prevent the loss of genius through war, but I am afraid that such a petition as the one you suggest would be merely embarrassing to the poets. How would it be to urge exemption for the latter without being prepared to recommend similar consideration for novelists, dramatists, painters, musicians, scientists, etc.? Where would the list end? Besides, the men themselves would no doubt strongly oppose such exemption. To accept it would be to deny their common status as human beings—and once they had been placed, so to speak, in the citadel, it would probably be the end of their talent. I imagine that there would be even less hope of the world's evolving beyond war, if poets enjoyed the same prerogatives as generals and statesmen.

Sincerely yours, / George Dillon

Karl Shapiro to George Dillon   *Baltimore, 31 March 1940*

Dear Mr. Dillon:

Thank you for accepting my poems for POETRY. I am happy to join such a distinguished magazine as a contributor. Here is the autobiographical note you asked for:

I was born in Baltimore, attended public school there, in Norfolk, Virginia, and in Chicago, Illinois. After graduating from the Baltimore City College, I enjoyed a brief career at the University of Virginia and another at the Peabody Institute of Music. In 1937 I entered the Johns Hopkins University with a grant awarded, I believe, on the merits of a book of poems I had published (POEMS. The Waverly Press. Baltimore. 1935.) and the following year I won a scholarship to continue. With all this, I am still a member of the undergraduate world, but next year I hope to enter the School of Higher Studies in English.

Some of my poems have been printed in magazines and newspapers. I am a member of the Maryland Poetry Society, and give lectures on poetry in the city. My age is twenty-six. I hope this information will suffice.

Sincerely yours, / Karl J. Shapiro

"University," "Midnight Show," "Love Poem," and "Necropolis" were printed October 1940. Shapiro was paid $31. K.S. recorded his stunned reaction to this first acceptance in chapter 9 of his autobiography, *The Younger Son*.

Oscar Williams to George Dillon   *New York City, 10 July 1940*

Dear Mr. Dillon:

I should like to protest strongly against the inane review of my book [*The Man Coming Toward You*] in your July issue. In your attempt to be over-honest you succeeded in being mainly unjust to me and to your readers. It is hard to understand why you chose Lionel Abel to review my book when poets who have produced are available to give a seasoned judgement, people like William Carlos Williams, Muriel Rukeyser, Robert Penn Warren, Willard Maas, and perhaps even Louis MacNeice . . . .

Now it shouldn't be so wrong, in an insane world, for a worm to turn, and I have written "A REVIEW OF A REVIEW", and ethical or not, right or wrong, I believe I am within my constitutional rights as a poet in asking that you print this review in full in your next available issue. I believe it ten times as informative to your readers as Abel's review, and a darn sight more interesting to the poets. I am enclosing it herewith and I look forward to hearing from you soon.

Sincerely yours, / Oscar Williams

Oscar Williams to George Dillon   *New York City, 16 August 1940*

Dear Mr. Dillon:

In view of the injustice and senselessness of your review of my book and the insult added to injury implicit in the slipshod way you ignored my protest and answer, it would be meaningless for my poems to appear any longer in POETRY under its present editorship. I therefore request that you return the manuscripts of the four poems you have accepted (including the poem VACATION 1940): I am today sending these elsewhere for consideration.

And please cancel my subscription . . . .

And please give De Vries my respects and congratulations: in the short time he has been associate editor he has achieved a first class reputation for inanity: I am sure that with his diligence, ambition and extraordinary ability to get rid of poems and poets, he should have no difficulty in landing the job of editor of VOICES.

Yours very truly, / Oscar Williams

P.S. I am writing to the subscribers of your fund and stating my grievances, in the hope that at least one out of 46 will have a word of sympathy for me: it's awful odd that with W. H. Auden, Stephen Spender and George Barker all thinking and *writing* that my poems are good, POETRY should go out of its way to call my book bad and rash.

George Dillon to Oscar Williams   19 August 1940

Dear Mr. Williams,

We give our reviewers entire liberty. There is, of course, the matter of choosing a reviewer in the first place, but you are wrong in thinking that we "went out of our way" to print an attack on your book. The fact is that we went out of our way to save it from worse treatment. A number of our regular reviewers were approached, including some of those you mentioned as possibilities, but all replied that they would have to give the book an unqualified slam. Mr. Abel's partially adverse comment was the best we could get. It didn't represent my own opinion—however, when I recall your ugly attempt to "fix" the review of your book in POETRY, I have no regret for printing it.

For the same reason, although I like the enclosed poems, it is a pleasure to be able to return them as you request, to cancel your subscription, and to bring our correspondence to an end.

Sincerely, / George Dillon

In April 1939, Williams had complained about De Vries's rejection notes, though he admitted he had sent "more heavily than most of your accepted contributors: I notice I have sent in 64 poems (including some long ones) since last June." Despite these exchanges, Williams sent many more poems—the archives hold dozens of undated cover letters to De Vries, Strobel, North, and Peters—and *Poetry* awarded him its Fellowship Prize in 1944.

Nelson Algren to Peter De Vries   Chicago, 14 August 1941

Dear Pete,

Glad to see you've decided to take a chance on "Local South" [September 1941]. I've taken the liberty of making a couple changes in it . . . .

I got the boot off the local writers' project a couple weeks ago and would therefore have the time to do some reviewing for you—if any-thing that requires no especial background happens to come along. Books in words of two syllables, profusely illustrated, are just my dish— or don't they write them that simply any more?

Best, / Nelson

Karl Shapiro to George Dillon   *Camp Lee, Va., 28 August 1941*

Dear Mr. Dillon,

... May I say a word about BUICK. I was shocked to think that any-one might take it for satire, and I can easily understand that today's poetry critics are so keen with suspicion that they might mis-read even love poetry. You are right; it is a simple love poem; but if it seemed to you to be over-idealized then there is a true fault. I remember that Mr. De Vries made the same comment on HOLLYWOOD, a poem I sent him about a year ago, and PARTISAN REVIEW, which took it up later, accepted it I believe with satire in mind. Many people have read BUICK, soldiers here and my friends at home, and they considered it as a warm tribute, which was what I intended. At any rate, I'm glad of your warning and I shall make no mistake the next time I fall in love with something and try to tell about it.

Sincerely yours, / Karl Shapiro

CHAPTER XV

World War II

In July 1942, George Dillon was inducted. When he left for boot camp, he gave instructions that all correspondence to him be sent on plain stationery; he was afraid if the army learned he was an editor he would be stuck behind a desk writing instruction manuals. Trained for the Signal Corps, Dillon spent most of the war in West Africa. He was with the vanguard during the Liberation of Paris, 25 August 1944, and announced the news to the world from his radio post in the Eiffel Tower. He then served in Paris as a translator while awaiting his discharge late in 1945. He returned to the States and, rather reluctantly, to the editorship in 1946.

In the interim, with Peter De Vries and Jessica Nelson North at the helm, the magazine carried on. For the first time, the magazine was run by committee. Marion Strobel came back to lend a hand; like North and Dillon, she had kept close to *Poetry* since the twenties. While De Vries was listed as Co-editor, both women deferred to his literary and administrative judgments. Certainly Dillon was pleased, and congratulated De Vries for seeing *Poetry* through the 30th Anniversary Issue.

Early in 1943, De Vries himself was drafted, and from Camp Joseph T. Robinson, Arkansas, he sent mordant letters describing his misery in basic training. In March he was given a medical discharge, for sinus problems and high blood pressure, and returned to the magazine. In October, he married Katinka Loeser, herself a poet and thus someone who considered the poverty of his profession no impediment. Originally from Iowa, Loeser received her B.A. from the University of Chicago in 1936. Her first poems were printed in *Poetry* in January 1941; the next year De Vries (who hadn't yet met her) voted to award her the $100 Jeannette Sewell Davis Prize. She was named an Associate Editor in March 1943, and shared the burdens throughout De Vries's tenure. Amid his several duties at *Poetry*, De Vries continued to write book reviews for the Chicago *Sun*, and completed his second novel. He also published one of his most famous essays, "James Thurber: The Comic Prufrock" (December 1943), with an illustration by the cartoonist—the first appearance of the whimsical Pegasus that has become the magazine's logo.

The Thurber Pegasus made its first appearance in *Poetry* in December 1943,
accompanying Peter De Vries's article, "The Comic Prufrock."

Soldier-poets passing through Chicago during the war frequently
stopped by the offices at 232 E. Erie and were entertained or taken out to
dinner by the staff and Board members. However straitened its circum-
stances, *Poetry* maintained its tradition of hospitality. Maintaining sol-
vency, however, was a particular challenge during these years, when the
fate of one little magazine must have placed low on most potential
donors' lists of priorities. But for poets, especially younger ones who
hoped to be featured there, *Poetry*'s continuation mattered a great deal. In

Peter and Katinka De Vries sorting mail in the *Poetry* office, mid-forties.

a memoir in the 75th Anniversary Issue (October–November 1987), James Dickey recalled: "I conducted my whole poetic education by means of its issues; the Southwest Pacific war was made possible to me, in terms of survival, only by means of what appeared, month to month, in its pages."

Several readers who were called up for duty wrote to say they eagerly awaited the late-arriving monthly issues at distant outposts. *Poetry*, in turn, regularly published late news from the several fronts. A May 1942 News Note, for example, reported: "Word has come from the so-called protectorate of Bohemia-Moravia (the former Czechoslovakia) that the newly appointed Reichsprotektor Herr [Reinhard] Heydrich ["the butcher of Prague"] has ordered a mass burning of literature. Among the books seized by the Gestapo were the poetical works of Pushkin, Heine, Wolker, Bezruč, and many others." It added that notable Czech poets had been arrested as "subversive elements" and sent to concentration camps. A June 1942 item commended Soviet poets for aiding the war effort by writing war poetry and "stinging and pithy, easily remembered rhymed verses" for posters, both intended to unify the people and "inspire courage and endurance and confidence and will to victory."

Poetry's entire issue for August 1943 was devoted to "Poets in the Service," including Karl Shapiro, Stanley Kunitz, Randall Jarrell, Roy Fuller, Howard Nemerov, and Louis Aragon, a leader of the French Resistance. Throughout the war, the prose section also featured letters from writers in the armed forces in a new column, Our War Correspondents, which related their varied struggles and accomplishments and gave updates (so far as the censors allowed) on their whereabouts. It also listed deaths in combat. Month after month, servicemen wrote about the important role *Poetry* played in keeping them in touch.

On 2 April 1943, Major Merrill Moore, a psychiatrist serving in the South Pacific (and a prolific sonneteer), said he was using *Poetry* and poetry books as therapy for "shell-shocked fighting men who have been freshly evacuated from places you read about in the newspaper." With his subscription order, one newly promoted soldier attached a note: "When I was a private I thought that I couldn't afford such a luxury. With four dollars more a month, I know it is a necessity, not a luxury." An April 1943 News Note advised: "Henry Rago, writing from Camp Beale, California, says that POETRY is a lifeline in an isolated Army barracks." A January 1944 Note conveyed this unexpected message:

As we go to press word comes that a Liberty Ship soon to be launched at a Richmond, Calif., shipyard is to be named after Harriet Monroe .... We have no more details than this to give, as yet, for we heard about it ourselves for the first time through an item in *The Chicago Sun*. . . . Harriet Monroe would be intensely pleased to have a ship named after her. She did not care greatly for busts or plaques or shrines for poets, but a ship is a lively and useful form of a monument. There is a pleasing appropriateness in giving the name of a poet whose interests were as world-wide as hers were to such a vital link in global communication.

The October 1945 issue was devoted to "Poets of the French Occupation and Resistance." On his days off, Dillon had visited poets and collected their work, including Paul Éluard's "La Liberté," the most famous poem of the Resistance. Dillon wrote De Vries in May that he did most of the translations "while waiting around in jeeps."

Throughout the war years, De Vries had to devote more and more time to fund raising. Decades later, in a *Chicago Daily News* interview (13 April 1963), he recalled: "Editorial toils on that monthly regularly alternated with time-outs to beg, borrow or bludgeon our tiny salaries out of civic-minded persons. I say civic-minded because Chicago has always been proud of Poetry's deficit. The magazine's annual critical financial illness was always reported in the newspapers somewhere near the obituary page."

After Monroe's death, efforts to increase support from "civic-minded" Chicagoans had enjoyed only limited success; in 1940–1941, donations totaled about $1,500. In 1941, Adlai E. Stevenson sent out letters asking subscribers to become "sustaining members" at $10. When Dillon made his dramatic announcement that the May 1942 issue of *Poetry* might be its last, the sense of emergency elicited almost enough donations to wipe out the deficit. In Washington, D.C., a benefit was arranged by Inez Boulton and Katherine Chapin Biddle, with Mrs. Franklin D. Roosevelt and Mrs. Harlan Stone, the wife of the Chief Justice, as sponsors. On 10 June, a group gathered in the Phillips Memorial Gallery (now Collection) to hear Archibald MacLeish give a stirring reading. Duncan Phillips himself opened the program with a speech on the importance of the arts in wartime.

Though the response was encouraging, De Vries, a veteran of many such soirées, knew that donations from the usual patrons would not be enough. Squadrons of volunteers were organized in Chicago and the suburbs to arrange additional benefit programs to attract new and larger audiences. One major production, the "Midsummer Night's Jam," was staged 14 August 1943, featuring "outstanding Boogie Woogie Artists." Using more conventional methods, the magazine also sponsored a series of five noontime lectures at the Arts Club of Chicago. Though these programs didn't generate much income, the series ran for four seasons, beginning in 1943. Among the speakers in the first year were Frank Lloyd Wright, Rudolf Ganz, and Robert Penn Warren. The second series featured an "impromptu" lecture by James Thurber and Oliver St. John Gogarty on "Poets I Have Known." The expense of spirit involved with the last lecturer may be surmised from De Vries's sardonic letter to John Nims in March 1944.

Eunice Tietjens to George Dillon   Coconut Grove, Fla.,
                                                      14 February 1942

Dear George:

Enclosed is a short fulmination [against Ezra Pound's radio speeches from Rome] which I hope you can see your way to printing in the prose section, as I feel rather strongly on the subject.

I did not hear the broadcast myself, but I trust the source of my information implicitly. Four people whom I know happened to hear it together. . . . They tuned in in the middle of the broadcast on the Rome band, heard "a middle westerner voice" talking as described and waited till the end to hear what it could be. They then heard the announcer say, "You have been listening to Ezra Pound, broadcasting from Rome." . . . I have seen nothing about it in print—nor whether he does it regularly. But there it is! I don't know whether you agree with me, but I feel that such a thing throws a shadow over the whole craft, and that it is up to us to say so in some form or other.

I confess that I have been sick of Ezra for years, as I think lots of us have been, but if you think the expression too violent, perhaps you could print it as a letter to the editor, which would put the whole responsibility on me personally, with an editorial comment by yourself. I do feel that the magazine, with which he was associated for so long, ought to repudiate him officially in this matter. . . .

G.D. returned E.T.'s screed for revision; "The End of Ezra Pound" ran in April.

Evalyn Katz to Peter De Vries   Baltimore, *17 March 1942*

Dear Mr. DeVries:

I am writing at the request of Private Karl Shapiro, to let you know that he has left the country to a destination which is still unknown. I received one letter from him, which was censored, at sea. That was three weeks ago and I have heard nothing since. I can only uneasily speculate from there on. It was his intention to write you that I was taking care of his work, his poems, his files, his manuscripts, etc., and that you were to communicate with me for any information that you might want. . . .

Stanley Kunitz to George Dillon   *New Hope, Pa., 13 June 1942*

Dear George Dillon:

Here—and not too late, I hope—is my review. Please do not pay me for it, but accept it as my small contribution to POETRY in its War for Survival. I had been hoping to send you some real honest cash, but a minor operation killed that possibility.

When the Wilson Library Bulletin resumes publication in September, after the summer hiatus, I will do what I can to boost your circulation. If POETRY goes, a part of our civilization goes with it.

Sincerely, / Stanley Kunitz

Kunitz's review of *Five Young American Poets*, Second Series 1941 (Paul Goodman, Jeanne McGahey, Clark Mills, David Schubert, and Karl Shapiro) was printed in July.

Karl Shapiro to Peter De Vries   *[V-Mail from Australia]*
3 August 1942

Dear Mr. De Vries,

May POETRY has reached me—in August. Not an extraordinary delay either. I want to thank you for printing my group and for giving them such a prominent display. I've begun to send new things to Miss Katz who will, I am sure, turn them over to you. My new volume [*Person, Place and Thing*] is now at the printers', but I am at such a distance from them that communication is difficult. If there is any difficulty in procuring American copyrights I may call on you for help. . . . The censor will have to review the book of course. I hope he doesn't think it's all a code.

Miss Tietjens' remarks on Pound in April were a little disturbing. Isn't the issue a little wider than [propagandist Lord] Haw-Haw? As she says, isn't it the technicality of citizenship that brings the matter into the open? . . . Pound is one of the few good American prose writers. Shall we forget the debt of Joyce, Hemingway, and Eliot to him? Yeats has gyres and things: wasn't that part of him? If Fascism has Ezra it's our loss, I think, not Ezra's. I speak as an old Popular Fronter and worse. You know my opinions.

I'm glad you all missed the shoals again. I wish I could send a thousand pounds. My very best to you and Mr. Dillon and the magazine.

Sincerely yours, / Karl Shapiro

Evalyn Katz wrote De Vries 23 September, hoping to send more poems, but "demand is now greater than the supply. . . . It is wonderfully gratifying to believe that Karl's talents will be and are being recognized. Certainly you have done much to fashion the pattern."

George Dillon to Peter De Vries

Camp Crowder, Mo.,
18 August 1942

Dear Peter,

. . . My basic training is now finished, which means that my real Signal training can begin . . . . I hope that the final work on your book is progressing satisfactorily and that you won't find the magazine interfering too much. It's a great satisfaction to know that you are carrying on. In fact, it seems almost too good luck, to be accepted in the branch of the Army I particularly wanted to get into, and to know at the same time that *Poetry* is being continued. Also, I've been wanting to say that I hope you and Jessica and Marion won't hesitate to make any changes, in the magazine itself or the office or anything else. It is a fact that when you begin doing a job you have a freshness of vision that you can never recapture . . . .

Weldon Kees to Peter De Vries

Denver, Colo., *6 October 1942*

Dear Peter De Vries,

It was nice of you to think of me [as a reviewer] for the Jarrell, but I'm afraid I must say no. My own feeling about Randall is that he should be tossed to some convenient hatchetman or werewolf like Dunstan Thompson or Wyndham Lewis or William FitzGerald. I don't mean because of Jarrell's reviews (they were pretty steadily mean but contained more sense than most people like to admit, and they *did* enliven the columns of the New Republic, which is quite a trick); I mean I am simply unable to see much merit in Jarrell's verse, nor can I understand what the fuss is all about. I can play hatchetman myself now and then, but truly, I shouldn't much care to review the book [*Blood of a Stranger*]: the reading of it, I'm afraid, would be too much, far too much. Thanks, though, for thinking of me; I'm sorry not to be cooperative this time. . . .

John F. Nims to Peter De Vries

South Bend, Ind., *29 October 1942*

Dear Mr. De Vries,

. . . What I'm really excited about is a clipping from the Daily News which seems to say that one of *Poetry*'s annual prizes [the Harriet Monroe Lyric Prize] has been awarded to someone with my name. Since I haven't received any notice, perhaps it's indelicate of me to mention it, but I am excited. Is it true? Good Lord, it's wonderful, if it is! I can't think of anything mentionable that would make me happier. And I'm almost as excited about Karl Shapiro's being given the Levinson Prize. He's my favorite modern poet these days. . . .

John F. Nims to Peter De Vries   South Bend, Ind., 1 December 1942

Dear Mr. De Vries,

. . . That was only a still-born rumor—about going into the Navy. I sent them an application and a lot of forms, and, judging by what had happened to friends of mine, I said that I expected to be called into Chicago for an examination. But they weren't even interested. Said I apparently had bad eyes, since I wore glasses. I can't understand some of their mediaeval notions. What are telescopes for? . . .

Peter De Vries to Geraldine Udell and Staff   *Camp Joseph T.*
Robinson, Ark.,
[January 1943]

Dear Geraldine and Company:

I feel guilty, knowing I should have written long, long ago, and have no excuse to offer. I landed here, as you probably know from the dizzy blonde [Katinka Loeser], a few days after I returned to Fort Sheridan. Camp Robinson (named, I believe, after the Senator?) is for the most part a general basic training camp. . . . Then, there is a substantial medical corps division here and, I believe, ordnance. That, except for [actor] Melvyn Douglas who is a buck private somewhere around here if not on his way to the Personnel School out east for which he has been ticketed, about sums up Camp Joseph T. Robinson—which Walter Winchell that great American epithetician once called the Alcatraz of the Army.

My reactions about it are mixed. I can't say I much care for the non-commissioned officers; they strike me as small time Napoleons. However I have lately begun to conceive a sympathy for them. I know why they bark; they are mercilessly barked at themselves, and worked to death. As a sergeant said of his portion, "I wouldn't recommend it for a dog." For the commissioned officers I have had occasion for nothing but respect. Those I have dealt with have struck me as intelligent, discerning, and considerate—though I can never get my rifle clean enough for the bastards by inspection time, work at it though I do with every available device including my toothbrush. In the course of processing I encountered another officer, by God, who, glancing at my occupational report, leaned back, sucked on his coke, laced his fingers behind his head and asked for my opinion on every contemporary poet in the land while buck privates pile up behind me like a log jam.

Arkansas (or Orkansas as even I am beginning to say) you can have. It is the most miserable patch of earth you will ever see—meagre, grudging crops, dilapidated farm houses and a climate good for nothing but the cultivation of nasal and respiratory infection. And if you tell me, well, after all there is John Gould Fletcher, I will reply that every state gets the poet it deserves. . . .

Peter De Vries to Poetry   *Camp Joseph T. Robinson, Ark.,*
9 March 1943

Dear Friends:

I believe when I wrote you last there was some doubt as to my remaining. Now there is none. I'm in the discharge wing of the hospital with some two hundred other culls, all of us waiting to be sent back. I have been receiving treatments for my sinus condition, at present quite severe, but I'm going to put a stop to that promptly, because now that they are sending me back I want to get out of here as fast as I can and those receiving treatment are apparently delayed. So I'm telling them I feel better, in the hopes that I can get out of this madhouse Friday or Tuesday (the two days of the week on which the gate swings out). It's a continuous din all day and half the night, drunken arguments, fights and the general uproar characteristic of these wards. Down the hall a drunk stabbed two men in a card game, one of them in the liver. Somebody stole my shoes.

The blood pressure has been down a bit lately and doesn't seem to be as bad a matter as I had thought. My sinus infection has, as I say, been quite beastly, with terrific headaches again like I had a year or so ago. . . . There has been one doctor around here once, and then only to attend to the discharge routine. I made the point again that I don't want to go but—yesterday I had my clothes checked in.

All this is extremely discouraging to me. Yet I am at least moderately capable of facing the fact that no great blow is being dealt the Allied cause by the removal of one lank and sore-throated ghost stumbling and sniffling his way through the dank dawns of Arkansas under a full field pack. Oh well . . . .

The thing about all these discharges, most of them soon after induction, is, they make the army angry with the local draft boards, who care only about getting their quotas in. There's one boy here in the ward all crippled up from infantile paralysis! . . .

Randall Jarrell to Peter De Vries   *[Chanute Field, Rantoul, Ill.,*
spring 1943]

Dear Sir:

Would you care to print these poems? I'd like to send them on an all
or none basis, though—I wrote them at the same time and I believe I'll
try to get them printed together.

I enjoyed the review [by Jessica North] of me [*Blood of a Stranger*]. I
was in a hospital at Sheppard Field [Wichita Falls, Texas] with nothing
but *Penrod* to read, the day it came; I liked it considerably better than
Penrod.

The most genuinely imaginative thing in *Poetry*, these days, are the
letters from poets describing the army. I enjoy them more than I can say.

Yours sincerely, / Randall Jarrell

Randall Jarrell's cover letter with his first submission to *Poetry*, spring 1943.

R.J.'s "Absent with Official Leave," "Point of Embarkation," "Come to the Stone," and "The Emancipators" were printed in August 1943.

May Sarton to Marion Strobel   *New York City, 16 May 1943*

Dear Marion Strobel,

What a blessing it was to have your note about *Navigator*,—I had to keep quiet for two months last fall and it was a time for poems. I wonder when there will be another.

Here I am working hard and the work is good—writing scripts for documentary films about America for OWI [Office of War Information] distribution in Europe among our allies. They will go in with the troops. Now we are in the middle of a film about the TVA—thrilling material of course because it is such [a] positive achievement. On the other side is one's growing awareness that the reactionary powers are getting ready for a fight—and while the physical battles go on outside America, the fight for ideas, the fight to make clear the real issues of the war and that fascism is likely to be a home-product—that fight is just beginning. Muriel [Rukeyser] has just resigned from the Graphics division of OWI because every honest poster has been turned down. Now she is being attacked in the press as a red. According to the F.B.I. one is a dangerous person if one was un-American enough to be anti-fascist before Pearl Harbor! But now Muriel will write poems again and I am glad of that. . . .

Stanley Kunitz to Jessica Nelson North   *Fort Benjamin Harrison, Ind., 18 May 1943*

Dear Miss North:

I seem to conduct my correspondence with you solely from Army hospitals! (Scarlet fever is my current affliction.) If I weren't already as bright as a pomegranate, I should blush for shame at my failure to produce that promised review of Ettore Rella's poems . . .

Thus far, as the result of so much illness, I appear to have been a bad investment for Uncle Sam, but I'm hoping to prove not a total loss after my release from the hospital, when I am to be transferred to Public Relations at Fort Harrison. Am I glad to get out of Finance!

All best wishes to you. Each issue of *Poetry* shines like a good deed in this naughty world!

Sincerely, / (Pvt.) Stanley Kunitz / #33486772

John F. Nims to Peter De Vries   *South Bend, Ind., 4 July 1943*

Dear Mr. De Vries,

I was very happy to get your letter and to find that you think several of the poems satisfactory. I'm a little uneasy too; I feel about you and the rest of the staff as I would about a bright-eyed individual who would start passing out hundred-dollar bills on the street. Something must be wrong.

Congratulations on your new book [*The Handsome Heart*]. I've not been able to read it yet, but I hope to read it very soon—probably within a day or so. The reviews I've seen are very friendly and approving—hope all the rest are. Best wishes for a large sale too (or is that too vulgar?)—so large a sale that you can take care of all the expenses of *Poetry* and not even have to give up your penthouse.

Things are quite different here—the [Notre Dame] campus is white with sailors and dark green with marines. None of the nice silly college boys just lying around in their sloppy clothes. I've been talking to some of the marines. After their first lectures from some pretty tough top-sergeants, they're not sure whether the real enemy is the Japs and Nazis or the U.S. Navy. Last night at the country club, I'm told, one of the marines, an ex-football player, threw the mayor of South Bend over a table (I don't know how large a table) and knocked out three sailors before being quieted by the sight of several large pistols. It should be an exciting year, but I hope to miss most of the excitement. . . .

Karl Shapiro to Peter De Vries   *APO San Francisco, 28 July 1943*

Dear Peter,

I'm inclosing a letter written for publication, if you think it worth while. It has been on my mind for a long time and had begun to fester. . . . I avoid Criticism like poison, or I think I do. Consequently I haven't dished up any of the jargon and have said what I thought rather than what I had "concluded" from other conclusions. If my letter is not suitable I hope I've at least put you on the lookout for plain talk about poetry. . . .

The war is still with us. My time in the combat zone is I think much longer than that for most men already. We have hopes and beliefs that we shall be relieved soon, even to get home! The current rumor is that Mussolini has abdicated. After sticking pins in his effigy for fifteen years it's about time he began to wilt.

Let me hear from you, please.

Best wishes, / Karl

[*attached letter*]

Dear Peter,

A few weeks ago I received four consecutive numbers of *Poetry* and had an opportunity to catch up on the current contributors and to think about them. I read, for once, with a pencil, using the vocabulary of the camp for my marginalia. Resultantly I burned the magazines for fear they'd fall into the hands of the censor or chaplain. . . .

I think I could take any four *Poetrys* of the last six or seven years and see the things I see now: a predominance of good reviews, outstanding articles, and poor poems. I could mark, as I have marked here, one or two contributions of great value (by a known or an unknown writer) out of a possible hundred and ten; and for the rest, a body of verses more or less penned by the same hand, largely of neutral or belated opinions, weakly constructed, without even interesting versification, and with wild ranges of subject matter—and yet all vaguely of the same subject. . . . With some surprise I turn to the Notes on Contributors and discover that So-and-so is a farmer or a soldier or a Welshman or a woman! How can we account for all this want of personality and individuality?

Or is it possible that I am asking too much? Maybe two out of a hundred and ten is a good average. But that's impossible; I think a glance at the original volumes of *Poetry* would disprove anything of the sort.

Or am I being simply nostalgic? Check me up on this. I think that there is a seduction, a drawing off of poets into other departments of literature. I can think of several good names off-hand who have become novelists, literary critics, or historians. What is the significance of this? And for all the others who persist, why is the level of composition and inspiration and thought so low? . . .

After reading my four *Poetrys* I find myself leafing through the reviews and articles trying to pick up a crumb of Spender or Yeats or Hart Crane, like a beggar. . . .

It seems almost out of place to say such a thing in *Poetry*. But why? Isn't our divorce from active participation in thought and action also a symptom of our persistent weakness? I wonder how many generals and diplomats read *Poetry*. I wonder whether [Lewis] Mumford, Einstein, or [Wendell] Wilkie would review a book for *Poetry*. Why does this sound so idiotic—because they haven't time?

Again, I don't ask for a corrective, but I would like it to come to our conscious[ness] that we are a wee small voice miles and miles away from a roar of resurgence that is rocking the whole world. The journalists, the very radio announcers are making better poetry than we are.

School's out for a while. I should think with all this loving and hat-
ing and living and dying together that poetry would also get out in the
world and do some loving and hating and living and dying on its own.
                                    My very best wishes, Peter, / Karl

De Vries did not print the letter.

John F. Nims to Geraldine Udell   South Bend, Ind., 20 August 1943

Dear Miss Udell,
      . . . Could you please send me five extra copies of the Sept. issue and
deduct the dollar from the check? I send copies of all my work to the
Dionne quintuplets.
      Congratulate Peter De Vries on the smooth way he handled the
mike the other night [at the Boogie Woogie benefit]. He's wasting his
time behind a desk. What he needs is a handful of chorus girls, (that
should flush a pun), a performing seal, a little place on State Street, and
he could finance *Poetry* all by himself. . . .

Karl Shapiro to Peter De Vries   *[V-Mail] APO San Francisco,*
                                           28 October 1943

Dear Peter, August *Poetry* here at last. All my thanks for such bold
showing of my work. You give me courage. I liked your analysis
immensely, with its eye cocked on the sceptic *and* the patriot. The issue
held more than an anthological meaning to me, which reminds me of
my letter to you of a couple of months back. I don't think it said what I

In the service: Karl Shapiro and William Van
O'Connor, New Guinea, 1944.

thought it said; at any rate it was not criticism in any of the accepted styles; it was grudge-writing at best & probably not suitable for publication for that reason. I despair of criticism and I haven't it in me to refrain from playing the judge. That I am not a judge is evidently apparent to some readers. *Poetry* has been very generous. However, I have no concrete news of *V-Letter*. I keep after poor Evalyn to keep after them. But because I feel Time's winged chariot at my back—oh not calling me I hope, but calling off the smoke of battle. Isn't there a proper time for a book to be born? I'm sure there is. . . .

Evalyn Katz to Peter De Vries   *New York City, 28 January 1944*

Dear Peter De Vries:

Will you be interested in any of the enclosed? Karl's new book *V-Letter* will be out April and I thought—that which you already anticipated—a double-header might be possible? Now that the book is at the printer's, it's difficult to realize that *all* of the poems were written overseas. It has been that long.

I know you've been hearing from Karl because he's written so, but in the last two months you may not have heard that he was pretty active in a bullet-fray and *didn't like his looks getting all the ammunition!* It was one of those non-stop, non-sleep, non-eating, non-washing mud and grime episodes. I gather he's now on a boat in the same seas with no chance for any kind of a furlough. But he's still writing. . . .

E.K. wrote P.D. three weeks later that Shapiro would be transferred in April, and thanked him for writing a recommendation for a Guggenheim Fellowship.

Nelson Algren to Peter De Vries   *[Fort Bragg, N.C.],*
                                      31 January 1944

Dear Pete,

I'd rather you wouldn't send those books right now, much as I'd like to look them over, because I won't have the chance to write even a hasty review. This outfit is run like a damned chain-gang six full days a week—and I've never missed a Sunday detail yet. So culture will have to suffer, I'm afraid. . . .

I applied twice for overseas duty and been rejected twice. Not that I'm feeling particularly sanguine these days—it's just that the endless tedium of doing right face and left face for six months would make anyone prefer to take his chances in action!

If I get a Sunday off or a couple Sundays—I'll write you a goddamn poem. . . .

Oliver St. John Gogarty to Katinka Loeser
New York City,
3 March 1944

Dear Miss Loeser,

You are very kind to go to such trouble to arrange talks for me in Chicago. . . .

Ask Poetry not to go to any lengths in entertaining me. It has been very good already and I prefer to live in some quiet place where I shall be out of the way of devastating Irish hospitality. . . .

Peter De Vries to John F. Nims
15 March 1944

Dear John,

If you want to come up here Saturday for dinner, should you be in town, O.K. But we have had four days of Gogarty (and by that time we may have had six or seven) and absolute quiet is required, with a simple, nourishing diet and no excitements. Books will be passed out to those who wish to read—looking up and reading "interesting passages" to others will be barred, as a possible double strain not advisable. The radio will be turned on, softly, in the other room, for those who wish to lie down and listen to it.

No whispering. No unnecessary stirring or movement allowed. Tiptoeing to the toilet will be permitted. Subjects barred: the Irish question, the proper preparation of tea, Yeats, Shaw, Churchill, obscure references in Joyce, George Moore's impotence, roots (as, for instance, "an artist's roots"), Druidic myths, AE [George William Russell], and Gogarty.

Guests will not be found missing at the Medinah Club an hour and a half after the dinner is fully cooked. Guests will not arrive or depart in drunkenness, nor make assertions concerning sexual intercourse while passing Mrs. Wolff's (the landlady's) door, even when such assertions apply to great men of letters, ancient or modern. Under *no* conditions will the recitation of long passages from the poets be allowed. Under certain conditions quotations limited to four lines will be allowed. There will be no exception whatever in the use of contemporary Celtic writers.

Beer only will be served, and guests will be limited to three glasses. Conduct cannot be regulated after the guest has left the apartment building, but guests are kindly requested not to be found standing at midnight on Elaine Place, hatless, peeing in the rain. And though the hosts will cooperate in every way possible to see guests to their nearest transportation points, they must decline to drive guests through the mazes of Lincoln Park in pursuit of cabs, whether in rain or no, or to chase, at the behest of guests, after lights which when they are overtaken turn out to be traffic signals, while the guests distract them with a recitation of obscene limericks. . . .

Stephen Stepanchev to Peter De Vries   APO New York, 6 June 1944

Dear Mr. De Vries,

I'm awfully sorry I left Chicago as suddenly as I did, without letting you know that I was leaving; but things like that happen, when one is a soldier. In any case, be assured of my high regard for you and the *Poetry* staff. I left Chicago for Camp Reynolds, Pa., which is an ASF [Army Service Forces] Replacement Depot, and there I stayed until about two weeks ago, when I was moved to a camp "somewhere on the East coast of the United States" to await shipping space for overseas transport.

Say! The news has just been flashed over our camp loudspeaker system that the invasion of France has begun! It's 7:25 A.M. I'm sitting on my bunk. Wait, I'll go over and see what the story is.

Yes, it's time, apparently. We've captured Caen, ten miles inland, and everything seems to be going well.

But what I was going to say is this: Is there anyone abroad whom you'd like to have me look up for you? I can't tell you where I'm going, but you, knowing what I've been trained for, should have a pretty accurate guess as to my destination.

My A.P.O. number, incidentally, is temporary, but you can reach me by writing me at it. I'll send you the permanent one as soon as I've been located.

Regards to all. / Sincerely, / Stephen Stepanchev / 2d Lt., A.G.D.

George Dillon to Peter and Katinka De Vries   Paris, 8 August 1945

Dear Peter and Katinka,—

Thank you for your two good letters, the last one (Katinka's enclosing the picture of the baby), and the other one (Peter's) which I realize with shame I have not yet answered. It gave me a great deal of pleasure. I have delayed writing, primarily, of course, because of this kind of reform-school life which our new garrison Commander, Gen. Rogers (who ought to be Grand Wizard of the Boy Scouts) thinks is appropriate for U. S. troops to lead in a wicked city like Paris . . . .

Finally, I am sending some clippings about Valéry's funeral in which you and Julia Bowe may find something for the News Notes. I was surprised by the tremendous amount of attention given to Valéry's death. It coincided with the opening of [head of the Vichy government, General] Petain's trial, but not even that could keep it from getting a large share of the front page in the two-page Paris newspapers. There has probably been no more impressive ceremony since Victor Hugo lay in state under Napoleon's arc. And this week the newsreel "Actualités Françaises" starts out with the sound of a dirge and the subtitle "Paul Valéry est mort," then gives about 1/3 of the footage to scenes of the funeral, at Paris and at Sète (where he was buried in the "Cimetière Marin").The rest of the reel being devoted to the Trial. Can you imagine a poet's death receiving such attention in the U.S.? . . . I went to attend a farewell reunion of the radio team of which I was formerly a member.They are about to go to the Pacific. At this moment I'd like very much to be going with them, despite the 60-day trip.That is a "safe" wish, however, for the Army is not sending the 39 year olds. . . .

Give my love to Geraldine, Marion, Julia and Inez. I owe them all letters and it has gone past the point where apologies are even acceptable. Someday I'll snap out of this gray mood.—Jan [the De Vrieses' baby daughter] looks so self-willed and confident, not at all befuddled, no, but with her father's rather artistic eyes. I am delighted to see her. Decidedly she belongs to the generation of Atomic Energy—and good luck to her and it!

George

George Dillon to Peter De Vries   *Paris, 3 September 1945*

Dear Peter,—

Thanks a lot for your letter of the 23rd. Immensely pleased, and surprised, to hear that the French number is a reality. . . .

Try as I may, and do, to *peer* into the future, the business of my personal reconversion looks just as nebulous as ever—to such a point that I sometimes think the simple and sensible thing, in my case, would be to *stay* in the Army . . . But to do that I'd have to be about twice as crazy as I am. . . . It remains to be seen whether I can get a job, or whether I can stand any regular job, after 3 years of continuous duty in Army offices and radio installations. At nearly 40 it is doubtless time I thought about earning a living and building a small security for the future—which would mean leaving the direction of *Poetry* to those who can afford to do it or who can combine it with other work.You, as I've said before, should feel no responsibility to continue—though if you like doing it and don't find it too great a sacrifice of time, energy and income, I can think of no better arrangement than the present one. At all events I hope to see you before long, or call you up on the telephone and hear your own ideas on the subject.—It is too much to

Sgt. George Dillon, Paris, 1944.
He broadcast news of the Liberation
from the Eiffel Tower.

hope, I guess, that the U.S. Employment Service can find me a part-
time job, yet that's what I keep hoping for—some work that would not
tie me down to regular hours. I suppose about 6,000,000 other GI's are
dreaming the same dream. . . .

CHAPTER XVI

Period of Adjustments, 1944–1949

1. Peter De Vries and *The New Yorker*

In the December 1943 issue of *Poetry*, De Vries published "James Thurber: The Comic Prufrock." He began by recalling his Thurberesque moment searching for Ford Madox Ford's glasses under the table at the 1938 banquet, then announced his thesis:

> I am not sure what poetic sensitivity is, but I am practically certain Thurber has got it. This is a magazine of verse, and critics especially, with their bootlegger's passion for boundaries, will probably thank me to get back in my territory. But . . . he has more in common with modern poets than, for instance, he has with any other present-day humorist you might mention. . . . If fancy and the imagination and "subjective" as opposed to "objective reality" is the emphasis we are talking about, then Thurber can certainly be included. . . . It is hard to think of anyone who more closely resembles the Prufrock of Eliot than the middle-aged man on the flying trapeze.

De Vries sent Thurber an advance copy of the essay—the first serious critique of his work—and they struck up a correspondence. Thurber invited him to New York, and early in 1944 the De Vrieses visited the Thurbers at their East Side home. They hit it off immediately, and Thurber agreed to appear in *Poetry*'s Arts Club lecture series.

Thurber's program was set for 13 April 1944 and billed vaguely as "If You Ask Me." It was intended to be, not a formal lecture, but a question-and-answer session. Knowing that public speaking made Thurber extremely nervous, De Vries and his guest speaker took the precaution of getting together the night before. Many years later, he revealed that they colluded in making up several fictitious "questions from the audience"—camouflaged on bits of paper of different sizes and colors—just to make sure the ball got started and kept rolling.

He needn't have worried. The show was a huge success, as Thurber

proved "one of the great monologists of our time." De Vries's introduc-
tion was a brilliant stand-up performance itself. (Among his many puns,
he said Thurber "hit the male on the head.") The *Chicago Sunday Tribune*
review on 14 April reported that many in the audience thought *he* was
Thurber. Early on, De Vries's fiction was compared with Thurber's. In
thanking Jean Burden in May 1940 for sending a review of his first novel,
he protested: "It's of course a dirty lie that I write like Thurber. It's
Thurber who writes like me."

De Vries's quick wit convinced the older humorist that the sophisti-
cated young editor-critic-novelist would make a splendid addition to
Harold Ross's menagerie at *The New Yorker*. All that remained was to con-
vince the Editor of the obvious. Just as De Vries had primed him for the
Arts Club program, Thurber prepared the way for De Vries's interview
with Ross with a stratagem of his own. The story of their initial
encounter—another example of De Vries's striking first impressions—and
his letters to *Poetry* describing his first months at *The New Yorker*, seem
taken from a comic novel by James Thurber, or Peter De Vries.

In his version of the story, recounted in his memoir of *The Years with
Ross* (1959), Thurber said he told Ross he had found "a perfect *New Yorker*
writer," and handed him a bundle of De Vries's work. Ross said he'd read
it, but was sure it wouldn't be funny. Two hours later, Ross wanted to get
"DeVree" on the phone. (For some reason, he thought the name was
French, and always pronounced it as if it rhymed with "debris.") Thurber
warned him the Editor could be very unpredictable, and when they met
for lunch at the Algonquin, Ross didn't disappoint. His first question to
"DeVree" was: "Could you do the Race Track department?" "No," he
replied, "but I can imitate a wounded gorilla." (It had in fact been one of
his roles on the radio.) Thurber reported: "Ross glared at me, realized I
had briefed De Vries, and then his slow lasting grin spread over his face.
'Well, don't imitate it around the office,' he growled amiably. 'The place is
a zoo the way it is.'"

De Vries was on the job in July, which meant splitting his efforts
between *Poetry* and *The New Yorker*. While he continued to vet manu-
scripts, handle book reviews, and oversee such basic tasks as copyediting
and proofreading from New York, Marion Strobel took charge in
Chicago. Margedant Peters, who began as subscription manager in 1942,
became an Associate Editor. Although not listed on the masthead, her
husband, S. I. (Don) Hayakawa, also helped with prose. Late in 1944, John
Nims joined the staff part-time to read manuscripts and advise on prose.
He was teaching at Notre Dame, but made frequent trips to the city
while working on his Ph.D. at Chicago.

In Manhattan, De Vries was in an ideal position to line up prominent

James Merrill, age 19, in snapshot sent to *Poetry* in 1945, upon his first acceptance.

authors and other artists for *Poetry's* benefit programs. Topping his list of prospective lecturers were Martha Graham, Aldous Huxley, even Peter Lorre; but despite often lengthy negotiations, he didn't manage to sign them up. Meanwhile, Harold Ross kept finding new ways to keep him busy: editing prose, writing Comment pieces and reviews, "helping out" in the Art Department with the cartoons. It was not until many years later that he revealed he not only edited captions but came up with original ideas that the artists then executed.

During this transition period, *Poetry* continued to make "discoveries." Gwendolyn Brooks, who had begun sending poems when she was in high school, first appeared in November 1944. James Merrill was a student at Amherst when the magazine gave him his first professional publication in March 1946. Kenneth Koch and John Ashbery both debuted in November 1945—Ashbery inadvertently, after a prep school classmate stole some of his poems and submitted them as "Joel Michael Symington." Ashbery discovered the theft only after he had sent some of his work himself when he entered Harvard—and picked up the November 1945 issue. As he first explained over forty years later, in *Poetry's* 75th Anniversary Issue, when his poems were returned with "Sorry" on the rejection slip, he assumed the editors thought *he* was the plagiarist. He feared he'd be blackballed. "It seemed to me that my career as a poet had ended before it began. It was quite a few years before I was able to summon up enough courage to submit more poems to *Poetry*."

Writing to De Vries from Paris in September 1945, Dillon had expressed uncertainty about what his new civilian occupation would be, and seemed reluctant to return to the magazine. Finally, in March 1946, he agreed to resume the editorship. Katinka asked that her name be taken off the masthead, but Peter continued advising until September 1947. In the October 1948 issue, Dillon offered a tribute, which read in part:

Peter De Vries, when he came to us in 1938, was already a popular young writer demanded by editors. The long hours he put in here were a substantial loss to his own writing time and business pursuits, but it was a willing sacrifice . . . . If P.D. had done nothing else in his versatile life he would still be remarkable for the number of good writers he discovered and stimulated during his seven years in this office. In addition he lectured widely in behalf of *Poetry*, raised money for it, and kept up everyone's spirits with his amiable wit.

Katinka Loeser De Vries to Poetry   *Hotel Algonquin, New York*
                                          City, Thursday [July 1944]

Dear kids,

. . . Pete's had several Comments accepted (you know, page 1 in Talk of the Town) and some used already. I'm sure you have been diligently perusing your New Yorkers and have spotted items about the Chicago Republicans, phosphorescent meat, etc., and a fine one next week on judges & precedent. We got the rough copy already on that and he's also sold a nice casual, a satire on the Unforgettable Character of the Reader's Digest. So far, in his daily work there (he has a nice little office, and a simply unbelievable new big typewriter which runs away with him) he's been doing rewrite. For instance, the horse-racing man seems to be notorious, sending in such items as "many new faces are seen in the saddle this year," etc. Nothing specific has been worked out yet. . . .

The Thurbers came in Wednesday for a few days, and Jim adds to the general picture. Last night he told me that on the day Pete first met Ross, he, Pete, regarded him calmly, listened quietly, and then said, "Mr. Ross, you can pace up and down without leaving your chair." . . .

Peter De Vries to Poetry *Staff*   *New York City, 26 July 1944*

Dear Everybody:

It being ten to ten and nobody down here yet except for coca-cola bottles, I thought I'd better write you while I have a moment. Of course that's a lot of baloney to impress you, that about having a moment. I have sixty moments to an hour, up to at least twelve or so, when things get humming around here and the man in whose care and keeping I presumably am is visible darting about with page proofs and occasionally smiling at me through my open door to let me know that he is here, and that he knows I know it. Geraldine is right about nobody getting under way here till ten or eleven or more, except that they work till seven or eight, like as not.

What I have been given to do has been of a sporadic and totally
unpredictable order—rewrite, second reading, Going Through the Art
Basket, tearing down the corridors southeast to Ross' office when he
summons me to wrangle over a phrase in a piece of Comment. So far
I have been an appeaser, feeling that nothing really critical has been in
question, but I am girding myself for the first big showdown on
something for which I have determined to fight to the last, carrying
on a guerrilla warfare from Chicago if necessary. It involves a pun in a
piece of Comment on [the columnist Westbrook] Pegler, in which I
make reference to "the noted newpaper calumnist." Why this will be a
terrible thing you can't know, until you realize the Law Against Puns
in Talk, one of the many sacred precepts and bugaboos around here.
This one is particularly Ross', but of course respected in fear and
trembling down through the hierarchy. He has accepted the piece in
question, but I have not put the pun in the original copy. My plan is
as follows. After he has put it through, I will slip it in the galley or
page proof, arrangements having already been made with the Talk
editor who handles all that copy in its various stages and who is also
my immediate superior, a sweet, flexible guy of thirty-odd. When my
phone rings and Ross summons me, my defense will be simple, and
also the New Yorker's in the event of libel proceedings: it was a typo-
graphical error.

So it goes. This is a wonderful place but something of a madhouse,
with nobody ever quite knowing what he is doing. It doesn't take you
long to realize that the NYer is not written, it is rewritten. Everything
is ground three times through a terrific mill—and that goes for every-
thing from department copy to the pronouncements and prognostica-
tions of the track guy . . . . It's a dull and tortured road to perfection, all
right. . . .

Ross doesn't think they'll need my services (?) till the first of Octo-
ber, so we've made arrangements to return then. The apartment situa-
tion here is absolutely *frightful*. But luck has been with us. We
explored the Riverside Drive and East River sections over the week-
ends. Nothing. Then yesterday Katinka went out to the Village and
walked into a vacancy [at 32 West 11th Street], which we snapped up
so fast it made our heads swim. Now we are firmly sandwiched in
between the Episcopal and Presbyterian churches but a block and a
half from Cummings. . . .

We'll leave tomorrow or the next day. Will call you when we get in.

Love, / Pete

Ross will pay expenses on trips to Poetry till the end of the year any-
how. After that he doesn't want to make any commitments. He's afraid

(sic) the war will end any minute. Then he doesn't know what will happen. So..... Meantime he says he is more than glad to see all the dough go to the writers. He says there are two places he by God doesn't want to see it go—the government and the business office. . . .

Paul Engle to Peter De Vries and Marion Strobel　Stone City, Iowa, 2 September 1944

Dear Peter and Marion:

This has a double purpose, even if it is a stinking little card: to tell you that there was a negro girl at the Evanston conference who wrote some pretty good stuff—Gwendolyn Brooks. She will send, or has sent, some poems to you.

Second—I am leaving here the first week of Oct. for New York, where I will be a while before going to Europe for OWI. I hope to see you on the way, or in New York. My point is, I'd like to have Peter's New York address in case I can look him up there. Rural greetings,

Paul Engle

Gwendolyn Brooks to Marion Strobel　Chicago, 4 September 1944

Dear Miss Strobel,

I'm so glad to have poems of mine accepted by POETRY! . . .

Gay Chaps at the Bar, along with the other poems entered in the Northwestern U. poetry contest in July, was to be printed in a little brochure in November or December. . . .

Will this make a difference? I desperately hope not. . . .

Here is my "autobiography":
Birth—Topeka, Kansas, June 7, 1917
Residence—623 E. 63rd Street
Occupation—Housewife
Married Name—Mrs. Henry Blakey
Books—No books published or scheduled to be published . . . .

Brooks debuted in the magazine in November 1944 with "Gay Chaps at the Bar" and "Still Do I Keep My Look, My Identity." *Poetry* also first published "We Real Cool," her best-known poem, in 1959. G.B. sent the photograph in 1945.

Peter De Vries to Marion Strobel   *New York City,*
                                                      17 November 1944

Dear Marion:

Thanks for sending the letter from MacLeish. . . . I am thinking of asking Peter Lorre, who is endlessly flitting around and popping in and out of odd corners of the Algonquin, but I never get him in a corner. Why couldn't he give us a lecture both suitable to our high plane and consonant with his own professional bent: to wit, "Culture Vultures: A History of the Famous Paintings Stolen or Almost Stolen from the Museums of the World."

Shall I ask Oscar Williams to lecture for us? You better not irritate me in any shape, manner or form, because I have got that to hold over your head and threaten you with at any time. He asked to be remembered to you. He "took me out" to lunch yesterday, having phoned again. I saw to it that he took me to an inexpensive place, a little French restaurant over on 47th St., or it might have cost me a lot more than it did. As it was his hospitality only set me back a couple bucks. He's really not bad, by the way. Completely self-absorbed but in a monotonous, rather than offensive, sort of way. . . . He has some new unpublished poems by Dylan Thomas which he promised to give us. Because of his anthology, I guess Thomas gave them to him. Thomas asked him, when he sent them, to try to get some immediate magazine money for them if he could, and for that reason he sent the one he is particularly enthusiastic about to Harper's Bazaar. I can't see H. Bazaar buying any Thomas and neither can he, and he said he'd let us have it when it comes back. . . .

Thomas's "Poem in October" appeared in *Poetry* in February 1945, "A Winters Tale" in July 1945.

Peter De Vries to Poetry *Staff [telegram] 10 January 1945, 9:18 A.M.*

FIRST BORN LAST NIGHT   6 LBS   TOOK ALL OUR RED POINTS
CONDITION MOTHER DAUGHTER FINE   WOULD RATHER NOT
DISCUSS MINE   PETE

Peter De Vries to Geraldine Udell   New York City, 20 January 1945

Dear Geraldine:

Everything is O.K. along the obstetrical front. The baby is doing all right, though she has been returning her dinner lately. However I guess that's a rather common thing among babies. Katinka is getting along fine, and is starting to get up now, though she's been bored and lonesome all week because I haven't been able to get out there [to Columbia University Medical Center], being sick in bed. We hadn't decided on a name at all, but the baby gets letters addressed to Gretchen. Thurber inscribed her name thus in a copy of his new book, the first copy he gave out, etc., so it seems a sort of write-in campaign against which we can't do much. We like it very much, but have had one or two others we were thinking about too, notably Jan and Jennifer. (Somebody told us once we were going to have twins, you know, in which case we were all set to call them Jennifer and Conifer.) . . .

Everything else from now on will be bad news. Not only is [S. J.] Perelman out, but Martha Graham fell through too. . . . Now we are up a tree all right. I haven't got an idea in my head, and am frankly so weary and disgusted and bowed down I have half a mind to go across the street to church, confess my sins and pray. . . .

Peter De Vries to Marion Strobel   *New York City, 3 May 1945*

Dear Marion:

. . . I spent Monday afternoon at Reynal and Hitchcock's new only half built offices reading Shapiro's long poem—or rather trying to, with hammer and saws going all around me and the editor in the editor's office I was using. Too, there is some uncertainty about what [parts] Kenyon and/or Partisan [*Reviews*] are taking of it, if any, and nothing was satisfactory about it—least of all, incidentally, the poem itself, which is just what it says it is, Essay on Rime, a long discussion of prosody and technique, and content, in English poetry, mostly modern, which is good enough as it goes (a good poet looking the field over), but not a smidgeon of poetry in it. Completely prose, completely. So I was disappointed. . . . Shapiro, however, seems to have begun writing *poems* again, judging by the single the mail at the New Yorker contained this morning. He's in town for a few days, now again, preparatory to some final transfer to Washington . . . . I want very much to meet him, tell him to write some more poems, to save up a good batch and give them to us, rather than pass them out to Evalyn as he writes them and let her send them to the big-paying markets, as she wills. I'm glad anyhow he's got this long lucubration out of his system. He said in his letter he hoped it was important. I fear it is not important (except to him), and I know it is not interesting. Except perhaps to some of the other poets themselves, and scholars, and so on. . . .

None the less, two sections from the *Essay* were printed in the July 1945 issue: "Dialectic and Criticism" and "The Dead Hand and Exhaustion of Our Rime."

Peter De Vries to Marion Strobel   The New Yorker,
                                                   12 October 1945

Dear Marion:

Talked to [Thornton] Wilder and Sinclair Lewis and they are out.
They both hit me fast low grounders which bounced off my glove. I
said "But, uh—", but they were already whirling through the Algon-
quin's revolving door, as from a plague. Looks as though I'm beginning
to need some good stiff Dale Carnegie in Handling People. I've been
trying to phone Martha Graham for days but every time she's out or in
class or something, so I've written her a note, as I also have Shapiro.
Expecting to hear. . . .

Kimon Friar to Poetry   *Amherst College, 6 February 1946*

Dear Editors:

Mr. De Vries informs me from New York that you have accepted the
poems of James Merrill which I sent you, and he requests that I send
you some biographical details for the Notes on Contributors.

Mr. Merrill will be twenty on the third of March. He attended
Lawrenceville School, and is now, after his honorable discharge from
the army, entering his senior year at Amherst. He has never published in
any magazine other than the school publication at Lawrenceville
where, however, his father had his school stories and poems collected
and privately printed in book form [*Jim's Book*, 1942]. . . .

Peter De Vries to Margedant Peters   *New York City,*
                                                   7 February 1946

Dear Marge:

Last week Oscar Williams phoned and said he wanted to see me. He
came to the office. As I came into the reception room he was looking
over this—not only did he happen to have it in his briefcase when he
called on me, but he just happened to be glancing at it at the very
moment when I came in. It is the proof of his introduction to his new
forthcoming anthology of modern poetry (this one to cover fifty years)
which Scribners will bring out around April. He thought it might do as
a separate article for Poetry. . . . So greatly developed have my recupera-
tive powers become that I cannot clearly remember what the piece is
about, though I read it only last week . . . . I would take exception to at
least one or two of the remarks, especially about science. . . . He cites
radio as a case of something not appearing at the exact moment when
it would answer a need in the enrichment of the human mind. This is

all putting the cart before the horse. The only way you can make your-
self equal to a thing is by experience with it and the results it produces,
and this cannot come till after it has been invented. So he is talking like
the mother who wouldn't let her child go in the water till she had
learned how to swim. . . .

But you and George decide, or you decide. . . . Or maybe George
will want to write him. If he has some sign like that to show that I'm
no longer with the firm, maybe he'll go away. . . .

George Dillon to Peter De Vries   *[Richmond, Va.], 16 March 1946*

Dear Peter:

At last I can write to offer you relief. It was good of you to consent
to continue with the Poetry work until April 1st, and I wish it could
have been earlier still. . . .

Well, thanks for these months of grace, which have enabled me to
get a number of things straightened out. You and Katinka have been
wonderful in your devoted service to Poetry, and I would do every-
thing I could to persuade you to continue, for the sake of the magazine,
if it were not too much of a burden for you. . . .

I hope very much that when you are free of this chore you will at
least send us something for publication whenever you can. Also that
you will still consent to be one of the editorial board, and listed as
such . . . . I have been working steadily on direct-mail advertising and
articles for trade journals, which is something that goes on and on
because there is no end whatever to the peace-time applications of
aluminum. . . .

George Dillon to Marion Strobel   *[Richmond, Va.], 6 April 1946*

Dear Marion:

Slim pickings! Although I don't look at the comments, except by
accident, before reading the poems, I find we agree perfectly nearly
every time. Which is monotonous but pleasant—makes me feel like a
musical little echo, way off in space. If only something new would
come along, or something old, resuscitated. Something with life.

The March issue is nice. It was good to feature a conspicuously tal-
ented young poet like Merrill, though to me his verse is just an exqui-
site arrangement of words. That is doubtless enough at his present stage,
since his is so ingenious about it. Who knows that he, or one of the
others, may be the ONE. . . .

Merrill was given the honor of leading off the March issue, making his professional debut with "The Green Eye," "The Cosmological Eye," "Perspectives of the Lonesome Eye," and "The Formal Lovers."

Karl Shapiro to John Frederick Nims   *Gaylordsville, Conn.,*
                                                        13 June 1946

Dear Mr. Nims,

Thanks for the invitation to participate in the symposium on criticism [A Hard Look at Criticism, a special section in the August 1946 issue], but I must refuse. I feel that any statement I might make would be a rewording of some part of my one critical essay. Further, I try to avoid the practice of criticism as much as possible, in the belief that it is a side issue, a parlor sport—at least as far as poets are concerned. Still further, I think our poets should stop trying to catch up with criticism.

. . . By now the lines of division between "appreciation," evaluation, factual scholarship, linguistics and symbology are so thoroughly muddled that it will take a new Aristotle to clarify and reclassify our terms and our motives. I had to write my essay [*Essay on Rime*] in a kind of poetry because I saw no system of definition that could encompass the "signs" of criticism. Except for one more paper, which I have promised to write for The Lockwood Library, I intend to go into critical silence for good. . . .

John F. Nims to Peter De Vries and Marion Strobel   [*South Bend,*
                                                        Ind.], *9 July 1946*

Dear Marion and Pete,

Please read this with a fine-tooth comb and see if it passes mustard. Give it the eagle-eye and see if it rings the bell to the tune of one cigar. I mean, scrutinize it if you have to do so on bended knee ~~worn to the bone~~ (excessive). See what I mean?

Is it too topical? Huh? Too didactic? Huh? Too journalistic?

Please don't take it unless you're SURE, since it will probably get me fired, anyway. Myself, I think parts of it are swell, but as a whole, I don't know. New Republic (Mayberry) read it with "pleasure" but found it too long for them.

This is not the long one I told you I was working on. That is still unfinished, and prob. will be till I finish typing my goddam thesis. That will be late in August, I hope.

                                                        John

Gee, I wisht I was in Chicago so I could stop in in person and point out the beauties of this-here pome.

James Merrill to Peter De Vries   New Canaan, Conn., 28 July 1946

Dear Mr. De Vries,

Enclosed is a group of poems for your consideration. One of them, "The Broken Bowl," was in the group that won the Irene Glascock Memorial Prize at Mt. Holyoke College this spring.

Yours truly, / James Merrill

Interoffice memos: Nims: "End of *White Unholy Ghost* is weaker than rest. Last 2 stanzas could well be omitted, but that would lose the good last line. Ask him to cut or revise? Broken Bowl *ok. Accumulation of the Sea* I like the 1st 3 stanzas. Less sure of the last section. Would certainly take *most* of it." De Vries: "accept Accumulation, White, Broken Bowl, From Morning."

Dillon (on the back of Merrill's envelope): "Afraid I can't quite agree about him. There is some fine detail but the total effect is prolix and often pedestrian. Poems seem an almost equal combination of fresh, vivid perceptions and tired banalities (and oratory), all smoothly unified and well knit, and set to a sleep-producing rhythm. There is no doubt of his talent. But since he seems to be fairly prolific, I think we should take only his very best at this point. 1st 3 stanzas of Albino are good (last 2 pretty awful) and perhaps he will consent to printing only those 3, as the complete poem is in them, or at least omit stanza 4. In addition, I'd take *Broken Bowl.* (*Morning* is precious and the sea poem, all in all, pretty tame.) But of course I'll abide by a majority vote—it's the only system in these cases."

Peter De Vries to Geraldine Udell   *[New York City],*
                                                        29 December 1946

Dear Geraldine:

We have purposely postponed responding to your letter about getting the grant [from the Bollingen Foundation], out of a certain inveterate, long-established skepticism about all those things, which you will appreciate. We have been expecting a rude-awakening follow-up from you stating it was all a mistake, or that it has all fallen through. It was not, and still is not, possible to believe. This letter is still a kind of wary hosanna, one eye cocked on the possibility of the news being all a mirage. You can see what the years of pessimism have done to old Poetry hands. . . .

Anyhow, a Happy New Year to all.

As ever / Pete

We saw Cummings at a party the other night and told him to send some poems to the magazine. If he hasn't, you might send a follow-up letter. There was a horrible confused conversation with Cummings, at first, because he said he was grateful for the Percy Bysshe Shelley award which Jean Starr Untermeyer and I wrangled for him, even though he was ashamed of the prize proper. Also Cyril Connolly (for whom the reception was) kept calling me Mr. Van Vries, and it was a three-cornered mixup in which I didn't have any idea what was going on, the kind I'm always getting into, it seems. I finally straightened out with Cummings (who hadn't gotten my name in the first place of course) what prize I was really instrumental in getting to him. We gave Cyril Connolly official greetings from Poetry. I also believe Connolly asked me whether I had painted anything lately, but at that point I picked up the punch bowl in my arms like a child and drank.

2. "The Age of Criticism," Controversies, and Hayden Carruth

Although George Dillon returned to *Poetry* in April 1946, he did most of the editing from Richmond, Virginia, where he looked after his seriously ill parents—thus, incidentally, saving the magazine money. Dillon, Strobel, Nims, and Peters got equal billing, and shared the mere $2,067 budgeted for the Editors. Dillon continued to augment his salary by writing ads extolling aluminum siding. Because of postwar inflation, hard times at *Poetry* were not expected to end soon. So, like De Vries, Dillon and the staff were much relieved when the Bollingen grant was promised in December.

Editorially, the postwar years were among the more interesting in *Poetry*'s history. Nearly all the notable poets of the time, senior and junior, made appearances: Stevens, Pound, Graves, Williams, Marianne Moore, Cummings, Spender, Berryman, Robert Lowell, Jarrell, William Stafford, David Wagoner, W. S. Merwin, William Meredith, Roethke, Donald Justice, Merrill, Howard Moss, Richard Wilbur, Weldon Kees, Margaret Avison, and Gwendolyn Brooks. *Poetry* also published three sections of Williams's autobiography-in-progress (June, August 1948; November 1949) and generous selections from MacLeish's *Notebooks, 1924–1938* (October, November 1948).

On the financial side, *Poetry*'s haphazard ways were straightened out when Thomas C. Lea, a retired Chicago businessman, volunteered to take over the bookkeeping. As paper, printing, rent, and other costs continued to skyrocket, Lea approached over three dozen foundations for support. Almost every application was rejected outright. In July, Lea made another try and found a more sympathetic ear in Huntington Cairns, a trustee of the Bollingen Foundation. Dillon shared De Vries's "long-established skepticism"; invariably foundations said they did not fund literary journals.

To everyone's surprise, on 5 December the Bollingen Foundation awarded $10,000 for 1947, and later raised it to $15,000. The Foundation said it would consider similar awards for 1948 and 1949, if "the educational benefits resulting from your program justify the expenditure." As part of the "program," between March 1947 and February 1950 *Poetry* published a series of "Critical Supplements" for use in university classes; the guides offered explications of poems in current issues, with discussion topics. John Nims wrote most of them; Hayden Carruth, John Berryman, and others completed the series. *Poetry* also isssued *A Glossary of The New Criticism*, a reprint of articles by William Elton in 1948 and 1949. Enlarged as *A Guide to the New Criticism*, it ran to five editions.

Perforce, if not always by preference, *Poetry* had become deeply involved in what Randall Jarrell ruefully called "The Age of Criticism." Since the twenties, the magazine had printed reviews and essays by prominent critics, "New" or otherwise. Now more space was devoted to literary analysis, theories, and criticism of criticism. Shapiro, who professed to be against criticism, provided a number of specimens. In 1947, the magazine even started printing "previews," critiques in the back of the book of poems in the front.

After much debate among the staff, in September 1946 *Poetry* printed a section of Canto LXXX from Pound's *Pisan Cantos*, along with commentaries by Dillon, T. S. Eliot, and R. P. Blackmur. (The issue led off with Robert Lowell's first appearance, "Ghosts: After Sextus Propertius.") Pound had been indicted for treason in 1943 for his infamous radio broadcasts from Rome during the war. His obscene diatribes against F.D.R., Churchill, bankers, and Jews, among others, were considered enemy propaganda. (They also were so incoherent the Italians thought Pound was crazy, or speaking in code.) In 1945, he was arrested, held near Pisa, then brought to the United States. Judged incompetent to stand trial, he was incarcerated in St. Elizabeths, a mental hospital in Washington, for the next twelve years. Sentiment against Pound, within and outside literary circles, ran high. In her article "The End of Pound" (April 1942), Eunice Tietjens had denounced him as a Benedict Arnold. Dillon felt the new Canto deserved to be printed and judged "as a poem," he wrote John Nims 9 June 1946, "and not for its academic interest, or topical interest, or anything else."

Politics and personalities aside, the growing emphasis on prose in *Poetry* troubled many readers. The worst example, September 1948, consisted of only eleven pages of verse (seven poems by Jarrell), with the remainder reviews and critical articles. Inez Boulton wrote Dillon that she was "dismayed" and "revolted": "Receiving the September issue of Poetry was like getting a letter from home with one's allowance cut to ten per cent."

Marion Strobel Mitchell,
John Frederick Nims, and
Geraldine Udell, c. 1947.

For his part, Dillon was dismayed about the poetry submissions—which may explain the shift to prose. He wrote Udell in April 1947: "Unless we can uncover some genuine new talent pretty soon the prospect of publishing a poetry magazine, even with financial support, is going to be bleak. . . . Slight as the possibilities are of finding anything in the first reading, we must not forget that it represents almost the ONLY possibility of keeping the magazine alive."

Unfortunately, the task of identifying new talent became harder when, in May 1947, John Nims asked to be relieved of his duties. It had become very difficult to do the first readings and edit the prose while teaching and writing the supplements at the same time. He felt what *Poetry* needed "most of all [was] a full-time resident editor." He told Dillon that Strobel agreed. Despite his "resignation," Nims continued to serve as co-editor until 1950. Strobel also soldiered on. In the spring of 1948, Hayden Carruth, then a graduate student at Chicago, was hired as Associate Editor and eventually took over the critical supplements. They had become drudgery for Nims, because he could find little to say about the material in recent issues. Nims wrote Dillon 16 October that some of the poems seemed "to belong not in *Poetry* but in *The Florida Magazine of Verse*."

General fatigue had set in. For Dillon, the strain of long-distance editing and constant worry over money finally took their toll. In March 1949, he resigned. Announcing "A Change of Editorship" in the May issue, Dillon explained the need for "a single, unifying editorial direction." After much consultation, Carruth was chosen with a recommendation to the Board "that he be given a free hand to put his ideas into effect." But the new Editor's other hand was tied, and direction was in fact anything but unified.

Carruth first entered the *Poetry* office in 1947, through a window. He helped his good friend Henry Rago jimmy it open, to get some advance copies of a new issue containing Rago's work. Carruth made his first appearance in *Poetry* with "The University of Chicago" in July. He had come for graduate studies in 1946, after serving in the Army Air Corps in Italy. In naming him Editor, the Board felt that, at twenty-eight, Carruth was too inexperienced to have complete authority. He was given control over the back of the book, but his decisions on verse had to meet the approval of Nims or Strobel. Restricted in the poetry section, Carruth soon made his mark with prose.

In the spring of 1949, the Library of Congress awarded Pound the first Bollingen Prize, for the *Pisan Cantos*, and controversy erupted. Protests were heard across the land. The most influential, and devious, came from Robert Hillyer, a Harvard professor and poet of the old school. In two articles in the *Saturday Review of Literature*, he insinuated that the Bollingen Foundation and the judges were part of a vast conspiracy to impose the New Criticism upon the world. Karl Shapiro and Katherine Garrison Chapin had voted for Williams. They and most of the other judges (and, of course, Pound) were long associated with *Poetry* but hardly proponents of the New Criticism. Still, Hillyer claimed that the magazine was "falling into the hands of the new esthetes."

Ludicrous as Hillyer's accusations were, they seemed plausible enough to the *Saturday Review*'s readers to generate great distrust and many letters to the editor. Rep. Jacob Javitz of New York called for an investigation, then settled for a resolution of Congress that ordered the Library to stop making awards.

Carruth was outraged by the smears, and felt Hillyer had to be answered. In "The Anti-Poet All Told" (August 1949), Carruth pointed out the errors in Hillyer's articles, and presented a general defense of freedom of expression. He had his essay reprinted in a pamphlet, "The Case Against *The Saturday Review*." Along with additional rebuttals by Archibald MacLeish, Mark Van Doren, Yvor Winters, and others, it included an article by Malcolm Cowley, "The Battle Over Ezra Pound," that demolished each of Hillyer's charges and claimed the professor was a failed, jealous poet trying to wreak revenge on his betters by stirring up the philistines.

Some *Poetry* readers and trustees were not pleased by this foray into (literary) politics. At the 75th Anniversary celebration, Carruth reiterated his stand and said: "We felt *Poetry* really was the spokesman for all poets in the country." He recalled that some skeptics suggested the pamphlet was a way of currying favor with the Bollingen Foundation. Carruth denied that was his motivation, and all evidence supports the purity of his intentions. "I was very naïve at that time," he said in 1987.

In fact, the Foundation had already told Carruth that the third Bollingen grant would be the last. Carruth went East to seek donations. In Washington, Inez Boulton offered advice and hospitality. (But, he wrote Geraldine Udell 11 September, she "spoiled the evening a little bit by bringing out her own poems. Why do people always do that? What do they expect me to say about them?") George Dillon had already written directly to Paul Mellon, founder of the Bollingen. He replied 23 August that the Foundation had limited funds—and its own problems because of the award to Pound. Even so, Mellon said that he would talk with the other trustees. Allen Tate also met with Bollingen trustees and wrote glowing letters of support. But, he told Carruth 18 November, they were still uncertain because of "their stubborn fear of getting committed to indefinite support."

Nothing came of Carruth's mendicant tours. On 16 September, he wrote Tom Lea from New York: "I'm just not the man for this job, and I'm afraid I'm making a botch of it. . . . I don't like this work, and I hope I never have to do it again. Furthermore, I don't think any editor is good at money raising. The two talents are too far apart."

By fall, the situation became so desperate that Carruth wrote to Robert Maynard Hutchins, asking that the University of Chicago take over *Poetry*, with its $20,000 deficit. He told Hutchins the magazine had cut expenses to the bone, raised circulation to 4,000, and increased advertising 300 percent. Carruth was informed the University couldn't help. At the end of November, the situation appeared hopeless.

Carruth, Strobel, and Udell debated who should call the printers and tell them to stop the presses. "It was a dramatic moment," Carruth recalled in 1987. He prepared an announcement that *Poetry* was closing. An hour later, a telegram arrived. The Bollingen had decided, after all, to give the magazine another, absolutely final, grant.

In December, with money on the way, Carruth felt that he should have full editorial authority. But some of the older trustees, particularly Inez Boulton and Marion Strobel, were put off by Carruth's ideas and attitude. As his colleague Margedant Peters put it, H.C. had problems with "public relations." The Executive Committee met twice but couldn't come to a decision. A meeting of the full Board was set for early January. Each side prepared reports in the interim. Margedant Peters spoke for Carruth's supporters, who felt H.C. had earned his freedom. Peters also feared that the Bollingen grant would be in jeopardy if he left. She said that he would certainly resign if his demands were not met.

In her report and in a personal letter to Dillon, Boulton revealed the main objections of Carruth's opponents: the magazine printed too much criticism and H.C. just couldn't "get along." To Carruth's complaint that errors crept into issues because the Editor was continually harassed, she replied: "To be Editor of *Poetry* is to be harassed." As for H.C.'s literary taste, Boulton found the "bracketing" of Cummings and Stevens with Berryman "hard to take." She didn't like the "fancy diction" in H.C.'s editorials, either.

She and Strobel and Julia Bowe did like Karl Shapiro, however. *Poetry* had "discovered" him, printed him often, given him prizes. The magazine brought him to Chicago in 1947 for a lecture, and the crowd was so large people had to be turned away. Boulton had become friendly with

Shapiro while he was Consultant in Poetry at the Library of Congress in 1946–1947, and everyone on the Board admired him. Shapiro was teaching at Johns Hopkins, in fact had tenure, but didn't like the job. He was available.

"I must have had a desire for poverty," Shapiro recalled at the 75th Anniversary program in 1987. "I needed to escape the academy, and Editor of *Poetry* seemed like a beautiful and exotic alternative." By the time the full Board met on 9 January 1950, Marion Strobel had Shapiro and the votes lined up. Julia Bowe, seconded by Strobel, moved that Carruth's resignation be accepted since they felt his conditions could not be met. The vote was seven in favor, two against, with one abstention. Bowe was asked to phone Shapiro and offer him the job. That evening he accepted.

Peter De Vries wrote Geraldine Udell on 7 February: "We're happy the recent crisis resolved itself as handsomely as it seems to have. You've probably been going around with a wet towel around your head for months, and are due for some calm sailing." The Board believed tranquillity had finally come to *Poetry*. They soon discovered they were in for a bumpy ride.

Karl Shapiro, winner of the 1946 Pulitzer Prize for
Poetry, with Robert Frost at Bread Loaf, 1947.
K.S. was then the Consultant in Poetry at the
Library of Congress.

CHAPTER XVII

Karl Shapiro: 1950–1955

1. High Hopes

Announcing the appointment on 22 January 1950, the Chicago *Sun-Times* declared: "With Shapiro as editor the future looks bright for both *Poetry* and the chances for a literary renaissance in Chicago." The Board shared these great expectations. Shapiro was thirty-seven and at the height of his fame: acclaimed "war" poet, Pulitzer Prize winner, former Consultant in Poetry, and much-quoted dissenter in the Bollingen-Pound affair. At the very least, the glow of his celebrity promised to brighten *Poetry*'s recent lackluster image.

Shapiro's editorship indeed had sparks, but the excitement occurred as much behind the scenes as between the covers of the magazine. Icono-clastic and outspoken, Shapiro courted controversy. Despite his laurels from the Establishment, he seemed bent on appearing an outsider. His acerbic articles, like his first assaults on literary dogma in *Essay on Rime*, created resentment among academic poets and critics, who hastened to point out the gadfly's self-contradictions.

In fact, just as he came aboard, Shapiro did a major about-face. During the Bollingen fiasco, he had voted against Pound, and by extension New Critical "objectivity." But when he realized the serious damage caused by Hillyer's sinister accusations, Shapiro switched positions. In "What is Anti-Criticism?"—printed in March 1950, the first issue of *Poetry* he edited—Shapiro dissected the anti-intellectual prejudices against Mod-ernism that Hillyer and his kind promoted, and gave an incisive defense of contemporary poetry—and criticism. Shapiro's disdain for the hob-goblin of consistency was admirably Emersonian. But his editorial policy at *Poetry* (or, as he told reporters, his *lack* of a policy) was sometimes dis-concerting.

Although it desired stability, the Board overlooked the fact that Shapiro didn't like to stay put, in either his literary opinions or his career. Shapiro attended three institutions, but never took a degree. Johns Hopkins had given him tenure none the less, but within a year he wanted to leave. The

Evalyn and Karl Shapiro in the *Poetry* office, 1950.

English department asked him to finish out the term; so, like Dillon, he edited through the mail. From Baltimore, Shapiro solicited material and tried to find new donors on the East Coast, with the help his wife, Evalyn, who had demonstrated her skill at promotion as his agent during the war. Within weeks of their arrival at the office in June, the fireworks started.

One of Shapiro's first decisions, after removing the Whitman motto from the magazine, was to remove Gerry Udell. He later said he regretted the hardship to Udell, but felt he couldn't work with her. Further, he had to cut expenses. Evalyn Shapiro took over her duties, without pay. During her twenty-five years at *Poetry*, Udell had shouldered major responsibilities and had befriended many trustees and poets. Peter and Katinka DeVries were shocked. Tom Lea, the Hayakawas, and Julia Siebel, the secretary, all resigned in protest. The old Board had been contentious; now Shapiro could shape a new one.

He convinced the trustees that the Board had to be enlarged, preferably with people of means, influence, or expertise. It grew to over twenty members. Most important among them were Daniel Catton Rich, Director of the Art Institute; Ellen Borden Stevenson, the wealthy ex-wife of presidential candidate Adlai Stevenson; and Scott, Foresman executive Robert McNamara, who was particularly helpful in dealing with unpaid printers. His wife, Cornelia, volunteered as publicity director and saw to it *Poetry* got the widest coverage since the death of Harriet Monroe.

On the editorial side, too, Shapiro was able to start with a fairly clean slate. Because Carruth's selections had seldom met his overseers' approval, K.S. found very few accepted poems in the files. In his first editorial, "The Persistence of *Poetry*" (March 1950), the new Editor essentially restated the Founder's pledge of the Open Door, and stressed his desire to discover and encourage emerging talents. Shapiro added he would accept work by known poets only if it showed "growth or change."

Many of the younger poets he printed in his first years had already been "discovered" or presented in *Poetry* in the forties: Brooks, Justice, Meredith, Merrill, Merwin, Stafford, Wagoner. Among the most notable of those who eventually debuted under Shapiro were May Swenson, Frank O'Hara, James Dickey, Anthony Hecht, Philip Booth, Galway Kinnell, and Adrienne Rich. Successful aspirants typically had their submissions returned two, three, or more times, usually without comment, before they were published.

Throughout his term, Shapiro tilted heavily toward his contemporaries and friends. Delmore Schwartz, Muriel Rukeyser, Randall Jarrell, Richard Wilbur, Theodore Roethke, William Jay Smith, John Ciardi, John Nims—the so-called Middle Generation—were printed fairly regularly. Like him, they were well schooled in the Great Tradition. (Ciardi, Jarrell, Nims, and Wilbur made names as gifted translators, as well.) Nearly all of them taught, and in their own work they followed New Critical practices: compression, allusion, irony, "intellectual" content, and masterful technique displayed in forms polished to high finish—in short, the artistic values that would be called into question or abandoned by the rebellious generation that came to the fore in the late fifties and sixties.

Shapiro repeatedly tried to get the unprolific Elizabeth Bishop to contribute, but she was under contract to *The New Yorker*. He rejected one poem she did send. Shapiro had no more luck with the old masters. William Carlos Williams, one of Shapiro's idols, had nothing available in 1950. In 1951 he had a stroke, but in 1952 he offered sections of *Paterson* and other work. Williams also reviewed Carl Sandburg's *Collected Poems* for *Poetry* in September 1951, shortly after it won the Pulitzer Prize. It was probably the most damning critique of Sandburg's career. The two had been paired since the teens, and Williams did not like the comparison. He had kept experimenting, but (he noted in his review) Sandburg's work of almost forty years showed "no development of the thought, in the technical handling of the material, in the knowledge of the forms, the art of treating the line." Sandburg was not the only noted poet to be roasted during Shapiro's years.

Among his peers, Shapiro's favorite by far was Randall Jarrell. Though they were not close friends—as "war" poets they were rivals, and Shapiro won—the two shared an admiration for Auden and Whitman, and preferred the American idiom in poetry. Both were also noted (and, in Jarrell's case, feared) for their caustic criticism. Shapiro welcomed everything Jarrell sent, and wished for more. Because Shapiro printed his poems exactly as written, Jarrell paid him the compliment, "You don't act like an editor at all."

Shapiro followed *Poetry* tradition by arranging issues on single themes and devoted to foreign poets. The June 1951 number on modern Greek poetry, gathered and translated by Kimon Friar, featured George Seferis, Nikos Kazantzakis, Odysseus Elytis, and several others then unknown in the United States. September 1952 was devoted to postwar French poets. The work of the Spanish poet Juan Ramon Jiménez was highlighted in July 1953, three years before he won the Nobel Prize. French Nobelist St.-John Perse got star treatment in October 1951 with a dual-language presentation of "Et Vous Mers." Shapiro had hoped to do other foreign numbers, but complications set in and they were delayed.

Creative writing courses were spreading in the early fifties, and one of the more publicized of Shapiro's special issues was the Workshop Number (February 1952), featuring work from the pioneering programs directed by Paul Engle at Iowa and Theodore Roethke at Washington. Most of the student-poets in the issue dropped from view, but Roethke's essay on "The Teaching Poet" was often reprinted.

Shapiro worked particularly on changing the prose section. As early as April 1950, he wrote Julia Siebel, the secretary: "I feel unhappy about the whole reviewing policy of the magazine: there are too many reviewers who aren't really critics . . . there is much too much literary bowing and salaaming between poets." He preferred shorter, more subjective appraisals, not long, "scientific" analyses. He also said he wanted group reviews to cover more books. Leslie Fiedler panned fifteen books in eleven pages with "Bad Poetry and the Tradition" in January 1951. Many of the highly idiosyncratic reviews Shapiro published made him enemies. One by Edward Dahlberg created an uproar.

Shapiro assembled a new stable of reviewers, including his army buddy, William Van O'Connor; Wallace Fowlie, who also handled French poetry; and an obscure, recent Yale Ph.D., Hugh Kenner, who had contributed his first article in June 1949. Kenner held to New Critical standards, and his acerbic critiques in *Poetry* made him notorious. At the 75th Anniversary celebration, Shapiro reflected that Fowlie "was never too scholarly and always fair," while Kenner "was more than scholarly and almost never fair."

While Shapiro might not agree with Kenner or *Poetry*'s other reviewers, he insisted on letting them have their say. But when Kenner produced a scathing review of Delmore Schwartz's *Vaudeville for a Princess*, he

felt in a quandary. Eleven poems in the collection were first printed in
Poetry, and Schwartz was awarded the $100 Guarantors' Prize for 1950.
Shapiro put off printing the piece for nine months, got O'Connor to
write a more favorable notice to follow Kenner's (after Berryman turned
him down), then warned Schwartz what awaited in the October 1951
issue. Schwartz didn't hold grudges, and later wrote a fine essay on Eliot
for *Poetry*.

Edward Dahlberg did hold grudges. Largely self taught and resentful of
the privileged classes, he had been writing for years without much recog-
nition. In January 1951, *Poetry* ran a negative review of his autobiographi-
cal *The Flea of Sodom* by Edouard Roditi, who pointed out Dahlberg's
errors, pedantic style, and "fascist" tendencies. Dahlberg fired off angry
letters and demanded he be allowed to reply. (Roditi wrote Shapiro 17
August 1951, "What a psychopath!") In March 1952, K.S. printed
Dahlberg's nasty, ad hominem riposte, "How Do You Spell Fool?"

Instead of being suspicious when Dahlberg asked to review Conrad
Aiken's *Ushant*, Shapiro gave him the go-ahead. At the 75th Anniversary,
Shapiro confessed he didn't realize then that Dahlberg "had been lying in
wait for Aiken for years and was now about to bushwhack him." In his
"review," a bizarre mishmash of classical quotations, Dahlberg called
Ushant "an ill-conceived cento," and used most of his space to make irrel-
evant comments about Henry James. Aiken was understandably upset,
wrote Shapiro several times to protest, and threatened to sue for libel.

At first the Editor defended Dahlberg; but when several letters came in
pointing out his numerous distortions and misquotations, Shapiro began
to question the reviewer's motives. In the June 1953 issue, Shapiro apolo-
gized to Aiken and printed two pages of corrections of Dahlberg's mis-
spellings, partial quotations, and other misleading handling of Aiken's
text. He also printed a letter from Elizabeth Pollet (Mrs. Delmore
Schwartz), which denounced Dahlberg and succinctly showed that his
remarks about *Ushant* were "astonishingly false." Shapiro included an edi-
torial, "Does *Poetry* Have a Policy?", reaffirming his goal to publish the
best poetry he could find, and asserting that the reviews were secondary.
He rejected the "operating-table approach" of the quarterlies, adding:

> *Poetry* does not favor edited literary criticism or party-line criticism or
> laboratory criticism. Systematic and impersonal criticism does not seem
> to us to belong to literature, but to science and philosophy. We take the
> view that literary criticism should be subjective (but certainly not *ad
> personam*), passionate, humanly decent, and stylistically unique: we are
> inclined to judge a piece of criticism by how well it is written and not
> how "right" it is. *Poetry* does not attempt to legislate about poetics.

But after getting burned by the Dahlberg affair, Shapiro told reviewers to tone down the negative. Aiken had had tangled relations with *Poetry* since 1912, but he had been very kind to Shapiro. The review ended their friendship. Aiken didn't appear again until 1962, when "Love's Grammarians," his final contribution, led off the 50th Anniversary Issue.

Randall Jarrell to Karl Shapiro   *[Greensboro, N.C.,*
January/February 1950]

Dear Karl:

I was astonished to have you answer me from *Poetry*—astonished and pleased. I certainly will send you some more poems, but I believe I'd rather not do any reviews; I wrote an omnibus review for *Partisan*, and it was extremely depressing to see how bad the books were, and how hard it was to find anything at all good to say about most of them. I think I'll write some articles about poets I'm crazy about—I am certainly going to write a couple of articles about the Auden poems I like best, and I could give you one of those if you wanted it. . . .

Jarrell's "An English Garden in Austria" and "Seele im Raum" appeared March 1950; they had been accepted by Carruth. R.J. never did publish an article in *Poetry*.

T. S. Eliot to Karl Shapiro   *London, 6 March 1950*

Dear Shapiro,

When your cable arrived, telling me that you had accepted the editorship of "Poetry", I was in South Africa . . . .

For a good many years, I think, "Poetry" has ceased to belong to the category of the "little magazine." One of the distinguished marks of the "little magazine" is that it should be not only little, but short-lived. The little magazine, if no vicissitudes overtake it sooner, is limited in life to the literary editorship of one editor. . . . Now, "Poetry" has never changed its form: it remains obstinately the same in appearance as in the days when it printed "Prufrock." (I have sometimes hoped to see a different quotation, whether from Whitman or somebody else, on the back of it; but even this conservatism is expressive of tenacity.) . . .

"Poetry", in fact, is not a little magazine but an INSTITUTION. It was in existence before most of its younger contributors were born: to some of them it must seem as ancient of days as the American Constitution or the *Atlantic Monthly*. It can look back upon its past with satisfaction; but it remains perennially young and does not appear to need any drastic amendments. I congratulate it on passing into your hands;

and I hope that the heavy responsibility will not bring you to a premature grave, or impair your own creative activity.

With best wishes / Yours sincerely / T. S. Eliot

George Dillon to Geraldine Udell   [*Richmond, Va.*], *13 March 1950*

Dear Geraldine,

Thank you for sending me a copy of the excellent letter from T. S. Eliot. I can't think of anything that would be more valuable, at the moment, for promotional purposes. Karl is to be congratulated on getting such a declaration from "Old Possum." . . .

I admire Karl's patience in dealing with the reluctant tribe of art patrons; for example, he found the man at the Bollingen office in New York very sympathetic, although the man told him that Bollingen hoped "to be relieved of the burden of Poetry as soon as possible." . . . I should think that from the standpoint of Paul Mellon, who says that he has a personal interest in modern poetry, such a "burden" would be a very light and appropriate and welcome one to assume—permanently. But it is true that a foundation, any foundation, will not be likely to pledge its support for more than a year or two at a time. Nor is it likely that more than that degree of security would result from any annual campaign to enlist contributors. Therefore, though Karl speaks of Poetry's "financial crisis," the truth is that the magazine has always been in such a state of crisis, and that this can be regarded as its normal state. . . .

Gwendolyn Brooks to Geraldine Udell   *Chicago, 14 April 1950*

Dear Geraldine,

You must know how overjoyed I am, and how grateful to you people for allowing a consideration of my book to consume FIVE PAGES.

Something horrible must be about to befall me, because I have been so fortunate in the recent past.

Enclosed is a note which I hope you will forward to Mr. Kunitz when next you have to write him. He is a reviewer whose observations in the magazine I have frequently found instructive, and because of that I am particularly pleased.

Sincerely, / Gwen

Kunitz's review of *Annie Allen*, her second book, appeared in April; it won the Pulitzer Prize.

Kenneth Rexroth to Karl Shapiro   Sequoia National Park, Calif.,
[spring 1950]

Dear Karl Shapiro—

Perhaps *Poetry* is planning some sort of memorial issue to John Gould Fletcher. I looked on myself as a friend of his and was deeply moved by his death. I should like to be informed of any such issue and would be very happy to take part in it.

I was greatly surprised to hear of your assuming the editorship of *Poetry*. I had been travelling almost continuously for two years and just heard of it. I wish you luck. I think you'll need it.

Please give my best regards to Gerry Udell—I hope she is still there. She, it seemed to me, provided the magazine with vital organs & skeleton—whatever the editors provided.

Faithfully / Kenneth Rexroth

Fletcher had appeared regularly since 1913; troubled by severe depression, he drowned himself on 10 May. His "Los Angeles Smog" and "Along the Highway, Rogers to Fayetteville" (July 1950) were dedicated to his wife, Charlie May Simon, who wrote Shapiro about his last days. On 18 March, he had written Shapiro about the magazine's importance to him, and of his relief that K.S. was now Editor. In August 1954, *Poetry* printed a twelve-page review by Ben Kimpel of Mrs. Fletcher's *Johnswood*, with four of J.G.F.'s poems.

Richard Wilbur to Karl Shapiro   So. Lincoln, Mass., 6 October 1950

Dear Karl:

I am suffering slightly over your deletion of a paragraph from my review [of John F. Nims's *A Fountain in Kentucky*, October 1950], but having had some editorial experience I am aware that slashing is sometimes unavoidable. . . .

Today I had a glance at a ms. by a Radcliffe girl named Adrienne Rich. Have you seen any of her work? Her book [*A Change of World*] will come out in the Yale Series very soon, and very little of it has had periodical publication. If I get the chance I shall urge her to submit some things to *Poetry*. Very clean and witty poetry. Formal: she can write a stanza as few nowadays can. As "hard" as one would wish a woman-poet to be. And not too swamped by Frost & Yeats.

Yours, / Dick

Rich first appeared in *Poetry* in January 1951.

Randall Jarrell to Karl Shapiro   *[Princeton, N.J., early 1951]*

Dear Karl:

I'm doing two things at Princeton: I'm a Fellow in Residence teaching creative writing, and I'm also doing some lectures in a seminar. . . . I also gave "A Girl in a Library" [April 1951] to *Botteghe Oscure*, and I just had a letter from *Harper's Bazaar* asking whether they could print it in this country: so that except for *Poetry* I could be appearing among gaunt models in pedal pushers and maillots. See what you saved me from.

Yours, / Randall

Tennessee Williams to Karl Shapiro   *New York City,*
4 February 1951

Dear Mr. Shapiro:

Your lumping of Oliver Evans' work with that of fourteen writers of verse under the title "Bad Poetry and the Tradition" is a staggering piece of misjudgement [sic]. I don't question the right of Mr. Fiedler to attack where he chooses. He has certainly chosen to sally forth single-handed against an imposing number, numerically speaking. The energy of venom as it is particularly displayed by certain minor poets is never easy to understand. With that much steam in their vituperation, why is their verse so flabby?

What I do question, and most earnestly, is your own extreme indiscretion in submitting the work of Oliver Evans together with all those others to this single mass-executioner. Does he make a reduction for a job-lot? Seriously, I think you owe Mr. Evans an apology. I don't think it. I know it. And I know that you owe some explanation to all the rest of your readers.

Cordially, / Tenn. Williams

Karl Shapiro to Tennessee Williams   *7 February 1951*

Dear Mr. Williams:

I think I ought to defend Leslie Fiedler and take the responsibility for his article myself. We have been trying to review more books of verse than we used to, and it was my idea to send large packages to good critics and let them have their own say. Fiedler is not a malicious writer in the least; his judgment of Oliver Evans may be wrong but I know it is objective and sincere. It is always the case with literary magazines that the reaction of the reviewer is unpredictable. Recently we had a completely damning analysis of a poet to whom we had given a prize [Delmore Schwartz]. All the editor can hope for is some kind of balance between his own judgment and that of the reviewer he selects.

None of this is very soothing, of course, and I do intend to write an editorial presenting the case for unfavorable reviews. If Evans' work is really better than Fiedler thought, his judgment on Evans will be rectified.

This is probably the wrong time to ask but we would like to see some poems of your own when you have them.

Cordially, / Karl Shapiro

Several poems in Evans's *Young Man with a Screwdriver* appeared in *Poetry*. Williams did not submit his own work again; his "We Have Not Long to Love" was published posthumously in *Poetry* in February 1991.

Josephine Miles to Karl Shapiro   *Berkeley, Calif., 4 January 1951*

Dear Karl Shapiro,

Here are 3 poems "for New York" you might like; I'm not sure. If you remember the long poem on us-&-Russia called "A Foreign Country," you may be amused to know that I sent it to *Hudson Rev.* & they liked just the parts you didn't, that is, the first and last sections, & disliked the middle which was the part you [praised?]. I guess I *could* split it up your way and say, "see Hudson Rev. for the beginning & end", but that feels a bit silly, doesn't it? What I need now is a referee!

Truly, / Josephine Miles

"Three Poems for New York" appeared March 1951. K.S. printed parts I and II of "A Foreign Country"; one of the few poems in *Poetry* that dealt with the Cold War, it led off the March 1952 issue.

Edward Dahlberg to Karl Shapiro   *New York City, 25 January 1951*

Dear Editors:

I have just read the violent, garbled review of my book, *The Flea of Sodom*, by Mr. [Edouard] Roditi [January 1951]. It has become the slattern habit of calling people fascists on any pretext whatever and I think that since you printed such a bitter invective against my book, it would be civil and just of you to let me make a reply.

I should like to take up some of the Greeks, the "proto-Nazi" Plato as well as such "fascists" as Blake and Nietzsche, who I am sure, considering that Mr. Roditi is a very literal rather than a symbolical reader, [he] would call fascists. It is easy to feign that Blake is all right but I can abstract lines too from the total text, a villainous custom today, that will make Mr. Roditi's bland, Marxian bowels rage! The essay is hardly a review as there is absolutely no idea of the book generally or particularly given. Mr. Roditi seems only concerned with typographical errors and petty grammatical mistakes, that is certainly pedantry.

I can only say here that I do not care for the educated classes or the working classes or the malignant writing classes to which Mr. Roditi seccumbed [sic]. I only care about good workmanship, a cultivated human being and a poet. Since Mr. Roditi writes poetry, I wish to heaven that he himself were enough of an honest artisan, and not so fatuous a phonetic pedant as to blame me for the bad errors of printers in London, and enough of an imagination to have read my book like a poet instead of a man slaughtering myrmidon.

If you will let me answer Mr. Roditi will you kindly tell me how many words I may have for my reply.

Sincerely yours, / Edward Dahlberg

John Berryman to Karl Shapiro   *Princeton, N.J., 5 February 1951*

Dear Karl

Christ. One of my worst habits is not even opening letters when I am to blame, as in correspondence I usually am. I thought this letter (of Jan 8th) was to say, of course, *when* the *hell* the [Pound] *Patria Mia* review? What now made me open it was finding (with horror) a stampt & addrest but not sealed letter of mine to you of Oct 10 thanking you for the Levinson award, obviously lost in the nightmare of my desk & forgotten. *What* you have thought of me on 3 counts now, I don't care to wonder.

Well. I won't send the Oct letter, because it was grateful-but-very-gloomy though not so gloomy as I feel now. Why you gave my stuff a prize God knows;—perhaps the others were even worse. The money was v. useful & gave me a moment's breathing. The encouragement let me finish an atrociously bad poem I had (correctly) lost faith in. . . .

And now Delmore. Rotten luck altogether about Kenner. Is he any good, really? I mean has he any taste? So wonderful is our critical machinery that a man who couldn't distinguish between Dante & Patmore's odes might easily get a full professorship at Yale *as a literary critic.* Let me read the *Vaudeville* book carefully, I have not done so for lowness, and then . . . maybe I can help. I'll let you know in 2 or 3 days. But I'm doubtful—who else to suggest—? The writers who can *hear* poetry are not very numerous, and younger ones I know v. little about because I never read magazines anymore or as seldom as possible. Wait a day or so.

Very sorry about all this mess.

Best / Yrs / John

Berryman

Princeton, 5 feb.
51

Dear Karl

Christ. One of my worst habits is not
even opening letters when I am to blame,
as in correspondence I usually am. I thought
this letter (of Jan 8th) was to say, of course,
when the hell the *Patria mia* review? What
now made me open it was finding (with horror) a stamped
& addrest letter but not sealed of mine to you of Oct 10
thanking you for the Levinson award,
obviously lost in the nightmare of my desk
& forgotten. What you have thought of me
on 3 counts now, I don't care to wonder.

Well. I won't send the Oct letter, because
it was grateful-but-very-gloomy though not
so gloomy as I feel now. Why you gave my
stuff a prize God knows;— perhaps the others
were even worse. The money was v. useful &
gave me a moment's breathing. The encourage-
ment let me finish an atrociously bad poem
I had (correctly) lost faith in. — My first
deal with the 'Karl' do 'John' you brought up, let us.

Then Pound. Orkeletons, I see I told

John Berryman to Karl Shapiro, 5 February 1951.

Berryman wrote a few days later, turning down the offer, since he could not coun-
terbalance Kenner's negative review. He suggested K.S. kill Kenner's piece or at least
warn Schwartz what was coming.

Robert Frost to Karl Shapiro   *South Miami, Fla., 6 February 1951*

Dear Shapiro:

Your offer of a whole number of your esteemed magazine to fill
with my unsatirical ironies didn't amuse me as you thought it might. It
scared me for my virtue. It was like putting temptation in my way to
write a whole lot in a hurry or to go to Hollywood for the big money.
But nonsense aside. I knew that your proposal was meant to be nice to
me. My chief objection to it was your timing. If I give something I
don't want it to be used to celebrate my birthday. Let's forget the Ides,
Nones, and Kalends and all the rest of March. I have been looking back
at your poetry. You're a good poet and we're friends. If you want to
please me as your friend you can give me the place of honor in some
number pretty soon with some single poem I have on hand. I have one
seventy or so lines long I have half a mind to send you if you say the
word.

Ever yours / Frost

Frost did not send K.S. any work; his next (and final) appearance was in October
1962, the 50th Anniversary Issue.

Karl Shapiro to Hugh Kenner   *7 February 1951*

Dear Mr. Kenner:

I am sorry I have not acknowledged your review of Schwartz. It cre-
ates a special problem for me. We awarded Schwartz a [Guarantors']
prize for eleven of the poems in the volume you criticized. For this rea-
son I feel that we should publish a double review of the book—yours
and one more sympathetic. If this plan is repugnant to you I will return
your article. I hope, however, that you will see the merit of my sugges-
tion. In any case, I should consider it a great loss to this magazine to
have to forego your criticism because of this dilemma.

Sincerely yours, / Karl

Hugh Kenner to Karl Shapiro   *Santa Barbara, Calif.,*
28 February 1951

Dear Mr. Shapiro:

Thank you for your letter of the 7th. I don't know whether to be
more appalled that Poetry has decided to bemedal that volume, or

impressed by your readiness to run the review anyway. I can indeed see how you would find the situation embarrassing.

I should not be in the least averse to a second review running alongside mine; since, however, I should then be stacking myself against the editorial judgment of the entire magazine, I feel I should usurp your editorial capacity sufficiently to request no cuts, or no major ones. If I'm going to play devil's advocate, I've got to PLAY it. I can't afford to be a sitting duck....

In any case, I admire your calm re l'affaire Schwartz. I can think of at least two editors who would have tried to wriggle out of printing the review.

Sincerely, / Hugh Kenner

Theodore Roethke to Karl Shapiro   *Seattle, Wash., 18 June 1951*

Dear Karl:

I'm glad you liked the two poems, and are going to run them in September.

If you wish to split the [workshop] issue with Engle, that's all right with me. However, since this represents something considerably less for us than what was originally planned, I don't think I am being unreasonable in asking that the University of Washington work should lead the issue and be kept together as a group—the poetry, that is; (I don't care where my remarks go or how they're handled). I say this particularly because Iowa has had considerable publicity and these people have had nothing. Also I am assuming that everyone gets paid....

T.R.'s "Sensibility! O La" and "O Lull Me, Lull Me" received the Levinson Prize ($100) for 1951.

Kenneth Patchen to Karl Shapiro   *Old Lyme, Conn., 31 July 1951*

Dear Karl Shapiro:

Thanks a lot for your invitation to send poems to *Poetry*. As soon as I get a bit more strength back I'll put together a batch for you. I'm very grateful to you and to your wife for such generous efforts to help during my trouble.

Sincerely yours, / Kenneth Patchen

Patchen sent five poems and K.S. accepted them all on 8 August. Patchen was bedridden from rheumatoid arthritis, and out of money; Auden, Eliot, and MacLeish set up a fund to help raise $10,000 for cortisone treatments. On 14 April, Shapiro, J.V. Cunningham, Reuel Denney, Elder Olson, and Selwyn Schwartz gave a benefit reading in Chicago at Henry Miller's studio on East Fifty-seventh Street.

Karl Shapiro to Delmore Schwartz   *13 September 1951*

Dear Delmore,

We are printing an unfavorable review of *Vaudeville* [*for a Princess*] in our October issue and I want to explain that this happened unintentionally. I like the book very much and tried for a long time to get a favorable review; it turned out that the people I asked declined on the grounds of friendship for you. I finally got a review by Hugh Kenner which I held for a long time while I was looking for a counter-review. Kenner at last insisted on publication of his piece and I went through with it. The "counter-review" is written by Van O'Connor and is not strong enough to offset the effect of his.

I guess it makes matters worse telling you the background of this thing but my only aim in doing so is to keep you from being caught by surprise. I try not to govern the opinions of poetry reviewers and this policy, as in the present case, sometimes backfires.

With best wishes, / Karl

D.S. replied 22 September that he wasn't upset, since Kenner "really likes no one but Pound." In his review (October 1951), Kenner savaged the book as incompetent, silly, and sentimental.

2. Conflicts and Continual Crisis

Recalling his predicament over the Kenner review at the 75th Anniversary Celebration, Shapiro said that after that his "relations with Schwartz, which had never been of the best, suffered considerably." Shapiro soon discovered the non-editorial side of his job was even more vexing. In 1950, *Poetry* had a budget of $35,000, and a projected deficit of $20,000. The Bollingen Foundation reminded Shapiro in February that in awarding the latest $15,000 grant it made "no further commitment."

In December, Evalyn Shapiro went to New York and Washington to lobby the Bollingen trustees. K.S. wrote them that, with just one more $15,000 grant, *Poetry* would have a "period of grace" to resolve its "last financial crisis." He promised that, once on its feet again, the magazine would not need further aid. In January, the Foundation pledged $7,500 for 1951 and $5,000 for 1952. Shapiro wrote to thank them and "to repeat our promise to you that we shall not at any future time request funds for support."

In 1951–1952, the Board tried to raise funds with a new reading series. Shapiro invited MacLeish, Williams, Stevens, Marianne Moore, and E. E.

Cummings, with limited results. Dylan Thomas gave a well-attended reading on 23 April 1952, but receipts were only about $200. Shapiro tried to interest the Library of Congress in buying *Poetry's* post-1936 papers. Conrad Aiken, then Consultant in Poetry, wrote in September 1951 that they didn't have the funds, and besides the archives really belonged in Chicago.

Despite his $6,500 Editor's salary at *Poetry* (the highest to date), Shapiro had to take a teaching job, at Loyola University, to make ends meet. He also accepted out-of-town speaking engagements and led workshops, as in

Dylan Thomas after his reading for *Poetry* at The Arts Club of Chicago, 23 April 1952.

the summer of 1951 at Utah and at Nebraska in April 1953. Engle invited him to give a writing course at Iowa for a year, beginning fall 1952. Midway through the first term, Shapiro quit. He found the weekly commute taxing, and he didn't care for conducting workshops. In December 1952, Shapiro took still another job, as editor of the *Journal of Acquisitions* at the Newberry Library. Within a month, he persuaded Stanley Pargellis, director of the Newberry, to join the Board. Dr. Pargellis and the Library would eventually rescue the magazine.

In the spring of 1952, Evalyn resigned her multiple duties, to take care of the growing Shapiro family. In June, Shapiro invited Isabella Gardner to join the staff as first reader. The wealthy grandniece of Isabella Stewart Gardner, founder of the eponymous art museum in Boston, Belle served without pay. She wrote many letters of advice to aspiring poets, and became Shapiro's closest confidante. Nicholas Joost, an English professor at Loyola, volunteered as copyeditor, then became Associate and Acting Editor during Shapiro's several absences.

After his unpleasant experience with Edward Dahlberg, Shapiro turned over most of the back of the book to Joost, with instructions to keep the prose short. Joost wielded the blue pencil with a heavy hand. When Delmore Schwartz protested cuts Joost requested on an essay K.S. had accepted, the Editor allowed his excellent analysis of "T. S. Eliot's Voice and His Voices" to run as written (December 1954 and January 1955). When Joost lost his teaching job and left Chicago in the fall of

1954, Henry Rago took over and also exercised tight control on prose, as he would during his own editorship.

Wallace Fowlie became Advisory and then Foreign Editor, remaining on the masthead until 1969. Robert Mueller and Joseph Wiley, Loyola graduate students, also joined the staff. Both stayed on under Rago, and Wiley continued as an unpaid first reader for over twenty years. While living in Rome in the fall of 1951, James Merrill got word that Shapiro wanted to offer him a position at *Poetry*. K.S. wrote on 13 November to say they could discuss it when he was in Europe. Merrill was flattered, but ultimately preferred Rome to Chicago.

Shapiro had been invited to lecture at the Salzburg Seminar in January 1952, with a six-week U.S. Information Agency tour of Switzerland and Italy to follow. When he returned from his tour in late February 1952, he discovered that *Poetry* was bringing in $2,000 but spending $2,500 per month; at that rate, the magazine would be out of business by August or September. The ten-year cycle was repeating itself, and it looked like *Poetry* wouldn't make it to its 40th Anniversary. The Board tried to get support from several foundations; as usual, it got nowhere. The only hope seemed to be to approach the Bollingen again—an awkward proposition, considering the promises Shapiro had made. Finally, Mrs. Stevenson was delegated to ask for a grant—termed a "renewal"—and once more Tate and Dillon wrote letters. The Foundation came through with still another award of $5,000 for 1953—and then another, *truly* final, grant of $5,000 in 1954.

Poetry squeaked into October. The 40th Anniversary double number sold well and was the first issue to recover its costs. It featured ninety well-known contributors, from Aiken and Auden to Williams and Zaturensky. Harold Swift donated $500 for a prize for the "best" poem in the issue, which was awarded to Auden for "The Shield of Achilles." *Poetry*'s birthday party, held on 18 October at the Newberry Library, got big write-ups in the papers. *Newsweek*, *Time*, and *Life* covered the story, *Life* with a six-page spread.

It was at this rare happy moment that Shapiro chose to fire the publicity director, who had just demonstrated her effectiveness. Cornelia McNamara was well liked by the Trustees, who were very upset by Shapiro's abrupt action. At a testy meeting on 22 November, Board President Daniel Rich demanded to know why, and by what authority, the Editor had dismissed her. Shapiro explained, vaguely, he felt some of the p.r. work she had done was damaging *Poetry*. Privately, Shapiro suspected Mrs. McNamara was leaking items to the press and it was hurting fund raising. The papers were curious about *Poetry*'s possible political connections with Mrs. Stevenson, a staunch Republican who didn't hesitate to express her opinions about her ex-husband or his party. Rich said he should have been consulted, and Shapiro cited the bylaws. Rich threatened to resign. Shapiro agreed to consult on such matters in the future.

Mrs. Stevenson became Board president in January 1953. At first, she threw herself into the job. Negotiations opened with the University of Chicago Press to have it take over printing, distribution, and advertising. Early in May 1953, *Poetry* was evicted from it offices of over twenty years, as 232 Erie Street was to be razed for a parking garage. Mrs. Stevenson offered the magazine space in the Borden family's chateau-style mansion on Lake Shore Drive, which she was turning into the 1020 Art Center.

At the Board meeting of 23 May, on the eve of the move, Shapiro announced he had received a Guggenheim Fellowship for 1953–1954. Again, his timing was unfortunate. The Trustees had been annoyed by his 1952 trip, and were none too pleased when he requested a six-month leave of absence, beginning in October. He assured the Board that Nicholas Joost and Belle Gardner could handle things. From then on, relations with the Board were strained, and grew more unpleasant after a series of major and minor crises. But, as Dillon remarked, such was *Poetry*'s "normal state." The Board lurched from one stop-gap measure to the next to keep it going. Mrs. Stevenson loaned $2,000, the office's extra set of bound volumes of *Poetry* was sold for $1,500, readings and benefits were held. In September, the rest of the *Poetry* archives were sold to the University of Chicago, for $2,600. The price was paltry, but the magazine was desperate for cash.

On 2 October 1953, Shapiro left these troubles behind, and sailed for Europe with his family. He had told the Board he would continue to choose the poems, but wrote Joost that he should accept work, but from "name" poets only, if the files got low. Shapiro had planned to stay in Rome until March 1954, but he was soon low on funds. When the Shapiros' daughter Kathy became ill, they decided to return to the United States at the end of December. They stayed in Virginia until April. The Board was most anxious to have the Editor in Chicago. The deficit was now projected at $6,000, and a new problem had arisen. When the contract with the University of Chicago Press went into effect in January, it was discovered that one little clause had been overlooked: payments to *Poetry* were to be issued only twice a year. Meanwhile, all its operating capital was frozen.

Mrs. Stevenson had promised to assume financial responsibility until the end of the year. Then she changed her mind. She thought income from her Art Center would cover expenses, but her business manager informed her otherwise. She wanted her money back. (K.S. had mistaken the $2,000 loan for a gift.) In her unpublished memoirs, Julia Bowe recalled, "The meals were wonderful, but we had no money coming in and Ellen refused to raise any funds." She did attract unwanted publicity, however, and reporters lurked about hoping to get anti-Adlai quotes. Shapiro feared Mrs. Stevenson wanted to take over the magazine if it went bankrupt. *She* suspected he was trying to oust her—a stunningly bad move, if true: *Poetry* had only $100 on hand. The Board met in emergency session on 18 June. Shapiro reported the obvious: "The financial condition of the Association is alarming." Then Mrs. Stevenson's letter of resignation was read. Since *Poetry* was no longer welcome in her house, Dr. Pargellis offered it rent-free office space in the unheated top floor of the Newberry Library.

K.S. exiting the 1020 Art Center with the original
Poetry sign, after Ellen Borden Stevenson ordered
the office out of her house in 1954.

E. E. Cummings to Karl Shapiro   *New York City, 29 March 1951*

Dear KS—

how did you guess I'd forsworn all socalled
readings;or does Satan in dis guise tempt
me from the unpublic path:not, sotto rosa, that
all Hell's armies ever proved sixfifteenths as
fatal as(hence "democracy")1 goodcause

item; our non(vacationless possibly 13 years)
hero may very well find himself elsewhere next
autumn. If not, & if "poetry" expects nothing
but "the usual fifty minute performance"(no oto-
or-phautographing,banket-or-junqueting) shall
adventure Shekahgoe on October 26. But hereby
give fairest warning that "expenses" must comprehend
travel-de-superluxe . . .

Marion asks to be remembered to you each
                              —et bonne chance!

James Merrill to Karl Shapiro   *Rome, 7 November 1951*

Dear Mr Shapiro,

I have received your letter telling of the prize for my poems, also a
letter from Kimon Friar [his teacher at Amherst] about your thought I
might be interested in a position on *Poetry*. Whatever comes of the lat-
ter, I'm extremely grateful for both bits of news, having tasted over the
past months something of the curious fruitlessness that seems to be part
of putting out a book [*First Poems*]. Not that mine drew more or less
attention than it deserved, but that the quality of the response was for
the most part so very low. . . .

In respect to my working for the magazine, I can say at once that I *am*
interested, and should like to hear from you what might be expected of
me. . . . My situation at the moment is simple enough. I plan to stay
abroad, in fact steadily in Rome, for at least another eight months. I have
no external commitments here and, following my return to America,
most likely in August of next year, none outside of family visits.

Apart from interest and circumstance, however, I have any number of
suspicions as to my qualifications. I've had no experience worth men-
tioning of editorial work, and tend to feel myself, by contrast with most
of the literary people I've met, either ignorant or dense. Nevertheless, I
hope to hear from you. . . .

Merrill had just been awarded the Harriet Monroe Memorial Prize for "Hotel de L'Univers et Portugal," "The Lovers," and three other poems in the September issue. K.S. wrote him 13 November that they could talk about the job when he was in Rome in February.

Kimon Friar to Karl Shapiro   New York City, 26 December 1951

Dear Karl:

. . . I wrote to Jimmy Merrill about your proposal, and he answered me some time ago that he was going to write you and to accept, and to ask for further information. But I've not heard since: I don't imagine that the two bottles of champagne which he sent me for Christmas is to celebrate anything in particular! I hope that you will both work out some arrangement: the magazine will be good for Jimmy, and Jimmy good for the magazine. Marianne Moore told Kathleen Raine the other day that she considered Jimmy to be the best of the younger poets.

I'm enclosing three of my poems. If Jimmy is on the staff now, don't send them to him for decision; that would be too strange. . . .

Theodore Roethke to Karl Shapiro   [Seattle, Wash.], 23 May 1952

Dear Karl:

Here's this damned [Dylan] Thomas piece, and I'm of a very divided mind about it: one minute I think it's a hot item that says things that should be said and effects a rough justice; another, it seems a damned impertinence to say such things in print about a contemporary. And, of course, I am v. fond of the little bugger.

So you call it, old chum. And I won't be sore if you say no. . . .

Roethke's review of Thomas's *In Country Sleep and Other Poems* was titled "One Ring-tailed Roarer to Another" and appeared in December 1952; he used the pseudonym "Winterset Rothberg."

Allen Tate to Karl Shapiro   Burlington, Vt., 22 June 1952

Dear Karl:

Certainly I will send a letter to the Bollingen people. The magazine seems to me to be in excellent shape. If the verse you print is not always too good, that is scarcely your fault. You can't write it all your-self; you can't print better poetry than is being written. I do wish the Bollingen people would set up this subsidy as a permanent thing, so that you would not have to go through the routine all over again every year. But I suppose that's too much to expect.

I'm glad you liked the poem [unidentified]. A good many years ago a reaction began to set in in me against "explicating" poems; so that I was disqualified as a new critic before I could become one. . . .

May 23, 1952

Dear Karl:

Here's this damned Thomas piece, and I'm of a very divided mind about it! One minute I think it's a hot item that says things that should be said and effects a rough justice; another, it seems a damned impertinence to say such things in print about a contemporary. And of course I am v. fond of the little bugger.

So you call it old chum. And I won't be sore if you say no. But I don't want to make changes — not any, except possibly to delete the sentence beginning 'And there you have it, etc.' in the

Roethke to Shapiro, 23 May 1952: "Here's this damned Thomas piece...."

Fr. M. James, O.C.S.O. to Karl Shapiro   *Our Lady of Gethsemani Abbey, Trappist, Kent., 5 July 1952*

Dear Mr. Shapiro,

Your letter of June 17 addressed to our good Father Louis (Thomas Merton) in regard to his contributing to the October issue of your magazine has been received.

Unhappily our higher superiors have forbidden our authors to write for such purposes.

Therefore, dear Mr. Shapiro, we regret that we are not in [a] position to cooperate with you in that particular way. However, be assured that all the 270 monks of Gethsemani will continue to pray for you, for all your needs, in the daily round of our Trappist Cistercian Life of prayer and sacrifice.

All for Jesus—thru Mary—with a smile,

fr. M. James, O.C.S.O. / Abbot

Merton entered the monastery in 1941; he had last appeared in *Poetry* in October 1949.

Robert Lowell to Karl Shapiro [postcard] *Verona, Italy, 20 July 1952*

Dear Karl,

We hear that C. Day Lewis (who is with us here) has won the $500 [prize for best poem in the 40th Anniversary Issue]. We are trying to borrow some of it now. Allen [Tate]. — I have written to Dr Sitwell correcting her. I am writing poems which won't win prizes for other numbers. Here is a winner: AS I ENTER MY 2ND CHILDHOOD. Stephen [Spender].

Could I have the cheque by return post, please, as I am paying for all their dinners. C.D.L.

[P.S.] This is all by me in disguised handwritings. Cal.

Lowell is mocking Sitwell and Spender, who refused to be in the issue, thinking it was also a "contest." Apparently Day Lewis apprised him of the fact; but all the poets, including Sitwell, were in Italy at the time. See letters below. Auden won the prize for "The Shield of Achilles."

Stephen Spender to Karl Shapiro   *Gstaad, Switzerland,*
                                                                          9 August 1952

Dear Karl,

Just after I wrote to you three days ago about the poems I had lunch with Dr Edith Sitwell who told me she had decided not to send poems to you because she would not enter into a competition for $500.

Knowing this puts me in the position where I certainly cannot enter into such a contest myself. To send something in would imply that I disagreed with her. But in fact I do support her in this because I do not think it very wise of Poetry to write round to poets as distinguished as Dr Sitwell asking them for poems to support the magazine and then telling them that the poems are going to be marked by a prize-awarding committee. It had not occurred to me that I would possibly win such a prize, so previously I had felt indifferent about the competition, but now I feel I should support Dr Sitwell in her action by my own non-action.

At the same time I am pleased to have been asked. Please treat this letter as personal. It is written without the knowledge of Dr Sitwell.

Yours / Stephen Spender

Karl Shapiro to Stephen Spender   *12 August 1952*

Dear Stephen,

Your letter about submitting a poem to our anniversary issue was a disappointment here. Only one other poet raised the objection you did about the prize, but we received poems from almost everyone else including Auden, Cummings, Marianne Moore, de la Mare, Day Lewis, Graves, Wallace Stevens, W. C. Williams, and about fifty others. I do think you misunderstood the intention of the prize and I would be obliged if you would correct Edith Sitwell on this point. POETRY magazine has given about ten prizes a year since it was founded forty years ago. The intention of these prizes has never been to create a competition but to help support the poets. I myself have felt scruples about awarding annual prizes for poetry but the great majority of poets seem to be grateful for this kind of interest. The $500 award for the anniversary issue is intended primarily to draw attention to the magazine in the hope that the public will help solve our financial problem. You probably know that it is easy to obtain money for prizes and almost impossible to obtain it for the more practical purposes of running a magazine. I do hope you will send us poems for use in a later issue of POETRY.

As ever, / Karl

Karl Shapiro to Oscar Williams   *28 August 1952*

Dear Oscar:

I could kick Dylan in the rump for not sending us a poem for the October issue, because I think he would have stood a wonderful chance of winning the $500 prize. Anyhow, we are interested in going ahead with a Dylan Thomas number of POETRY, if we can shove D.T. in our direction. We already have an excellent review by Theodore Roethke (really a kind of poem) of his last book and we can hold this as a nucleus.

One thing we would insist on, as we are a literary magazine and not a scholarly journal: we must have a new poem of Thomas' to feature in an issue devoted to him. Then we could use sections of work sheets of the previously printed poem. As you know, we cannot publish anything which has appeared in print in any form before. Of course we would like to publish his letter to you along with the work sheet material. And of course we could use photographs of Dylan in an issue of this kind.

We cannot pay anything in advance, not because we don't want to but because we simply are operating hand to mouth. Payment in this issue would be made as follows: verse 50¢ per line and prose $5 per page. These are the usual rates but they could be increased by counting the work sheets as verse instead of as prose.

We are really interested in doing something for Dylan and for many reasons. I hope you will act as a middle man for us. I can't get a word out of him.

Cordially, / Karl

Max Bodenheim appeared on the scene yesterday, apparently to become a Chicagoan. If you have any advice about him I would certainly appreciate it.

Oscar Williams to Karl Shapiro   New York City, 12 September 1952

Dear Karl,

I've written to Dylan asking him to let us have a new poem. But I am afraid that there isn't much of a chance we'll get a new one. The six poems in his last book took him, it seems, exactly six years to write. And if you'd look at the 140 odd working sheets of his *Poem on His Birthday* you would realize how pains-taking and time-consuming his special kind of writing is. . . .

My best to Evalyn, Isabella and yourself, as always, / Oscar

P.S. I don't know what to say about Bodenheim; give him as much as you can spare of the milk of human kindness in the digestible form of cash, to make his last days a bit less gruesome. Dylan and I helped him out a bit in New York when we ran into him in the Village.

Nelson Algren to Karl Shapiro   Gary, Ind., 3 November 1952

Dear Karl,

Your party [for the 40th Anniversary] was a success, thank you for asking me. My sole misgiving is whether I was right in insisting that Mrs. Ellen Stevenson wear my Stevenson button. I'm not sure I was right about this. But I do feel that you ought to have a party every week, as I have any number of friends who are fond of parties. . . .

Karl Shapiro to Edward Dahlberg 4 *December 1952*

Dear Edward:

I think the review [of Aiken's *Ushant*] is extremely good and we are going to use it in the Feb., 1953 number of POETRY—thereby ending my friendship with Conrad Aiken. I would like to call the article "A Long Lotus Sleep". This is a phrase from your opening page and I think describes the text.

All the best to you, / K.S.

Edward Dahlberg to Karl Shapiro *[Berkeley, Calif.],*
9 December 1952

Dear Karl:

Thank you very much for your kind words about my review. The title you suggest is very agreeable to me. I am troubled by your predicament. I would not have asked you for the book had I suspected that I would have to negate the work. I knew that he was a consultant for Poetry magazine, and imagined that there was a friendship between you. Then there is the publisher, Charles A. Pearce, my friend, who brought out the book. . . . I can tell you very plainly that I had no stomach for the task, and that I had the least will to impugn this author. I had met him once at Brewster and then at a party at Jones Street. I believe I wrote you that I considered him a fat, sleepy Silenus, but I did not care to rely upon my impressions of his face. It is true I am often very dogmatic about books I have not read, and sometimes I go to the book to prove my own feelings. . . .

I deeply hope that Conrad Aiken will not believe that either you or I is the Iscariot. I owe him honesty and you can give him no less. . . . All of us write badly much of the time, at least more often than not, so why should we blame and hate those who remind us of it when it is essential to do so.

Affectionately, / Edward

Conrad Aiken to Karl Shapiro *London, 2 March 1953*

Dear Karl:

That piece of Dahlberg's on USHANT—I won't dignify it with the name of review—seems to me to go altogether too far, and in more directions than one! Into most of these, since they are in part matters of taste, I don't here propose to go; but there is one which I *do* want to discuss and that is the question of whether or not it is libelous. To call

USHANT an "ill-concealed cento" and then follow with a page of implications as to plagiarism, concluding with the statement that Aiken's pilferings do not amuse is, it appears to me, damaging in the extreme, and I am going to take up the matter with Cap Pearce and Charlie Duell as soon as I get to New York. It doesn't help Dahlberg either that approximately 90% of his quotes from USHANT are inaccurate, garbled, or distorted, including one entire sentence, which he puts in quotes, and which does not exist as such in the book. Naturally, I am most unhappy about all this, as it concerns us personally, and I want to assure you that it in no way affects my feelings towards yourself. On this score, I can only hope, when you have had time to consider the situation, that you will agree with me that something should be done about it, and some sort of amends made. What form this should take, I don't know—perhaps something will occur to you. A *riposte* by someone not so obviously and maliciously biased, or a statement by yourself, or both? Anyway, I suggest that you give it thought, and perhaps drop me a line at my New York address, as above—I shall arrive there March 12th.

Yours as always, / Conrad

Karl Shapiro to Conrad Aiken   24 March 1953

Dear Conrad,

We have Elizabeth Pollet's letter, the Eithne Wilkins, and several others from less known people. We intend to use one of these protests only and follow it with an editorial apology for Dahlberg's bad manners.... We have let Dahlberg rave because I credited him with a sense of honor and a sincere belief in the bad state of letters, etc. Apparently he [is] only another mad dog....

I try to put myself in your place in a matter of this kind, but I find it hard to do. I have seen so many of these literary betrayals, as I know you have, that I am more curious than shocked by them. I can't tell you how much I went out of my way to help Dahlberg. I've never met him and had no desire to. He wrote pitiful letters about the ascetic poet, the evil of the age, etc. etc. and sent long poems which I worked on for him, advised him about, published. When he asked to review *Ushant* I did not give it a thought. I had read the book and was quite carried away by it. I was stunned by his review but did not feel it was my right to censor it. It was only *after* the acceptance of the piece that I began to receive letters from him asking for a big-scale Attack on the moderns. Then my heart began to sink. This is beside the point, no doubt, but I thought I would let you know a little of the background of the piece. The whole point is that a critic may hold a strong and even violent viewpoint which is the opposite of mine, and we will give him space.

As ever, / Karl

Karl Shapiro to Edward Dahlberg   *24 March 1953*

Dear Edward,

We have a number of protests about your review, protests on the grounds that you were personally abusive and that you misquoted Aiken many times. I have decided to print one of the letters and to append an apology for the misquotations and the personal element in your article. It would please me very much if you yourself would apologize for these things. One man who wrote in [Rolfe Humphries] said that he had frequently roasted Aiken in print himself but could not understand how we could pass on a personal attack. Reading your review again in the light of your most recent letters I can see that the personal element is there. I don't mind saying that I consider this a kind of betrayal of trust. We never question a critic's opinion of the work he is reviewing, and we give him every liberty we can; but we do not mean this as an opportunity to express private peeves and rant. I have watched your work a long time and thought enough of it to encourage it in print; it seemed to me that you had strength and true conviction. Now I am inclined to wonder whether you are just another embittered writer who is out for the kill. Your proposal to launch a full-scale attack on the moderns is very disturbing to me because it puts your previous work in a baleful light. If you want to write us a note explaining the mistakes in the review and the idea of your approach to Aiken, we'll print it. Or maybe you'd rather reply to the letter we intend to publish. If so, I'll send you a copy. We're not going for feuds or symposiums. We want honest opinions within the ordinary limits of literary order.

As ever, / Karl

Edward Dahlberg to Karl Shapiro   *Santa Monica, Calif.,*
                                          26 March 1953

Dear Karl:

I hope I was not peevish with you. I do not care one jot about the piece. I worked hard on it, and the errors were very niggling. I would not garble any one's book for the purpose of destroying or praising it. I have poor eyesight, one eye, in fact, and sometimes I feel that it is as dim as old Isaac's. Dropping an s or a comma cannot mar even a good book. You must believe me that Mr. Aiken's volume was a poor one. I have no subtle reason for impugning him, and I was playing neither Machiavel's fox nor the lion in assailing him. . . .

I wish you could find sufficient space in your own head and heart to realize that Poetry magazine is very far from good. . . .

Conrad Aiken to Karl Shapiro   *New York City, 27 March 1953*

Dear Karl:

I'm not too damned happy about all this, for I can't help feeling that you show a tendency to run with the hare and hunt with the hounds. God knows I agree wholeheartedly with your defense of the reviewer's right to say his say uncensored; but when this is carried to the lengths of permitting him to make an obscene (for that is the word) and libelous and mendacious (in misquoting) attack I think you must agree with me it is beyond all bounds of morality or decency, and almost suggests an editorial condonation.

How could you honestly, if you say you were "carried away" by USHANT, lend yourself to that sort of disloyalty to the right interests of literature—? I don't get it. Nor can I for a moment agree with you that there can EVER be any justification for "personal criticism", as you put it: true criticism is *never* personal. In all this you seem to me to be begging the question, or trying to get out from under.

I can only say that I *hope* you will make proper amends, but that if you don't I must naturally reserve the right to take the affair elsewhere, or even to court, much as I would dislike having to do the latter. But I do think, and will say again, that there should be a resounding and emphatic disclaimer of the entire charge of "centoism" and plagiarism and pilfering, and in my opinion you should print *both* the Wilkins and Pollet letters, and list the others. Together with a listing of the "errors", if that is what they were! . . . [sic] And finally, it's all very well to express pity and sorrow for Dahlberg, but holy cats what about a little pity and sorrow for the Injured Party, ME? Nor, may I add, is this the first time in the past forty years that POETRY has manhandled me: the record ain't so hot. . . . [sic] And let me add just one thing more—that if you don't feel you can print the two letters then I will suggest to Delmore Schwartz that PARTISAN print the other. This seems to me only fair—it will help to repair at least a *little* of the inestimable damage *you* have done me.

as always / Conrad

Karl Shapiro to Conrad Aiken   *30 March 1953*

Dear Conrad,

Neither am I happy about this. I am still trying to explain to you that I do not impose my opinion of books on our reviewers. You seem to be willing to hold it against me that I liked *Ushant*. I do not, as you say, run with the hounds: I am against hunting, literary or otherwise. You have every right to feel injured and angry but I think your anger should be directed to the proper source. We stick with the idea of freedom of opinion in criticism; we are one of the few magazines in a position to do this. . . .

Your threats of bringing down the law on us only make me wonder about your temper. Dahlberg did not libel you; maybe he libeled Henry James. I do think his *tone* was offensive and we are going to apologize for that. The misquotations were not as serious as you at present think; they were definitely not deliberate. As Dahlberg did not return the book we did not recheck his citations. But we shall also apologize for these errors.

I fail to see how the review did "inestimable damage" to the book, but I can understand that the hurt to your pride was deep. I am sure that everyone who has ever published a book has suffered in this way.

As ever, / Karl

Dahlberg wrote yet another letter to K.S. 4 April, saying: "I am very sorry that any one should have thought that I attacked Conrad Aiken's USHANT for any other reason than that it is an untalented book."

Karl Shapiro to Elizabeth Bishop   *4 August 1953*

Dear Elizabeth:

I never thought I'd see the day when we would reject a poem of yours [unidentified] but we do so daringly today. I hope that our courage will be rewarded with a long poem of yours.

Evalyn and I are going to Italy this fall. I got myself a Guggenheim and hope to do some writing in Rome. We hope you are well and we send our love.

Nothing has happened about the L.C. [Library of Congress]. Williams got sick and never took up the reins and I think that [Luther] Evans [the Librarian] is leaving the L.C. for UNESCO. It is all unusually fishy. . . .

Kenner wrote K.S. 12 February 1953 that he had heard the reason W.C.W. was objected to as Consultant in Poetry was that he was accused of being a Communist; the "proof": he had been to Europe several times.

John Ciardi to Karl Shapiro   *Medford, Mass., 5 September 1953*

Dear Karl,

All goes well, I hope. Ciardi's blossoming and Judith did me a son to go with her previous very superior job of daughtering. Hope you are the same. . . .

I'm shifting to Rutgers to have a shot at organizing a Creative Writing Program. Should you know of any geniuses who will write great literature which I can then pretend I taught them how, by all means throw them in this direction.

Best to you and Evalyn, / John

Edith Sitwell to Karl Shapiro   *London, 30 March 1954*

Dear Karl Shapiro,

Your letter gave me the greatest pleasure, both because it was written by a poet for whose poetry I have a high esteem, and because of its contents.

I hold it a great honor that I should have been asked by you to write this elegy for Dylan Thomas, and I will, of course, do so.

I cannot believe he is dead. I knew him since he was twenty-two. Was he a friend of yours? One could not know him without loving him. . . .

Sitwell's "Elegy for Dylan Thomas" was printed in the memorial issue, November 1955, which included facsimiles of his mss. and work sheets, some of them owned by Ellen Borden Stevenson.

Randall Jarrell to Karl Shapiro   *Laguna Beach, Calif., 7 June 1954*

Dear Karl:

. . . I had an awfully good time in Chicago and hardly minded the unfinancialness of the trip. All they did was send me a check for $75 and my air and airport-bus expenses were $102; if *Poetry* can fix up the difference, or get them to, that would be nice. . . .

I have several funny poems, mostly short, one longer; if you decide to have that funny issue tell me and I'll send the funny poems.

I'd like to send greetings to *Poetry*'s secretary and to tell both her and you that *Vogue*'s asked me to write an article on sports cars and sports car racing ["The Little Cars"]—isn't this a case of Heaven smiling on one's vices or hobbies or sillinesses or whatever they are? And we really are going to buy that Mercedes—*Pictures [from an Institution*, R.J.'s satiri-cal novel] has been doing pretty well. . . .

Jarrell appeared on 21 July 1954 in a lecture series directed by Galway Kinnell and co-sponsored by *Poetry* and University of Chicago Downtown Center; it ended after one season.

Randall Jarrell to Karl Shapiro   *[Laguna Beach, Calif., July 1954]*

Dear Karl:
. . . Thanks a lot for the Chicago-Reading-Tour-expense-check—I certainly had a good time. It's hard for me to imagine *Poetry* moved so soon, but it's a lot better to be on the second floor of a library [actually, the attic] than on the second floor of an evaporated milk fortune, I guess. . . .

James Wright to Poetry   *Seattle, Wash., 21 July 1954*

Dear Sirs:
I realize that you must have to go through thousands of poems; and that it is therefore presumptuous of me to submit so long a manuscript. I apologize. However, somebody has got to fight for a hearing for the kind of poetry which, as far as younger people in America are con-cerned, is being neglected. I mean the kind which seeks not for bril-liant and purely lyrical effects, but which tries to simplify and harden its purely linguistic devices (perhaps in the manner of somebody like Crabbe) and to exploit the areas of story-telling and the development of character.

The enclosed poem is not primarily about war, of course. It is proba-bly about guilt, even about suicide. But in spite of its general themes, I hope its details are localized enough to give it a certain concrete validity.

I have been pessimistic about sending it anywhere, because it is so long. But I know that your policy involves an interest in every kind of poetry; and I hope that reading this poem will at least be of some inter-est to you.

Thank you. / Sincerely, / James Wright

"The Resurrected" and "Elegy in a Firelit Room" appeared in July 1954. "A Pre-sentation of Two Birds to My Son" was printed in January 1955, followed in Sep-tember by "Morning Hymn to a Dark Girl," "Erinna to Sappho," and "Sappho's Child," which won the Eunice Tietjens Memorial Prize for 1955. Auden chose Wright's first book, *The Green Wall*, for the Yale Younger Poets series in 1957.

Frank O'Hara to Karl Shapiro   *New York City, 13 August 1954*

Dear Mr Shapiro,

I hope you had a very good year in Europe. It was kind of you to write me good luck in that Iowa Fellowship thing. I didn't get one but Robert Lowell wrote me about my manuscript of poems and that was even better. He liked, with reservations, the long poem I've included in this batch, which is why I'm sending it; it isn't anything you'll want to print, so if you are very busy you may want to skip it (*Second Avenue*). The others were all written after you went away and I take the liberty of sending so many because you've always taken an interest in them. I hope it's not too big a batch. . . .

I was sorry to see Harry Roskolenko's review [July 1954] of Kenneth Koch, whose work I admire. If it is at all feasible, I'd like to write a short letter defending it—it seems to me that there is a great precedent for his style and that he is both open and skillful at it; his true talent appears in the light of Whitman, early Stevens, the Cavalier poets, and in French people like Benjamin Péret, Jacques Prévert, Raymond Queneau, André Breton. In the latter connection, he seems to have been influenced by the French poets who were most influenced by American writing, notably Queneau. But it is right that your space be devoted to poetry rather than to literary cross-references; I did think it too bad that Koch, who is quite felicitous, was made to seem like a School Wit who couldn't think yet but was learning.

Anyhow, I hope you like these poems.

Sincerely yours, / Frank O'Hara

As a juror for the Hopwood Prize, K.S. had helped O'Hara get a scholarship to Michigan. In December 1951, *Poetry* gave O'Hara his first major publication with "Ann Arbor Variations." The November 1954 issue led off with "Aus Einem April," "Poem in January," "Romanze, or the Music Students," "Meditations in an Emergency," and "Chez Jane." O'Hara defended Koch in the March 1955 issue: "His technique is opposed to that academic and often turgid development by which many poets gain praise for their 'achievement,' an achievement limited usually to the mastery of one phase of Yeats . . . . Most important of all, he is not *dull*." In his riposte (June 1955) Roskolenko insulted Koch's work as "verbal nonsense" and "infantilism." O'Hara wished to reply to him again, but Rago thought the debate should stop there.

T. S. Eliot to Karl Shapiro   *London, 14 August 1954*

Dear Shapiro,

Any powers of persuasion I possess are at the disposal of POETRY in any appeal for public support.

I don't believe many people in the U.S.A. realise how important

POETRY looks to people abroad: I mean, to English-speaking poetry-lovers and lovers of poetry who read English. There is nothing quite like it anywhere else: POETRY has had imitators, but has so far survived them all. It is an American Institution. To poetry-readers abroad it is still the magazine to which we look first, to make us aware of whatever new poetic talent appears in the U.S.A. And American twentieth-century poetry, as an export article, is bringing in higher returns in the way of "cultural prestige" in foreign countries than most American citizens realize.

And POETRY could do still more for poetry if it could do more for the poets: the more support it gets from the public, the better it can pay the poets. I can hardly believe it possible that POETRY should be allowed to die: but what I want is to see it *flourish*.

Yours sincerely, / T. S. Eliot

In thanking Eliot, 24 August, K.S. noted: "We have always suffered as a magazine from too much fame; people take *Poetry* for granted and are always surprised to be told that we need assistance."

Karl Shapiro to Hugh Kenner   *14 September 1954*

Dear Hugh:

. . . This is just to answer one question of yours. I have no sheepskins of any description. The extent of my education was two undergraduate years at Hopkins. Five years after I left there, I returned as an associate professor. Consequently, I have a record of teaching but no record of learning. As a matter of fact, the only thing I would ever dare try to "teach" is what is called "creative writing." That's the only kind of job I would apply for and the only kind I would take.

Henry Rago and I have been discussing your articles for *Poetry*. They are by far the best criticism we have, and we hate to drop them. George Dillon wrote the other day that we should give a critic's prize and that you are the only person who would be eligible for it. I'm going to try to dig up some money for that purpose, but I don't know if I can. Rago and I want to get rid of as much of the prose drivel as we can, and we are working out plans to hold down all reviews to about a paragraph and to turn over the whole prose section of *Poetry* to one critic per month. Meanwhile, we are trying to find ways to use up stuff we have already accepted and to hold onto you as our main reviewer. You may not get much direct response from the articles of yours we publish in *Poetry* but I know that your reviews have strengthened the magazine considerably.

Many thanks for your information again.

Cordially, / Karl

3. The Final Months

After almost five years of turmoil, Shapiro started thinking about a change. On 27 September, he wrote Joost, "I feel that I can't go on working at two jobs forever." He told the Board he would leave within six months or a year. By late fall, Shapiro was offered a visiting professorship at Berkeley, starting in January 1955. At a special meeting on 29 November, he informed the Board and said he would be willing to edit the magazine, without pay, from California. As his replacement, he recommended Henry Rago, who had been on staff only a few months. By early spring 1955, Shapiro had decided definitely not to return, but he asked the Board to make his resignation official as of September. In the summer of 1955, Shapiro made a tour of Ireland, Italy, and India for the State Department, and started to gather poetry from those countries for special issues. Rago was already firmly in control months before the masthead was changed in October.

Ironically, almost as soon as Shapiro left Chicago, *Poetry*'s fortunes turned. Benefits were held, new donors were found, bankruptcy was narrowly avoided. The magazine's contract with the University of Chicago Press was renegotiated, and subscription income was released. In his last

Henry Rago, prize-winner W. H. Auden, and Karl Shapiro a 40th Anniversary party, October 1952. Note photograph of Edna St. Vincent Millay.

two years, drastic economizing had forced Shapiro to slash printing expenses. *Poetry* was put out with ugly typography on cheap paper bound with staples, reflecting the cut-rate production. It was in this amateurish, low-budget format that Philip Levine, William Dickey, Donald Finkel, Thom Gunn, Donald Hall, Mona Van Duyn, James Wright, and other newcomers made their first appearances in *Poetry*. Henry Rago made it a priority to restore the magazine to its former elegance. At its November 1954 meeting, the trustees had voted to make Rago "temporary" Editor, at half Shapiro's salary, "until the Board was in a position to choose and pay a new editor." They added: "his position was not to be regarded as a succession." Rago stayed for almost fifteen years.

Stephen Spender to Karl Shapiro   London, 15 September 1954

Dear Shapiro,

Poetry must be unique among all magazines which have supported poets, in being representative over a great many years of the best, and simply the best, poems being written. All other magazines fall down sooner or later over supporting the "conventional" against the "advanced" or some clique against all the other poets. *Poetry* has never made poets members of an established institution of past poetry, it has never set the old against the young or the young against the old. . . .

K.S. asked Spender and several other poets for endorsements, to help raise funds; they ran on the inside covers of the magazine, Spender's in January 1955.

Delmore Schwartz to Karl Shapiro   Pittstown, N.J., 27 September 1954

Dear Karl:

I'm extremely sorry to have to say I can't consent to the cutting of my piece: how an essay of seventeen pages could be reduced to three hundred words is, under the circumstances, a mystery to me . . . . I consulted you about the length of the essay before writing, spoke to Joost also, worked at it for two weeks, and counted on payment for it as part of the extremely small living by means of which Elizabeth [Pollet, his wife] and I are trying to get through the present year without the interruptions of teaching. . . .

There are other considerations too, which would make me feel that your suggestion that I cooperate in this way is quite unreasonable, apart from my own financial problems. For example, you have had the essay for more than three months, and if, during that time, you had expressed misgivings about its merits, or some other difficulty, I would have with-

drawn it and been able to publish it elsewhere . . . . [I]n the twenty years
that I've written for reviews I've not heard of anything of the sort: but
the contrary is the case, articles are paid for, though a magazine sus-
pends publication, and commissioned pieces are paid for even when
they prove unusable.

. . . If you like, I'll waive the question of publication, though with
acute disappointment. But I can't waive the question of payment in full,
which, as you must know, is customary practice. So will you please
decide about publishing the essay—which I regretfully make a matter
of your option—and however you decide in that regard, see that I
receive the payment in full on which I've counted for months, immedi-
ately if it's possible at all, or if that is too difficult, let me know when I
can expect it.

                                      With best wishes, / Delmore

William Carlos Williams to Karl Shapiro   *Rutherford, N.J.,*
                                                   29 October 1954

Dear Karl:

How the time runs on! It's almost time for me to grow young again.
We're reading Proust's À la recherche du temps perdu for the first time,
it is an enlightening experience—which only confirms my suspicion
that if you dig deep enough as I knew as a child you will come to
China.

Thank you for transmitting Mrs. Levinson's check. I will write to her
at once thanking her for her generosity. How are ya, anyhow? I never
did get it clear in my head what happened to Poetry's central office
except that it has been moved. No matter, you are comfortably housed
somewhere near where you have always been and carrying on as
always. Keep it up.

                                      Sincerely yours, / Bill

George Dillon to Karl Shapiro   *Charleston, S.C., 6 November 1954*

Dear Karl:

I have been occupied with visitors or would have written sooner to
thank you for your letter telling me of the California appointment. As
much as I regret the loss to the magazine, I cannot doubt that this is the
best thing for you and your family, and I am glad to know that the
decision is off your mind.

Poetry can seem the most thankless job in the world, while one is
doing it, but I am sure that you will not eventually regret the experi-
ence. The rewards are of the delayed-action variety; it is necessary to

await the gradual un-numbing of the sensibilities.You will keep the sat-
isfaction of having carried the magazine on for five years, through a
time of difficult (and very necessary) changes and increasing costs.You
will be leaving it in what appears to be an alert and serious phase, with a
good staff and a good organization behind it. No-one whose opinion
you could value will fail to estimate that accomplishment. In any event,
the record speaks for itself, and it stands on the library shelves from
Bangor to Berkeley. . . .

CHAPTER XVIII

Henry Rago: The Early Years, 1955–1962

1. A New Era and a Wider Door

Henry Rago seemed fated to be Editor of *Poetry*. Rago began writing verse at age seven and started submitting to the magazine when he entered high school. He had letterhead printed: "Henry Wadsworth Rago, Litterateur," with the adopted middle name after Longfellow, his favorite poet. His father was a businessman (Rago Brothers Funeral Homes), and took a businesslike attitude toward his avocation. He brought the embarrassed fourteen-year-old to Harriet Monroe for a professional opinion. She understood the situation perfectly, encouraged the boy, and recommended he read more modern poets. She commented on pieces she returned, then gave her "protégé" his first acceptance when he was fifteen. Like the Founder, Rago would frequently offer comforting words and detailed criticism to fledgling poets when he himself became the arbiter at *Poetry*.

Between his debut in December 1931 and his appointment as Acting Editor, Rago had over thirty poems and a dozen articles or reviews in the magazine. Monroe and Zabel wrote him recommendations for college. After studying law at DePaul University and passing the bar exam, he took degrees in theology and philosophy at Notre Dame, where he became good friends with John Nims. He served in counterintelligence during the war—he met T. S. Eliot in London during the Blitz—and was among the first soldiers to enter Paris after the Liberation. Several times in his three years there, Rago visited Alice B. Toklas and talked poetry with Gertrude Stein on long walks along the Seine.

In 1947, he started teaching at the University of Chicago, where Hayden Carruth was in graduate studies. Soon they were boon companions. Henry liked to take Hayden to a club run by "Bottles" Capone, brother of Al, whose funeral Rago Brothers had handled. By all accounts, Rago was a brilliant lecturer and highly popular with students. Even so, the University failed to reappoint him in 1954, and he was very pleased to accept Shapiro's invitation to join *Poetry*.

The *Poetry* staff in the attic of the Newberry Library, 1956: Robert Mueller, Margaret Danner, Elizabeth Wright, Henry Rago, and Frederick Bock.

Rago never practiced as an attorney, but his approach to both the business and the literary sides of the magazine was lawyerlike: measured, methodical, meticulous in every detail. While Shapiro kept the title until fall 1955, Rago took over more and more of the Editor's work. Although the latest crisis had passed, *Poetry*'s future was still in doubt. There was no time to lose in getting affairs in order.

As Editor in chief, Rago ran a tight ship. The offices of *Poetry*, which had always had a clubby atmosphere, became much more professional. Probably no editor ever expended more energy than Rago on every aspect of running the magazine and establishing policies, right down to the use of paperclips (bronze only). Certainly no previous Editor spent more time communicating with poets, even aspirants whose chances of seeing print were slim. A great number of letters in the voluminous files he left run to two, three, or more pages. Often Rago gave detailed suggestions for changes, always with such gentleness that it was difficult to argue with him. His explanations for returning manuscripts were so courteous that he got letters of appreciation from poets he rejected.

In the first half of his tenure, Rago's diplomatic skills were tested with perennial problem cases like the prickly hipster Kenneth Rexroth and the paranoid Edward Dahlberg, while his kindness was demonstrated by the help he offered Delmore Schwartz, Kenneth Patchen, and other writers in emotional, physical, or financial distress. Rago's tact and generosity continued through the quarrelsome sixties, and sustained his friendships with a remarkable diversity of writers who were often not on speaking terms with each other. Many proponents of the emerging styles were contentious, carrying on factional disputes even more heated than the theoretical and technical debates during the early days of Modernism. It is a measure of Rago's openness, and the magazine's continuing prestige, that old practitioners and young experimentalists alike were accommodated in *Poetry*.

Considering his conservative background and self-limited range as a lyric poet, Rago was surprisingly broad-minded in his selections. He was deferential to senior writers, and managed to win back a number of people who had been offended during the Shapiro years or held grievances going back further still. But he was particularly responsive to younger poets, whether formalists or free spirits. Rago's choices for *Poetry's* annual prizes in 1955—Thom Gunn, William Carlos Williams (for "Of Asphodel, Book 2"), John Ciardi, Philip Booth, James Wright, and V. R. "Bunny" Lang—indicate the catholicity of his tastes from the start. Equally diverse were the poets he presented in the January 1956 issue, all making their first appearances in *Poetry*: Ann Stanford, Carolyn Kizer, Vi Gale, John Hollander, Richard Howard, Leonard Nathan, John N. Morris, and Christopher Middleton. The prose section held essays by Williams on Wallace Stevens, Kenner on Wyndham Lewis, and Kenneth Burke on Marianne Moore's *Predilections*.

Throughout his tenure, Rago made Monroe's Open Door wide enough to admit almost every literary innovator or trendsetter of note. While maintaining a place for tradition, the magazine closely mirrored what was developing into the second revolution in America poetry—a return to the radical ideas and methods of *Poetry's* original Modernists, which had been tamed by the Academy in the thirties.

In the early fifties, the influence of Eliot's later poetry and criticism was still strong, particularly his notions of emotional restraint and "impersonality." Elaborating on Eliot's ideas, I. A. Richards, William Empson, and John Crowe Ransom (whose 1941 book *The New Criticism* fixed the name) preached the virtues of control, ironic distancing, ambiguity, and scrupulous handling of form. The poets coming of age in the fifties were trained to read and write poetry according to the code of the New Criticism, as neatly expounded in Cleanth Brooks and Robert Penn Warren's *Understanding Poetry* (first edition, 1938), a standard textbook in undergraduate English classes well into the sixties.

Shapiro had begun attacking New Critical doctrine in the mid-forties. By the late fifties and early sixties, an increasing number of younger poets (and a few older ones) rebelled against or simply ignored the academic strictures and started to pursue a variety of new directions in poetry. Many found inspiration in the example of Whitman and, above all, Dr. Williams, who received house calls from young acolytes.

Whatever his personal preferences, Rago showcased a wide spectrum of these shifting aesthetics in the magazine. He was especially welcoming to the poets associated with Black Mountain College. By 1962, he published nearly two dozen poems by Robert Creeley, and almost as many by Robert Duncan and Denise Levertov. Charles Olson, the theorist of this Projectivist group, appeared more selectively in 1962 and after.

James Wright in a snapshot sent about the time of his first appearance, 1954.

Rago was extremely supportive to James Dickey, and the two were fairly close for a time. Rago also had cordial relations with Robert Bly, and regularly featured Bly and others sometimes labeled as the Deep Image "school," particularly Donald Hall and James Wright, a favorite of the Editor's. Frequent contributors likewise were Galway Kinnell, David Ignatow, and W. S. Merwin, among others loosely linked as Surrealists.

Most of the poets in the "New York School" were presented in *Poetry* years before that misleading title was applied to those rather disparate individuals. John Ashbery, then living in France, sent "As You Know," "Grand Abacus," "The Pied Piper," and "The Painter" in 1955. The poems were credited in the December issue as his first appearance, although that had actually occurred (with poems a classmate of his stole and submitted under a pseudonym) in November 1945, the same issue that featured Kenneth Koch's earliest work in *Poetry*. Frank O'Hara debuted under Shapiro in 1951, and continued to receive eager acceptances from Rago. James Schuyler began to appear in the mid-sixties.

Although the assertion is often repeated that *Poetry* gave a cold shoulder to the Beats, the record indicates it was the other way around. In May 1957, Rago sent an eloquent letter of support to Lawrence Ferlinghetti for use by the defense at the *Howl* obscenity trial. The highly respected Editor of *Poetry* was a not-inconsiderable witness, since, incidentally, he was also a member of the City of Chicago's censorship board, appointed by Mayor Richard J. Daley. The *Poetry* staff entertained Allen Ginsberg, Gregory Corso, and Peter Orlovsky at the office in 1959.

Throughout his years, Rago welcomed and printed other counter-cultural and Eastern-influenced poets from both the East and West coasts—Rexroth, Lew Welch, William Everson (Brother Antoninus), Gary Snyder—and would have published Ginsberg, too, had he been given the chance. But an editor cannot present work by authors who decline to submit any. (Louis Ginsberg suggested a father-and-son appearance, repeatedly, but Rago wasn't keen on the elder's verses.) Rago in fact invited Allen Ginsberg to send poems early in 1966, and immediately accepted "Wichita Vortex Sutra (I)" when it arrived in April. Unfortunately, *Poetry* couldn't present it: Ginsberg informed him student pacifists in Omaha had already printed it in a mimeographed magazine (*Do It*). In any case, *Poetry* published reviews of most of the Beat poets' books. Ferlinghetti's *Pictures of the Gone World* received *two* notices, in October 1956.

Besides keeping up with the evolving American scene, Rago offered surveys of poetry abroad. Shapiro had initiated a number of foreign issues, but it was left to Rago to complete the complicated work of assembling them. Long after Shapiro left, Rago saw through the press the Japanese (May 1956), Israeli (July 1958), and Indian (January 1959) issues. And he was successful in getting grants to pay the guest editors and trans-lators. Rago regularly presented translations from French, Italian, Greek, and other European poets, as well. Two years after Dylan Thomas died— he drank himself into a coma in New York City on 9 November 1953— Rago finally got the much-delayed special issue on the Welsh poet, now a Memorial Number, into print in November 1955.

Within the year before that issue came out, *Poetry* went from what Rago later described as "the leanest and meanest time in the history of the magazine" to unprecedented prosperity. When Shapiro departed for California, *Poetry* was teetering on the brink. Then, as he explained to Delmore Schwartz on 22 December 1954, "Just about two weeks ago there was a sudden change: we found a printer whose price we could meet and several thousand dollars appeared miraculously at about the same time."

At the critical juncture, another angel had stepped from the wings. Largely self educated, J. Patrick Lannan was a financier, art collector, and longtime friend of Gus and Julia Bowe. Judge Bowe liked to write, recite, and talk about poetry, and he got Pat Lannan interested in it as well, introducing him to *Poetry*'s editors and to many of the authors the Bowes entertained. Although not a Trustee, Lannan sat in and advised at Board

Robert Frost at the first Poetry Day, 13 November 1955.

meetings, and now promised to underwrite deficits for the first quarter of
1955.

Still trying to raise money the old way, the Board brought Oliver St.
John Gogarty to the Arts Club in November 1954 and Dame Edith
Sitwell to the Art Institute in January 1955 for benefit programs. Both
appearances generated lots of publicity; but when Lannan saw the
receipts ($120 and $1,298), he had a better idea. Instead of several small
gatherings and appeals to the usual sponsors, Lannan proposed one big
event—to be called Poetry Day—featuring a reading, followed by a for-
mal dinner and an auction. As one of *Poetry*'s earliest contributors and, by
this time, America's most famous poet, Robert Frost was invited to be
guest of honor. Lannan got prominent publishers, booksellers, and art
dealers to donate rare first editions, manuscripts, paintings, and other
items. Frost read to a packed house on 13 November. The auction
attracted 168 high-bidding guests, including presidents of corporations
from IT&T to Lipton Tea, as well as directors from major libraries and
museums. When the party was over, *Poetry* was richer by almost $29,000.

So the pattern was set (although the auctions were dropped in later

Guest of Honor T. S. Eliot and Valerie Eliot at the
Poetry Day Dinner, 7 November 1959.

years), and Poetry Day continues as the longest-running reading series in the country. In 1956, Carl Sandburg spoke, without fee, and drew an even bigger audience than Frost. John Crowe Ransom and Archibald MacLeish, though lower profile, had high attendance in 1957 and 1958. Rago tried for three years to get T. S. Eliot; after the Editor arranged additional speaking engagements during his stay, Eliot agreed to come for Poetry Day 1959. The crowd that lined up at Orchestra Hall could have filled the auditorium twice over.

W. H. Auden and Marianne Moore were only slightly less popular in 1960 and 1961. For the auction, Moore herself was very generous, donating manuscripts, signed editions, and her famous correspondence with the Ford Motor Company about the naming of the Edsel, as well as letters and inscribed volumes from H.D. In 1962, Frost returned to give the reading, one of his last, in celebration of *Poetry*'s Golden Anniversary.

After two and a half years in the Newberry's dim and drafty attic, where vodka was always on hand to provide warmth, *Poetry* was able to move to rented space at 1018 N. State Street. Rago and the staff received raises, and payments to contributors were increased. Rago changed printers and asked Greer Allen, head of the University of Chicago Printing Department, to redesign the typography and layout of the magazine. The new format, basically unchanged since, was introduced with the January 1957 issue.

After the first Poetry Day, the *Poetry* staff were freer to concentrate on editing. But Rago spent much time, and was very effective, too, at raising funds. He worked tirelessly at promotion, and in each annual report to the Board after 1955, the Editor reported steady increases in subscriptions, advertising, donations, and national publicity. By the spring of 1961, Rago was able to announce that monthly circulation had hit 5,500, making it the largest of the "little" magazines, and second or third in rank among the institution-sponsored, general literary quarterlies.

Cid Corman to Karl Shapiro   *Paris, 31 January 1955*

Dear Mr. Shapiro,

The news has reached me deviously that you are planning to leave POETRY shortly and go to Berkeley to teach. If the information is correct, as I suspect it may be, and if POETRY is in as dire straits as I hear, I would like to be nominated as editor. Provided I were given the strings to hold, without any other strings attached. I am very certain I could give the magazine a tremendous boost in every important sense. I could enlist the vigor and enthusiasm of a brigade of young people, of my own generation (a major failing in POETRY has been this backward gaze), and could improve circulation while cutting expenses. I have no illusions of the difficulties involved. In editing ORIGIN (which has had the acclaim of my generation without fail and the applause of people as diverse as Stevens, Williams, Rexroth, Marianne Moore, Ransom, etc.) I have undergone every editorial experience possible, alone. Including distribution to bookstores nationally, addressing envelopes by hand always, never once sending a blank or printed rejection slip .... I know you are unlikely to have much "say" in a successor, if the magazine is to continue at all. But if I could be guaranteed a modest living wage, I would forego what I have intended here (to start a journey around the world) and return. I would not offer my services, which will entail tremendous personal sacrifice in time and energy, if I did not think the magazine were capable of generating a whole new era in the art....

This is not, on the other hand, to kick you. Or to crow over you. Despite all disagreements, etc., I have respect and even affection for anyone like yourself, any sincere poet, who tries to do, something, [sic] in times when such attempts are almost suicidal.

My best, always, / Yours / Cid Corman

Karl Shapiro to Henry Rago   *[Berkeley, Calif.], 13 February 1955*

Dear Henry:

I can't answer this lout. Would someone write him that we have an editor; or something; or better still, nothing. He is a large economy-size thorn in the side of everything. One of the few people I feel no pity for. File the letter under Documents.

Karl

Louise Bogan to Henry Rago   *New York City, 2 July 1955*

Dear Henry Rago:

Thank you for your letter, asking me to contribute to your series of "appeals" on the behalf of POETRY. . . .

The July number came this morning, and I think that it is particularly interesting. The fact that poets are now doing some reviewing of poetry is a virtue, I think; and Kenner gets at the hack modernists in a v. subtle way. I think you (yourself!) are doing an excellent job.

Sincerely yours, / Louise Bogan

Louise Bogan to Henry Rago   *New York City, 20 July 1955*

Dear Henry Rago:

Harriet Monroe gave me, in 1921, my first acceptance, and in 1931 my first prize, and was a sympathetic and helpful friend. But my memory of *Poetry* goes back to the year of its founding, when I was still in high-school. It took some time for me to find a copy of the magazine—the mechanics of subscription were then somewhat beyond me. I finally tracked it down in the Periodical Room of the Boston Public Library. I learned a great deal, throughout the years, from a close scrutiny of its pages. One of its reiterated lessons—that poetry is an art—had been passed over by my other mentors. . . .

Kenneth Rexroth to Henry Rago   *San Francisco, Calif.,*
7 October 1955

Dear Henry Rago—

As I guess you know, Patchen's operation a few years ago seemed to have, as so often happens with herniated disc jobs—only made his back worse. He is now pretty close to being unable to get around at all. He was trying to get some dough to go back for another operation when Miriam (the only support for the family) became ill and got a diagnosis of diabetes mellitus and multiple sclerosis. Multiple sclerosis—as you may have learned from the Lou Gehrig case—is an incapacitating, eventually fatal disease of completely unknown etiology. Not only is it incurable, but it makes the patient an invalid for years.

I don't know of anything that Poetry can do—but anything you can do—any way you can help—would certainly be welcome.

This is a terrible year—did you know that Weldon Kees threw himself off the Golden Gate Bridge this summer?

My best to you personally. Let's hope you can make something of Poetry. Nobody else ever did or could.

Faithfully / Kenneth Rexroth

P.S. Poetry Center out here going great guns. Its only thoroughly ungracious guest to date was K Shapiro who certainly seems to have got himself disliked! I never met him.

After an injury in the thirties, Patchen suffered from severe back pain the rest of his life; he had surgery on a herniated disk in 1950 and a spinal fusion in 1956. In 1951, Auden, Eliot, and other poets started a fund to help pay for his treatments. See Patchen's letter to Shapiro, 31 July 1951.

Thomas Cole to Henry Rago   *Baltimore, Md., 20 October 1955*

Dear Mr. Rago:

I am angered (as I believe numerous others of your readers must be) by Edouard Roditi's brash and uncalled-for statement, "Long before becoming insane, Ezra Pound . . ." Roditi implies a sanity before and while *Personae* was being written, and seems to foresee insanity as the ultimate goal of Pound because of the idea of masks. This is all presumed, no doubt, by Pound's present predicament and is a rather silly instance of poor thinking.

Don't you think it is about time that certain critics and especially poets awoke to the fact that Pound is not insane? When he was committed to Saint Elizabeth's [sic] he was in a state of physical illness and mental shock after having sustained many months of *outdoor* internment at Pisa. If he was not completely lucid at the time, who would expect him to be after the prison camp? Wasn't it notorious for harsh treatment? But the Army psychiatrists said Pound was sane. It was the government (State Department?) that found him not capable of defending himself. Has Mr. Roditi read the recent *Classic Anthology*, *The Women of Trachis*, the *Analects*, and the new cantos in the *Hudson Review*?

No, Pound is not insane, and our younger poets should know this. Our older poets should know better than to say that he is. He is still alive, sane, and *producing* great poetry. . . .

In "The Several Names of Fernando Pessoa" (October 1955), Roditi said in passing:

"Long before becoming insane, Ezra Pound had thus chosen *Personae*, meaning masks, as the title of the early collection of his poems where he revealed . . . the complexities of his own identity while hinting unconsciously at his own future alienation."

Stanley Kunitz to Henry Rago   Seattle, Wash., 6 November 1955

Dear Henry Rago:

Congratulations on your official appointment as editor of *Poetry*! It's a good many years—too long!—since I've sent anything Chicago-ward. Hope you will like these as a group. . . . I'm visiting prof. of poetry here, while Roethke's off Fulbrighting. The Word's very much alive in these parts—poets lurking under each camellia bush!—& I like the feel of the place. I'd be interested in doing some reviewing again—I used to be a *Poetry* regular, but got surfeited with mediocrity & held my tongue. Think of me if something exciting turns up!

Sincerely, / Stanley Kunitz

Carolyn Kizer to Henry Rago   [Seattle, Wash.], 6 December 1955

Dear Henry Rago,

I've been wanting to send you the enclosed poem (Hera, Hung from the Sky [not printed]) for some time, but hesitated, because I hadn't received proof of "Complex Autumnal" [January 1956]. I hope you are still going to print it. What ho?

I'm sending "Hera" anyhow, mainly because I can't stand not to. So glad you are printing a wad of Kunitz. We are still delirious about having him here at the University this year. What a teacher! He is giving a public reading tomorrow night: Roethke, himself, Wagoner, and me. This company is a little fast for baby, but exciting.

Yours cordially, / Carolyn Kizer

Richard Howard to Henry Rago   New York City, 29 December 1955

Dear Mr. Rago,

Although I am delighted to discover my poems ["Landed: A Valentine" and "Agreement with Sir Charles Sedley," his first appearances] are to appear as soon as January, I cast back, with a sense of missed intentions, to a recollected communication from you to the effect that I was to be paid for them upon receipt of the corrected proofs . . . [sic]

I trust it does not seem merely venal of me to inquire this way about money for the poems—the amounts received from the total of my appearances in *Hudson Review* and the *Paris Review* are indeed minuscule, yet somehow, as George Eliot, I think, pointed out, there is a world of difference in getting paid for writing from getting, simply, praised.

I have decided against buying additional copies of the January number—the two complimentary ones must do for myself and my family, and the milieu must shift for itself, even if that means shifting without the poems of RH, a deprivation my friends have survived remarkably well so far.

Most cordially, / Richard Howard

Kenneth Rexroth to Henry Rago   *San Francisco, Calif.,*
10 January 1956

Dear Henry Rago—

Damned if you aren't resolved to ketch me in that sheet you run— via the dead or maimed if no other way. Dad—I just won't blow for Poetry a Magazine of Verse—I just don't make that scene. Like nothing happens—it's not just like one of those moldy fig scenes—like nothing ever did happen—like they just don't blow, dig?

However, you can quote me from elsewhere or letters.

Weldon Kees' car was found on the approach to the Golden Gate Bridge. He told people he was going to kill himself. He was in a state of extreme excited depression if you can visualize the combination. His personal life was in a pretty chaotic state. He appealed to his parents for psychological NOT financial support, in a sort of last minute frantic gesture. They told him to mind his own business and now mostly seem to resent his suicide as a personal affront & family disgrace. They are strictly Midwest scissorbills from Central Casting—real Balzac characters. Anne, his wife, broke down before him and was institutionalized, but out and living away from him at the time. . . .

Of what Patchen calls the generation born in one war and destroyed in a second, I would say that Weldon Kees was one of the best. At first glance his poetry seemed to owe much of its subject to the early Auden, but on closer inspection—Kees' world really was like that. He really saw horror spreading on the walls and the towns in ruins and bones breaking through the pavement. Others have called themselves Apocalyptics, Kees lived in a permanent and hopeless apocalypse. This, of course, is what our 20th century world really is, all the time, but we all let on it isn't so, at least usually. It is impossible to live fully conscious of the contemporary world. We all accept one sort of decerebration or other, Religion, Politics, Art, Shock Therapy or Lobotomy. Kees insisted on facing it all the time, so it killed him, as it has killed so many others and maimed and gnawed us all. In an age of treason to mankind on all hands, he held fast.

Now I hope you print that. If you do—intact or nothing. It'll sure look funny in that house organ of retired high school English teachers! Presumably, you're trying to reform same. I wish you all the luck, but you've got an Augean task, for sure. . . .

Love & kisses, / Kenneth

On 6 January, H.R. had asked Rexroth to "say something" in tribute to Kees, who disappeared 18 July 1955. Rexroth's remarks on Kees in the second-last paragraph were printed (intact) in the June 1956 issue.

Kenneth Patchen to Henry Rago   *Palo Alto, Calif., 9 May 1956*

Dear Henry Rago

Today I mailed you the second final offering of my work in silkscreen reproduction—that is, final as far as this particular venture goes.

On May 28 I am scheduled for a second spinal operation; this one a fusion, which involves three months in a cast (about six weeks of that in hospital bed) and another three to six months of very limited movement. This with my wife's illness presents a rather unpromising picture.

So far I might well be on another planet in terms of support through foundations, awards committees, etc.—for I have received no help of any kind whatever, not one penny, or the promise or prospect of any such awareness-in-aid of our worsening plight.

I inform you of this because of your magazine's most concrete and generous expression of concern with that plight; it seems to me fitting that you be told about the nature of our present situation.

Warm good wishes to you. / Sincerely yours, / Kenneth Patchen

Patchen was trying to support himself by selling his self-published "Painted Editions," limited runs combining verse and art work. *Poetry* ran ads for them, without charge. H.R. wrote 11 May, asking if he might put an emergency appeal in *Poetry*: "We would say only and exactly what you would tell us to say, so that there would be no more imposition on your privacy, and your wife's, than is strictly necessary."

Kenneth Patchen to Henry Rago   *Palo Alto, Calif., 15 May 1956*

Dear Henry Rago,

Your letter of yesterday heartened us more than I can express in this hurried note. (I am just now in the thick of tests, briefings, etc, connected with my hospital entry and rapidly nearing surgery.) . . .

While I agree that my situation does call for an appeal to any and all sources which might promise help, I can not bring myself now to believe that an open campaign of solicitation is the immediate answer. My past experience has been that returns from such an appeal do not amount to more than a stop-gap lessening of pressure in terms of the real situation, which is one of a continuing need; and it does have the unfortunate effect of creating an impression that the problem is by way of finding an at least partial solution. It is a trickling away into the sand . . . . To put it more directly: say that through your columns two hundred dollars came in, for that two hundred dollars I would be selling whatever chance I might have for a substantial and meaningful (in terms of my prospect for continuing need) sum from any of the several artists' awards and aid-in-need organizations. I speak from experience. It may be objected that a small help is better than a large one which shows no sign of materializing anyway; in the abstract sense this is quite true, but in the sense of a drowning man who is given a straw to keep him afloat it is not—the question is one which has to do with survival on the open sea, not in a duck pond.

But it would be serviceable from the stand[point] of keeping my predicament in the open, so to speak, to have an item like the following printed in your News Notes:

> Our readers will remember that, after a campaign to raise the necessary funds was undertaken by a committee headed by T S Eliot, W H Auden, Thornton Wilder and Archibald MacLeish in 1951, Kenneth Patchen underwent surgery for a spinal difficulty. We now report that a second operation was performed on May 28th, and that Kenneth Patchen will be confined for some months at the Palo Alto Hospital in Palo Alto, California.

I hope to be able in the next few days to devote time to the copy for the ad which you have again so very generously made possible for us to have in *Poetry*.

So—in haste—thank you!

With every good wish, / Sincerely yours, / Kenneth Patchen

The paragraph was the lead item in News Notes for June 1956.

Philip Booth to Henry Rago   *Wellesley, Mass., 18 June 1956*

Dear Henry Rago,

Proof for my July four ["Green Song," "Chart 1203," "Shag," "The Seiners"] goes your way with this note, and I must say I'm delighted to see these finally in print. As a matter of fact, they come to me on a day when I somehow doubt myself as the person who *might* someday (tomorrow?) write something else, and it is surprisingly encouraging to find my name at the end of these lines. Did *I* really write these? I wonder, look twice, and—reassured that it was me—make ready to try again. . . .

Richard Aldington to Henry Rago *Montpellier, France, 25 June 1956*

Dear Mr Rago,

Edward [Dahlberg] suggests that you might allow me to review for you his SORROWS OF PRIAPUS which New Directions are issuing this fall. I should much like to have this privilege. The book, he says, is illustrated by Ben Shahn.

I believe I may claim to be one of Poetry's oldest surviving contributors since, if my memory is not at fault, I published the first Imagist poems with you in November 1912.

Yours sincerely / Richard Aldington

Edward Dahlberg to Henry Rago *Svaneke, Denmark, 14 July 1956*

Dear Mr. Rago:

. . . I am deeply pleased to hear that Richard Aldington has asked to review THE SORROWS OF PRIAPUS. He is a man of letters, and even an attack by him will give me deeper pleasure than the scurvy praise of some biped of our ignorant literati.

In the past six years I have sent my verse only to Poetry and New Directions. The other little magazines are the sterile adjuncts and the parched oracles of our colleges of lower education. I don't even know whether there are other magazines except The Partisan Review (which I founded!), but my name is never mentioned there as I regard [Philip] Rahv, a pseudonym for that ancient and esteemed name of rabbin, and [William] Phillips, as the dreariest of locusts who have eaten up the foliage of Parnassus, and Kenyon Review which is another sort of Cerberus. . . .

Henry Rago to Carl Sandburg *23 July 1956*

Dear Mr. Sandburg,

We are all delighted to hear from Mr. [J. Patrick] Lannan that you consent to be the guest of honor on Poetry Day this coming November. We cannot help thinking how felicitous the event will be, your homecoming to a city that found its first speech in your poetry, and the help you now bring for the future of a magazine that already owes you so much of its past.

I want to say that the day will have a special meaning for me. You were the first famous poet I ever saw. When I was fifteen years old, I introduced you to an audience of my fellow students in the assembly hall of Austin High School in Chicago. That was back in 1931. I myself was glowing with my first acceptance from Harriet Monroe who for several years before that time had been scribbling criticisms on my poems. So we have already met, and worked from the same platform.

With my kindest regards and in happy anticipation.

Sincerely, / Henry Rago

Elizabeth Bishop to Henry Rago   Petropolis, Brazil, 11 August 1956

Dear Mr Rago:

I'm sorry I have been so long replying to your kind letter, written May 8th . . . . I do indeed hope I'll be able to have some poems in *Poetry* before this year is over. I have also thought of sending you a selection of short bits translated from the best young poet here—or around 40, that is—João Cabral de Melo. He's received the most important prize here and I think he's about the best of all I've read. . . . The older, better-known poets have appeared in English, and all seem rather pastel and not nearly as interesting—at least, to me.

Thank you again. / Sincerely yours, / Elizabeth Bishop
P.S. I want to say how very tragic I think the death of Weldon Kees was. I met him only once—I took him to call on Pound one afternoon in Washington—but I liked him immediately. And if you were responsible for the note following Rexroth's remarks I'd like to add that I think you're right. It's useless to say that "Art"—among the other odd things he mentions—is a "decerebration"—useless and wicked, surely!

H.R.'s note stated that "this sorrow will be anything but diminished . . . by a belief in the illuminations sometimes vouchsafed by art." Bishop's translation of João Cabral de Melo Neto's play *The Death and Life of a Severino* was printed in the October 1963 issue.

Edward Dahlberg to Henry Rago   Malaga, Spain, 26 September 1956

Dear Mr. Rago:

I must advise you that Mr. Richard Aldington does not wish to do the book. We had a literary altercation, one of those wounds and shames in life, without which we are morose brutes, but with which we are further lashed by vanity, and the wind we imagine thought, and the necessity for more icy solitude. . . .

Richard Aldington to Henry Rago   *Montpellier, France,*
                                                       10 October 1956

Dear Mr Rago,

There is no controversy—merely a sick man who ought to see a psychiatrist.

I think it would be very pleasant if after all these years I could do something in the way of reviews or articles for *Poetry*. The fact cannot be disputed that *Poetry* was the head and centre of the so-called "revolution of 1912" partly because of Miss Monroe's skill and openmindedness as editor, partly because Ezra Pound was in touch with young writers, but also because Chicago is away from the literary rackets of New York, London and Paris. . . . I still recollect how pleasant it was to be working for Chicago from a village in Berkshire (Eng) or the island of Port Cros or even Paris. It was outside the tiresome cliques. . . .

Aldington explained on 18 January 1957 that Dahlberg wanted him to read his long book in his presence: "And before I'd had time to read more than half of it he wanted me to say it is a masterpiece. . . . I'm very sorry about it, and wish I could serve him. But we can't any of us expect lavish and unqualified praise."

Carl Sandburg to Henry Rago   *Flat Rock, N.C., 14 December 1956*

Dear Mr. Rago:

We did not get to the talk we should have had when I was in Chicago but we can hope to have it along late January or early March when I am to be in Chicago again. Across the period 1912–1928 there was definitely a quality of fellowship among poets which is very slightly in evidence today. There were fewer definite cults and vague movements than now. If by the poetry of a man he seemed to belong somewhere he and others who seemed to belong did not form an open or covert movement. About this as I have seen it for forty years I shall probably never have time to write. Whatever comment or interpretation of it I might have is implicit in my writing. Once for two weeks while she was on vacation Miss Monroe put me in entire charge of the manuscripts flowing in. And I want to hear you tell about the ups and downs, the ins and outs, of the daily manuscript mail and the callers in person, how it looks as compared with forty years ago.

Warm regards, / Carl Sandburg

Delmore Schwartz to Henry Rago   *Pittstown, N.J., 21 January 1957*

Dear Henry,

Many thanks indeed for your note. I would have written a piece for you on Graves' book long before now, had the past year not been extremely difficult, so difficult that the Kenyon fellowship was a kind of melodramatic thing which I kept thinking of as a ransom, for otherwise I would have been looking for any kind of teaching job whatever in the middle of the academic year. The reason for the trouble was, for once, not a matter of my own ineptness: we were supposed to go to one of the small colleges of the University of California [Santa Barbara] for a year, at an extremely good salary, and then, in the middle of summer the chairman called the whole thing off and explained that it was not his fault if the man I was to substitute for had changed his mind about taking a sabbatical. It turned out that the hero in question was Hugh Kenner, who, as you may remember, feels rather strongly about my work. As a result of his stand, a fracas developed and Kenner ended up as chairman, which is all quite flattering to me in a peculiar way. . . .

Harry Brown to Henry Rago   *Los Angeles, Calif., 21 March 1957*

Dear Mr Rago,

After a lapse of several years, during which time I have been laboring in the Sicilian mines, as a result of Alcibiades blowing the duke at Syracuse, I seem to have seriously taken up the writing of poetry again. Enclosed is a certain amount of the end result. Would any or all of them be suitable for you?

The letterhead above [Jaguar Productions] is a disguise, also a snare and a delusion. My proper address—at least, where I sleep—is below; and the enclosed stamps should suffice for you to tell me whether you like these or not. Or, more important, *want* them desperately.

Most sincerely / Harry Brown

As a teenager, Brown had been printed by H.M. in 1935; see Chapter XIII. "The Wheel of Love, Like All Wheels, Comes Full Circle" appeared June 1957. When his check went astray, Brown wrote 1 October: "It's boring to have to be so persistent, but I'm raising a pet behemoth out behind the barn, and I planned to use the money to buy him fodder. I need not remind you that Hell hath no fury like a behemoth unfed."

James Wright to Henry Rago   *Seattle, Wash., 11 April 1957*

Dear Mr. Rago;

You will recall that recently I asked your permission to review the selected poems of Stanley Kunitz, and that you wished to wait till the book appeared before making a decision. Just recently I heard from Mr. Kunitz. He is ill in New York City—laid up with an injured leg. Among other things he said that he is not succeeding in finding a decent publisher for his selected poems. The New York publishers, it seems, find his poems too "bitter" and "violent" for their taste.

I think this is a disgrace. If the bitterness and violence of a poem, and not its grandeur of conception and skill of execution, were to be the standards of judgment, then certainly the New York publishers would reject the Book of Amos, the works of Charles Dickens, and about two-thirds of Shakespeare's plays. My own feeling is that the present generation of poets in the United States are not bitter and violent enough. In any case, we are not skillful enough. Skill is not the manipulation of meter. Skill is the ability to grasp and present reality without flinching from it (to use one of Kunitz's words).

If Kunitz were a young fellow searching for a first publisher, matters might be different. But he is actually one of the few really accomplished poets alive.

He suggested that, since hell will probably freeze over before his poems are published, I might want to do a piece on his poetry in general—not a review, but a brief essay. That is what I wish to suggest to you. . . .

No essay appeared; David Wagoner reviewed Kunitz's *Selected Poems, 1928–1958* in September 1958.

William Stafford to Henry Rago   *San Jose, Calif., 13 April 1957*

Dear Mr. Rago:

Something in the *care* of both acceptances and rejections from *Poetry* recently makes me offer the enclosed as the result of a kind of complicated impulse: I am grateful and want to see good things get into *Poetry*; and I don't know whether I help or not by sending some awkward-sized things, and perhaps awkward-slanted things, that may be a clutter on the desk rather than a help on the project.

Also I have a kind of trust that you'll help keep me from putting out damaging things! . . .

Sylvia Plath to Henry Rago   *Cambridge, England, 7 May 1957*

Dear Mr. Rago:

I was very pleased to hear you'd accepted my four poems for publication in *Poetry* and am just now jotting down the few relevant items that might be appropriate for your Notes on Contributors column.

Since last writing you, I've had poems accepted for the first time by *Accent, The Antioch Review* and the *London Magazine*. After my tripos exams in English lit. this month, I'll proceed home with my British husband [Ted Hughes] to write on the Cape all summer and then to Northampton, Mass., where I begin teaching freshman English at Smith College this fall. . . .

"The Snowman on the Moor," "Sow," "Ella Mason and Her Eleven Cats," and "On the Difficulty of Conjuring up a Dryad" were published in July 1957. Between 1959 and 1961, *Poetry* printed eight other poems by Plath. On 27 December 1962, a month and a half before her suicide, Rago accepted "Fever 103°," "Purdah," and "Eavesdropper," which appeared in August 1963.

Aileen G. Melchior to Henry Rago   *Huntingburg, Ind.,*
1 March 1958

Dear Mr. Rago,

I don't understand traditional poetry very well and modern not at all. I am not familiar with your magazine however I have been told that you are one of the most astute judges of modern poetry in America. For that reason I hope you will be good enough to read the enclosed work which was done by my daughter who is now twelve years of age. . . .

I hope you will give me an honest appraisal of her work. Since my husband was killed in a tragic accident almost two years ago my duties as a parent have taken a more important aspect and it would be a tragedy indeed if the child had talent which I failed to recognize.

May I hear from you?

Sincerely yours, / Aileen G. Melchior

Henry Rago to Aileen G. Melchior   *10 March 1958*

Dear Mrs. Melchior,

Thank you for letting us see Julie's poems. It's very hard to say anything at a distance, and we usually avoid questions of this sort altogether; we simply look at the poems that are sent to us and decide whether we want to publish them in POETRY. Also, I'm always afraid of over-encouraging young talent. Any number of vital decisions can be influenced in this way, and sometimes a whole life can be turned off the course that might lead to just a good, not very exciting but happy life.

But I think you can be sure that your little daughter has genuine literary talent. It's too early to say whether it will find its final expression in verse or in prose; many, if not most, prose-writers begin with verse. But she does have a feeling for language, and there is some evidence that she lives an important part of her life not only with words but in them. Of these poems the best are CALENDAR and NEON. . . . She ought to work with concrete things that are familiar to her, and with the sentiments and feelings of not just *a* little girl (too often this can be a little girl in the movies or "literature") but of the little girl that she is. . . .

Right now it would be good if she did much reading on her own. Among poets, she should read Emily Dickinson, William Carlos

Williams, Gerard Manley Hopkins, Chinese and Japanese poets in translation, H.D. (Hilda Doolittle), and the others that these will inevitably lead to. . . .

I was a child-poet myself, and I know that she can do justice to her talent and at the same time have all the fun that any child should have. She shouldn't be deprived of this—even poetry isn't a good enough reason. And she shouldn't feel that she absolutely has to turn out to be a poet, to succeed in it at all costs. Again, don't over-encourage her. She should feel free to pivot into any number of directions—perhaps some of the other arts, perhaps teaching, perhaps journalism, perhaps even business, perhaps no career at all except her home. She should feel free to stop writing poetry at any time.

With every good wish to you both. / Sincerely, / Henry Rago

Julia Anne Melchior to Henry Rago   Huntingburg, Ind.,
                                                  [March? 1958]

Dear Mr. Rago,

This is to thank you for reading my tiny contributions to the field of literature. Mama should never have bothered you with them, but I

Miss J. Melchior
500 Geiger St.
Huntingburg, Ind.

Dear Mr. Rago,
This is to thank you for reading my tiny contributions to the field of literature. Mama should never have bothered you with them, but I know Mama. All she thinks about is us. I think she can write a thousand times better than I but you could never get her to admit it. And as for writing poetry, I don't write, I just put words together and they come out poems

disguise. Now! I have never seen a meaner child.
I better close this letter now before she sees it and decides to cover the above paragraph with a big splotch of ink.
Very Sincerley
Julia Anne Melchior
P.s. Thanks again, and I'll be sure to take your advice.

Thank-you letter from Julia Anne Melchior, age 12, to Henry Rago, March 1958.

know Mama. All she thinks about is us. I think she can write a thousand times better than I but you could never get her to admit it. And as for writing poetry, I don't write, I just put words together and they come out poems.

I don't know if I'll be a poet though, Mama says there's no money in it and I do want to eat. I really do love words, especially adjectives. They seem to know how to describe exactly what you're feeling.

Mama might have given you the impression that I'm a studious, hard working, young genius overflowing with literary talent. Boy is she misleading you! I am really very inclined to be lazy. I am a daydreamer, and as for talent—well, if I have any pray to the good Lord Mama keeps hounding me till I use it.

As I said before Mama always brags on us. To all her friends we are the most adorable, sweet, talanted [sic] young angels who ever wore skirts.

By "we" I mean my sister and I. I don't want to sound prejudiced but if I am a little cherub—she must be Satan in disguise. Wow! I have never seen a meaner child.

I better close this letter now before she sees it and desides [sic] to cover the above paragraph with a big splotch of ink.

Very Sincerley [sic] / Julia Anne Melchior

P.S. Thanks again, and I'll be sure to take your advice.

J.A.M. did not appear in *Poetry.*

Alfred Kreymborg to Henry Rago   *New York City, 23 April 1958*

Dear Mr. Rago:

I am answering your card of December 1, 1956 belatedly. It may be I've grown somewhat touchy at my age regarding rejections. However, one of the poems, "Man in the Meadow," dedicated to Robert Frost, has appeared elsewhere and all is forgiven, as it were. I am now submitting several poems again. "Warm Sun" is somewhat related to the Emily Dickinson birthday ballad of 1955. The Elegy to Maxwell Bodenheim almost broke me apart before I got it down or old Bogey finished me. Yet it is strictly objective as a whole. It has not been submitted elsewhere because we have no poetry magazine in New York worthy of the name.

With continued good wishes, / Alfred Kreymborg

"Warm Sun," Kreymborg's last contribution, was printed December 1958. Coincidentally, Ben Hecht depicted Bodenheim and the Greenwich Village Bohemia of the twenties in his play *Winkelberg*, produced off Broadway in 1958. They had been friends from their teenage years in Chicago, but later feuded. M.B. gave an unflattering portrait of Hecht in his novel *Duke Herring*; Hecht retaliated with *Count Bruga*, a novel based on Bodenheim's "misadventures."

Robert Creeley to Henry Rago   *Veracruz, Mexico, 10 August 1958*

Dear Mr Rago,

I've had no mail forwarded from Oaxaca, so I've been concerned that, if you have written, I've not received any letter. Which depresses me, always. In any case we have at last settled for what time remains. Las Casas was an incredible place, but at this time of year cold and wet— and also inhabited by a young English professor who showed me the first day we met a carefully mimeographed sheet of examples, 19, of enjambment etc. By one o'clock that same morning he had thrown me out of his house. So I'm reminded that the battle, like they say, is real. Anyhow we came here—finally much simpler, being a city of some size, and much more to the point, having excellent beer, shrimp & what have you. We will be here till about the 25th, and then back to teaching Latin, which I'm embarrassed to have forgotten almost completely, as ever. But will remember quickly enough in that form. . . .

Patrick Galvin to the Editor   *Norfolk, England, 20 September 1958*

Sir—

I have just read Mr. David Wright's review of my book "Heart of Grace" and I write to congratulate him on the title of his own work "Monologue Of A Deaf Man". I take it that the work is of an autobiographical nature?

I have no objection to the term "British" if, by the same token, Mr. David Wright can be described as having enough "Irish" in him to know what he means. For the benefit of your readers, however, I should point out that there is a great deal more "Irish" to be found in the humble carrot. And, Sir, have you thought what one could do with a carrot?

Finally, I understand that it is not done for an author to criticise his reviewer. I apologise.

Yours faithfully, / Patrick Galvin

James Dickey to Henry Rago   *Atlanta, Ga., 1 February 1959*

Dear Henry Rago,

. . . One thing that working in business has taught me, although in a rather negative way: one must preserve certain important areas of one's life where one does nothing at all for effect, or for advantage: certain areas where honesty and fundamental beliefs are the only things that exist. For me, this area happens to be poetry, which includes the reviewing of poetry. Since I don't teach poetry, or lecture on it, or read it from platforms, or make a living on anything connected with it, I feel there is really no excuse for me if I am not honest about it. This is not to say that the others, the teachers, are not honest; they are, but I must be doubly so.

Please excuse this harangue; you don't deserve it, but because you are so unfailingly sympathetic, and because you are doing more for American poetry than any other living man, you have to get it anyway.

My best to you. Send some new poems in typescript if you have them, and if you want to, and if it's not too much trouble. I'd like to see them.

Yours, / Jim Dickey

Richard Hugo to Henry Rago   *Seattle, Wash., 28 September 1959*

Dear Mr. Rago—

If unsolicited notes on contributors to POETRY are acceptable, I wanted to say a word about the poems of James Dickey. I always recognized what I considered a real originality in Dickey's poems, but always felt the poems were too slow, or too long. With the eight poems published in the July issue of POETRY, I began to really get with Dickey for the first time. What, I think, makes the poems seem slow is that the lines are slow—they end, often with multisyllable words, or with the next to the last word a multisyllable word—propeller, unheard-of, trembling compound, etc. This slows the line down, but the pace of the *total* poem is not as slow as the lines indicate. The poems develop evenly, and move along quite briskly once one stops reading them *in lines. . . .*

I hope to see more of Dickey's poems. He has his own voice, I think, and of all your contributors may be the one to leave the most original voice with us. I do have a couple of negative comments. One, is that he is so serious about the 'art of writing' that he sometimes tends to use words that are affected—not normal to speaking—'wherefrom', 'Farewell', 'awaver' etc. Things nobody says. This probably comes from the urge to be 'poetic'—a difficult thing to escape, but a thing that ought to be escaped from.

Hope this kind of quick, unthoughtout, spontaneous comment is welcome there, tho I know you're plenty busy. Anyway, hope to see more of Dickey in POETRY, and vice versa.

Sincerely / Richard Hugo

Dickey's poems in the July 1959 issue were: "The Game," "The Landfall," "The Signs," "The Enclosure," "The Performance," "The String," "Below the Lighthouse," and "Into the Stone."

Frank O'Hara to Henry Rago   New York City, 21 October 1959

Dear Henry Rago,

I haven't sent you any poems for some time and I'm sorry to send you such a batch at once, but they are all recent and perhaps you'll find something you like. Actually I had been trying (and still am) to get together another book, and there's nothing like looking through old poems to make you feel you've left practically everything undone, so I got to work again, which was a relief. . . .

A. R. Ammons to Henry Rago   Northfield, N.J., 26 October 1959

Dear Mr. Rago,

So very pleasant talking with you in Chicago. We had a good trip . . . I was astonished at the price first, then the size of the cheeseburgers. Had one for lunch and had to forego dinner. . . .

I haven't done any reviews. But would like to try. Thank you for asking me. I don't think I should try the better established poets, as their critical and original literatures are not easily accessible here. May I try a few first books, preferably of men? I know something personally of Josephine Miles [his teacher at Berkeley], Galway Kinnell. . . . I think there is some unreported thunder in Josephine Miles, and I would like to say so but I feel I do not deserve her critically yet.

What do I do now? I'm totally ignorant of the mechanism. . . .

Ammons reviewed books by Robert Duncan and Charles Reznikoff (but not Miles) in April 1960; he recalled Miles's influence on him in his memoir for the 75th Anniversary Issue in 1987.

James Wright to Henry Rago   [Minneapolis], 25 November 1959

Dear Mr. Rago:

Of course your suggestions for revisions in my review were reasonable; and all your points are well taken—with the possible exception of the phrase "classic comics" on page 4, line 3. The fact is that I don't know whether the word is "classic" or "classics." I always use the latter word when I mention these comics in conversation. (I guess I should buy some . . . long ago I read *Hamlet* in classics comics, and it is marvelous. Hamlet's dying speech: "I, too, must go to join my dead father. Aaaaaaaaaaaaargh!") . . . .

2. The 50th Anniversary Celebrations

In June 1960, Rago received a Rockefeller travel grant. He asked the Board for a year's leave of absence and recommended John Nims, his friend and an old *Poetry* hand, to serve as Visiting Editor. Rago departed in October with his wife, Juliet, and their four young children. But he left enough accepted poems for several issues—and expected his stand-in to print them. Nims did not care for some of the material, so he solicited work and published his own selections. With genial understatement, Nims later recalled that his "delay" in presenting Rago's choices "may have irritated him. Then too he may not have liked all of the poems I accepted." Rago was in fact furious, and never spoke to him again. He also excluded Nims from the 50th Anniversary number.

Work on the Anniversary issue and the year-long celebration began early in 1961. As part of the project, Rago arranged *Poetry*'s third British number, edited by Charles Tomlinson; published in May 1962, it included Donald Davie, R. S. Thomas, Austin Clarke, Ted Hughes, and several others. The entire July 1962 bilingual issue was devoted to Yves Bonnefoy, translated by Galway Kinnell and Jackson Mathews. The special double issue itself, October–November 1962, was actually triple-size (the largest to date, at 160 pages), and featured work by almost sixty poets from both sides of the Atlantic. The most notable of the younger generation—Merrill, Merwin, Dickey, Gunn, Levertov, Lowell, Creeley, Sexton—mingled with several of *Poetry*'s longtime contributors—Aiken, Frost, Cummings, Graves, Jarrell, Rukeyser, Schwartz, Spender, Williams, Zukofsky.

Rago was even able to get a piece from the increasingly silent Ezra Pound. Along with a section from Canto CXIII, Rago presented a facsimile of the opening of the "Three Cantos" from 1917, and reproduced the marked manuscripts of "Prufrock," "Sunday Morning," and several other early poems from Joyce, Williams, Frost, Moore, Crane, and Yeats. The number quickly sold out, and the Golden Anniversary Issue was reprinted as a paperback book. The U.S. Information Agency ordered 2,000 copies, for distribution abroad. By the fall of 1962, *Poetry*'s circulation had reached almost 6,000 and the magazine was now sent to every state in the Union, four U.S. territories and possessions, and eighty-two foreign countries, seven behind the Iron Curtain.

To coincide with the Anniversary, the Library of Congress put on a three-day National Poetry Festival, 22–24 October, with the general theme "Fifty Years of American Poetry." Supported by the Bollingen Foundation, the Festival was organized by Rago and Louis Untermeyer, the Consultant in Poetry and one of *Poetry*'s earliest contributors and most good-natured critics. One hundred poets were invited and eighty-five attended. Rago gave the welcoming address, followed by Morton Dauwen Zabel, who offered pointed remarks about "The Poetry Journal in Our Time" and the unique role of the magazine in the development of modern poetry. Shapiro's topic was, "What Is a Public?" All thirty-four other guest speakers, except Ogden Nash, were longtime *Poetry* authors. Frost, whose status as Grand Old Man had been confirmed by his reading at the Kennedy inauguration, gave the longest program. He recalled Harriet Monroe as "a great little lady": "she wanted to be thought as good a poet as anyone, and she didn't get that recognition . . . she just hid her poetry by being such an editor."

Randall Jarrell gave a brilliant brief history of the past fifty years, with capsule critiques of significant American poets—several of them sitting before him, anxiously waiting to be mentioned. Pound received careful notice by Jarrell and several other speakers. Mrs. Kennedy had invited poets and spouses to the White House, but had to cancel the reception. Still, everyone had a fine time, some, too much so. Mary Jarrell recalled that Berryman and Schwartz were under the influence throughout, and Schwartz was hauled away in a paddy wagon after he broke up his hotel room.

Unfortunately, the festivities were upstaged. President Kennedy appeared on TV on the evening of 22 October with the news that troops were on alert and the United States was on the brink of war, because of the Russian buildup of bases in Cuba. Despite the pall cast by the Cuban Missile Crisis, every seat was occupied during each session. The first such event offered under government auspices, the Festival was the most popular program held until then at the Library of Congress.

Frost repeated most of his Festival recitations at Poetry Day, on 16 November. Twice as many people had to be turned away as could fit into the Studebaker Theater. Reporters and photographers from the major newspapers and *Life* magazine covered the reading and the splendid party afterward. The gala came midway in Rago's tenure, and marked its high point. But on the larger poetry scene, the Golden Jubilee represented both the culmination and the end of an era.

On 29 January 1963, Frost died. Williams was gone two months later. Hilda Doolittle had died in 1961, her former husband and fellow *Imagiste*, Richard Aldington, in 1962. Harriet Monroe's other original contributors and oldest collaborators soon followed: Morton Zabel in 1964, T. S. Eliot in 1965, Carl Sandburg in 1967, Witter Bynner and George Dillon in 1968. Though Ezra Pound and Marianne Moore lived until 1972, their creative lives ended in the sixties. Moore's last collection, *Tell Me, Tell Me*, appeared in 1966; Pound's final *Drafts and Fragments of Cantos*

CX–CXVII in 1969. Before the decade ended, Henry Rago, too, would be gone.

Kenneth Patchen to Henry Rago   Palo Alto, Calif., 6 February 1960

Dear Henry Rago,

. . . Four years have passed since we received the nightmarish verdict of the doctors that my wife had fallen victim of multiple sclerosis. Four years in which I have done everything I could to bring our plight to the attention of the various committees which announce themselves as being interested in the welfare of the artist of merit in this richest of nations, in this democracy whose stock in trade is the selling of itself to the world as the enemy of inhumanity to man; and during this unceasing, four-year effort of mine (and a few others) to get one of the awards *which have been passed out to every poet of recognized worth not just one time but three-four-five-six times,* I have received nothing, not a word, *not a red cent from any of them!* Perhaps one day, when this story is told, it may be of interest to some people of good will—and with a regard for the state of health of our American letters—to know why this should be so. . . .

Philip Booth to Henry Rago   Concord, Mass., 6 May 1960

Dear Mr. Rago,

God knows a gimmick *is* inhuman, and, however awkwardly, I want to say some inadequate thanks for the courage your letter lends me. Given the backlog of Bright Young Men who want to ice their doctoral hopes for tenure with a few Distinguished Poems, I begin to gag. . . . I care *about* poems more than any Chair of Comparative Ironies; talk *about* poems has become a profession in itself, as inhuman as advertising Brand Names. I think poems are the maybe simplest thing in the world; the poems we try to write, and sometimes even live-out, if we can only see *through* the worldly complexities we create—to prevent us, with self-indulgent pain, from reaching through to pure love and hate. I may be fallible as hell, but I'm beginning to get convinced that the heaven of perfect poems is a dangerous place for humanity. Frost says it: "Leave something to learn later." . . .

James Merrill to John F. Nims   Munich, Germany, 5 October 1960

Dear Mr. Nims,

Thank you for your kind letter. Indeed you did do an analysis of that Accumulations poem [in July 1946]; it pleased me no end!

I have spent a few hours trying to think what to send you. 'A Tenancy' came back [from *Encounter*] not long ago, all wrinkled by Mr Spender's tears. I don't know how well it 'goes' with the others; together they make what is probably too long a group. While you are welcome to both, I should perfectly understand your sending back either. . . .

J.M.'s "A Tenancy" and "Six Leaves from the Album in the Waiting-Room" appeared June 1961.

X. J. Kennedy to John F. Nims   Ann Arbor, Mich., 3 December 1960

Dear John,

Thanks for your letter. Harvard and tea with cummings sounded nice. ~~One way to get one's lumps~~.

I'll be looking for the books to review. Can certainly do it within six weeks. Gads, you pay $6 a page for prose? My 50-page review will be along promptly. It may take a little cutting. . . .

Robert Lowell to John F. Nims   New York City, 3 May 1961

Dear Mr. Nims:

Here are two more Baudelaires to swell the group I sent you. . . .

That Frost National Prize is odd. I suppose nothing is too good for Frost, but one feels it is all being done in a heavy steam-rollerish fashion. I voted for W. C. Williams, who is ill and dying, and after a lifetime of courageous and brilliant service has had little of the gravy that has [been] raining on Frost. Each letter from the National Award group is

Robert Lowell, early fifties; he was first printed
in *Poetry* in September 1946.

more grandiose than its predecessor—they should import De Gaulle or Churchill or Nehru (all authors) to give the award.

Yours, / Robert Lowell

Lowell's Baudelaire translations were printed September 1961. Frost was voted the Congressional Gold Medal in 1960; President Kennedy presented it to him in 1962 on Frost's birthday, 26 March.

Marianne Moore to Robert Mueller   *Brooklyn, N.Y., 26 June 1961*

Dear Mr. Mueller,

Your considerateness, generosity, completeness—thinking ahead so carefully—make me wish *very* much that I might be able to do as you suggest—come and give a reading, stay overnight and be present at the Auction on behalf of POETRY, returning the third day—come by train and return by night train if you approve. . . .

As you may know—I have been disabled the past winter—am obliged to ration myself and not multiply engagements (indeed make any); but I cautiously am promising to appear once or twice in the autumn not later than November. I have thrived in Chicago and thank you very much for not looking upon me as a hazard. If you could have me early in November—as suggested—I shall do my best, try not to disappoint you.

Sincerely yours, / Marianne Moore

Robert Mueller to Henry Rago   *NewYork City, 24 September 1961*

Dear Henry, et al,

. . . I called M. Moore who chatted on for 45 minutes about everything that came to mind. She definitely wants to keep our expenses down and wants to come in a sleeper coach, "which some friends tell me is perfectly adequate", etc. But I have urged her to think about taking a roomette ("but that would be 23$!" she said . . . etc.). Will keep after her to worry less about the costs. I will also try to suggest (as I already hinted at tonight) that she shd come on Sat to get a good night's rest that night. It might help to send off a letter to her (a note) saying that we *want* her to come on Sat to make *sure* she gets a full night's refreshment. I think she did agree tonight that it *would* be more restful for her. And you cd also insist that she take a roomette.

She wants to help very much about items [for the auction]: spoke about digging out odds and ends out of her trunk—antiquities that *might* be interesting; but I made the definite suggestion that (as in the case of Eliot & Auden, etc.) the manuscripts themselves are the things

which we feel to be valuable from the Poet of Honor—those which are
written out, that is. She has all kinds of ideas about other things which I
shall advise her about. . . .

The manuscripts, letters, and books Moore donated for the auction brought a total
of $1,800.

Mona Van Duyn to Henry Rago   *St. Louis, 24 January 1962*

Dear Henry—

Believe me, this is not a posthumous letter! Don and Connie Finkel
told me yesterday that they had received a letter from Carolyn Kizer,
commenting sorrowfully on my death, about which she said she had
been informed by you. Since I am in excellent health and spirits,
though since yesterday feeling a bit ghostly, please tell me all you can
about how the rumor came about. I am intensely curious. *Her* misun-
derstanding? Yours? Someone else's? *What* on earth could it have been?
When and from what was I supposed to have died? When are the
poems coming out?

All good wishes for your and my longevity / Mona

P.S. Don & Connie telegraphed Carolyn immediately, so she's no
longer under any misapprehension.

Robert Mueller wrote Van Duyn on 26 January claiming responsibility for misin-
forming Kizer that she had died. It was, in fact, Eda Lou Walton who died.

James Dickey to Henry Rago   *Perugia, Italy, 17 March 1962*

Dear Henry Rago,

Now *here's* a switch! Until yesterday I was at our beloved Florence,
from which I really should have written you, and you were (and I guess
are) back in the States. How I wish we could have been in Florence at
the same time, and walked around the Boboli Gardens talking about
poetry! Well, I like to think that it will some day happen, even yet!
Meantime, Florence is very cloudy and cold, with the wind whistling
down the Arno as from the North Pole. . . .

I hope to have some new things to show you before too long,
though I am an awfully slow worker. The new book [*Drowning with
Others*] is finally out, though, and seems (at least to me) a good one. I
hope it will stand up. Certainly I was delighted to see what James
Wright had to say about the first book [*Into the Stone and Other Poems*],
in the December issue. It would be doubly hard to fail after a send-off

like that! Hard, and crushing if it happened. But I am already fairly far along into the third book, called now (tentatively) *Goodbye to Serpents*.

Incidentally, thanks for the good space you gave the four poems in the January issue. Thanks, and *thanks!*

Write me c/o American Express, Rome. . . . After that we may go to meet Jimmy Merrill in Greece. But most likely we'll hole up in Sicily for a month or so until I can get some work done. Ah! The land of the Mafia! My son and I both have switch-blades, and we pop them out endlessly, striking bloodlessly the classic attitude of switchbladery, for our own mutual admiration. . . .

Barney Rosset to Henry Rago   *New York City, 5 April 1962*

Dear Mr. Rago:

I am writing to ask your help in bringing to a halt the current book-banning crusade which is sweeping the country. As you perhaps know, we have been fighting a battle against censorship during the past six months. With Judge [Julius] Epstein's decision in Chicago, this battle now appears to have entered upon a new and more hopeful phase.

As of this writing, *Tropic of Cancer* is effectively banned from distribution in over half the country. We have undertaken to defend booksellers arrested in their respective communities, and there are still some 60 criminal cases pending throughout the country. It appears that the *Tropic of Cancer* case has developed into the largest single case of literary censorship in modern times, and its outcome will be of decisive importance for the future of American publishing. But *Tropic of Cancer* is only one of the books which have suffered in the current crusade; almost every day brings word of a new literary or film repression in some community or other. . . .

A group of leading writers, critics, and publishers who believe it is time for the literary and publishing community to make its voice heard on this issue has signed the enclosed statement of support for Judge Epstein's ruling.

If you agree with what the statement has to say, you will help the anti-censorship battle immeasurably if you put your signature on one copy of the enclosed statement, and return it to us in the enclosed return envelope. Once several hundred people in the literary and publishing world have put their names to the statement, it will become a potent weapon in arousing public opinion against censorship crusaders. . . .

H.R. note: "Statement signed and returned."

Delmore Schwartz to Henry Rago   *New York City, 27 May 1962*

Dear Henry:

I hope you like the enclosed, which is part of a long poem you have already printed: "The Kingdom of Poetry." Possibly you can give an advance on this or other poems, for as usual I'm extremely hard-up. . . .

I'm looking forward to seeing you at the Library of Congress meeting in honor of poetry. It's been a long time since the spring of 1954; so much has happened that I feel two thousand years of age.

Best, / Delmore

James Laughlin to Henry Rago   *Norfolk, Conn., 29 May 1962*

Dear Henry,

Thanks so much for your kind letter of May 25th. I agree with you that it would be most fitting that Ezra should be represented in the Golden Anniversary issue of "Poetry."

I'm afraid, however, that there is not much point in your writing to him about it. He is somewhat better in health now—visiting down in Rapallo, a place he loves so much—but the report is that he is still very weak, and fairly melancholy, and not writing anything new, or answering any letters. His affairs are now being conducted by Dorothy, his wife, and the most able young Mr. Herbert Gleason in Boston, the attorney who looks after things for them here, and we at New Directions lend a hand when we can.

I think that there might be a few fragments from unpublished Cantos around, if one or more of those would interest you. Donald Hall has been able to get some material of this kind from Ezra for the "Paris Review" interview, but I don't think they are going to use all of it. If I can lay hand on it, perhaps you might like to see what there is.

What would your rate of payment be for Ezra? That is quite important in the present situation.

With best wishes, as ever, / J.

Richard Wilbur to Henry Rago   *Portland, Conn., 4 June 1962*

Dear Henry:

To admit that one has no new poems on hand is always unpleasant; it's like announcing one's impotence; but that is the situation, and I fear I shall probably not be able to send you anything before the July first deadline. But *deo volente* there shall be some new poems this summer,

and what *The New Yorker* spurns I shall send along. The Tartuffe transla-
tion crawls ahead. I'm glad to hear of your good year in Europe, and
wish the Grecian rumors of our advent were true.

All good wishes for the Golden Anniversary Number. I expect I shall
see you in Washington for the October festival.

Yours, / Dick Wilbur

James Dickey to Henry Rago   *Paris, 20 July 1962*

Dear Henry Rago,

I haven't communicated for a long time, for we have been travelling
steadily for six months now. . . . Well, it is good to be writing, though
just in hotel rooms and in fields beside the tent. In January I go out to
Oregon to be Poet in Residence at Reed College for a year and a half.
It seemed a good offer, and I took it. Surely it beats working in busi-
ness, which was killing me and making me rich. . . .

Lawrence Ferlinghetti to Henry Rago   *San Francisco, Calif.,*
[August 1962]

Dear Editors Thank you for the review of Ginsberg's *KADDISH And
Other Poems*, even tho' your reviewer did not recognize Allen Ginsberg
to be *the greatest living American poet*. (Who is greater, daddy?)

—lawrence ferlinghetti

Anthony Kerrigan to Henry Rago   *Palma de Mallorca, Spain,*
20 August 1962

Dear Henry:

Thank you for your interesting letter of July 17. I have been away in
Madrid for a month, doing a piece for The Atlantic on the bullfight . . . .

I'll write you something about the mushrooms when I have time to
send you "a small packet" of poems. . . . But you might like to know
that the Harvard Institute of Behavioral Studies (I think it's called),
through the person of Timothy Leary, its director, has been distributing
Psilocybin (synthetic mushrooms) to writers, in a special program
designed to learn about the reactions to this Face-of-God-seeing drug
among the scribblers. (I'm reviewing the mushroom book in Spanish,
perhaps I can send you an English version.) For the moment, with best
greetings, to you both,

un abrazo [a hug], / Tony

CITY LIGHTS BOOKS
261 COLUMBUS AVENUE, SAN FRANCISCO 11

Dear Editors Thank you
for the review of Allen
Ginsberg's KADDISH
And Other Poems, even
tho' your reviewer
did not recognize
Allen Ginsberg to be
the greatest living
American poet. (who
is greater, daddy?)
—lawrence ferlinghetti

Lawrence Ferlinghetti to Henry Rago, August 1962

Anne Sexton to Henry Rago   *Newton Lower Falls, Mass.,*
                                              30 August 1962

Dear Henry Rago,

   I returned home from The Cape two days ago to find your letter and your suggestion I do a review for you. I am badly tempted . . . the three books [by Dickey, Koch, and Levertov] interest me and would, I know, provoke strong opinions. It would be a damn good batch to review! Part of me wants to . . . but I must say no.

I have been asked to do reviews before and said no with greater ease than this. But I have always read the reviews in POETRY and liked the quality and the differences . . . And as a poet I know how badly we need good critics . . . each book deserves a fair shake. But I am afraid I would become caught up in the role of the critic and that my spontaneity would wither and my own poems decay. I have a sneaky feeling I am being neurotic about this . . . or, to speak more plainly, that I am a coward about it. I have a special trouble there . . . I love poets and poetry is family to me. Although, of course, I have reactions and opinions about the quality of other poets' work, I think I would have trouble expressing them in print.

So you see . . . and I have reread your letter many times these past two days . . . being tempted and really wanting to say "yes," but I think I might do a disservice to poetry by trying to do something I am not actually equipped to do well.

I am flattered to be asked and then to think of following our friend, John Holmes . . . makes it even harder. I am sure that you understand that my regret is sincere. And let me add that I may change my feeling about all this and I hope that I will and someday I may be able to do a review for you.

In the meantime I will try to write new poems . . . and please know that I am really touched that you thought of me.

Yours ever, / Anne Sexton

All ellipses in the original.

Robert Bly to John F. Nims   *[n.p., September? 1962]*

Dear John,

. . . The Winters pieces are what made me throw up. Charles Churchill, indeed. All those people are trying to do is to race each other back to the sixteenth century.

Lowell's review of Winters was even worse—*this* is criticism? It wasn't your fault—but I thought the review, or Lowell's part, was a disgrace. It was embarrassing, as when a young professor gets up for his first speech to the student body, and spends the whole speech praising the President of the University.

As ever— / Robert

Yvor Winters's "The Poetry of Charles Churchill" ran in two parts, April and May 1961. Lowell reviewed Winters's *Collected Poems* in September 1962.

Henry Rago to Ezra Pound   *12 October 1962*

Dear Mr. Pound,

As you know, each year *Poetry* offers some eight prizes . . . for the
best poems published in the magazine during the year. This year,
because it is *Poetry's* Golden Anniversary, the donor of one of the
prizes, the Harriet Monroe Memorial Prize, provided us with five hun-
dred dollars and left it to me to decide whether I should like this time
to widen its scope to include any poet who had published in *Poetry* any
time in the past fifty years. I decided instantly to do this, and in the
same instant I knew that one poet was the inevitable choice. My col-
leagues agreed heartily with that choice. So I enclose, *very* happily, a
check for five hundred dollars and a copy of my statement, which will
be published in our December issue . . . . The amount is small, though it
towers over our other prizes; but because the prize includes *Poetry's*
entire life of fifty years, it is simply the most distinguished we have ever
been able to give. . . .

I hope that your health is much better.

Yours ever sincerely, / Henry Rago

Ezra Pound to Henry Rago   *Rapallo, Italy, 18 October 1962*

Dear Rago

If you think it will sustain Harriet's glory, go ahead.

If it gives me a chance to admit the multitude & depth & gravity of
my errors, go ahead.

If it claims that I did advertise the magazine, & encourage Harriet,
that may be a justification. I. e. that there were good years in which I
was of some use to someone, go ahead.

Yours sincerely
Ezra Pound,
a minor satirist who
at one time contributed to
the general liveliness by scratching
a few barnacles off the language.

Afterword

"Make it new," commanded Ezra Pound, reformer and prophet, as he helped to scrape off the excrescences of nineteenth-century verse and usher in the first Poetry Renaissance. But the prime mover saw himself displaced as his "protégé" T. S. Eliot became *the* arbiter and the Academy advanced Eliot's critical principles. Ironically, though Pound disdained universities, it was ultimately English professors who passed on his work and scholars who turned the Cantos into a cottage industry. Wallace Stevens, William Carlos Williams, Marianne Moore, and other early Modernists were also overshadowed by Eliot. But, of course, they, too, continued to create, and most were lucky to live long enough to be "rediscovered" and to see their achievements widely recognized.

Pound's call for renewal was heeded again, with a vengeance, from the sixties onward. Dissatisfied with the status quo, anti-Establishment poets identified with the iconoclastic motives of the old avant-garde. As they rejected Eliot's conservative ideas and the academic dogma they had been taught, a second poetry renaissance burst forth. It, too, became a revolution, but in the primary sense: a return to the original principals and radical methods of Pound and the other experimentalists *Poetry* first championed.

By the late sixties, the very notion of arbiters, poetic orthodoxy, and a dominant style became unacceptable to the Now Generation. The diversity of approaches to poetry reflected the social and political upheavals of a culture again in rapid flux. The Generation Gap discovered (or at least labeled) by sociologists became pronounced in the art world, as a multiplicity of literary sectarians segregated themselves in ideo-aesthetic subgroups.

In his second seven years as Editor, Rago kept up a far-flung correspondence with the leaders and freelancers in the increasingly fragmented provinces of American poetry, amassing a detailed record of this tumultuous era in the *Poetry* archives. While the extraordinary growth of new voices and viewpoints was matched by the proliferation of publishing outlets, *Poetry* maintained its leadership as a unique place where both

established and emerging authors vied to appear. Despite the unprece-
dented competition, circulation of the magazine approached 9,000 by
the end of the decade. But even with his stamina, Rago began to feel the
strain of keeping the enterprise going after almost fifteen years. When
the University of Chicago invited him back, he accepted. On 26 May
1969, nine months after leaving *Poetry*, he died of a heart attack, at the age
of fifty-three.

In the *Poetry* archives, thousands of letters to Rago and his successors
hold spirited testimony to the immense social changes, cultural contro-
versies, and artistic transmutations that have marked the last four decades.
Surrealists in their many guises; countercultural and Confessional poets;
feminists, blacks, gays, and other liberation movement activists; anti-
Vietnam war protesters; New Formalists, regionalists, postmodernists,
experimentalists beyond description—all are well represented in the files
after 1962.

As in the first fifty years, poets of every stripe continued to write to
the magazine, usually from the start of their careers. Maxine Kumin,
Adrienne Rich, May Swenson, Wendell Berry, Mark Strand, and Charles
Wright are among the other notable correspondents from the sixties. In
his nine years, 1969–1978, Daryl Hine also presented these poets, as well
as early work by Stephen Dobyns, Louise Glück, Erica Jong, Tom Disch,
Lisel Mueller, William Dickey, Stephen Berg, Mark Jarman, Sandra
McPherson, Sandra M. Gilbert, Marilyn Hacker, Margaret Atwood, Dave
Smith, David Bottoms, and Robert Pinsky. During his third term at
Poetry, 1978–1983, John Frederick Nims kept up with a wide network of
friends throughout the poetry world. As his missives in the present vol-
ume indicate, Nims was a very witty letter writer himself, and the corre-
spondence from his relatively short tenure is particularly lively.

During the years of the present Editor, *Poetry*'s circulation has grown
to its highest in history, and with it the number of submissions. Today's
leading poets have continued to send their best new work, as well as
engaging letters. The highly eclectic mix of contributors has included—
to give but a sample from the wide gamut—Agha Shahid Ali, Eavan
Boland, Neal Bowers, Raymond Carver, Amy Clampitt, Billy Collins,
Carl Dennis, Gregory Djanikian, Rita Dove, Stephen Dunn, Alice Fulton,
Seamus Heaney, Edward Hirsch, Andrew Hudgins, Ha Jin, Mary Karr,
Jane Kenyon, Yusef Komunyakaa, William Matthews, Sharon Olds, Mary
Oliver, Reynolds Price, Pattiann Rogers, Kay Ryan, Timothy Steele,
David Wojahn, and Robert Wrigley.

And in keeping with the magazine's Open Door tradition, the editors
have been particularly interested in finding and promoting new talents.
Over the last decade, about a third of the poets printed each year have

been First Appearances, many of them published while still in school or as recent graduates. The missives of this latest new generation recall the originality, enthusiasm, and unpredictability of Harriet Monroe's first correspondents.

Their letters to the editors, with those of the other acutely independent talents who have contributed to *Poetry* and the evolution of poetry over the last forty years, wait in the archives—a cache of candid comments, running arguments, and inside stories to fill another volume.

Copyrights and Permissions

Karl Shapiro: Permission of Sophie Wilkins Shapiro.

Edith Sitwell: Copyright © 2002 Francis Sitwell. Used by permission.

Osbert Sitwell: Copyright © 2002 Frank Magro. Used by permission.

Stephen Spender: Copyright © the Spender Estate. Used by permission.

William Stafford: Printed by permission of the Estate of William Stafford.

Stephen Stepanchev: Printed with the permission of the author.

Wallace Stevens: Permission of Peter R. Hanchak.

Allen Tate: Permission of Helen H. Tate.

Sara Teasdale: Permission of the Wellesley College Library.

Dylan Thomas: Estate of Dylan Thomas, Harold Ober Associates.

James Thurber: From *The Years with Ross* by James Thurber. Copyright © 1957, 1958, 1959 by James Thurber. Copyright © 2001 by Rosemary A. Thurber. Reprinted by arrangement with Rosemary A. Thurber and The Barbara Hogenson Agency, Inc. All rights reserved.

Eunice Tietjens: Permission of Jennifer H. Dougall.

Louis Untermeyer: Published by arrangement with the Estate of Louis Untermeyer, Norma Anchin Untermeyer, c/o Professional Publishing Services. This permission is expressly granted by Laurence S. Untermeyer.

Mona Van Duyn: Permission of the author.

Ernest Walsh: Permission of Sharon Cowling, sole owner of the rights and only daughter of Ernest Walsh (posthumous).

Richard Wilbur: Permission of the author.

Thornton Wilder: Permission of the Wilder Family.

Ellen Williams: Ellen Williams for kind permission to quote from *Harriet Monroe and the Poetry Renaissance 1912–1922* (Urbana: University of Illinois Press, 1977).

Oscar Williams: Permission of Strephon Kaplan-Williams and Alison Williams.

Thomas Lanier (Tennessee) Williams: Letters by Tennessee Williams from *Selected Letters: Volume I, 1920–1945*, copyright © 2000 by The University of the South. Reprinted by permission of New Directions Publishing Corp.

William Carlos Williams: "Excerpt" by William Carlos Williams, from *The Autobiography of William Carlos Williams*, copyright © 1951 by William Carlos Williams. Reprinted by permission of New Directions Publishing Corp. Letters by William Carlos Williams, from *Unpublished Materials*, copyright © 2002 by Paul H. Williams and the Estate of William Eric Williams. Printed by permission of New Directions Publishing Corp., agents.

Yvor Winters: Unpublished letters of Yvor Winters courtesy of Daniel Lewis Winters. Letters dated 4 March 1919, 23 March 1919, 28 January 1920, 7 February 1920, 3 December 1920, 27 November 1926, 28 June 1927, 31 July 1928, 10 February 1930, and 23 September 1930 from *The Selected Letters of Yvor Winters*, edited by R. L. Barth. Used by permission of Swallow Press/Ohio University Press.

James Wright: Permission of Anne Wright.

William Butler Yeats: Permission of Michael Yeats.

Morton D. Zabel: Permission of Matthew A. Sutton.

Marya Zaturensky: Permission of Patrick Bolton Gregory.

Illustration credits: All photographs are from the office archives of *Poetry* and used by permission of the Modern Poetry Association, with the following exceptions: The Newberry Library graciously permitted reproductions of the photographs of Harriet Monroe at her desk, p. 38 (Harry Hansen Papers); Robert Frost, p. 60 (Eunice Tietjens Collection); and young Edna St. Vincent Millay (Floyd Dell Collection); and of the cartoons from the Chicago *Daily News* and the Philadelphia *Public Ledger* (Eunice Tietjens Collection). The photograph of young Marianne Moore is reproduced by permission of The Rosenbach Museum and Library, Philadelphia. Photographs of all letters are used by kind permission of the Department of Special Collections Research Center, Regenstein Library, University of Chicago, with the exception of the Harriet Monroe letter to Wallace Stevens of 21 October 1914, p. 119, which is reproduced by courtesy of The Huntington Library, San Marino, California, and the Lawrence Ferlinghetti letter to Henry Rago of August 1962, which is reproduced by courtesy of the Lilly Library, Indiana University, Bloomington, Indiana.

Index

Page numbers in **boldface** refer to letters and follow the names of their authors.